The War Against Oblivion

Zapatista Chronicles 1994–2000

John Ross

Common Courage Press

Monroe, Maine
Philadelphia, Pennsylvania

Library of Congress Cataloging-in-Publication Data

Ross, John, 1938 Mar 11-
    The war against oblivion : Zapatista chronicles, 1994-2000 / John Ross.
        p. cm.
    Includes index.
    ISBN 1-56751-175-9 (cloth) -- ISBN 1-56751-174-0 (pbk.)
        1. Chiapas (Mexico)--History--Peasant Uprising, 1994- 2. Ejârcito
Zapatista de Liberaciân Nacional (Mexico) 3. Indians of Mexico--Mexico--
Chiapas--Social conditions--20th century. 4. Mexico--Politics and government--
1988- I. Title: Zapatista chronicles, 1994-2000. II. Title

F1256.R72 2000
972'.7506--dc21   00-060116

Common Courage Press
PO Box 702
Monroe, ME 04951

(207) 525-0900; fax: (207) 525-3068
orders-info@commoncouragepress.com

www.commoncouragepress.com

First Printing

To Los Muertos of the Zapatista Army of National Liberation—and Los Vivos!

La lucha sigue y sigue y sigue y sigue y sigue y sigue y sigue y sigue y sigue y sigue y sigue y sigue y sigue y sigue y sigue y sigue y sigue y sigue y...
—EFREN CAPIZ, Purépecha leader, Michoacán

Everywhere and always, go after that which is lost.
—CAROLYN FORCHÉ,
from the book *The Country Between Us*

The War Against Oblivion could not have been written without the contribution of two valiant souls—Elizabeth Bell, my sharp-eyed editor and wisewoman confidante, and Hermann Bellinghausen, who lived these adventures and survived to tell the tale day after day on the pages of La Jornada. In addition, I am indebted to many colleagues for their wisdom and testimony: Amado Avendaño, Luis Hernández Navarro, Blanche Petrich, Jaime Avilés, Juan Balboa, Elio Henriques, Pepe Olmos, El Flaco Garduño, María Teresa del Riego, Daniel Pensamiento, Trina Kleist, Michael McCaughan, and many more whose reportage and advice has been compressed into this volume. My gratitude too to Andrés Barreda, Tim Russo, Chip Morris, the Very Reverend Emmett Fitzgerald (SJ), Gaspar Morquecho, Gerard Rannou, the staff of the Hotel Isabel which has kept a roof over my head for 15 years, and my compañeros at the Cafe La Blanca, particularly Carlos Diez, who never failed to ask about the health of Oblivion during its long gestation, and Arthur Stamoulis of Common Courage Press. Finally, to all those who came to the War Against Oblivion and did their part to win it, this is your story.

PREFACE

The central plaza of San Cristóbal de las Casas, the throne of the Mayan high-lands of Chiapas, is a dank and hollow space at 3 a.m. on a New Year's morning. Yellow vapor lamps illuminate the glazed paving stones, further accenting the emptiness. The chill is so intense that ice crystals form inside the bone. In the early morning silence, one listens for what the future might hold.

Or the past...

> The pitch-black night suddenly came alive with darting shadows... The slap-slap of rubber boots against the slick pavement echoed through-out the hushed neighborhoods on the periphery of town. Sleepy *chuchos* stirred in their patios, stretched and bayed, the howling catching from block to block, barrio to barrio. Across the narrow Puente Blanco, down the rutted Centenario Diagonal, up General Utrilla from the market-place district, dark columns jogged in military cadence. With their fea-tures canceled behind ski masks and bandannas that left their collective breath hanging in the still mountain air like vapors from a past many Mexicans do not want to recognize as being present, the *sin rostros* ("those without faces") advanced on the center of the city....
>
> (from *Rebellion From the Roots*, Common Courage, 1995)

So it began, that freezing New Year's morning, 1994.

The Zapatista Army of National Liberation marched up to the alabaster gov-ernment palace built stone by stone by the Indian day laborers of San Cristóbal and using sledgehammers, the tool and weapon of the *peones* of the old city, smashed down its doors, emptied out the contents of the offices, climbed to the balconies, declaimed the first Declaration of the Lacandón Jungle, declared war on the Mexican Army, and launched the first post-Communist, post-modern, anti-neoliberal uprising in the Americas. To make their point palpably clear, the

Zapatistas timed this unique uprising to coincide with the very first hours of that beacon of globalization, the North American Free Trade Agreement.

The challenge did not go unnoticed. As soon as the New Years' Eve hangovers had thinned in Mexico City and Washington, attention swiveled south in the unlikely direction of Chiapas. But that was many years back down this rutted highway. Much has happened since then, and that story will indeed be told on the following pages. Preface, though, tells us what came before.

In an earlier volume, I carbon-dated the seeds of the Zapatista rebellion to that frozen moment in October 1492 when the Spanish sailor Juan Rodrigo Bermio shouted "¡Tierra! ¡Tierra!" from the crow's nest of the caravel Pinta. But the story of course begins considerably before then, in the Popul Vuh and the Chilam Balam, the sacred books of the Maya that survived the bonfires of Bishop Landa's inquisition, and tell us, as did Old Antonio in the stories passed on by Subcomandante Marcos, of the first gods, the ones who gave breath to the world.

Fast-forward from this Mayan Eden to the 1950s, when the Mexican government throws open the gates of the lush and foreboding Lacandón jungle to the landless Indians of the south. The pioneers pour into this "new agrarian frontier" from Los Altos (the highlands) to the west, and the sun-baked savannahs to the north and east, marching down the canyons (Las Cañadas) like the Chosen People, ripping down the great groves of cedar and mahogany and carving ejidos from the jungle floor.

The consequences of such mistaken exuberance were unavoidable. Within a generation, the settlers had burned the nutrients from the soil, and corn and coffee yields plummeted. The campesinos applied to the government for relief, seeking extensions to their ejidos—agricultural tracts granted by the government as communal property—but the petitions only gathered dust in the offices of the Agrarian Reform Secretariat.

Instead of ceding to the mostly Indian farmers the land they demanded, the federal government tried to evict them from that which they already possessed—first in 1972 and again six years later, when President José López Portillo sought to mollify the outcry of the international environmental community by having the fast-receding Lacandón jungle declared a United Nations biosphere.

Eviction proceedings began forthwith and resistance became generalized throughout what was left of the jungle. The ejidos formed unions of ejidos to defend themselves against not only the intentions of the government to move them out but also the depredations of the ranching oligarchy with their great fincas and haciendas and World Bank credits and private armies called "white guards." To the finqueros and hacenderos, the Mayans of southeast Chiapas were of far less value than their prized cattle.

Up in Los Altos, the Indiada, that historical flashpoint when the indígenas of the rural highlands would overrun San Cristóbal and murder the burghers in their feather beds, was always on the agenda. Rebellion in the highlands rises like a dark underground river, bursting into the blazing sunlight once or twice a century.

It had happened in 1722 in Cancuc when the Indian Army of the Virgin had marched to their doom on the steps of the royal city. It happened again in 1869 in Chamula, when the talking stones had prophesied war and the Indians swirled into San Cristóbal only to be cut down by the hundreds on the very plaza the Zapatistas would take in another century.

And it happened again in the Spring planting of 1974, up above the Valley of Jovel in what the map labels "San Andres Larráinzar" and the EZLN "Sakamchién de los Pobres," a place name synonymous with the Zapatista story, when radicalized Tzotziles—the People of the Bat—forced the whites and mestizos off Indian communal lands.

By the mid-1970s, the Mayans of Los Altos and the jungle were fast coalescing into a social force that the government, the Catholic Church, and the Marxist-Maoist Left were each seeking to control.

It was into this activist cauldron that a young radical from the north plunged in 1983, armed with ideological firepower and a few fast-oxidizing weapons, prepared to make a revolution. "When we first came here, we thought we were invincible. We thought we were the light of the world sent here to organize the Indians," Marcos once told Mexican journalist Blanche Petrich.

The volunteers had come as a unit of the Forces of National Liberation (FLN), one of the last surviving guerrilla *focos* (small localized groups) dating from the 1970s when 15 such groups roamed the land, holding up banks and kidnapping governors and U.S. consuls. By the 1980s, the FLN, originally formed in the northern industrial city of Monterrey, had been battered by informers and the nation's draconian security apparatus—its historical leaders were gunned down in Mexico state in 1976. The same year, the leader of its southern wing, Comandante Pedro, was hunted and killed by army troops near El Diamante in the Lacandón jungle.

During its early years on the Chiapas front, the FLN was often at odds with other radical missionaries. One particular irritant was the Maoist "Proletarian Line" (*Línea Proletaria*), also out of Monterrey, whose ideological leader Adolfo Orive had struck an uneasy alliance with Samuel Ruiz, the bishop of San Cristóbal, an apostle of liberation theology. Years later, as an Interior Secretariat policy maker, Orive would take personal revenge both upon those who were once the FLN and on Bishop Ruiz.

The revolution, of course, did not work out the way Marcos had planned it. The Tzeltales and Tojolabales of the Cañadas soon relieved the newcomer of his pre-packaged ideological baggage. The children dying of perfectly curable diseases, the brutality of the finqueros and their *guardias blancas* (the "white guard" paramilitary squads), the beauty of this deadly landscape in all of the stations of the year, the resiliency and deeply spiritual mindset of the communities that told their authorities what to do and not the other way around, changed the young intellectual who now operates under the name of Subcomandante Marcos. He was not the first missionary to be so transformed.

Samuel Ruiz came to San Cristóbal as a novice bishop fresh from the orthodoxy of the Vatican, and for years he saw nothing wrong with the way his Indian parishioners lived their lives. "I was like a fish, sleeping with my eyes wide open," Don Samuel is fond of confessing.

The Bishop finally woke up during the 1974 Indian conference commemorating the 500th year of the birth of Bartolomé de las Casas, the first bishop of San Cristóbal and the first defender of the Maya. Speaker after speaker at the conference rose to articulate the same indignation that the Zapatistas would shout from the balconies of the city 20 years later. They demanded to know whether the Church stood with them. Ruiz was forced to choose sides.

The Bishop was not unaware of the competition he faced in this battle to save the souls of the Indians. His Tzeltal and Tojolabal catechists would bring the news of the ferment in the Cañadas, and sometimes they would defect and join the rebels' secular ranks. For years, there were alliances and break-ups between Don Samuel's social organization in the communities and the radicals. The bickering was loudest in the ejido unions of the Cañadas.

San Cristóbal first found out about the EZLN during tumultuous demonstrations October 12, 1992, to mark 500 years of heroic resistance by the indigenous peoples of the continent against would-be European conquest. Then masquerading as the campesinos they would still prove to be under their ski masks and *paliacates* (kerchiefs), the "Emiliano Zapata National Association of Indian Farmers" (ANCIEZ) attacked a statue of Diego de Mazariegos, the Conqueror of Chiapas, yanking him from his pedestal and torching the bronze figure with gasoline before disappearing back into the jungle.

Now the days of civil resistance were narrowing towards war. The signs were posted by then-president Carlos Salinas as he sold off the country to transnational investors. The final notice was the revision of Article 27 of the Constitution, which governed land reform and is the fruit of EZLN namesake Emiliano Zapata's martyrdom that ended the monumental 1910-1919 revolution. "We had no other choice after that but to go to war," Marcos told Petrich early in this impending chronicle. The mutations in Article 27 allowed transnational agribusiness "to buy, rent, or enter into association" with the ejidos and the Indian communities, protected from any sale or fragmentation of communal landholdings under the original law. The change was an obligatory stepping stone to NAFTA.

Even as the EZLN trained with wooden rifles in the Corralchén sierra in the Spring of 1993, corn import quotas were being negotiated in Washington and Ottawa that threatened to displace the Indian farmers of Mexico from the domestic grain market and eventually from their land. Chiapas is the third largest maize producer in the Mexican union, with a half million farmers dependent on its cultivation. 300,000 of them who work tiny wedges in the jungle or up in the Altos stood to lose it all to NAFTA.

How important is corn to the EZLN? Well, armies are said to move on their bellies, and the rebellion did not begin until the corn harvest was secured in November in their base communities. The Zapatistas are, after all, Mayans, and the Maya are known to history as "The Men (and Women) of Corn."

By May, after the shadowy slaying of two military officers near San Cristóbal, the EZLN's cover was in danger of being blown. Rumors spread like brushfire, and troops from the 31st region at Rancho Nuevo, outside San Cristóbal, were sent to fine-comb the Cañadas for verification. A firefight broke out in the Corralchén near La Garrucha, in the canyons of Ocosingo. The military conceded two casualties, but Marcos insisted there were many more. A rebel *comandante*—"Raúl"—was also killed. The army climbed further into the sierra and stumbled across the EZLN training camp up in the caves. The camp contained many clues—uniforms, weapons, and propaganda, even a kind of stage set that served to rehearse scenarios for the coming war. Caught red-handed, the guerrilleros fled into the deep bush.

Then, abruptly, Army field commanders issued orders to pull back—orders, that Marcos considers could only have come from Carlos Salinas.

By 1993, the now-reviled ex-president was fixated on making NAFTA the crowning glory of his political legacy before he left office the following year, and a guerrilla war in southern Mexico would fatally damage the treaty's prospects in the U.S. Congress. Although the guerrilla threat was an open secret in Mexico during the Summer of 1993, both Salinas and his neophyte counterpart Bill Clinton conspired to keep Congress in the dark. The Salinas government hired Burson-Marsteller to burnish Mexico's image as a stable environment for U.S. investment. The White House gagged analysts from the intelligence community when they testified before House committees. "It's my opinion that had the House known about the situation in Chiapas, NAFTA would have been dead," Ross Rogers, the U.S. embassy's senior political officer, told me on deep background when I interviewed him in San Cristóbal a week after the uprising.

By the time NAFTA cleared the House by a narrow 34-vote margin on November 17th, the Ejército Zapatista de Liberación Nacional (Zapatista Army of National Liberation—EZLN) was in the final stage of its preparations for war.

For most of the world, the Zapatista legend kicked in January 1st, 1994, with the taking of San Cristóbal and six other municipalities in Los Altos and the lowlands. In *Rebellion From the Roots*, I told the story of the first 10 months of the uprising, and some of that material I reprise in the early seasons of this chronicle.

No matter when or where they were written (and the bibliography now includes over 200 titles), most "chronicles" of the Zapatista rebellion do not go much further than the 12 days of the January shooting war. There is, of course, *un chingo* more to tell.

The final chapter of *Rebellion From the Roots* was entitled "The End of the Beginning," and I trust these pages will serve to decipher the middle. There is no end in sight to this ceaseless war against oblivion. Even the corporeal obliteration of the Zapatista leadership and all its base communities, always an option for the *mal gobierno* (bad government), will not derail the resurgence of Neo-Zapatismo in the jungles and highlands of southeastern Chiapas. "In order to wipe us out," Marcos once proclaimed, "they will have to wipe this piece of territory from the face of the earth—not just destroy it but erase it completely—because there is always the danger from the dead below."

The War Against Oblivion is not my title. The EZLN always speaks of their struggle as *una guerra contra el olvido,* and when at New Year's midnight 2000 under a moonless sky down in La Realidad, I heard "Claudia," the tiny, emphatic representative of the community, say the name of that war, I realized now I had the title for this chronicle—which is, in itself, an attempt to rescue the memory of the myriad tragedies, the jubilees, and most of all, the enduring resistance of a rebellion that now enters its second millennium.

The War Against Oblivion: Zapatista Chronicles 1994–2000 is essentially a sequential résumé of the rebel experience between January 1994 and the Mexican presidential vote in July 2000. The chronicles end very much as my first book ended, with a presidential election. For this I apologize to the EZLN, which does not take such ballotings very seriously. Elections are hardly the watershed events that politicos make them out to be, but they are bookmarks and weathervanes, moments in which to measure which way the wind is blowing.

In Mexican journalese, *crónica* does not refer just to the serial recounting of who what when where and why, but is also a style of telling the story by inviting the reader into it, to notice the living details—how the sky looked above San Andrés on the February day in 1996 when the never-implemented autonomy accords were signed, the cries of Zapatista women as they physically pushed soldiers out of X'oyep in January 1998, the stench of the corpses at Acteal and the autonomous community of San Juan de la Libertad…

Crónica is not chronology, but the two are tied to time, and the pace of this narrative moves inflexibly ahead from day to day and year to year and yes, century to century. I have sought to soften this long march by arbitrarily dividing the Zapatista experience into distinct "Times" and the "Times" themselves into seasons, the most congruent blocks of remembrance for an agricultural people such as the Zapatista Mayans.

One caveat on the geography of this chronicle. Although I have touched down in Chiapas during each of the seasons that I record here, I remain based in Mexico City and as a writer cover a whole nation where social movement is ubiquitous and must be attended to. It is inevitable then that this "War Against

Oblivion" takes place as much in the capital and the country at large as it does in Las Cañadas and Los Altos of Chiapas. I have in fact sought to integrate the Zapatista story with that of this very wide political stage that calls itself Mexico.

The new millennium does not seem a propitious one for the indigenous peoples of the planet. The Masters of the Universe now wear the mask of Globalization and vie to consolidate control of the world's resources and peoples. It is an irony of the passage from one millennium to the next that the oldest peoples, amongst them the Mayan Zapatistas, should find themselves in the vanguard of this battle to the death with the new false gods of markets and money. But then it is always the first peoples that fight more diligently for their land and their trees, their languages and their cultures—their way of doing things— because it is the indígenas of this world that have the most to lose. This war is always a matter of the corn patch vs the World Bank, the hoe against the stock market, the poorly armed guerrilla band against a military armed to the teeth by the Pentagon, the village against the World Trade Organization, the smallest of the small against the Fortune 500, the local against the global, the many against the few... There is a clear choice to be made.

"All we want is a new kind of world," Subcomandante Marcos told the multinational mob that descended on the EZLN outpost with the haunting name of La Realidad for the "Intercontinental Forum in Defense of Humanity and Against Neo-liberalism," i.e., "The Intergaláctica," in July 1996. "All we want," the Sup intoned, "is a world big enough to include all the different worlds the world needs to really be the world."

Table of Contents

BOOK FOUR: The Time of Re–encounter and Resistance

ZAPATISTA TIMELINE

Nov. 17, 1983—The Zapatista Army of National Liberation is founded near Lake Miramar, deep in the Lacandón Jungle.

Autumn 1991—Modification of Constitutional Article 27 governing agrarian reform by President Carlos Salinas, leading to an eventual declaration of war by the EZLN.

Oct. 12, 1992—500th anniversary of the European invasion of Indigenous America. Zapatistas lead march in San Cristóbal.

May 23, 1993—First skirmish between Mexican Army and EZLN near La Garrucha.

1994

Jan. 1st—EZLN seizes San Cristóbal, Ocosingo, and five other municipal seats in southeastern Chiapas and issues the First Declaration of the Lacandón Jungle, declaring war on the Mexican government.

Jan. 12—President Carlos Salinas declares a unilateral cease-fire. The shooting war ends.

Feb. 21–18—Negotiations between the EZLN and the Salinas government in the Cathedral of San Cristóbal.

March 23—Luis Donaldo Colosio, PRI presidential candidate, assassinated.

June 10—Zapatistas turn down government offer, issue the Second Declaration of the Lacandón Jungle.

Aug. 8–10—Thousands attend the EZLN's National Democratic Convention deep in the Lacandón Jungle.

Aug. 21—The PRI's Ernesto Zedillo is elected President of Mexico.

Dec. 19—EZLN peacefully occupies 38 Chiapas municipalities.

Dec. 20—The peso collapses and Zedillo blames the Zapatistas. Mexico plummets into deepest depression since 1932.

1995

Jan. 1st—The EZLN issues the Third Declaration of the Lacandón Jungle,

Feb. 9—Zedillo orders thousands of troops into the jungle to capture the EZLN leadership.

April 9—First negotiating session between the EZLN and the Zedillo government. Negotiations will be ongoing for the next 18 months.

Aug. 27—More than a million Mexicans participate in a Zapatista "consultation" on the EZLN's political future.

1996

Jan 1st—The Fourth Declaration of the Lacandón Jungle is issued.

Feb. 16—The EZLN and Zedillo's representatives sign the Accords on Indian Rights and Culture at San Andrés–Sakamchíén de los Pobres in the highlands.

June 28—The Popular Revolutionary Army (EPR) appears in Guerrero and declares war on the Zedillo government.

July 28—The EZLN welcomes thousands of Mexican and foreign visitors to the Forum for Humanity and Against Neo-liberalism, or the *Intergaláctica*.

Aug. 29—EZLN suspends peace talks with the government.

Oct. 12—Comandante Ramona arrives in Mexico City for the founding of the National Indigenous Congress.

1997

Jan. 11—EZLN rejects Zedillo's modifications of the San Andrés accords. Months of silence ensue.

July 6—Left leader Cuauhtémoc Cárdenas becomes the first elected mayor of Mexico City.

Sept. 10–18—1,111 civil Zapatistas visit Mexico City to attend the founding of the FZLN or Zapatista Front for National Liberation.

Dec. 22—46 Tzotzil Indian supporters of the EZLN are massacred by paramilitaries at Acteal in the highlands.

1998

January—Mexican army troops invade dozens of EZLN villages in the jungle and highlands.

March/April—Immigration agents expel hundreds of foreigners from Chiapas, some for life.

June 10—Interim governor Roberto Albores orders the dismantlement of the EZLN autonomous municipality of San Juan de la Libertad (El Bosque); 10 are killed.

July 20—The EZLN breaks its silence and issues the Fifth Declaration of the Lacandón Jungle.

Nov. 20–22—First meeting between the civil society and the EZLN in two years.

1999

March 21—5,000 civil Zapatistas travel throughout Mexico to conduct a consultation on the San Andrés accords—3 million Mexicans cast ballots in their favor.

May 11—Second encounter between the EZLN and the civil society. Subcomandante Marcos makes his first appearance in public since 1996.

Aug. 15—EZLN villagers and the military clash in Amador Hernández, on the edge of the Montes Azules biosphere. Hostilities continue for months.

Nov. 3—Samuel Ruiz, liberationist bishop of San Cristóbal, tenders his resignation to the Pope.

Dec. 30—Ruiz's carefully groomed successor, Raúl Vera, is transferred out of Chiapas by the Vatican.

2000

Jan. 1st—EZLN rejects global celebration of new millennium, begins its seventh year of the War Against Oblivion.

Feb. 6—Federal police break 10-month strike at the national university (UNAM)—a thousand students arrested.

July 2—For the first time in seven decades, the PRI loses the presidency of Mexico. The winner is right-wing PAN party candidate Vicente Fox Quesada.

BOOK ONE

THE TIME OF THE TALKING GUNS

"If the way of the arms only served us
to be heard, then that was good…"
—*Comandante Tacho*
(*to French Historian Yvon Le Bot*)

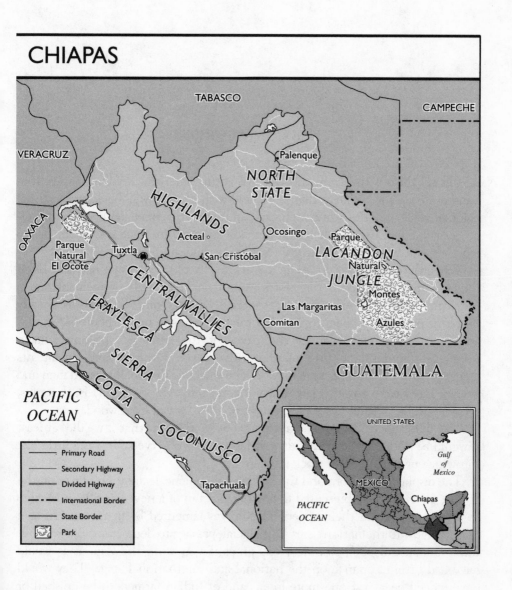

CHIAPAS

TABASCO

CAMPECHE

VERACRUZ

Palenque

NORTH
STATE

OAXACA

HIGHLANDS

Acteal

Ocosingo

Parque
Natural
El Ocote

Tuxtla

San Cristóbal

Parque

LACANDON

CENTRAL VALLIES

Natural

JUNGLE

FRAYLESCA

Las Margaritas

Montes

Comitan

SIERRA

Azules

COSTA

GUATEMALA

PACIFIC
OCEAN

SOCONUSCO

Primary Road

Secondary Highway

Divided Highway

International Border

State Border

Park

Tapachuala

UNITED STATES

Gulf
of
Mexico

MEXICO

Chiapas

PACIFIC
OCEAN

WINTER 1994

THE CURTAIN RISES

Political theater throbs in the veins of Latin American revolutionaries from Sandino to Che to Sendero Luminoso, and with its narrow cobbled streets, high colonial walls, graceful stone archways, and dramatic street lighting, the jewel-box city of San Cristóbal de las Casas made an exquisite stage set for one of the most innovative pieces of political theater ever mounted on the continent.

When the curtain was drawn up in the bitterly cold dawn of January 1st, 1994, the first morning of both the North American Free Trade Agreement and a Mexican presidential election year, the EZLN's black-and-red flag was already fluttering over the old heart of San Cristóbal. Indians in rubber boots, ski masks, and paliacates huddled under the eaves of the damaged, leaking Palacio Municipal around bum fires blazing with broken furniture and documents dragged out of the civil registrar's office. The weapons the small masked men and women toted were a mixed bag: a few Mach Sten, AK-47s and -15s, shotguns, revolvers, a lot of single-shot .22s, even toy rifles, carved from wood.

"We didn't go to San Cristóbal to die, but we thought that if we did, at least it would be noticed," Subcomandante Marcos once observed. "It was a little like throwing our blood on the stock market."

The display of weapons and the EZLN's subsequent declaration of war on the Salinas government represented the first apparition of a new guerrilla in Mexico in a generation, and their materialization was lamented by many citizens as a bruising blow to the nation's steady, if glacial, passage to democracy. But without these dramatically bellicose devices—props if you will—the Zapatistas would have had little resonance on the national and international stage. They would have indeed been just one more loser band of Indian farmers to be crushed or coopted by a government that has been dominated by one party for more than seven decades, a Guinness book of records for modern dictatorships.

Who were these masked men and women? In the first hours of the uprising, state and federal authorities denounced the insurgents as Guatemalans and Salvadorans. Their leader was a green-eyed stranger who spoke four languages. Several priests and the radical Bishop of San Cristóbal, Samuel Ruiz, were implicated. So were moribund guerrilla grouplets whose leaders had been killed off years before. A Venezuelan bird-watcher working in Chiapas on a Smithsonian grant was mistakenly detained as the rebels' leader.

In Mexico City, the illuminati dismissed the uprising as an election-year scheme devised by armchair Lefties or the old guard in the long-ruling Institutional Revolutionary Party (PRI) or even Carlos Salinas himself. For his part, Salinas considers the Zapatista rebellion to have been a plot masterminded by ex-president Luis Echeverría. NAFTA foe H. Ross Perot was mentioned as a possible instigator and right-wing "economist" Luis Pazos accused human rights groups of staging the uprising to give free trade a black eye.

As usual, no one gave the Indians any credit for taking matters into their own hands. 600 Tzotziles and Tojolabales, Tzeltales and Choles under the command of Mayor (Major) Ana María had been sent against San Cristóbal, and they were just as invisible as they would have been if they hadn't come masked. Racism has been the subtext of this rebellion for more than 500 years now.

MEETING THE PUBLIC

Curious townsfolk had begun to drift into the plaza to inspect the more or less uniformed rebels in their hand-stitched brown-and-olive shirts, black pants, and rubber farmer's boots. Munda Tostón, who had unwittingly costumed the Zapatista Army of National Liberation from her market stall, wandered downtown, "and there I saw them all, all my customers in my brown shirts and black pants" and even the 500 ski masks she had ordered from Puebla state.

One of the insurgents, taller than his compañeros, wrapped up in a black *chuj* (short serape) crisscrossed by bandoliers of shotgun shells, had begun to work the gathering crowd of Indians, tourists, and *coletos* (white and mestizo burghers so called because centuries ago they affected ponytails), even saluting crusading newspaper editor Amado Avendaño by name. "The coletos will get what they deserve," Subcomandante Marcos joked with Avendaño. "We're not all bad here," a woman admonished from the edge of the throng.

By noon, the plaza was thrumming with anxious tourists. Were they prisoners of or witnesses to the revolution? A group of anxious Italians had called their embassy in Mexico City, which in turn had called the National Human Rights Commission (CNDH).

The Comandantes appeared on the high-windowed balconies of the palace. "Felipe" pushed to the rail and read the opening words of the (first) Declaration of the Lacandón jungle, a document that enumerates 500 years of cruel oppres-

sion of the indigenous peoples of Mexico by the mal gobierno in its various forms.
The small Indian warrior recited the EZLN's succinct 11-word program: *"Trabajo,
Tierra, Techo, Pan, Salud, Educación, Democracia, Libertad, Paz, Independencia, y
Justicia"* (work, land, shelter, bread, health, education, democracy, liberty, peace,
independence, and justice).

Accusing Salinas of theft and treason, the Zapatista comandantes demanded
his resignation and the substitution of a transitional government. Then the
Zapatista Army of National Liberation declared war. "Today we say, *¡Basta ya!*
Enough!" shouted the Comandantes, a cry that has become their signature down
the years. "We will march on the capital, defeating the federal army on the way,"
they said, a challenge that soon became the justification for the permanent occupation of the state of Chiapas by a fifth of the Mexican military, leaving the other
four-fifths to cover the remaining 30 states and the federal district.

Did the EZLN really mean what it said about marching on Mexico City? Was
this political theater or prophecy? Years later, Marcos would draw a map for the
French political scientist Yvon Le Bot and detail a battle plan that called for several units to hook up and first take the complex of dams above the state capital
of Tuxtla Gutiérrez, which supplies 45% of the nation's hydroelectric power, and
then seize the regional military headquarters outside of Tuxtla before setting out
for the center of the country. The Mexican military apparently took the threat
seriously, mobilizing 2,000 paratrooper-fusiliers to guard the dams. And although
the offensive collapsed before it got out of the highlands, the EZLN has taken the
capital many times since. But those are other chapters in their story.

Now, Marcos summoned the public to dialogue. But the first questions came
from so deep in the crowd that the Sup had a hard time catching the drift and
descended into the street to facilitate the exchange. The worried tourists pressed
in around him demanding to know if they were free to leave. "We have reservations to visit the ruins at Palenque tomorrow," one Swiss couple pleaded. "Forgive
us," Marcos responded amiably, "but this is a revolution."

A handful of reporters on holiday in the old royal city pressed Marcos about
the roots of the rebellion. "We have been training for 10 years," the
Subcomandante told Gianni Prociettis, who sold the interview to L'Unità, the
Rome-based left-wing daily; it was the EZLN's first international notice. "Today
we have taken four cities in Chiapas because there are no conditions for free elections in this country. This is a warning to the government that we are fed up with
the lack of democracy in Mexico."

The Subcomandante said he was a *ladino* (non-Indian), one of three within
the Zapatista ranks. The General Command of the Clandestine Revolutionary
Indigenous Committee (CCRI) which he served was composed of Mayans from
the highlands and the jungle who, although they spoke six distinct indigenous
languages, spoke collectively with one heart. He had been chosen to communicate their directives because he had "a facility with *Castilla*" (Spanish). Marcos

confessed he was just a subcomandante, but the press got it wrong and he would be identified as commander for many weeks.

"Today the white people of San Cristóbal respect the Indians because they have guns in their hands," Marcos told the witnesses to this remarkable colloquy. Although the elegant tourist town had suffered little damage at the hands of the rebels, Marcos warned that if there was retaliation against the Indian people there after the Zapatistas left, "we will return and take San Cristóbal apart stone by stone…"

"Of course what we are doing here today has to do with the 'Tay-Ele-Say'" (the TLC, Spanish initials for NAFTA), he responded to the Italian journalist's queries, laying out how cheap U.S. grains would soon be pouring into Mexico and obliterate the People of Corn's possibilities of competing in the commercial market. "To us, the free-trade treaty is the death certificate for the ethnic people of Mexico," the ski-masked spokesperson lamented, a pull quote that made the overnight AP wire and jolted Washington awake on the bleak, snowbound Sunday morning of January 2nd.

By mid-afternoon, the Zapatistas' tone had grown ominous. A few minutes after 2 p.m., the first government response to the rebel uprising appeared on the horizon: four light-framed Mexican air force fighters, flying in from the west, dipped low in formation as if to salute and circled back in the direction of the military base down in Tuxtla. "Pilatus," Marcos observed, correctly identifying their Swiss manufacturer as he traced their trail through the thin mountain air. The signs were clear. The military would soon be here.

As evening began to drape itself over the colonial city, Marcos returned to the balcony. He had a few announcements to make. Tourists would be free to leave at 7:30 the next morning for Tuxtla only, the Subcomandante told the hundred or so hardy souls that remained in the plaza, emphasizing that the EZLN was complying with a request faxed to the municipal palace by the CNDH asking the safe conduct of foreign visitors. Finally, Marcos announced that the Zapatistas too would be leaving early the next morning. "We have stayed too long already."

THEATER OF BLOOD

If San Cristóbal, with its artists and Indians, anthropologists and international tourist priorities, can be adjudged a theater of the absurd, Ocosingo, 60 kilometers downhill to the east, a cowboys-and-Indians city that bills itself as "the gateway to the Lacandón jungle," was the Zapatistas' theater of blood. The rebels would lose nearly 50 insurgents there and the civilian population suffer even more grievous "collateral damage." Six years after the siege of Ocosingo, the brutality of the Mexican military's counterattack there continues to outrage national and international human rights groups.

With its murderous "white guards" and smug, racist ranching elite, Ocosingo was a likely target for Zapatista punishment. For months, rumors of the coming attack had had the townspeople of Ocosingo cowering in their closets. But the regional commander, Brigadier General Miguel Godínez disregarded their fears with macho bravado. Helicoptering over the cañadas leading from Ocosingo into the jungle on December 30th, he spotted a gaggle of buses and trucks the EZLN had expropriated and concentrated at San Miguel to move its troops on to the city, but dismissed the vehicles as insufficient evidence of imminent uprising. The small military detachment assigned to Ocosingo was allowed holiday leave, but 40 heavily armed state judicial police were brought in to defend the Municipal Palace just in case. "There is no guerrilla," Godínez snapped to the press, painting the townspeople as paranoids. "There is no guerrilla!" Zapatista fighters gleefully scrawled on the walls when they came to town.

According to what Marcos told Blanche Petrich of the left daily La Jornada in his first national interview one month later, the EZLN deployed a double feint modeled on Pancho Villa's taking of Ciudad Juárez in the first days of the 1910 Mexican Revolution. Although Ocosingo was clearly the preferred target—a mock-up of the area around the palacio was discovered when the military took the EZLN camp in the Corralchén caves the previous May—the rebels launched their offensive first in the highlands, in San Cristóbal, a little past midnight on New Year's Eve. Columns were sent into Las Margaritas and Altamirano even earlier in the evening. It was not until the cocks were already crowing up the dawn that the sin-rostros moved into Ocosingo. To cover their backs, EZLN forces spread east towards the Tabasco state line to cut off the expected advance of troops moving in from Villahermosa. But the late arrival of the rebels in Ocosingo and the stiff resistance from the state police boxed up in city hall would keep the Zapatistas in town until it was too late.

Unlike in San Cristóbal, where the security forces had fled, the police held their ground in Ocosingo and the rebels had to fight their way through the darkened city from block to block to reach the town plaza just above the San Jacinto de Polonia cathedral.

The face-off on the square went on for hours. Exchanges of gunfire between the Zapatistas and the 40 police defending the Palace was intermittent. "The atmosphere was very special, like a fiesta," Father José Trejo from San Jacinto remembers. "Young men brought cases of soft drinks for the Zapatistas..." In between the bursts of gunfire, the townspeople and the rebels shared cigarettes. A lot of the bystanders had been drinking.

Efren Bartolomé, a Mexico City poet and psychoanalyst but an Ocosingo auténtico native ladino, was home for the holidays up the hill from the plaza. The bullets were sailing in from all directions as the EZLN fighters concentrated their fire on the city hall. Drunks kept wandering through the line of fire, walking away magically unscathed even when they questioned the manhood of both sides in the duel.

Finally, the exasperated Zapatistas shooed away all the *bolos* and launched their final assault on the palace. Stripped to the waist in the heat of the firefight, the cops slowly emerged from the bullet-pocked two-story building with their hands in the air in time for *comida* (lunch). Four officers had been killed during the 12-hour siege.

Ocosingo was under rebel control and the fiesta of vindication in full swing by late afternoon, the sledgehammers smashing jagged holes in the chipped walls of the palace. The Zapatistas set up shop in the municipal market at the bottom of town and invited their new neighbors in to drink *chescos* (soft drinks) and chat.

XEOCH, the state radio station in southeastern Chiapas that has all the jungle for an audience, had been in rebel hands since before breakfast, and the comandantes took turns broadcasting the details of the new war tax, announcing that the Banamex branch on the plaza had been expropriated, that all prisoners except narcotics traffickers and murderers would be released from jail. Tenants who had lived in one place for 15 years would no longer be required to pay rent. Wife beaters would be hunted down and severely punished. All families were encouraged to take in the homeless kids who roam the cities of the region. The Zapatistas also asked for donations for their wounded and their dead.

In between, ski-masked DJs spun rancheros, "The Internationale," the Zapatista hymn (to the tune of "Carabina 30-30," an old Pancho Villa favorite), and the aggressive political folk music of José de Molina—the last of which led Bartolomé to cringe. "Give them everything they want!" he wrote in his diary.

By late afternoon, the government supermarkets (ISSTE and CONASUPO) and the Calzimoda shoe salon had been pillaged, the beef-processing plant was burnt to the ground, and five members of the Solórzano ranching family had been taken hostage in their underwear.

MASSACRE IN THE MARKETPLACE

The Zapatista forces might still have survived the siege of Ocosingo if not for one critical omission. Assigned to blow the bridge at La Virgen, which troops storming in from Tabasco had to cross to reach the city, the EZLN unit delegated to do the job miscalculated the Mexican Army's ability for rapid mobilization and failed to take out the bridge in time. Troops from the 30th military region rolled into Ocosingo unimpeded.

The mood of the Zapatistas was still festive the next noon when Rodolfo Reyes Aguilar, a portly El Financiero stringer, was conducted into the market and offered a Coke. Reyes had driven in with four army battalions from Villahermosa, 200 miles east. They had met with no resistance, had driven across La Virgen bridge, which was still in one piece, and now the troops were encamped just outside of town. 14 Mexican Air Force planes were in the air, and the paratroopers would soon be dropping into Ocosingo.

Before their advance from Villahermosa, the soldiers had been briefed by Brigadier General Luis Humberto López Portillo, commander of the zone, and advised to have no compunctions about summary executions. Everyone was a rebel, the general instructed—take no prisoners, but be careful if the press is around, Mexican army captain Jesús Valles remembers being told. Valles, who objected to the kill-on-sight orders, later deserted with a hundred other soldiers and eventually escaped to Texas, where, five years later, he was granted political asylum by a U.S. immigration judge.

As the Financiero stringer sipped cokes with the rebels, troops encircled Ocosingo and roared in from the south, cutting off EZLN escape routes back into the jungle. The rebels, concentrated in the flatlands around the public market—a dark, narrow warren of booths—were caught in a rat trap by the military advance.

Roaring into town with mortars and heavy artillery, the troops bore down on the *mercado* (market). The first shots were fired by the rebels at 3:15 p.m. on Reyes' timepiece. The fat man scrambled for cover behind army lines. The first helicopter swung in low, reconnoitering the distances, circled back towards the hills, and roared in again, blazing machine-gun tracers. "You better get out of here before the good stuff begins," a soldier shouted at El Gordo.

The fighting in the Ocosingo mercado was the heaviest of the war. "We were pissed off at the soldiers," Captain Laura told reporters later. "They had humiliated us often and now we wanted to humiliate them." Although the military's big guns were neutralized by the closeness of the combat, the rockets fired by the gunships terrorized the Indians. "I've never heard such a terrible noise," Mayor Rolando, a young rebel officer, told me later. Fragmentation grenades hurled by the ground troops turned the market into an inferno. Surviving Zapatistas were forced to seek refuge in the surrounding barrio of San Sebastián. Others ducked into the rat-infested sewers.

The dead were fresh enough the next morning not to trouble the nose. There were as many bodies in the street as there were stones, one taxi driver recalled. The Reuters reporter counted 22 rebel corpses in the marketplace.

Nine more bodies were found huddled in the sewers—although dozens more had escaped through the drainage system. The bodies of seven young men lay in the market patio—five of the men appeared to have had their hands tied behind their backs. Each had been forced to kneel before being shot once, a coup de grace to the base of the skull. Five years later, ex-captain Valles would testify that Mayor Rodolfo Pérez Nava was responsible for the summary executions but, despite the pleas of both Amnesty International and Human Rights Watch to affix responsibility for the killings, the major has never been charged.

Undaunted by the massacre of their comrades, the rebels fought from house to house and the Army responded in kind, insuring a high civilian kill rate. Among the dead were at least eight civilians killed at a local hospital, some still in their beds. A lieutenant who later confessed to leading the hospital operation reportedly "committed suicide" while in custody at the Secretariat of Defense up in Mexico City.

The battle for Ocosingo continued on throughout Monday the 3rd. Zapatista snipers fired from the rooftops, and down below, the soldiers kicked in doors and ransacked private homes, hunting the rebels. HUEYs and P-7 Pilatus fighters streaked in from the hills, strafing rooftops and firing on Father Trejo's church, a reputed hotbed of Liberationist nuns and priests.

The remaining Zapatista troops tried to fight their way out of town again on the morning of the 4th. The civilian population bore the brunt of the skirmishes. 47 hastily buried bodies were exhumed in Ocosingo in subsequent days and 30 more were shipped off to Tuxtla for autopsies. Father Trejo thinks 150 were killed in Ocosingo between January 1st and the 4th, in the bloodiest fighting of this short, deadly war.

"Our troops did what they had to do—die for the people," Marcos would later rue.

THE BATTLE OF RANCHO NUEVO

Marcos and 600 Zapatistas pulled out of San Cristóbal before dawn on Sunday morning, January 2nd, leaving the Palacio Municipal smoldering behind them, and marched a dozen kilometers south to the headquarters of the 31st Military Zone at Rancho Nuevo, digging themselves into the deep pine forests to the north and south of the neatly landscaped complex. The EZLN's mission, Marcos told Le Bot, was not to take the base but to pin down the troops inside the perimeter long enough to guarantee escape back down to the jungle—but weapons stored on site were a giddy temptation. "An army that is hungry for weapons and ammunition must go where these things are," Marcos reminisced weeks later.

Reduced to a skeleton crew by holiday leave (as few as 180 troops may have been on duty), the defenders of Rancho Nuevo were outnumbered three to one by the rebels.

The gunfire continued on and off all morning, both sides taking pains to haul away their dead and wounded. Reinforcements were called up by noon. Helicopter gunships would soon arrive from Tuxtla.

Seven kilometers down Highway 188, a sinuous two-lane blacktop that slices north towards Ocosingo, young Zapatistas had just released all the prisoners from a new local jail that had recently been completed by Solidarity, Salinas's public-works program.

The inmates, 173 men and five women, virtually all of them Indians, had been awaiting liberation since the Zapatistas began broadcasting from Ocosingo New Year's morning. Now one group of escapees commandeered a public bus and were heading up 188 when they ran right into a U.S.-manufactured HUEY gunship roaring down the valley to blast rebel positions, the first U.S. participation in the war. 14 young men were killed instantly, their mangled, bullet-riddled bodies dumped on the roadside and deliberately allowed to rot there for days as a warning to those who dare to rebel against the rulers of Chiapas. Ten days later, the death van was still tilting precariously on the shoulder, dried pools of blood spread like late-blooming roses on the glass-strewn surfaces of the interior, in mute testimony to the massacre.

As night fell, the rebels reinitiated their offensive. Marcos's strategy was to draw the enemy out to the fence surrounding the base, where Zapatista snipers picked them off from concealed positions in the hills fronting Rancho Nuevo. Meanwhile, EZLN commandos circled to the undefended rear of the installation and penetrated the fence—the hit on the armory yielded 180 automatic weapons and an undisclosed number of grenades, a rebel dispatch boasted five days later.

After securing the arms cache, Marcos said, "we did what a good army does when it has accomplished its mission—run."

On the first morning that the military unsealed the roads out of San Cristóbal, some days later, I encountered five Tzotzil women walking single file along an uninhabited stretch of the highway, hunting down a strayed cow. Two of the women were leading black dogs on long strands of bright green ribbon. They chattered excitedly in Tzotzil—the women had just found a corpse and wanted to take me into the cool pine forest on one flank of Rancho Nuevo to view it. The dogs dashed eagerly ahead, smitten with the scent of decaying meat. The dead man was splayed on the forest floor. He had been thoroughly consumed by small mammals and birds of prey; and only his gristly ribcage and the structure of his skull were still intact. Like all the half-eaten dead in this land where the *calaveras* (skeletons) get up and dance every Day of the Dead, he seemed to be grinning.

This calavera was clearly a Zapatista—the white bones in his pant legs were planted in black rubber boots, and a staff, from which a ragged red flag flapped in the small breeze, was nestled next to him on the damp pine forest floor.

I turned back to the highway, leaving the dead Zapatista to mulch with the generations of bones that rattle beneath the military base. As it turns out, Rancho Nuevo, the campus-like site of the 31st Military Zone, was built upon a Tzotzil graveyard.

BACK TO THE JUNGLE

By daylight on Monday morning, the Subcomandante and the troops under his command were already moving southeast, climbing the alpine ridge above Ocotal, where the U.S. maintains an early-warning radar tower to detect drug-laden aircraft incoming from the south; the unit broke through the surrounding humpbacked hills at Chanal, and dropped down into the cañadas 150 kilometers as the crow flies from Rancho Nuevo.

As the rebels beat a tactical retreat to the jungle, Mayor Moisés and his men took a shortcut from Las Margaritas through the San Joaquín ranch, the home spread of General Absalón Castellanos Domínguez, the iron-fisted governor of Chiapas (1982-88) whose penchant for jailing and killing Indian farmers was repeatedly assailed by Amnesty International in its earliest reports on Mexico.

Knocking politely on the ranch house door, Moisés and his men introduced themselves to the General's wife, begged pardon for the intrusion, loaded up the General, his valet, and two prized steers on one of Absalón's trucks, and continued on down the cañadas.

By the 4th, the Zapatista fighters were streaming back to their base areas. Behind them, they dug up swatches of the canyon routes that lead into the deep jungle and mined others with dynamite they had stolen from a drilling station run by the national oil conglomerate, PEMEX. Trenches were dug and trees were felled to slow the Army's impending ground assault.

BOMBING CHIAPAS

The skies were alive over Chiapas from the first morning of the uprising. 14,000 troops had been rounded up in the center of the country and airlifted in newly acquired U.S. Hercules transports to Tuxtla's military and civilian air bases. Paratroopers were dropped in to protect the dam complex on the western edge of the war zone. P-7s and HUEYs were active over Ocosingo trying to dislodge rebel snipers from fixed positions January 2nd and 3rd. By late Tuesday afternoon on the 4th, the P-7s were active around Rancho Nuevo, strafing surrounding hillsides to flush the guerrilleros from their dens. Civilian populations on María Auxiliadora mountain appear to have been deliberately targeted.

Despite military warnings that they were venturing into an active zone, journalists motored up the mountain to inspect the damage. In San Antonio, a collection of 40 Tzotzil families, only dogs and chickens scratched at the empty streets. Suddenly, the tense mountain silences were perforated by jet fighters streaking in from the east, firing rockets into the forest with imperfect aim. The flash and boom rattled teeth as the missiles plowed into the hillside. Sandina Robbins, working for Monitor radio, dove for cover in a nearby drainage ditch. Down at the bottom, several Tzotzil women gasped for breath but insisted they were not afraid. One pulled out her voter identification card and shook it at the incoming heavens: "*¡Somos del PRI!*" she hollered back in halting Spanish, "We're with the PRI" (the ruling party). "*¡Somos del PRI!*" her compañeras echoed.

The air war spread northeast on the 6th. In Tenejapa, the P-7s and gunships blasted the surrounding hillsides with missiles. "They look beautiful," one Indian farmer, who had never seen aircraft this lively before, told a Reuters reporter, "but the sound they make is like death."

Further to the south, on the ejido of Nuevo San Carlos near Altamirano, Agustín Lorenzo and his large family had run out of food after four days of sticking close to the house. The bean field was just 700 meters away, and for now, the skies seemed to be empty of war clouds. He grabbed up his kids and made a dash for it.

A trio of planes returning to Rancho Nuevo broke the bucolic silence. Abruptly, one of the P-7s peeled out of formation and doubled back towards Nuevo San Carlos. A terrified Agustín watched it drop three *bultos* (packages). He lost consciousness after the explosion.

When the farmer regained his senses an hour later, he told Jornada reporter Roberto Garduño his daughter Rosa was bleeding badly from a shrapnel wound in the neck. His 5-year-old, also named Agustín, was dead.

Late on the 6th, the military, fed up with nosy reporters poking about the war zone, closed off all access "for your own protection." Most of us suspicioned that the Army was whacking the hell out of the zone but could not get past the Rancho Nuevo checkpoint to verify the damage. Rumors flew on the 7th that the Army had taken out its own convoy up near the radar tower on the Hill of Strangers; perhaps 30 troops had been killed. But by the time reporters were finally allowed through the barricades to take a look, the only evidence was a few hundred meters of scorched forest up near the crown of the hill.

By the end of the first 10 days of the war in Chiapas, the bombs were starting to have an international echo. They were certainly on former U.S. attorney general Ramsey Clark's mind as he motored into the war zone early in January. "This is like Kurdistan," the well-traveled human rights lawyer observed, "or Iraq…"

Or Rwanda. Or Bosnia. Chiapas was on the global war map.

UNQUIET BONES

Although it is less than an hour out of Altamirano, the hard-core PRI municipal seat, the Ejido Morelia feels like it is days away, a green and solitary space set beneath the blue mountains on whose heights the Zapatistas have trained for years.

Early on January 7th, dozens of armored vehicles rolled into this tranquil Tzeltal coffee-growing community and 400 soldiers charged from hovel to hovel, dragging the men out and herding them onto the basketball court at the center of the settlement, the military's customary m.o. in Indian communities suspected of subversion.

The land of the Ejido Morelia was once owned by the kidnapped General Absalón Castellanos Domínguez, whose holdings extended into all the cañadas of the jungle. As with many jungle villages fashioned from haciendas on which the Indians had toiled for next to nothing for countless generations, the Tzeltales of Morelia fought for years to have the finca chartered as an "ejido"—a village organized as a communal agricultural production unit. The long struggle had turned the Morelia into a pocket of resistance in a zone traditionally dominated by the PRI and its farmers' federations.

Other than the attention focused upon this impoverished outpost on the morning of January 7th, 1994, the abandonment of Morelia by its government has been spectacular. The ejido had a basketball court but no baskets, a government clinic building but no doctor, a powerful thirst but no potable water, a full schoolhouse with one teacher three days a month, a priest who attended to the ejido every four months.

All morning long, the men were forced to lie face down on the ground, their noses driven down into the concrete. "Today is the day we turn Morelia into an orphanage," the soldiers barked. Their interrogators wanted to know about a doctor, a non-Indian, who sometimes visited the ejido. Three men were singled out, forced into the deserted hermitage of Jesus Christ of Good Hope, a square weatherbeaten building fronting the basketball court. For four hours, their compañeros listened to the screams of Sebastián Santiz López, 60, Severino Santiz, 47, and Ermelindo Santiz Gómez, 39. Severino's head was repeatedly dunked into the filled baptismal font. Electric cables were attached to the men's testicles and they were burnt. "The soldiers brought them out bathed in blood," said one witness. "All we could do is listen to their lamentations…"

The three prisoners were shoved into a military ambulance. Then a list of 30 or 33 more names was read out, and as each man meekly signaled his presence, he was hog-tied and thrown up in a military transport. Soldiers are accused of sacking the town's threadbare stores before they left the ejido and looting what valuables the Indians guarded.

In their odyssey from prison to prison, the men of Morelia lost track of time. In Altamirano, the soldiers burnt them with cigarette lighters. They were held naked in a coffee warehouse on the road to Comitán for a day amidst dozens of dead bodies. When the group was moved, gasoline was spread upon the corpses and they were burnt, a prisoner held with the farmers of Morelia told human rights workers.

Taken to Tuxtla in helicopters, the men were blindfolded, their hands tied behind their backs with yellow thongs, and crammed into Cerro Hueco, the state's most dreadful lockup. They were given no food for five days. Two weeks later they were released on bail posted by the National Indigenous Institute (INI, the government's Indian affairs bureaucracy) and the men began to drift back to the jungle. But three of those taken prisoner—Severino Santiz, Sebastián Santiz, and Ermelindo Santiz—did not reappear.

Weeks later, relatives out tracking the three men were told by a pigeon hunter about a pile of bones in a *zopilotera* (vulture pit) where dead animals were sometimes thrown to carrion birds, a few hundred meters off the Altamirano road. Strewn among the bones were articles of clothing: a blue kerchief, rubber boots, a leather one, false teeth. One by one, the relatives identified the articles as belonging to the three men.

The relatives summoned representatives of the diocesan-run Fray Bartolomé de las Casas Human Rights Center to witness the find. "It's my father that died here—the other two are my relatives," Severino's son spoke into a camcorder brought along to document the discovery. "Now I want to take them up. They've been here too long...even if its just dirt, I'm going to bring him home. It's my father. I've had a lot of pain for him..."

Of all the bones left to bleach under the midwinter sun of Chiapas, the bones of the Ejido Morelia would rattle around the longest and the loudest. Since the early days of the conflict, the martyrs of Morelia have been on the international human rights agenda from Washington to Geneva. Despite the embarrassment their bones have caused the Mexican government, the military continues to deny any involvement in the murders on the Ejido Morelia.

BREAKING THE ICE

Between January 1st and 12th, 15,000 troops poured into Chiapas, and Amado Avendaño's badly inked little daily paper, Tiempo, reported that most of them were advancing on Guadalupe Tepeyac, 80 kilometers south of Las Margaritas, where the Zapatista General Command was reportedly holed up. In September, President Salinas and his designated successor, Luis Donaldo Colosio, had flown into Guadalupe to dedicate a jungle hospital (a Solidarity effort, like the jail from which the rebels freed the prisoners on January 1st) even while the rebels lurked in the nearby bush—Comandante Tacho, posing as a waiter, reportedly served lunch.

The military had drawn a bead on the rebels. On January 8th, the Defense Ministry held a press conference at which a spokesperson listed the citizens band dial numbers the EZLN was using to facilitate communications, the location of its training camps, and the names of some of the base communities. Guadalupe Tepeyac was confirmed to be the headquarters for the rebels' General Command.

By the 9th, long lines of armored vehicles were lumbering down the uprooted dirt road that led into the rain forest, halting every hundred yards or so to remove obstacles and circumvent blown stretches. Central America hand Thomas Long, a journalist who had often accompanied Salvadoran troops into the field in the

1980s, marveled at the carelessness of the soldiers as they slowly removed barriers in low-lying valleys where they could easily be ambushed by guerrilleros positioned on higher ground in the trees. He was equally astounded by the Zapatistas' failure to attack.

The silence of the Zapatista command was unnerving. The Salinas government was being forced into a military option that could mire the Army for years in the swamps of the Lacandón jungle. Moreover, the troops were behaving badly, committing atrocities against the civilian population under the nose of the international press. Something had to be done.

On Sunday the 9th, a group of Tzotzil men approached independent television correspondent Epigmenio Ibarra in San Andrés Larráinzar in the hills above San Cristóbal. They asked Ibarra if he knew Amado Avendaño and handed him a folded envelope.

The first communiqué in 10 days from the Zapatista Army of National Liberation was published the next day in Avendaño's valuable little weekly—it had actually been dated January 6th, exposing a logistical lag in communications that would always plague Zapatista correspondence with the outside world. The communiqué insisted that there were no Guatemalans or Salvadorans or priests in the EZLN ranks. Arms had not been supplied by devious foreign backers— "We spent ten years accumulating these weapons," the rebels proudly asserted. The communiqué also made it perfectly clear that the Zapatistas were not laying down those arms anytime soon. But the guerrilleros did pledge to accept a ceasefire if the EZLN was recognized as a "belligerent force" and the rules of war, as codified in the Geneva Convention, were applied to the hostilities.

The communiqué was the first of a mighty Orinoco of such epistles that at this writing fill three fat volumes in the series published by ERA in Mexico City. Six years later, they are still flowing from the jungle.

A TURN AWAY FROM WAR

The moment the military adjutant summoned him from the elite New Year's Eve soirée to the presidential hot line and his Secretary of Defense informed him that San Cristóbal de las Casas had just fallen to a band of ski-masked Indians, Carlos Salinas must have had an inkling that the party was over. As the days drifted on, his pessimism was confirmed. Six years of rescuing the nation for the rich, of dismantling and selling off state industry to make a better Mexico for himself and his cronies, seemed suddenly to be slipping out of control.

Salinas's fury at his bumbling underlings and the cheeky rebels—the "professionals of violence"—grew daily. Not only had these upstart Indians spoiled Mexico's step up to the first world by reminding the nation of the debt it owed its Indian poor on the very day that NAFTA took over, but now these *pinche inditos* were intent on wrecking the presidential succession, too, specifically the campaign of his hand-picked successor Luis Donaldo Colosio, a functionary he had so closely groomed to take over that reporters were now calling Colosio "Salinas with hair."

Something was not "functioning," the President told the nation January 10th, and that which is not functioning has to be "fixed."

When Interior Secretary Patrocinio González, a cousin by marriage to Carlos Salinas and a former governor of Chiapas, was summoned to Los Pinos, the Mexican White House, he must have known the fix was him. Patrocinio was the obvious goat in this drama: as governor of Chiapas, he had allowed the Zapatista threat to ferment, and as Secretary of the Interior he had downplayed the guerrilla's existence, even after the May 1993 skirmish with the military, deliberately misleading Salinas about a problem the President did not really want to know anything about anyway. By mid-afternoon, Patrocinio González was booking passage to Germany.

Assigned to fill Patrocinio's shoes was the nation's attorney general, Jorge Carpizo, the former rector of the national university and pontificating ombudsman of the National Human Rights Commission (the CNDH was a piece of window dressing Salinas constructed to deflect criticism from international human rights organizations during the NAFTA run-up). Carpizo's appointment was a clue that the President was about to sue for conciliation.

But the bombshell dropped by the President January 10th was the selection of Manuel Camacho Solís, Mexico City's former unelected mayor, as the government's "Commissioner of Peace & Reconciliation in Chiapas," charged with bringing the Zapatistas to the bargaining table. Camacho's appointment confirmed that rather than slaughtering the rebels and risking further international condemnation, Salinas would now use a policy of co-optation, a crucial turnaround from shooting war. The president's abrupt, adroit veering of course disoriented Zapatista strategies, which were geared to the certainty of protracted war.

The choice of Camacho as conciliator was an astonishing one. Just 43 days previous, he had resigned as mayor of Mexico City in a snit because Salinas had chosen Colosio as his successor. Scuttlebutt had it that Camacho would leave the PRI, a party of which he had been president, and forge an independent candidacy, much as Cuauhtémoc Cárdenas had done back in 1988 when the son of the beloved president Lázaro Cárdenas had broken from the official party and formed the left-center opposition PRD (Party of the Democratic Revolution). Days later, though, Salinas lured Camacho back into the fold and he accepted appointment as Mexico's Foreign Minister. Now Salinas had fingered this agile politico who had long been the PRI's conduit to the Left, to rescue his regime from the deepest doo doo it had stepped in since the PRI blatantly stole the 1988 election from Cárdenas.

After the high-level switcheroos, Carlos Salinas's unilateral January 12th declaration of a cease-fire was an anticlimactic formality. Informed by his Defense Secretary that the invaded municipalities had now been secured by the Armed Forces, the President took to the airwaves. As Commander-in-Chief, he ordered his troops to halt their advance and fire upon the "transgressors" only if they themselves were fired upon.

One burning question remained. Would the military, stung by the goring it was taking in the international press for its atrocious behavior during the first 12 days of the war, and on the verge of cornering the retreating rebels in their own jungle lair, respect the cease-fire order?

Leon Lázaroff, an earnest, hustling freelancer, was covering the war that day from the Nuevo Momón finca, another of Absalón Castellanos Domínguez's former properties deep in the jungle, when the troops rolled by around 11:30 a.m., still advancing on the Zapatista General Command in Guadalupe Tepeyac, where General Absalón was thought to be held and where aerial attacks had been intense all morning. Lázaroff watched maybe 60 trucks and armored vehicles push past the abandoned estate, where dozens of fleeing Tzeltales and Tojolabales had gathered for mutual protection.

By mid-afternoon, while the refugees at Momón agonized about whether there was really a cease-fire or not, Lázaroff watched the Army roll right back up the same jungle track, turning away from Tepeyac. The turn-around, even with Absalón right at the end of the road, was emblematic of the turn away from war. Although 2,000 troops had moved into El Bosque and Simojovel in the highlands and the bombing in the cañadas would not tail off for days, the uneasy truce on the ground stood for the next 13 months.

Whether the generals had willingly followed cease-fire orders or had been coerced into compliance by the institution's constitutional subservience to civilian power remains a military secret. The dissatisfaction of the brass at the pullback with the Zapatistas on the run was well-documented, and chafing between the military and Salinas continued throughout his remaining months in office. Indeed, several high-ranking military officers were implicated—but never charged—in the assassination of Luis Donaldo Colosio months later.

Six years later, the final tally of 12 days of shooting war in Chiapas is still clouded by claim and counterclaim. In its annual 1993–94 report, the CNDH lists 159 dead, including 16 soldiers and 38 civilian security agents. The Commission affirms that 67 non-police civilians were killed, and another 38 bodies remained unidentified. The Zapatista death toll was calculated at 48. Of 427 civilians reported disappeared, 407 had been located by February. The CNDH count is considerably less than the first call of 400 deaths by the San Cristóbal diocese, an estimate that Bishop Ruiz has never corrected. The uncounted corpses strewn about the war zone—such as the grinning calavera we found behind Rancho Nuevo—or hidden away in rumored common graves, or cremated in coffee warehouses on the road to Comitán, challenge the government's bottom line of death and devastation in Chiapas between January 1st and 12th, 1994.

ANOTHER ARMY

As the troops trudged up from Nuevo Momón in the jungle dusk on January 12th, another army was filling the huge *Zócalo* (central plaza) up in Mexico City—the biggest outpouring in six years of Mexico's disenchanted "civil society," that unstated alliance of opposition rank-and-filers, urban slumdwellers, independent campesino organizations, disaffected union sections, human rights warriors, feminists and gays, Christian base communities, ultra-left students, mild-mannered intellectuals, peaceniks, beatniks, *rockeros,* punks, street gangs, and even a few turncoat PRIistas, all of whose red lights go on at once whenever there is serious mischief afoot in the land.

Although estimating crowd size is not a fine science in Mexico, veteran civil society watchers called the January 12th March for Peace in Chiapas the largest gathering since the huge protests following the stealing of the 1988 elections from Cuauhtémoc Cárdenas.

Behind a great banner that demanded *"¡ALTO A LA MASACRE!"* (Stop the Massacre!) and chanting *"¡Asesinos!"* (Murderers!) in thunderous unison at empty government offices, the marchers—many of them carrying flickering candles—packed in around the jerry-rigged stage to hear Cárdenas and Rosario Ibarra, the diminutive, red-headed *doña* of disappeared political prisoners, and many more veteran battlers for democracy in Mexico, demand a just peace in Chiapas.

Out on the perimeters of the enormous congregation, reporters spotted faces canceled by dark ski masks. It had taken just 12 days. The sin-rostros had arrived in the capital.

DOVES AND DUROS

After being glued to screens and radios and newspaper headlines during the first dozen days of January, the nation inhaled deeply and wondered about the whys of the rebellion. Why had Mexico treated its Indians so badly that they were driven into repeated rebellion? The bottom line was a sort of national sense of guilt about the "Indian problem."

Some sectors of the civil society supported the armed option as just retribution for the poverty and racism heaped upon Mexico's ten to twenty million Indians (depending upon whose perimeters one adheres to). Others forcefully resisted violence in favor of Peace—with Justice.

On January 8th, hundreds of members of San Cristóbal's civil society, led by CONPAZ, a network of progressive coletos, marched through the old city and into the Indian barrios to demand an end to the army's killer counterattack. The line of march was packed with Tzotzil women and international delegations that had hurried to Chiapas after an emergency call by Bishop Ruiz for foreign observers to bear witness to the atrocities being committed by the military in the region. Participation in such activities would later become a pretext for expelling hundreds of foreign human rights observers from the country.

As the doves were marching in San Cristóbal, the *duros* ("hards") were bombing Mexico City. A parking garage blast near the national university (UNAM) gave voice to those who espoused the armed option. Two days later, police busted five alleged members of the PROCUP—the Revolutionary Party of Workers & Farmers/Popular Union—which in the 1980s had joined forces with remnants of the Party of the Poor, the last guerrilla army to rise in Mexico. Whether or not the Mexico City blast really was a PROCUP stunt, the group did take credit for bombing an army bank on Acapulco's Gold Coast the following night.

With classic guerrilla élan, pro-Zapatista forces moving out in the land targeted electricity generation. On the 6th, Federal Electricity Commission (CFE) towers were toppled near Uruápan, Michoacán, and Tehuacán, Puebla. On the 8th, a dynamite charge took out a third pylon near Cuautitlán, an industrial Mexico City suburb where transnationals like Ford have production facilities. Police deactivated a second charge that could have plunged the whole Valley of Mexico into darkness.

That same night, a pick-up truck, reportedly attempting to lob mortars into Military Camp #1 on the western edge of the capital, blew up after a first launching went awry—the assailants got away. After midnight, a massive explosion ripped up a PEMEX pipeline 60 miles northeast of the city—the government called the explosion an "accident."

The bombs were not confined to continental Mexico. The consulate in El Paso, Texas, was firebombed January 5th; the embassy compound in Guatemala City was scorched January 8th; subsequent blasts were recorded in Berlin, Bilbao, and Sidney.

When the Mexican Bolsa de Valores opened for business Monday, January 10th, the capital was paralyzed by bomb jitters. 27,000 police were mobilized to detain suspicious motorists and track down bomb threats. Cops swarmed over Benito Juárez International Airport and set up security cordons around key PEMEX, TELMEX (the Mexican phone company), and CFE installations. Police dogs bounded through the high-gloss hallways of the spanking new glass-and-steel stock exchange on Reforma (some reports suggested that a bomb was actually found on the premises), but the real blast victim that day was the market itself, which at the conclusion of a panic-driven trading session was down a whopping 6.2%, its fifth steepest dive ever. "This (the Zapatista uprising) is evolving into a real crisis," the director of COPARMEX, the most powerful business association in the land, grimly muttered to the business press.

On the peace-without-violence side of the equation, the cataract of goodwill and recrimination that pressurized the Zócalo on January 12th, had begun to spill across the girth and down the spine of the nation.

In Puruarán, Michoacán, 1,100 striking sugar workers unanimously voted to join the EZLN. Up in Chihuahua in the north, where small farmers deeply in debt to the banks had come together under the banner of "El Barzón," protestors parked their tractors on public highways and voiced support. In the capital, small groups had begun to gather in the afternoons to celebrate the Zapatistas in song and speeches. Eventually, a tent was set up and folding chairs brought out, giving the EZLN its first sit-down beachhead in the big city, not 50 yards from the National Palace.

Nourished by guilt about racism, ethnic chic became the *onda* (wave) in civil society. Premier novelist Carlos Fuentes applauded the Indians' goals (but not their methods)—Nobelist poet Octavio Paz dissed them both. Boxing manager Ignacio Berenstein offered his star featherweight "Chiquito" González for a benefit match "to help the Chiapaneco Indians." The Ruta 100 bus drivers union in Mexico City sent their old uniforms to the jungle to clothe the naked indígenas, and schoolchildren in urban classrooms drew colorful pictures of soldiers beating up on Indians. Peace rallies were held in the central plazas of Morelia, Puebla, Cuernavaca, Acapulco, Chihuahua, Durango—more rock concerts than militant manifestations—where canned foods and sacks of rice and beans and old clothes and medicines were collected and caravans organized to drive south and deliver the goods. The first caravan, piloted by a band of middle-class Mexico City women on the Left, headed by PRD deputy Carlota Botay, reached Chiapas January 25th. The civil society was on the move.

THE CONCILIATOR COMES TO TOWN

The Commissioner for Peace & Reconciliation in Chiapas hit the ground running. "I've come to play!" Manuel Camacho Solís emphasized to the press corps jamming the patio of the Hotel Mazariegos January 13th. The photo ops included Camacho embracing Bishop Ruiz and pumping the beefy mitt of General Godínez. "The presence of the military will guarantee peace," he beamed to the General, lauding a military whose good name had recently been indecorously assailed by accusations of massacre.

On January 14th, Camacho formally proposed Don Samuel as mediator between the government and the EZLN, a motion that the Zapatistas had already made. An EZLN communiqué dated January 11th (but not delivered until January 17th) had set stipulations for the selection of a mediator. As a Mexican by birth, a seeker of solutions to social problems, and a member of no political party, the Bishop fit the Zapatista job description.

The rebel communiqué, the third received since the New Year's Day offensive, again requested belligerent status for the Zapatista Army of National Liberation, a designation that would give the guerrilla Geneva Convention standing. Camacho had been expressly warned by Salinas to avoid this option at any cost, because it would open a Pandora's box of international intervention at a delicate moment in the Mexican dynamic. Chiapas was to be strictly a local affair.

The urbane, preppy Camacho Solís was out of place in San Cristóbal's ethnicity-drenched ambiance but well positioned for the role of conciliator. His family was sprinkled with military men (his father had been Surgeon General), and his dead wife's uncle, the Cardinal of Monterrey, was an auténtico coleto. Moreover, as a younger man, Camacho had been part of the PRI's Maoist clique—as had Raúl Salinas, the President's brother. Some of these Maoists, under the rubric of Línea Proletaria, had been early outside agitators in Chiapas—and mortal foes of what had evolved into the Zapatista Army of National Liberation.

What exactly were the political ambitions of Manuel Camacho Solís, a rejected heir to King Carlos Salinas, who had unceremoniously dumped cold water on his bid to sit on the throne of Mexico? Camacho's staff broadly hinted that their man was still a presidential candidate, insinuating that this status would be helpful in luring the rebels out of the jungle. As Peace Commissioner, Camacho now represented a third force in the conflict, one that sought a return to domestic tranquillity, the price for which was now under discussion. "You are worth more than whatever candidate!" an elderly matron shouted at the Conciliator when he attended his first Sunday Mass in Don Samuel's cathedral.

Meanwhile, Luis Donaldo Colosio's campaign was in cold storage. When an excited woman with razor-sharp fingernails accidentally slashed the PRI candidate on the cheek in Guadalajara, drawing copious amounts of blood, no one even noticed. The Colosio campaign couldn't make it within 15 pages of the first one. Whatever Camacho said, whatever he did, wherever he went, was up there in eight-column headlines.

Colosio was not the only candidate playing second fiddle. The PRD's Cuauhtémoc Cárdenas was having a hard time drumming up crowds for his second run at the presidency. Moreover, wherever he whistle-stopped, handfuls of ski-masked rebel supporters would show up and shout annoying "¡Ya bastas!" The candidate had not been very forthcoming about the conflict either. His initial inclination had been to endorse the military (his father had been an army general), but by January 10th, he was urging soldiers to disregard orders to commit atrocities. Like Carlos Fuentes, Cuauhtémoc Cárdenas supported the EZLN's goals but not its methods.

HISTORY WILL ABSOLVE US

During his first weeks of feeling out the Zapatistas, Camacho shuttled between Chiapas and Mexico City, meeting with the President and the Secretary of Defense and the new Interior Minister Carpizo in lengthy closed-door sessions. The press releases were upbeat. On January 15th, Salinas was feeling so good about the situation that he proposed an amnesty that would pardon all insurgents who had been "pressured" into participating in the uprising.

The Amnesty edict did not at all please the Zapatista high command. Fuming over his pipe "somewhere in the Lacandón jungle," Subcomandante Marcos formulated a stinging reply to the Salinas offer that has since achieved the status of Fidel Castro's 1954 "History will absolve me" speech.

"Why do we have to be pardoned?" the Sup asked. "What are we going to be pardoned for? For not dying of hunger? For not being silent in our misery? For not humbly accepting our historical role of being the despised and outcast? For having picked up arms after finding all other roads closed to us? For having demonstrated to the rest of the country and the rest of the world that human dignity still lives? For having been well prepared before beginning our uprising? For having carried guns into battle rather than bows and arrows? For being Mexicans? For being primarily indigenous peoples? For having called upon the people to struggle in all possible ways for that which belongs to them? For not following the example of previous guerrilla armies? For not giving up? For not selling out? For not betraying ourselves?

"Who must ask for pardon, and who can grant it? Those who for years have satiated themselves at full tables while death sat beside us so regularly that we stopped being afraid of it? Those who filled our pockets and our souls with empty promises?

"Or should we ask pardon from the dead, our dead, those who died 'natural' deaths from the measles, whooping cough, breakbone fever, cholera, typhoid, mononucleosis, tetanus, malaria, and other lovely gastrointestinal and lung diseases? Our dead, the majority dead, the democratically dead dying from sorrow because no one ever did anything? Because the dead, our dead, went just like that, without anyone ever counting them, without anyone ever saying ¡Basta ya!

"Must we ask pardon from those who have denied us the right to govern ourselves? From those who lack respect for our customs, our culture, and ask for our obedience to a law whose moral basis we do not accept? Those who pressure us, torture us, assassinate us, disappear us for the serious 'crime' of wanting a piece of land, neither a big one nor a small one but a simple piece of land from which we could grow something to fill our stomachs?

"Who must ask for pardon, and who can grant it? The President of the Republic? State officials? Senators? Governors or Mayors? The Police? The federal army? The great gentlemen of banking, industry, commerce, and land?

Political parties? Intellectuals? Students and teachers? The workers? The campesinos? The people of the neighborhoods? Indigenous peoples? Our dead?

"Good health and a hug to you all, and in this cold weather, you should be thankful for both, even if they come from 'a professional of violence.'"

MEXICO PROFUNDO

In the remote Indian sierras and deserts of "México Profundo," or "Deep Mexico" (the term coined by anthropologist Guillermo Bonfils in the 1980s gained post-rebellion currency), the EZLN seed found fertile fields. In far-off Sonora, Mayo Indians encamped in front of the statehouse in Hermosillo and joined their land demands upon the governor with those of the Zapatistas. The Purépechas of Michoacán came together as a "nation" and blocked roads in the central highlands of the state, demanding indigenous autonomy. Otomí women went to see the governor of Querétaro to demand justice and endorse the EZLN program. In Quintana Roo, police grabbed a Mayan ejido leader and accused him of stockpiling weapons for the Zapatistas.

As the Zapatista phantom galloped through Indian Mexico, ghostly guerrilleros were spotted in the hills of Tlaxcala and Chihuahua and up at Palmar del Río in the Sierra Negra of Puebla. In the Mixtec mountains of that key central Mexican state, 25 villages banded together behind an old troublemaker named Gaudencio Ruiz and raised the banner of the "Chiapanecos." Military authorities got nervous about handing out the usual permits for five tons of gunpowder, the crucial ingredient in the wild Nahua Indian Carnival re-creation of the historic Battle of Puebla up in Huejotzingo. Real-life armed uprising was threatened if the fiesta was canceled.

Of most concern to government security planners were the highly Indian states of Guerrero and Oaxaca, where rebellion is endemic. In the latter, an entity with 18 distinct indigenous peoples living in 412 majority Indian municipalities, news of the rebellion spread like the forest was on fire. Near Juxtlahuaca in the Mixteca sierra, embattled Triqui Indians pledged allegiance. Down on the Oaxacan isthmus, where the COCEI—the long-lived left-wing alliance of Zapotec workers, farmers, and students—holds power, assemblies were convened to discuss the Declaration of the Lacandón Jungle. Thousands of Indians took over state and federal offices in support of both Zapatista and Zapotec demands, and the director of the Solidarity program flew in to talk turkey.

"The lesson from this for the Indians is that if you pick up the gun, the government will finally listen to you," Jenaro Domínguez, advisor to the National Coordinating Body of Indian Peoples (CNPI) told me in early February.

Next door to Oaxaca, along the tropical Pacific coast in Guerrero, the EZLN uprising had stirred memories. It had been 20 years since the rebel chieftain Lucio Cabañas and his Party of the Poor had been wiped clean out of the sierra, and now posters appeared calling for young men to sign up for the new guerrilla, reported La Jornada in mid-January. The military, edgy after the Acapulco army bank bombing, combed the mountains above the Costa Grande hunting for rebels. On January 13th, up in Tepetixtla in Coyuca municipality, a town where Lucio once held court, a new farmers' group was chartered. A year later, 17 members of that group, the Campesino Organization of the Southern Sierra (OCSS) would be gunned down by the Guerrero state motorized police, and the massacre would become the seed for a new Mexican guerrilla army in the state.

Across Guerrero, in La Montaña, demographically one of the most impoverished regions in all of deep Mexico, Amuzgos and Mixtecos, Tlapanecos, and Nahuas marched on the state capital of Chilpancingo. "In the name of our rivers and our mountains, our birds and our butterflies, in the name of our grandparents and all the generations that were sacrificed before them," the Indians of Guerrero proclaimed their support for the sin-rostros, the men and women of the Zapatista Army of National Liberation who had dared to stand up. ¡Basta ya!

COMMUNICATION FLOW

The communiqués had now begun to flow more fluidly from the jungle—eight in the first 17 days, including a note to Bill Clinton advising him that U.S. aircraft was liquidating Indians in southeastern Mexico, 31 in the first 31 days, 41 more in February, and February is a short month. Marcos's messages protested harassment on the fringes of the liberated zone but boasted of the EZLN's tactical advantages in a jungle where the rebels had been training for 10 years. Another poked fun at the popular television soap opera "Savage Heart" (Corazón Salvaje) and its star-crossed hero, Juan del Diablo. Occasionally Marcos would garnish his discourse with a fillip of English—"but of course"—tantalizing clues to a readership that was dying to discover his true identity. The communiqués were like a brilliant running commentary on Mexican life and their defiant, playful tone struck a nerve throughout the country—and the world—as, one by one, La Jornada, El Financiero (for a short while), and the opposition weekly Proceso circulated the epistles to a wider and wider audience. National and international diffusion was sped along by a press corps that numbered nearly a thousand in the first 23 days of the war. Activists in El Paso were already translating the communiqués and posting them daily on the Internet.

The EZLN first "welcomed" Camacho to the region (published January 18th), then endorsed the principle of "dialogue" (January 20th), insisting that it was not the rebels' intention "to hold the country hostage" and promising not "to impede the coming electoral process." "Change will not come with just one current or caudillo," Marcos wrote in a call for parallel action in other regions. All the communiqués flatly rejected the notion of laying down guerrilla arms until all their demands were fulfilled.

By the end of January, the interchange between the Commissioner and the Subcomandante had a manic-depressive tilt to it. The two spokespersons would flirt (*coquetear*, the headlines called it), then pull away from the table to hear out what their respective constituencies were trying to tell them. Curiously, through all of the push and pull of the first weeks of this dialogue, the fate of General Absalón Castellanos Domínguez was rarely mentioned.

THE CRIMES OF MI GENERAL

The Mexican government does not like to discuss the snatching of its aristocrats in public, lest such shared concern might spur the rabble to commit similar acts of retribution against the rich and powerful. During the first weeks of the war in Chiapas, General Absalón's name dropped out of common usage.

Where was he? Four days after the General was taken, Absalón's valet, René Ruiz, was freed and hoofed it back up to the San Joaquín. Ruiz had left his General with only a handful of cookies for lunch, and he was worried. On the 12th, medical personnel from the Solidarity hospital in Guadalupe Tepeyac were released by the rebels and staggered into Las Margaritas to report the ex-governor was being held in a hut behind the clinic.

Talk of a prisoner exchange was in the wind by the third week of the month. The January 20th communiqué hinted broadly that the time was ripe for such an interchange. On the 20th, 71 accused Zapatistas remained locked down in Cerro Hueco.

Reporters who got within a few miles of Tepeyac on the 27th (and were shooed off by three gun-toting rebels) asked the young men where the General was being held. "We haven't seen Absalón around here lately, and we really don't have the time to go visit him," one faceless Zapatista quipped. "He's probably out cutting firewood in some Indian village. At his age, my papa carried 30 kilos. We are proving to Absalón how we suffer here."

Spanish reporters were the first to find the General. In a January 30th interview, Maribel Herruzo described the hostage as being blindfolded 24 hours a day, unshaven, and disoriented. He had not been beaten, the white-bearded, hawk-faced Absalón thought, because he was a prisoner of war. He had been moved 15 times by his count but was well fed—beans and sometimes chicken, the General said, "very delicious." He had not bathed in a month.

On January 31st, 40 alleged Zapatista prisoners were released from Cerro Hueco. That left 31 government bargaining chips still inside.

Despite the tendency towards reconciliation, tensions were rubbed raw in the war zone. On February 1st, the military broadcast a false alarm that rebels were marching on Ocosingo, throwing that jungle city into panic on the eve of the feast of the Virgin of Candelaria, the town's patron saint. Copycat Zapatistas roamed Ocosingo and Las Margaritas rustling cattle. The army would not let more than three farmers go into their fields together to salvage what was left of the coffee crop or empty beehives of honey that was starting to ferment. When the campesinos returned, hauling their drums, soldiers stuck rods into the honey to see if they were smuggling bullets to the rebels.

On February 3rd, Manuel Camacho unilaterally announced the creation of two "free zones"—*zona francas*—one at San Miguel near Ocosingo and the other at Guadalupe Tepeyac, cañadas where support for the Zapatistas was overt. The two militaries were excluded from these zones—only the International Red Cross (IRC) could venture inside, bringing humanitarian aid to communities trapped by the war. For the next year, the zonas francas would institutionalize the military encirclement of the EZLN but, ironically, guarantee the Zapatistas a liberated chunk of national territory.

The creation of the free zones also defined a space in which prisoners could be released to the IRC—such an arrangement would give the Zapatistas international standing and bolster their demand for belligerent status.

Just then, the EZLN sent word that General Absalón Castellanos Domínguez had been sentenced to a life of hard labor "in some Indian community" for his many crimes against the indigenous peoples of Chiapas, felonies that included homicides and torture and kidnapping and the theft of Indian property. The bad news was that the General's sentence had been commuted.

Reporters who reached Guadalupe Tepeyac on February 4th looking for Absalón could not find him. He was not in back of the clinic, had not been there for weeks. Townspeople fed the press corps transparent soup with two tiny strips of cow meat floating on the filmy surface. "This is the soup we are saving for Manuel Camacho," one Zapatista supporter told La Jornada.

Handing over the General was the first step to the bargaining table, and the coquetry on both sides of the barricade grew intense. Absalón's family fretted. The army was growing impatient. Finally, on February 14th, the Commissioner and Bishop Ruiz jointly announced that the General would be freed within 48 hours, at Guadalupe Tepeyac, on Ash Wednesday.

SHORT PEOPLE

It had been five years since Samuel Ruiz—called "Father," or *Tatic* in Tzotzil and *J'Tatik* in Tzeltal—had set foot in Guadalupe Tepeyac, a distant corner of the huge diocese 20 kilometers from the Guatemalan border. Now the Red Bishop was planted in the middle of a jungle trail in the broiling heat, clad in glistening white robes and an embroidered surplice. He had brought with him the ashes that symbolize the Lenten season, with which to mark the faithful.

The Commissioner for Peace & Reconciliation and his team were also in place. 300 members of the working press, trucked in for the historic interchange, were confined to a white circle, chalked like some magic ring in a clearing at the bottom of the road around the far bend from Tepeyac. For hours, the sweltering media jockeyed for position, swatting at weird winged insects. The wait finally ended at 17:25 Lacandón jungle time when General Castellanos, escorted by five small masked Zapatistas, two of them women, appeared at the top of the rise and briskly marched down the road. *"¡Viva el E-Z-L-N!"* chanted the women and children in freshly laundered duds who lined both sides of the path. *"¡That all the landowners should die!"* rang in the stoic, Quijote-bearded Absalón's ears as he passed through this gauntlet of shame.

Don Absalón Castellanos Domínguez had been declared guilty by the Justice Tribunal of the Zapatista Army of National Liberation for "having obliged the Indians of Chiapas to rise up in arms," and he had been sentenced "to perform manual labor for the rest of his life," but the EZLN had commuted the punishment, "condemning him to live until the end of his days with the shame of having received a pardon and the good will of those he had killed, robbed, kidnapped, and plundered." The EZLN insisted that Absalón was being handed over in exchange for "all Zapatista combatants and civilians unjustly imprisoned" since the war began January 1st.

Then stubby Mayor Moisés, the architect of Absalón's kidnapping, nudged the General in the direction of Camacho Solís and Don Samuel. "We have given our word. You are witnesses that we speak with honor."

Moisés was followed by Aarón, a small dark man in a beautifully ironed short-sleeved shirt, who read a lengthy document, "The Clamor of the Lacandón Jungle," addressed to Manuel Camacho Solís, "the envoy of Peace." The "Clamor" lambasted the *PRI-gobierno* (the amalgam of the Institutional Revolutionary Party and the government it has sponsored for the past seven decades), brought life to the Zapatistas' 11 demands, and was, in essence, a rough draft of the *pliego petitorio,* the formal petition of demands the EZLN would present at the coming peace talks in San Cristóbal. The "Clamor" also accused General Absalón of embezzling state funds to build mansions in Tuxtla and the theft of 60,000 acres of good Indian land. Absalón, amazed at this last-minute impertinence, could no longer contain himself. "What you have heard here is totally false!" he grabbed the mike and rasped.

The nation watched these astonishing events with its mouth open. Such withering criticism of the PRI-run government as Aarón had just given breath to was forbidden on Mexican television. The exotic setting intrigued viewers. But what made the most lasting impression on a public that had already seen a lot since January 1st, was how small the rebels were. So magnified by the media and national aspirations had the Zapatistas become that their actual scale had been forgotten. Now Camacho had to bend to shake the small hands of the men and the women without faces, whose weapons seemed almost longer than they were. For the first time since New Year's Day, the Zapatistas had shown themselves to the world, and they were short.

Dusk, accompanied by a zillion fresh venomous bugs, was settling in over the jungle, and the truckloads of journalists groaned back up to San Cris to file. The release of General Absalón had not been an exchange—the 31 remaining presumed rebels in Cerro Hueco had not been released. What was going on here?

"The wars here are always brutal, but they have their own logic, and that logic leads to dialogue," veteran anthropologist Chip Morris observed to La Jornada's Hermann Bellinghausen up in San Andrés Larráinzar on the traditional day of Carnival. "The declaration of war is a way of saying 'I am.' When the other military replies with a strong attack, they too are saying 'I am.' With the Maya, you cannot talk until you know with whom you are talking. So the release of Absalón is a way of saying 'now we can talk.'

"But you must be patient. The EZLN has entered into a slow period of conversation in accordance with its own time and its own needs..."

CHINAMECA

At the end of January, TV producer Epigmenio Ibarra, who had delivered the first EZLN communiqué, received an intriguing phone call at his Mexico City offices: the Zapatistas needed more than Marcos's quirky, slow-arriving letters to get their message out. Now they wanted to tell the story of their rebellion in person. Would Ibarra be interested in interviewing and filming the Clandestine Revolutionary Indigenous Committee?

Around the same time, La Jornada had received feelers from the Zapatistas. A telephone call would soon be made. Blanche Petrich, one of the more diligent reporters in the country, took the call up in the capital and caught the first plane to Chiapas. Epigmenio and his French cameraman Philippe hooked up with Petrich and ace photographer Antonio Turok in San Cristóbal. That night they were crammed into a car, told to go to sleep, driven to the end of the road, unloaded, blindfolded, put into a truck, and when the dirt path ran out, mounted on mules. Watches had been confiscated at the beginning of the adventure and no one knew just how long they rode. It had begun to rain. Near dawn, they reached the EZLN encampment.

Petrich's interviews, Turok's stills, and Ibarra's film of tiny Comandante Ramona and the members of the Clandestine Committee, put a human face on the sin-rostros. Marcos's responses to Petrich's probings were devoured by a public hungry to know this witty, irreverent guerrilla myth.

"Living in the Lacandón jungle for a ladino (mestizo) is the worst thing that could happen to you, even worse than watching Televisa 24 hours a day," Marcos regaled. Peace talks were indeed at hand, but the Sup didn't know if he would sit at the table. "We see the threat of Chinameca in all of this," he told Petrich.

Chinameca?

On April 10th, 1919, a weary Emiliano Zapata rode into the Chinameca hacienda at the end of the Cuautla Valley in Morelos state, where he had fought the military to a standstill for nearly 10 years. He was tired and out of bullets and men, and had come to pick up a load of ammunition and guns promised him by an alleged turncoat federal officer, Jesús Guajardo. When Zapata rode alone through the archways of the hacienda, Guajardo's troops opened fire, cutting the great revolutionary leader down. 80 years later, the mere mention of the place name Chinameca still suggests government ambush.

"Chinameca's in this whole process," Marcos told the New York Times February 17th. "Our enemies know that the directors of our movement are going up there. They can ambush us in a minute and then bullfight with the protesters." Marcos summoned "compañeras and compañeros of good will" (i.e., the civil society) to interpose their bodies between the comandantes and the enemy. *"¡No nos deja solos!"* (do not let us go alone!) the General Command (CCRI) implored, and nongovernment organizations (NGOs) began organizing the *cordones de paz* or "peace belts" that would safeguard the imminent talks.

The Clandestine Indigenous Revolutionary Committee had reached consensus on attending the peace talks in early February after the first interviews were published and Ibarra's hourlong film on Marcos had aired on prime-time cable (a half-million viewers). Couriers crisscrossed the jungle mountains on foot, carrying the recommendation of the CCRI to attend the talks. Assemblies were convened in base communities in the Cañadas, the jungle, the highlands, and the north of the state—the four EZLN zones of influence—to preview the talks and pick delegates. "We are not going to send any pigeons—the delegates will be our best fighting cocks," Marcos boasted in a lengthy Proceso magazine interview on the eve of the talks.

The selection process was a complicated one. Communities that had prepared 10 years for protracted war now had to be convinced in four languages that talking to a government that had never listened to them before was the EZLN's best option. The concept that a "civil society" that had paid little more than lip service to Indian misery for 500 years was now prepared to defend Indian lives with their own, was a difficult sell.

Where the talks would be held was not even confirmed until the very last moment—Tapachula, Comitán, and Huehuetenango, the first Guatemalan city south, were mentioned. Ultimately, on February 19th, Camacho Solís leaked word to the press that the "Jornadas (Working Sessions) for Peace and Reconciliation" would be held in the Cathedral of San Cristóbal beginning Monday morning, February 21st.

The doors of the Cathedral were only a hundred miles northwest from the General Command headquarters at Guadalupe Tepeyac and a little less from the "gate" to EZLN territory at San Miguel, but the distances between the Zapatistas and Don Samuel's sanctuary were mined with all the treacheries that troubled the road to Chinameca.

STRAW JUST WAITING TO BURN

Three weeks after the shooting war had ended, Zapatista militia men and women had stripped off their ski masks and uniforms and become farmers again. The ground was hard and needed to be prepared for an uncertain Spring planting.

Rural Chiapas seethes with indignation at government inattention and the worst distribution of good land in the Mexican union. Campesinos battle the country bosses known as *caciques* and the agrarian authorities that back them up from one generation to the next for a wedge of land or an extension to their ejidos. Under General Absalón's governance, one farmworkers' union had 800 members jailed and its leaders butchered. Despite all the blood spilled out in the cornfields, nothing ever really changed. Rural Chiapas remained dry straw just waiting to burn. Then the Zapatista rebellion took wing.

"After a long night that seemed to have no end, it was necessary for the Zapatista thunderbolt to part the shadows," divined the Chiapas State Congress of Indian & Campesino Organizations (CEOIC), 280 farmers' groups that blurred party and ethnic affiliation, which came together in a stifling San Cristóbal coffee shed in the first days of the uprising. An alarmed Carlos Salinas replaced interim governor Elmar Setzer with another PRI flunky, Javier López Moreno, and instructed him to do his damnedest to corrupt the new farmers' alliance.

To this end, the government organized a "Peace" panel that became known as *Los Reyes Magos*, the Three Kings, because it came bearing so many gifts. Among the panelists were Eduardo Robledo, a PRI senator from Chiapas who would soon become his party's gubernatorial choice, and Eraclio Zepeda, the legendary leftist raconteur and one-time Fidel Castro bodyguard who would be Robledo's Secretary of Government.

On January 25th, Salinas was flown into Tuxtla under maximum security—his first visit to Chiapas since the uprising—and met with the CEOIC delegates for several hours. The tongue-lashing administered by the irate campesinos left the President wincing and his aides staring off into deep space just waiting for the session to end.

By February, political insurrection was sweeping through the state's 111 (out of 112) PRI-controlled municipalities (roughly equivalent to counties). In many towns in Los Altos, citizens questioned the whereabouts of unaccounted-for Solidarity monies. By February 12th, 26 town halls in the highlands were occupied by irritated residents, including four of the municipal palaces to which the EZLN had done significant damage January 1st. "This hasn't happened here since the Revolution," one elderly witness told La Jornada in Teopisca, a genteel town

30 kilometers from San Cristóbal, as 2,000 citizens stormed City Hall and ran the PRI mayor out of town.

The civil disobedience was most pronounced down on the farm. A wave of land occupations by independent campesino groups—most integrated into the CEOIC—made the maintenance of public peace problematic. On February 9th, the Mam Indian Supreme Council took over 11 coffee fincas in the Soconusco out on the coast. Far to the east in Chilon, near Palenque, Choles took 38 separate properties. In Ocosingo, a municipality that accounts for 17% of the Chiapas landmass, 27 ranches were overrun in the first valley alone. Mexico's Attorney General, Diego Valadés, flew into the state to investigate the occupation of 50,000 acres of private land in a hundred distinct land takeovers—plus the reported abstraction of 10,000 head of cattle. Since the 1992 Salinas-engineered mutilation of Article 27 that ended land distribution to the land-poor, any brave individual who occupies private land is subject to a maximum of 40 years in prison.

The revision of Article 27 was one of the matters the Zapatistas planned to take up with Manuel Camacho Solís when they got to San Cristóbal.

The cattle ranching elite did not respond kindly to the general insurrection sweeping the Chiapas countryside. The gnarly old cacique of the National Small Property Owners' Confederation flew into Tuxtla to warn ranchers that Don Samuel and the Church of Rome, German environmental groups, certain international financiers, and other not yet named co-conspirators wanted to convert Chiapas into an Indian reservation that would be beyond the reach of Mexican laws. The patriotic ranchers' associations of Ocosingo, Las Margaritas, Comitán, and Altamirano took up the cudgels. The maddest dogs were in the last-named cowtown, now bursting at the seams with 9,000 refugees from the war zone. Captained by the hunky (but short) Jorge Constantino Kanter, a "natural leader" as such demagogic types are labeled on the PRI's political tongue, the Stetsoned, fancy-mustachioed white ranchers of the region zealously witch-hunted suspect Zapatistas. Constantino's favorite target was the ramshackle nun-run San Carlos hospital, outside of which his klan gathered daily, threatening to burn the sisters out because they had once treated a wounded rebel.

On the eve of peace talks, Chiapas was electric with rumors. The "white guards," the bands of gunsels traditionally hired by the ranchers associations to protect the herds and kill Indians, were re-arming. In Ocosingo, the Citizens' Defense Group had received Army counterinsurgency training, Marcos revealed, and Guatemala-style civil patrols were being organized. The grapevine chimed with chisme that a Chiapas "contra" was training in the hills of Comitán, the Juarista National Army. The appearance of these early paramilitary groups obeyed a military campaign plan that called for the creation of counterinsurgent brigades in municipalities where the EZLN had influence.

The threat of a personal Chinameca notwithstanding, Subcomandante Marcos packed to head for San Cristóbal, ironizing over which of his rags to wear and pondering what price his "pestilent" ski mask might bring at auction and whether or not the positioning of a certain soft drink on the conference table would enhance the EZLN's war chest.

Despite the specter of Chinameca darkening their vision, the Zapatistas were coming in from the cold. What the hell, reasoned Marcos, we're already living *de prestado*, on borrowed time, having fully expected to be blown away New Year's Day. Now the EZLN was returning to San Cristóbal, but "not to beg anyone's pardon...

"We don't go to ask alms or recover the leftovers from the full tables of the powerful. We go to demand what is the right and reason of all the people: liberty, justice, democracy. For everyone, everything. For us, nothing...

"For the indígenas, everything. For the farmers, everything. For the workers, everything. For the students and the teachers, everything. For the children and the old people, everything. For everybody, everything. For us, nothing...

"For us, the smallest of these lands, those without faces and without histories, those armed with truth and fire, those who came from the night and the mountain, the true men and the true women, the dead of yesterday, today, and forever—for us, nothing. For everybody, everything!"

THE RED BISHOP'S CROSS TO BEAR

With its vaulted ceilings, gilded altars, burnished retablos of floating martyrs, alabaster columns, pews polished by centuries of the fannies of the faithful, and bleeding saints frozen in baroque niches, the Cathedral of San Cristóbal, now rebaptized the "Cathedral of Peace" and splashed with a fresh coat of yellow paint, was an auspicious setting for the return of the Zapatistas to the royal city for Las Jornadas Por la Paz y la Reconciliación.

Don Samuel Ruiz, the host of this House of the Lord, would later call the participants in Las Jornadas "actors," and the bishop himself played a leading role. Since the rebellion, "Comandante Sammy" had been vilified as the fountainhead of Zapatista mischief. Now, he was the favorite villain of the PRI, the television monopolies, the authentic coletos, and lunatic right fringe groups like Lyndon Larouche's "Ibero-American Solidarity Movement"—which printed posters accusing Ruiz of human sacrifice. "Samuel Ruiz—King of the Guerrillas" it read on the walls of Comitán and Altamirano. Homemade *corridos* (country ballads) cursed the Bishop as "a goddamn guerrillero." The Attorney General's office offered "proof"—CB radios bought with diocesan social development funds were being used by the rebels down in the jungle. Pablo Romo of the diocesan Fray Bartolomé de las Casas Human Rights Center and Jerónimo Hernández, a Jesuit down in Palenque, were both identified as Marcos.

The Army had taken more direct action against Samuel's Ocosingo outpost—machine-gun fire raked the roof of San Jacinto de Polonia and fragmentation grenades were tossed into the bell tower. The military made four separate searches for rebels the good fathers and nuns of the parish were said to be hiding in the church's 16th-century crypt.

Hounded for years by the auténticos, the ranching oligarchy, and the Vatican's ambassador to Mexico, Papal Nuncio Girolamo Prigione, and his accomplices in Rome, Don Samuel had grown obdurate in his defense of his Indian parishioners. For his efforts, he had been shot at, and his priests and nuns had been jailed and sometimes deported if they were non-Mexicans. On more than one occasion, the auténticos have tried to burn his church down. But still the Tatic soldiered on.

Down the decades, Bishop Ruiz had created solid social structures through which the Indians of the jungle and the highlands might struggle for a better life here on earth. Early on, young social agitators were invited into the diocese to organize Indian campesinos under the banners of the Union Quiptic, the Union of Unions, and the Rural Collective Interest Association (ARIC), the organizational sea from which the Zapatistas eventually emerged. Within the spiritual realm, greater participation in diocesan affairs by indigenous communities was a constant demand. "The ladinos think they own the holy spirit," Samuel once was told by a Tzeltal catechist. After that, the churches in the Tzeltal cañadas became increasingly autonomous. Today, in Zapatista communities, catechists with faces masked by bright red paliacates say Mass, and elsewhere in the diocese, women deliver the Host. At its height, when he was forced to retire in 1999, Don Samuel's army of catechists and deacons in the jungle and the Altos numbered 9,000.

The other army in the diocese—the Zapatista Army of National Liberation—has always had a conflictive relationship with Comandante Sammy. Sometimes the two competed for the same constituencies in farmers' alliances like ARIC and Quiptic, and there have been defections on both sides: Lázaro Hernández, Samuel's star deacon, was an EZLN comandante but defected after (he said) Marcos began attacking God, and Comandante David (Diego Ruiz), the highland leader from San Andrés, was an up-and-coming seminarian when he caught the Zapatista bug.

Although Samuel and Marcos, who has sometimes been accused of being a renegade priest, have known of each other for years, they are more veteran adversaries than intimates, and by the time of the rebellion, the Bishop's army and the EZLN had long since separated into estranged camps. Don Samuel vehemently opposed the Zapatistas' impending declaration of war and the violence that would invariably be unleashed against his flock. The Zapatistas, for their part, made their lack of religious affiliation a matter of public record in their first communiqué from the jungle: "We have not received orientation, direction, or support from any church structure, not from any diocese, state, Papal Nuncio, the Vatican, nor anyone…we want liberation without the theology…"

COMANDANTE SAMMY'S LITTLE MIRACLE

1994 had not figured to be a great year for the aging bishop (he was then 71). The previous November, the Nuncio and Cardinal Bernardin Gantin, the ultra-conservative African churchman who heads the Vatican's Sacred Congregation for the Doctrine of the Faith, had ganged up on the Red Bishop for "advocating a Marxist interpretation of the Gospel." Even a magnum protest by 10,000 of Tatic's indigenous supporters made little impression upon Rome. Samuel's removal appeared to be imminent

After January 1st, Carlos Salinas's first inclination was to finish off the wounded Bishop. José Córdoba, the house Svengali and conduit to the Church hierarchy, worked the phones to the Nuncio—a prelate so close to the Institutional Party that his last name was sometimes written PRIgione—and to Mexico City Cardinal Ernesto Corripio. According to La Jornada religious writer José Antonio Román, Córdoba urged Corripio to condemn Don Samuel for his ties to the EZLN.

Instead, at a January 10th Mexico City junta of the Mexican Bishops Conference (CEM), Cardinal Corripio, who once had headed the liberation-minded Pacific South (Oaxaca and Chiapas) archdiocese, publicly embraced Samuel and endorsed his "accompaniment" of the poor of Chiapas, a rude slap at both PRIgione and Córdoba. Many members of the CEM who had become disillusioned with Prigione because his hot line to Salinas now allowed him to bypass the Bishops Conference, applauded Corripio's hug.

It was the Miracle of Miracles! Within a few short weeks, the Zapatista uprising propelled the oft-maligned Ruiz from the dog house of his church to its very pinnacle. Influential members of the CEM suddenly saw Don Samuel as the Mexican Catholic Church's last best hope for social credibility. "Bishops who would never speak to us except badly, now come here and find a space," Father Romo exulted. Similarly, the Salinas regime, which initially had sought to pin the rebellion upon the Red Bishop, now saw Don Samuel as its political salvation. Federal bodyguards were assigned to protect the Tatic. Church attendance boomed. International luminaries like Bianca Jagger, Robert Kennedy Jr., and Rigoberta Menchú, in town to monitor human rights abuses, fought for pew space at Sunday Mass. TV crews jostled for the best shot. In February, just before the talks between the rebels and the government were to get under way, Brazilian supporters and a group of Cuernavaca taxi drivers nominated Samuel for the Nobel Peace Prize.

FETCHING THE ZAPATISTAS

Unlike New Year's Eve, when San Cristóbal had been caught with its pants down, the city was properly dressed for the Zapatistas' return. Three concentric circles of security—Military Police (400) and civilian volunteers (300 from the Mexican Red Cross, 400 from a dozen NGOs)—saturated the central plaza, draped in white to promote the aura of pacification and the environs of the Cathedral of Peace. They were there not so much to protect the people of San Cristóbal from the ski-masked insurrectionists as to safeguard the rebels from the wrath of the ranchers and the auténticos and other dark forces of reaction bent on teaching the uppity Indians a lesson.

On February 20th, Don Samuel finished up Sunday morning Mass and peeled off his robes. Pablo Romo knocked timidly at the door to tell him the Peace Commissioner was waiting outside in the car. Tatic prayed quickly and put the fate of this venture in the hands of the Creator.

The February morning was gray and streaked. Samuel Ruiz and Manuel Camacho left San Cristóbal driving north, escorted by the Highway Patrol, two International Red Cross ambulances, two other unmarked vehicles, and a rattling busload of reporters. The convoy was the last to leave—two others had departed in the dawn to pick up EZLN delegates at the gates in Guadalupe Tepeyac and San Miguel. Civilian vehicles had been added because the Zapatistas were coming in armed, and the IRC cannot transport armed combatants.

The press bus was halted at the turnoff to Chamula and told to wait. The Bishop's caravan continued north in the direction of San Andrés Larráinzar—called Sakamchién de los Pobres on the Zapatista map. 90 minutes later, Camacho and the Bishop were back, loaded with Zapatistas, nine of them in three civilian cars. Marcos was said to be among them. That Marcos and other delegates had come as far as San Andrés in the highlands to be picked up, skirting all sorts of military barricades down in the jungle, indicated the Zapatistas still had the capacity for mobility that had gotten them to San Cristóbal January 1st.

The convoy sped down Insurgentes into the tree-lined plaza and screeched to a halt in front of the Cathedral of Peace almost at the stroke of noon. Camacho and Ruiz bailed out first. Two small Indians, their faces masked by paliacates, emerged from the back seat, carrying enormous suitcases. Three armed Zapatista women popped out of the second car, then a ski-masked man, bent almost double under a bulky pack. Two heavily armed rebels, also ski-masked—one of them wearing a beribboned Tzotzil ceremonial hat—jumped from the third vehicle to cover the backs of their comrades.

The Zapatistas' reappearance in San Cristóbal was greeted by fervent "¡Vivas!" from the several hundred onlookers—many of them local Indian construction workers and house servants. But no group was more eager to greet the rebels than the hordes of paparazzi who surged forward to get a closer shot. The NGOs linked arms and wrestled with the determined press pack. "Yoo-hoo! You're Marcos—we know you!" yodeled one photographer at the Zapatista soldier struggling with the bulky backpack. The Subcomandante hesitated, then continued towards the open cathedral door, where Don Samuel and Manuel Camacho Solís were now stationed to greet the insurgents. "Yoo-hoo! Marcos!" the paparazzi persisted. Then, ever so coyly, the Sup reached down and pulled up a pant leg to display a muddy boot and a slice of hairy white flesh before he evaporated into the cathedral. *Enseñando pierna*, the maneuver is called in Mexican cheesecake argot: "showing some leg," a gimmick invoked by starlets at major motion picture premieres.

It was going to be that kind of a week.

CONVERSATIONS IN THE CATHEDRAL

The opening session was set for February 22nd at 6:30 in the evening. Reporters assembled early and spent the day squabbling over space. 370 newsgatherers had registered to cover the conversations in the cathedral.

The curtain went up right on time, a very un-Mexican note. Don Samuel, followed by 19 masked and armed Zapatistas, marched in from stage left and took up stations behind a long oak table. The Commissioner entered quietly from stage right. "This is a historic occasion," Don Samuel began modestly. Indeed the Gran Guignol spectacle of masked guerrilleros bringing large-caliber automatic weapons to the peace table in a cathedral filled with sailing martyrs had already achieved a perverse niche in the history of Mexican surrealism.

Don Samuel greeted the Commissioner, greeted the Zapatistas. The cameras zoomed to Subcomandante Marcos, hunched over to speak into the microphone to the Bishop's right. "Through my voice speaks the voice of the Clandestine Indigenous Revolutionary Committee," he breathed, establishing his identity as an interlocutor. The subcommander then asked each of the delegates to introduce themselves, which some rebels did, some in Chol, others in Tojolabal and Tzeltal and Tzotzil. Translating between the four languages and Spanish would extend deliberations for many days.

Now, with serendipitous timing, Comandante Ramona, the diminutive leader of the Zapatista women whom Petrich's interview had brought to national notice, produced a folded Mexican flag from her *moral* (woven shoulder bag) and handed a corner to Subcomandante Marcos, crouched in the first line of Zapatistas. As she struggled to drape it across the table, her size subverted her stretch. Gallantly, El Camacho stepped into the breach, grabbing a corner of the tricolored, snake-and-eagle-insignia'd cloth. The cameras rattled like a thousand Gatling guns, the flash bulbs blasted as if war had been declared all over again,

Even before they had begun, the peace talks had turned into a riot of patriotic symbolism.

By Tuesday evening, the country was on the edge of its seat, ready for the next installment of this national telenovela. By the end of February, Marcos Mania was sweeping the land—the subcomandante stared out from every magazine cover and daily paper in Mexico. The virus was liable to spread anywhere. On Saturday night at Bellas Artes up in Mexico City, at a performance of *Nabucco*, the stirring Verdi opera that tells of the Israelites' exodus from Babylonia, a young man had risen in the second balcony to shout *"¡Qué vivan los Zapatistas!"* and the tuxedo-and-evening-gown-draped gentry on the floor had responded with *"¡Qué vivan!"*

Now, outside on the streets of San Cristóbal, the assiduously mercantile matrons of Chamula were hawking "Marcos" and "Ramona" dolls (they still are), ballpoint pens, and tee-shirts featuring the Sup's visored visage. And then there were "Los Alzados" ("the risen-up ones"), the condoms produced by a safe sex group just for the peace talks, which so offended the Zapatistas. "They're selling the blood of our martyrs on the streets," complained Comandante Pedro, perhaps confusing bodily fluids.

"Buenas noches, compañeros, I'm going to speak for a long time, so you better change your cassettes now," the subcomandante warned the press. His voice sounded world-weary but quick-tongued, at first soft and grave but then deepening, swooping, sometimes cracking: "When we came down from the mountain, carrying our packs and our dead, we came first to the city to find the *patria* (fatherland).

"We came to the cities armed with truth and fire. We came to ask the patria why you have left us alone for so many years..." The subcomandante's slow oratory, replete with cadenced repetition, had the cant of the prophet-warriors of past centuries. "Why do we have to sleep with our boots on and our souls upon a string?" he asked. "We have become soldiers so that we do not have to be soldiers anymore." The Sup sounded a Lennonist note: "Now we have decided to give peace a chance." When the guerrilla-poet was done a half hour down the pike, there wasn't a dry eye in the house. The speech, filmed, printed, pronounced, repeated, and otherwise ritualized, has since become a sort of Zapatista sacred text.

BRASS TACKS

Negotiations replaced show biz by the third day of the Jornadas. The highlight of the EZLN's 34-point pliego petitorio, or list of negotiating points, was the demand for Salinas's resignation and the selection of a transitional government. Unlike their Latin guerrilla predecessors, the Zapatistas did not ask for state power. They did, however, demand the renegotiation of NAFTA and the revocation of the revisions to Article 27. Other demands included the creation of an independent electoral authority to oversee the coming presidential process and the autonomy of the nation's indigenous zones—in subsequent talks, autonomy would become the EZLN's fundamental goal.

Lodged inside the rambling yellow cathedral, the negotiations moved glacially. Camacho Solís had been instructed to restrict all concessions to those that could be realized locally—the Salinas administration was committed to maintaining the illusion that the Zapatista rebellion was confined to four municipalities in southeastern Chiapas and had no national ramifications. This persistent and deliberate misreading has poisoned all peace talks since.

Two of the stickier items on the table were indigenous autonomy, which Camacho was not authorized to discuss, and the cancellation of the mutilations to Constitutional Article 27. The Commissioner had been ordered to cede no ground on the constitutional revision. The powerful old PRI dinosaur, Carlos Hank González, Salinas's Agriculture Secretary and an agribusiness tycoon in his own right, attacked any return to the original text of 27 as "absurd and archaic," a signal to foreign investors that Mexican agriculture was too fickle a venture to dabble in. When Carlos Hank spoke, few dared to challenge him.

Other Zapatista agrarian demands such as land distribution, increased credits, fertilizers, and even revision of NAFTA, were stonewalled by the government's offer to create commissions that would render resolutions "within the next 90 days." Few commissions were ever created, and those that were, proved a joke. NAFTA, for example, was to be reviewed by a commission headed by Commerce Secretary Jaime Serra Puche, the man who had negotiated the treaty.

Camacho dodged the Zapatista social demands by assigning them to government assistence agencies like the Solidarity program. Other points, such as remunicipalization to give Indian towns greater representation, were to be settled by the state of Chiapas to emphasize the regionalization of the conflict. Salinas would not resign. There would be no transitional government.

As to the EZLN's demand for an independent electoral authority, Camacho said he was powerless. Eight weeks after the conclusion of the conversations in the cathedral, however, nine political parties voted to create an autonomous federal election institute—but the PRI government would still play the decisive role in the IFE during the 1994 presidential election.

The talks had groaned on for so long that only a handful reporters remained in town for the grand finale. They joined the principal actors in the cathedral a few minutes past 10 on a foggy San Cristóbal a.m. on March 1st. Under the spiring vaults, Don Samuel underscored the religious context: "Peace is a gift of God...to announce Peace, you must also be a constructor of Peace..." the prelate intoned obliquely.

The use of the word came to the Zapatista side of the table first. Marcos was now stooped over in the back row quietly chewing on the pipe stem inserted in the mouth hole of his *pasamontañas* (ski mask). Comandantes Ramona, Juan, and Humberto sat to the Bishop's right, and it fell to Humberto to summarize the Zapatista side of the talks. The Comandante's words were suprisingly hard-edged. "We want the great quantities of land that are in the hands of the finqueros and the national *terratenientes* (landholders) and the foreigners and the other persons who own a lot of land and are not farmers. We want these lands to pass into the hands of the villagers that have no land. We want the federal government to return to the Swiss the Pilatus airplanes that bombed our villages, and that the money accumulated by that exchange be used for programs to better the lives of workers in the cities and the country. We want the government of the United States to retire the helicopters that are being used to repress the Mexican people. For everybody everything. For us, nothing!" Subcomandante Marcos puffed away energetically on his pipe.

Looking a little gray around the gills, Manuel Camacho presented a 35-page document, the government response to 32 out of the 34 demands listed in the Zapatista pliego petitorio. "The Pledges for Peace and Reconciliation" were read page by page by an aide, and when he was at last done, the Commissioner congratulated the participants and anticipated a final accord—once, of course, the Zapatista communities had ratified acceptance, a foregone conclusion. "There are no winners and losers in this process," the Camacho riffed—but, of course, he himself was the big winner. Sent to do an impossible job, the ex–presidential hopeful had not only lured the rebels to the peace table but he had aced their demands with idle promises of commissions and regional improvements. Camacho was "very content." Peace was at hand, the shortest guerrilla war "since World War II" was virtually over, and best of all, the solution had been achieved by Mexicans!

The previous week, the Wall Street Journal had run an interview with Manuel Camacho Solís in which he announced he was still very much of a candidate for the presidency of Mexico.

Now the voice returned to Juan, to whom fell the responsibility for thanking the hosts for their honesty and hospitality, a gracious tradition that still prevails in Indian communities across the land. "We have encountered attentive ears here, prepared to listen to the truths that issued from our lips. The dialogue of San Cristóbal was a true one. There was no duplicity or lies. Nothing was hidden between our hearts and those of the people of reason and authority. We have the obligation to reflect well on what these words say. Now we must speak to the collective heart that orders us."

"This has been a great step forward in the construction of God's kingdom," Don Samuel hosanna'd, predicting the final accords could be signed "before the end of the month."

The Zapatistas sat coolly in their seats, the smoke billowing up around Marcos's masked ears. The outspoken voice of the rebels had said nothing, absolutely nothing, during the ceremony. Perhaps he was wondering if, after all the pomp and puffery, he was really going to get out of the Cathedral of Peace alive. This was also a concern of Camacho—he had warned against provocateurs in his remarks. Now, before some nut took a potshot at the comandantes and blew his coup right there on the spot, the Commissioner and the Bishop hustled the 14 remaining long-packed-and-ready-to-go Zapatistas out of the cathedral and into the waiting vehicles.

Virtually every story filed that day from San Cris had a similar spin: The Zapatistas had won unprecedented concessions from the government and peace was at hand. It was a matter of days, or at most, weeks, before the definitive peace treaty would be signed.

But the rebels themselves had a slightly different take on the conversations in the cathedral. "Until now, the only solution proposed to our problem has been pure promises and a mountain of paper," one delegate told La Jornada upon taking hurried leave of the Cathedral of Peace, drawing a fine line between government "response" and government "resolution." Moreover, since the opening salvo of the sessions, the Subcomandante had insisted that no decision would be made without the consent of the communal assemblies, and he had warned that there had been opposition in those assemblies even to sending delegates to the dialogue in San Cristóbal. In the Zapatista structure, the assembly is the crucial building block. Under the leadership principle of *mandar obedeciendo* (governing by obeying the will of the community) no decision is taken without extended consultation. This has been true for years—there would be no EZLN today if the immersion of the communities in the decision-making process were not a visceral reality. But such deep commitment to communal participation was not well understood by a government and its pundits accustomed to top-down leadership in which the approval of the *pueblos*—the people and their villages—is a mere formality that their leaders are charged with guaranteeing.

The Zapatistas knew better. Now, as they stuffed their belonging into the waiting cars, preparing to leave town still armed and masked and with their dignity intact, they knew the next step would be even more dicey: to take home this offer to their fathers and sisters, brothers and mothers and cousins and uncles, this piece of paper upon which, like so many others, the forked-tongue promises of the bad government had been inscribed. With this task heavy on their hearts, the Zapatistas returned home to the highlands and the jungle to begin the consultation that could end the war in Chiapas.

SPRING 1994

PLANTING THE SEED

Spring comes to the jungle of Chiapas overnight, Marcos writes. One day it is January and the next May. The trees fill out and the baking sun slows the pace of the day. Much as the fighters of the first Zapatista army up in Morelos state in the teens of the century, every Spring the rebels' attention turned towards getting their corn in the ground.

Spring planting in Chiapas is a tense time, as campesino organizations seek to sow land stolen from them by the hacenderos and their white guards, but 1994 was particularly charged. By the middle of April, member groups of the new farmers' federation, the CEOIC, had seized 350 fincas amounting to 250,000 acres, and the roster of takeovers and confrontations filled the newspapers. A killing a day was counted out in the fields during the first 15 days of April. The Zapatista civil leader Francisco Mena López was gunned down in Las Margaritas, and Mariano Pérez, a longtime organizer of the Emiliano Zapata Farmers Organization (OCEZ), was killed in Simojovel.

The coming Peace, so optimistically trumpeted inside the cathedral, suddenly seemed a fragile net. "The filthy Indians desecrated our church," a coleto tour guide was overhead instructing a clutch of tourists. "We're going to have to have an exorcism to clean it up."

As had been accorded up in San Cristóbal, the Zapatista delegates moved out into the villages, first to explain the government's 32-point offer. Voting would come later, in a second round of consultations. For now, the task was to listen. And to start the *roza y quema*, the burning of the fields for the planting.

But far from the conflict zone, dark forces were gathering in the wings for the next act in Mexico's nonstop political drama. On Monday, March 14th, Alfredo Harp Helú, the billionaire president of the nation's most venerable financial institution, Banamex, was snatched off a Coyoacán boulevard in the capital, one of a series of kidnappings of the extremely wealthy that had upped paranoia levels amongst the elite. Harp Helú's kidnappers, who months later reportedly received a Latin American record ransom—$30 million USD—for the banker's safe return, would ultimately prove to be hard-line Marxists who utilized the boodle to finance the Popular Revolutionary Army (EPR), an eventual rival of the Zapatistas on the armed Left.

A BULLET FROM WITHIN

Riddled by back-biting and dissension, the Colosio campaign got a big boost on March 16th when Luis Donaldo and the Commissioner of Peace pacted a truce. El Camacho would stand down in his pursuit of the presidency. For now. But the wily politician was not always to be taken at his word.

Luis Donaldo was not looking forward to the next stop on this grueling trail. Tijuana is a grimy, crime-ridden border town where, in the best of seasons, the mesh of politics, drugs, and bad cops can erupt in spectacular violence. Moreover, Colosio had had perilous problems with the Tijuana section of his party ever since his boss, Carlos Salinas, had summarily fired good old boy governor Xicoténcatl Leyva just a month into his presidency in January 1989—the guv was said to have opened the Tijuana corridor to a Sinaloa drug cartel, under the direction of the four Arellano Félix brothers, and the bodies have been falling everywhere on the Baja California peninsula ever since. So careless had Xico's governance been that Tijuana's state, Baja California Norte, had fallen to Cárdenas in the 1988 presidential race, a cardinal sin in the Salinas book. The unpleasant task of purging the Baja California PRI—and particularly its strident Tijuana section—fell to the national president of the PRI: Luis Donaldo.

It was also Colosio who, after July 1989 Baja gubernatorial elections, had gone on national television to announce that the PRI was conceding victory to the conservative National Action party (PAN), the first time in the ruling party's 71-year domination of Mexican politics that the PRI had ever given up a state to the opposition. When Colosio came to town a few days later to make peace with his party, PRI gangs followed him through the streets howling "Colosio should die!"

There were a lot of people waiting for him on the ground, an aide reported as the candidate flew up the Gulf of California on March 23rd. Colosio frowned. This was his first visit to Baja as a candidate, and La Jornada had noted just that morning that the anti-Colosios were preparing demonstrations. The candidate braced himself for the landing.

When the entourage touched down at mid-afternoon, the candidate sent his thin, terminally cancer-afflicted wife, Diana Laura, ahead to the hotel under military escort, to dress for dinner. Luis Donaldo would work his way into the city, touching bases in the hillside squatter colonies near the airport. Now his security wanted him out of the terminal quickly—airports had become nightmare alleys for bodyguards since Cardinal Juan Jesús Posadas was gunned down by the Arellano Félix boys at Guadalajara International in May 1993.

The crowd outside the doors was reluctant to move, recalls Germán Castillo, Colosio's longtime bodyguard. Castillo usually worked with General Domiro García of the Presidential Military Command (*Estado Mayor Presidencial*). That was all the protection the candidate wanted around him. The two-man team allowed Colosio maximum contact with the public, a signature of his revised campaign. Castillo put his shoulder into the crowd like a crack NFL blocking back and opened a path to the candidate's waiting Blazer.

The first stop was a Solidarity rally—Colosio was closely identified with the Solidarity funds he had dispensed to the PRI's electoral clientele for the past two and a half years, and the PRI was counting on its Solidarity committees in the impoverished urban colonies of Mexico to be its electoral shock troops come August 21st.

The meeting was set for the Lomas Taurinas colony, a gully that years before had been bought up by a pair of Tijuana bullfighters and sold off in lots by unscrupulous speculators to the poor of Michoacán and Guerrero and Oaxaca, who arrive in Tijuana by the dozens each day to make their fortunes in the *maquiladoras* (mostly U.S.-owned assembly plants) or pick garbage in the celebrated TJ dump or slide across the line, in the dead of the night, to the Golden Arches of the Golden State, California USA—the border was in view of the meeting site.

Colosio, who always drove himself, parked the rented blue Blazer a hundred yards uphill from the meeting site, a confluence of the colony's two paved streets. Castillo and the General moved him gingerly across a makeshift wooden bridge towards a pick-up truck from which the candidate would officiate. The crowd was as immovable as at the airport, but volunteer security teams opened a breach for Colosio.

The meeting was much bigger than expected and literally crawling with cops—besides the Estado Mayor, which General Domiro oversaw, national security agents from the top-secret CISEN (Center for Investigation & National Security) were on hand. So were the highway patrol and state judicial agents from the nearby La Mesa delegation. The Colosio campaign's national security coordinator had contracted 160 young men to control the crowds and run off hecklers, and a previously unknown "Grupo Omega" was assigned to form a diamond around the candidate and his two bodyguards. The Tijuana PRI fielded its own 45-man security team, mostly fired cops, under the rubric of TUCAN—its initials stand for "Everyone United Against the PAN."

The only local force not present at the rally was the Tijuana municipal police, under the direction of PANista Federico Benítez. Benítez, whose agents ultimately stationed themselves nearby, had been asked three times the previous day by the TUCAN security director, Rodolfo Rivapalacios, not to patrol the rally, because the presence of the PAN police might upset the PRI *colonos* (colony dwellers).

The Lomas Taurinas get-together was billed as a "neighborhood dialogue." The format of these seances is routine: representatives of the colony read their demands and the candidate writes them all down and promises to fix everything once he is elected to high office. This call and response was momentarily interrupted while a PRI goon squad scuffled with young men perched on the hillside waving a big hand-lettered sign that reminded the candidate that "Camacho and Subcomandante Marcos Are Watching You!" Colosio smoothed tempers. The candidate gazed up at the littered hillside above him, the cardboard shacks and undone cinder-block hovels, the discolored walls upon which his name had been scrawled in enormous letters. He responded to the neighbors' demands as he always did, smiling, assured, enthusiastic. No one seems to have taken down his exact words.

"We are going to win here!" Colosio shouted triumphantly, then stepped down from the pick-up bed into what his security had come to call "the public bath." A trademark *banda de guerra* struck up blaring martial music. The sound system kicked in with the rollicking quebradita *La Culebra*—"La Culebra (the Snake) is going to get you—you better move your feet." Castillo put his shoulder into the mob and started to push his way uphill, his boss right on his side, as always, and General Domiro covering the candidate's back. At the point of the diamond that surrounded them was Fernando de la Sota, chief of the Omega Group, a privately sponsored security formation. De la Sota, a convicted corrupt cop and onetime CIA informant, was later to be arrested for tampering with evidence at the scene.

Then what Castillo thought was a rocket went off somewhere behind him to his right. "The Culebra's going to get you!"—the sound system was shattering. The bodyguard felt Colosio go limp against him. Then Colosio was not there at all.

Castillo whirled around to see a hand emerge from the crowd and fire into Colosio's belly. By the time he reached his friend, the heir apparent to the presidency of Mexico lay face down in a pool of blood, his brains and his guts splattered all over a garbage-strewn gully a hair's breadth from the U.S. border. "This was a professional job," Castillo told reporters at Colosio's funeral.

The dying candidate was ladled into the rented Blazer for a wild ride to Tijuana General Hospital. World-famous surgeons were summoned, a helicopter chartered to lift the sinking candidate to the Scripps Medical Center in La Jolla. Outside, a frightened mob had gathered, cursing and screaming on the hospital esplanade in the dark. A little after 8 p.m., the death watch was over.

Carlos Salinas learned immediately of the shooting over tea with his new NAFTA trading partner, Canadian prime minister Jean Chrétien. Now the long black limousines and the armor-plated Grand Marquis were arriving at Los Pinos—the business leaders and the bankers, the directors of the Institutional Party's sectors, its labor czars and legislative leaders, the military. "The situation is grave," a clenched-jawed General Ramón Mota Sánchez muttered. Finally, after 10, an ashen-faced Carlos Salinas addressed the nation and put the official seal on the tragedy. "Luis Donaldo is dead," the President gulped, declaring Thursday, March 24th, a day of national mourning. The stock market would be shut down to hold off massive capital flight.

Three men had been taken into custody at the murder scene. One, the suspected shooter, had been beaten bloody by the mob. He was identified as Mario Aburto Martínez, a 23-year-old mechanic and native of La Rinconada, Michoacán. In his first statement released to the press, Aburto claimed to be "a pacifist." Aburto had been immediately pounced upon by an ex-state judicial cop and member of the TUCAN team, Vicente Mayoral, who was released within 24 hours. He would later be re-arrested, this time with three others, including Rodolfo Rivapalacios, and re-released.

The third suspect captured at the scene, José Antonio Sánchez Ortega, was ID'd as a CISEN agent. Sánchez Ortega was nabbed running uphill towards his car by members of Federico Benítez's Municipal Police, who had been hovering three minutes away—despite repeated requests by Rivapalacios to steer clear of Lomas Taurinas. When Sánchez Ortega fell into their arms, his shirt was splattered with Colosio's blood and he subsequently paraffin-tested positive for having recently fired a handgun. Federal agents snatched the CISEN man away from Benítez late on the night of the assassination, and Sánchez Ortega permanently dropped out of sight. Benítez, who had already begun his own investigation into these lurid events, was himself gunned down two months later near the Tijuana airport.

The trail from Lomas Taurinas has been a tortuous one. Like the Kennedy assassination, the Colosio hit has yielded a bumper crop of corpses, conspiracy conjectures, and blind allies. Five special prosecutors have failed to untangle the ambiguities. At one point, the killing was thought the work of a single assassin, then a complicated plot, then a single-assassin job again. The shooter, Mario Aburto—if it is the same Aburto—remains incommunicado in Almoloya penitentiary, Mexico's super-maxi lockup. Although a half-dozen other suspects have been jailed and released (not including Sánchez Ortega) and everyone from Carlos Salinas to Subcomandante Marcos has been pinned as the mastermind, no resolution is in sight. Multiple motives have been suggested—presidential selection, narcotrafficking, revenge for the stealing of the election from Cárdenas in '88, Colosio's 1989 snub of the local PRI—but no motive has ever been made to stick.

FINGERING THE COMANDANTES

The Zapatistas were an immediate target of investigation. "I did it to focus attention on Chiapas," Aburto is purported to have confessed during his first interrogation. Gustavo Hirales, an ex-guerrillero in the 1970s who signed on as a hired gun with Salinas's Solidarity mafia, blamed the EZLN "for constructing an atmosphere that made possible *magnicidio*" (killing a major public figure). Octavio Paz and Salinas's house pet intellectual, Hector Aguilar Camín, agreed. Paz lashed out at Zapatista supporters as "apologists for violence."

Marcos was near La Garrucha on the afternoon of March 23rd, giving reporters a sour earful about how Camacho was distorting the role of the Zapatista consultation on the 32 points. "Peace isn't just a signature away," he was telling Proceso when Mayor Mario brought news of the Colosio shooting far away at the opposite end of the country. The two hurried off together.

The reporters caught up with the distraught rebel leader an hour after Salinas's mournful announcement. "It wasn't us," he blurted. "We might have attempted to take out Salinas or Córdoba, but not Colosio. This hurts us. This hurts Camacho." He called the killing an *ajuste de cuentas*, a "settling of scores." "I never thought they would be so stupid as to stage a self-assassination to recover their lost prestige." Although he was troubled by the prospect of imminent army attack, Marcos did not see a military coup by morning. "Salinas will stay in power until 2000," he predicted and begged leave to huddle with the General Command.

RED ALERT

The throng that assembled on the 24th outside the PRI's national headquarters on Insurgentes North, the lengthy boulevard that transects Mexico City, was surly early. When Colosio's coffin was trundled in after 8 a.m., the mood grew ominous. One by one, the PRI honchos, kingmakers, bagmen, alchemists, governors, legislators, and lackeys filed into the party compound. Outside the stout iron gates, the rabble yelled "Justice!" and "*¿Quién fue?*" (Who was it?) and "Kill Camacho!"

On the morning after Lomas Taurinas, Manuel Camacho Solís's political ambitions were as dead as Colosio. When he arrived at the funeral parlor where the ex-candidate was laid out later that afternoon, the Commissioner of Peace was loudly booed and jostled by a whipped-up PRI mob.

A Mexican presidential candidate had not been assassinated since 1928, when a Catholic zealot gunned down General Alvaro Obregón in a plot probably masterminded by the Machiavellian Plutarco Elías Calles, founder of the party that has since become the PRI. Fittingly, the struggle to fill Colosio's boots began even as the candidate's corpse lay in the Plutarco Elías Calles auditorium at the ruling party's headquarters. The PRI is nothing if not timeless.

One wave of distinguished PRIistas after another took their grim-faced stance before their slain comrade's bier. Mentioned as possible substitutes were Finance Minister Pedro Aspe; the late candidate's campaign manager, former Education

Secretary Ernesto Zedillo; and the brittle president of the party, Fernando Ortiz Arana. They hovered now over Colosio's coffin. So did Carlos Hank González, the Godfather of the Institutional Party's old guard, who, after several years of biting his tongue, was about to try and take the PRI back.

A thousand miles south of these touching scenes, the EZLN watched with trepidation as the PRI government tore itself apart. 24 hours previous, the Zapatistas had known who the enemy was. Now they had no feel for who was in charge. A communiqué issued from the General Command on the 24th denied EZLN complicity in "this cowardly assassination" and said the rebels "profoundly lament that the governing group is not able to resolve its internal differences without covering the country in blood." "Colosio treated us with prudence," the communiqué continued—whoever had killed him had done so "to destroy hope." "Now they will crown this despicable act with invasion." Consultations on the peace pledges were suspended forthwith. The Zapatista Army of National Liberation was now on Red Alert. The roads into the jungle would be mined. Only "war correspondents" would be admitted into the zone. "Our steps will continue towards truth even if the path leads to death," the General Command warned darkly.

The EZLN statement received but one line at the bottom of that day's front-page New York Times dispatch, a portent of great inattention to come.

Death was more on Marcos's mind than ever. "The end of our cycle is near," he wrote to his "beloved fellow moles." "We are the dark side of the moon," he noted in uncadenced poetry, "but we have helped you to see the whole moon." "Farewell," the Sup bade his avid public.

Vanity Fair's Ann Louise Bardach and Medea Benjamin, the founder of the hip human rights aggregation Global Exchange, discovered the Subcomandante parked Buddha-style under a tree near La Garrucha on the 26th. He was fixated on the sky. "I can't talk, you have to leave. The Army will kill you and blame it on the Zapatistas." 50 planes had flown over EZLN territory already that day. The military was preparing "a surgical strike" that would have "low political cost" and "avoid killing large numbers of people." Despite his vow of silence, Marcos talked for four hours.

"They've arrested a pacifist for murder. It's JFK Mexican-style, and they have their own Oswald. It can't be a lone, crazy person. Look, he put his gun to Colosio's head. The bullet that killed Colosio came from somewhere within the government..." Marcos jumped up to pose Mayor Mario as a Colosio stand-in, his finger jammed to the ski-masked aide's temple. "No one could have gotten that close to him. Only someone of confidence, someone from within. They should have let the Zapatistas protect Colosio. We'd have done a better job."

THE SUBSTITUTE

Speed dictated the designation of a new candidate. The choice had to be made quickly to camouflage the damaging vacuum that was developing at the center of power, one that was bound to have devastating repercussions on foreign investment if it was allowed to continue. In an effort to stave off its NAFTA neighbor's collapse, less than 24 hours after Colosio's passing, the Clinton administration extended Salinas a $6.5 billion USD line of credit. Not 10 months later, Clinton would have to come to Mexico's rescue once again after the peso collapsed.

Now the PRI brain trust was meeting night and day up in the drab skyscraper on Insurgentes. Manlio Fabio Beltrones—Sonora governor, ex–National Security subsecretary, and a Colosio associate who had flown into Tijuana to question Aburto—stage-managed the putsch for Zedillo. The go-ahead came at last from the Carlos Hank group, after significant commitments were extracted from Salinas. One quid pro quo required by the Hank group was the exile of José Córdoba to Washington, D.C.—the old guard of the PRI wanted Salinas's Svengali out of the President's ear during his last days in office, the forthcoming Zedillo campaign, and the electoral process itself.

On March 29th, six days after Colosio bit the dust of Lomas Taurinas, the white puff of smoke burst from the PRI's inner sanctum. Carloads of supporters were trucked in from the Chalco misery belt in the wastelands east of the capital and taught to chant the name of the new candidate. Ernesto Zedillo, a Salinas protégé at the Budget Ministry and onetime shoeshine boy from Mexicali, who had never run for any public office in his life, mentioned the very dead Colosio's name 39 times in his acceptance speech.

WHO WERE THOSE MASKED MEN?

The bullets that Colosio caught also cut the Zapatistas down to size. For months, the EZLN had been flying high on its press ratings, stealing headlines every day from the traditional centers of influence. Suddenly, to the national and international press that had so avidly feasted upon them, the Zapatistas seemed like old meat. By March 24th, the rebels were disappearing from view under the hundreds of black-bordered in-memoriam squares for the late Luis Donaldo Colosio. Now an army that had been living on its press notices since January 1st had finally been victimized by a moving news front. In death, Colosio had extracted his revenge from the Zapatistas for having filched so much space for Camacho.

For the Zapatistas, the nut of the Colosio killing was that the nation's attention had gravitated back to its natural center, the capital, where all power in Mexico has been jealously concentrated since long before the so-called European conquest. One of the EZLN's greatest good deeds had been to turn the national spotlight, if only for a few short months, on the misfortunes of the faceless and the forgotten, the campesinos and the indígenas, who are always the last to be missed in modern Mexico. Now the rebels seemed an irrelevant hallucination lodged "somewhere in the Lacandón jungle." Who were those masked men?

VOTAN-ZAPATA

The turn towards war was unmistakable in the Cañadas as the hot tense days of early April ticked by. Troop movements were reported in Ocosingo, Margaritas, and Altamirano. 25,000 soldiers were reported in Chiapas on Good Friday, April 1st, when the Tzeltales of Garrucha gathered in their spare wood-frame church. Attack would come during Semana Santa (Holy Week), when all of Mexico goes on vacation and no one would be watching—I have heard the same rumor every Semana Santa since.

Silence resounded from the Zapatista zone. No communiqués were forthcoming for two weeks. But on April 10th, the 75th anniversary of the assassination of Emiliano Zapata at Chinameca and the 100th day of the war against oblivion, the EZLN finally let reporters pass down the canyons to the meadows of the Ejido América, where Marcos stood upon a rough-hewn platform and deified the old revolutionary as Votan, the Mayan Guardian of the Heart of the People:

"Votan-Zapata, light that came from far away and was born here again in our lands.

"Votan-Zapata, name that changes, man without face, tender light that is our salvation," the ski-masked rebel incanted as the Third Regiment of the Guardian of the Heart of the People paraded with long guns on the ejido grounds.

The spiritual catharsis of Holy Week and Zapata-Votan's death and rebirth seemed to ease the tensions in the sweltering conflict zone. On April 15th, the battling CEOIC farmers signed an agreement with the (interim) governor to halt further land occupations. In turn, the government would utilize federal funds to buy land CEOIC farmers had taken from absentee landlords.

On April 21st, candidate Zedillo paid a surprise visit to San Cristóbal to put on the chuj and buttonhole voters. That same day, the remaining 31 Zapatista civil prisoners were released from Cerro Hueco. Finally, on April 23rd, the EZLN called off its Red Alert. Camacho, back in the state now that war fever had mellowed, urged a quick resumption of the consultations in the villages.

Under cover of early morning darkness May 4th, Samuel Ruiz, his vicar Gonzalo Ituarte, Camacho Solís, and two assistants slipped out of San Cristóbal. No reporters were asked along. Six hours later, the Bishop and the Commissioner were seated in a hillside cabin above a jungle clearing just east of Guadalupe Tepeyac. Don Samuel and El Camacho met with 10 members of the CCRI for eight hours. They returned very late to San Cristóbal, and their pronouncements were discreet but hopeful that the lingering consultations would soon be resumed. Time was running out: a peace agreement needed to be signed now if the August 21st vote was not to be conducted under a declaration of war.

What actually transpired during the May 4th session in the jungle has never been publicly confirmed. In mid-June, Marcos told Proceso that Camacho had offered to allow the Zapatistas to remain armed if they would sign a public peace agreement and say they had disarmed. Don Samuel was presumably a witness to this offer. Camacho would later break a self-imposed vow of silence to deny the story.

POLITICS AS USUAL

The EZLN had cast a long shadow over the presidential election since it marched into San Cristóbal in the first hours of 1994. Not a few cynics suggested that the Indians were the stalking horse of some big player puppeteer to influence presidential succession, but the Zapatistas exhibited consummate disdain for all the political parties and their candidates, often truculently dispensed in Marcos's multiple communiqués.

In February, for example, the EZLN invited the parties to San Cristóbal as a sidebar to the peace talks. The PRI did not respond to the summons. The PAN's prickly presidential candidate, Diego Férnandez de Cevallos, said he would not meet with people who "wore socks on their heads," and the anti-Papist Popular Socialists, a geriatric clique, would not enter Bishop Ruiz's cathedral. But the Great White Father of the Green Environmental Party (PVEM), Jorge González Torres, showed up with a handful of Tzotzil Indians he had rented in Zinacantán. The hierarchy of Cárdenas's PRD came too. Marcos rewarded the handful of attendees by accusing them of only showing up for the photo op.

But if the EZLN had a soft spot for any of the entries in the coming horse race, it was Cuauhtémoc Cárdenas, the winner in 1988 who had had victory snatched from him in a fraudulent vote count, and the son of a patriotic hero who had expropriated Mexico's oil resources from the gringo moguls. Cárdenas had repeatedly endorsed the rebels' goals, "if not their methods."

Like the ill-fated Colosio campaign, things were not going well for Cuauhtémoc's second bid for the presidency. Gremlins tormented the tour. During an Acapulco stopover, "El Pasamontañas," the campaign bus, struck and killed a child, and the incident spooked the campaign. The polls were already leaning towards the PAN's "El Jefe Diego."

On May 12th, the PRD founder locked horns with the fulminating PANista and a mealy-mouthed Zedillo in Mexico's first-ever televised presidential debate and got scalped by El Jefe Diego, a blow from which his presidential bid would never really recover.

"We have the understanding that you are a candidate for the Presidency of the Republic," the EZLN's invitation to Cuauhtémoc Cárdenas began coolly.

"Actually, we did not think the PRD had much of a chance," Marcos admitted to Le Bot two years later. Mostly the Zapatistas wanted to know what would happen after the PRI committed the kind of massive fraud it had perpetrated in 1988.

RUMBLE IN THE JUNGLE

The prospect of an endorsement from the EZLN both thrilled and chilled the Cárdenas people. For months, Cárdenas had been desperately trying to deconstruct the bomb-thrower image the PRI and the PAN had hung on him, making a point of addressing bankers and shaking hands with industrialists. Now he was about to meet with the most wanted masked outlaw in the land. On the other hand, one embrace from Marcos could restore the animation of activist youth who, in increasing numbers, were thumbing their noses at electoral politics and picking up the ski mask.

Early on May 15th, a caravan of 27 vehicles disembarked from San Cristóbal, passing into the Cañadas at Las Margaritas and hugging the 80-kilometer, up-and-down track all the way to Guadalupe Tepeyac. By noon, the candidate and his 21-member campaign committee were cooling their heels just outside the rebel camp.

Hours later, Cárdenas and his group were escorted by heavily armed rebels down a dirt path, lined (as during Absalón's release at this same spot) by freshly scrubbed men and women. Some were holding banners that said "If You Win Your Candidacy, Don't Forget Your Country!" and "Don't Trade the Bread of the Poor for Junk and Plastic!" The chants were not all that friendly, either: "Cárdenas! Cárdenas! Get to work or the war will catch up with you!" Assailed from all sides by the militant cadences of the Zapatista bases, Cárdenas's normally stony countenance turned positively petroglyphic, the deep furrows deeper, his skin tone darker.

At the end of the gauntlet, the path opened into a huge clearing fronted by twin humps of treed hillocks. Cárdenas and his party were conducted to an empty stage. The site was filled with villagers—perhaps 1,500 Indians in fiesta mode. Some of the partygoers had walked three days from San Quintín, adjacent to Montes Azules, to see with their own eyes this first meeting of the Titans.

The notables—Cárdenas; his son Lázaro; the doña of the disappeared, Rosario Ibarra; the left venerable Heberto Castillo; a sweating Senator Porfirio Muñoz Ledo; Tiempo's Amado Avendaño—stood bug-eyed as 500 Zapatista horsemen poured out of the hill in synchronized formation and pounded past the bandstand.

At first Marcos seemed the perfect host. He warmly welcomed the candidate and his people, sounding a little awed to be sharing the platform with so many distinguished social agitators. The Subcomandante commended Cuauhtémoc's bravery in venturing into the zone, because getting his picture taken with masked desperadoes would not win him a lot of votes—in the Cañadas, there have never been any polling places anyway.

Later, Cárdenas would meet with the CCRI in the safehouse up on the hill, where the comandantes had recently sat down with Camacho and the Tatic. Marcos seemed eager, almost emotional, suggesting that the debate with Férnandez and Zedillo had been a trap. The fraud in the upcoming election would be much more sophisticated than in 1988, ventured the candidate. Marcos and Cuauhtémoc and young Lázaro continued the conversation out of earshot, under a shade tree.

The cow had been cooking all day, and as dusk descended, it was declared fit to eat. Zapatistas and Cardenistas broke bread together, and pretty soon it was time for the closing ceremonies. The candidate took the microphone to thank his hosts and then delivered what turned out be a standard campaign speech: the EZLN and the PRD shared many goals, he began dryly. But the PRD has taken the electoral path, the path of legality, and his victory August 21st would be "the breaking point with the PRI past." He invited the Zapatistas to accompany him in redeeming the Mexican Revolution. It was the usual no-frills Cárdenas pitch, and those poor souls who had walked three days from the heart of the jungle to witness this miracle meeting of myths must have wondered what all the fuss was about in the first place.

Marcos responded graciously: "Should the fraud repeat itself August 21st, those who prepare it calculate badly if they think the EZLN is only concerned about Chiapas." "We still have hope in Cuauhtémoc Cárdenas," the Sup sucker-punched. "But we don't have confidence in the PRD." Marcos listed the PRD's anti-democratic sins: Cárdenas's self-selection as candidate, the collusion between the party power groups to designate candidates and PRD officials, the deals brokered behind closed doors with the PAN and the PRI-gobierno. The Sup trashed the PRD as a house of "palace intrigues, disputes between cupolas, mendacities, and the worst ajustes de cuentas." "Show us what is the difference between the PRI and the PAN and the PRD!" the Subcomandante cruelly demanded. "If you can't handle the post-electoral struggle, the men and women without faces will," he warned.

"This was hard, very hard," Cárdenas told Blanche Petrich as he hopped in the car for the trip back to San Cristóbal.

The rumble in the jungle provoked much editorial comment—the gist being that Cárdenas had gotten his comeuppance and the PRD the boot. As usual, the Mexican Left had splintered before even getting out of the starting gate. Yet two days after the brouhaha in Tepeyac, crusading editor Amado Avendaño was named the civil society's candidate for governor of Chiapas. He would be running on the PRD ticket, with the tacit endorsement of the Zapatista Army of National Liberation.

NO-O-O-O-O!

Resumption of the consultations in mid-May, after a nearly two-month hiatus in which the power equation between the rebels and the surviving rulers of the nation had been dramatically altered, did not anticipate a happy conclusion. Confidence that the government would or could fulfill its promises was at a low ebb out in the communities. "The mal gobierno won't keep its word without a *bronca* (mêlée)" one representative told Hermann Bellinghausen before the vote was taken near La Garrucha.

Accepting the "pledges for peace" at this late date could only benefit the PRI in the coming election. The sole gambit the Zapatistas could play was to hold—hold out for a fresh dialogue, hold out for a new government, hold out to see what August 21st would shake out of the trees.

A coalition of independent Left groups had been asked by the comandantes to conduct a national sampling of opinion on Zapatista acceptance of the 32-point proposal—the survey would be the first of several subsequent national consultations organized by the EZLN. Now Marcos reported that 65,000 Mexicans voting under tents in plazas around the country thought the government was not to be trusted and would sell the rebels out.

On June 3rd, Marcos announced that the consultations were over. Photos appeared in La Jornada of masked rebels tallying the votes. A week later, on the 11th, the foregone conclusion was delivered to the press. Newspapers headlined the story with a big inky NO-O-O-O! "We looked for the word to surrender (*rendir*) in the Tzeltal language and could not find it. It was not in the Tojolabal or the Chol or the Tzotzil either," wrote Marcos. The NO vote was overwhelming: 97.8% were against acceptance of the government proposals. 3.26% wanted to start the war all over again, but 96.74% voted to continue the dialogue.

Manuel Camacho could not have been less surprised at the outcome. He had gotten these ski-masked skunks into the stable but he had not been able to make them take the bit. He had no alternative left but to quit. On June 16th, after taking a few desultory swipes at Zedillo, the Commissioner irrevocably retired yet again from politics, but no one really believed the final curtain had dropped on his political ambitions. Indeed, by 2000, El Camacho, long since an ex-PRIista, had postulated himself as the presidential candidate of a vanity affair he called the Party of the Democratic Center.

By the middle of June, the rains had begun to fall daily on the Land of No. "The rain and the mud stick to everything. Humans murmur and the water shouts," Marcos wrote. "Rain returns the green to these lands—the fires end and something new begins to emerge between the stones of the mountain." Above the camp, the arroyos were rising and "the clouds fight with thunder and lightning for the privilege of dying in the rain to nourish the earth."

As the skies closed in over his jungle hideaway, word came to Marcos that his beloved mentor Old Antonio, the Zapatistas' first conduit to the communities in the jungle, had passed on, become one with the rain and the mud, returned to the good earth to which the first gods had given breath.

SUMMER 1994

THE SECOND DECLARATION

The big NO from the jungle was accompanied by a resounding YES for that cross-class klatsch that bills itself as the "civil society." Issued six months after its predecessor, the Second Declaration of the Lacandón Jungle conceded that picking up the gun was not the only route to democratic change in Mexico. The second declaration lionized the role of the civil society in halting the war and demonstrating that dialogue was possible. Now, in turning away from pacting with the mal gobierno, the rebels were once again placing their fate in the lap of that ill-defined horde of do-gooders whose sheer numbers had shamed the government into cease-fire January 12th.

"What to do with that *bola* of people who had stopped the war was our problem," Marcos confessed to Le Bot. The solution was to put the civil society to work. The Second Declaration charges this abstraction, coined by the new-wave communist Gramsci, with the founding of "a new political culture," the writing of a new Mexican Constitution, and the creation of "a government of transition," the mechanisms for which would be debated at a forthcoming "National Democratic Convention" (CND) to be convened "somewhere in the Lacandón jungle" prior to the August 21st presidential election. The convention was to be modeled upon a 1914 "Revolutionary Sovereign Convention," joined by Zapata and Francisco Villa behind rebel lines in the central Mexican state of Aguascalientes, a failed effort to outflank Venustiano Carranza and establish a unified revolutionary government

Quoting Paulino Martínez, Emiliano Zapata's representative in Aguascalientes, the second Declaration of the Lacandón Jungle began, "The revolution is not just the launching of projectiles on the battlefield but the launching of new ideas and words of liberation. It is the wedding of the sword and the idea that overthrows empires…"

But the Second Declaration and the National Democratic Convention had a more pragmatic and immediate goal: "to organize the post-electoral struggle if the PRI should win again…" Post-electoral struggle has been recurrent in the nation's modern history—in 1929, 1940, and 1952, losing candidates staged mini-rebellions against the always triumphant state party. The most successful post-electoral struggle in the century was led by Francisco Madero after being crushed by dictator Porfirio Díaz in the 1910 presidential election, the stealing of which ignited the Mexican Revolution.

In 1988, Cuauhtémoc Cárdenas called a half-million supporters to the zócalo of Mexico City 10 days after the election had been stolen from him by Salinas, but rather than leading them into the national palace, he chose to avoid bloodshed and told his people to go home. Haunted by that turnaround, Marcos and the EZLN were determined not to watch the same movie in 1994. But organizing the post-electoral struggle this time around presented tactical booby traps. How could the EZLN spur on the now-traditional "second election," the one that takes place in the street following tainted balloting, without seeming to support the candidacy of the only entry in the race with whom they shared some sensibilities, Cuauhtémoc Cárdenas?

THE MOTHER OF ALL CARAVANS

In spite of the EZLN's intentions to invite thousands to their jungle for their convention, the Army kept tightening its vise grip on the checkpoints outside of Ocosingo, Margaritas, and Altamirano. Indians moving through the military barricades into the zonas francas were roughly searched, the women patted down by the young soldiers. Bringing extra bread or cooking oil back into the zone made the carrier suspect of feeding the guerrilla. On June 4th, at the Altamirano checkpoint, 30 soldiers dragged three young Tzeltal girls from Santa Rosita Sibquil into a nearby cabin and gang-raped them while their mother was restrained outside. Charges subsequently filed against the soldiers were turned over to the military courts by the National Human Rights Commission and, like the murders in Ocosingo and on the Ejido Morelia, were permanently ignored.

In this pernicious ambiance, the arrival of the mother of all caravans in Zapatista territory 10 days after the issuance of the Second Declaration was a sign from the gods. Not only was the "Caravan of Caravans" (actually four caravans representing distinct Left constituencies) bringing in 180 tons of food— a scarce commodity in the jungle once the rains began—but the 25 buses and trucks crammed with 350 caravanistas represented a dry run for the convention. They proved you could break the military encirclement, that the rebels could indeed invite the outside in.

Amongst the travelers was a certain gravelly-voiced folksinger that the EZLN had featured in its early morning broadcasts January 1st from Ocosingo—José de Molina. With his militant strumming as dinner music, the rebels "sacrificed a cow of solidarity" and chowed down with the outsiders, the vanguard of the masses of civil societarians to come.

THE LITERARY LIFE

During the early summer days of 1994, the attention of the civil society, normally a fickle chimera anyway, had, turned to the World Cup soccer matches being held for the first time ever in the U.S.

Down in the jungle, the Zapatistas too gathered around their radios to audit the misfortunes of the Mexican selection. The rains now came daily, falling in dense white sheets and soaking every surface. Such damp weather often nourishes the muse of poets. Subcomandante Marcos dashed off letters of invitation.

"My job is to make war and write letters," Marcos penned the celebrated essayist and social critic Carlos Monsiváis, whose work brilliantly chronicles the convulsions of civil society, trying to lure him to the convention. Monsi, an eminently urban Woody Allen sort, does not much cotton to snakes and attended the CND under protest.

In his epistle to Carlos Fuentes, Marcos quotes Macbeth and urges the novelist to present himself in the jungle. Fuentes responded from Salzburg, Austria, thanking Marcos for helping him to see that there are two Mexicos (Fuentes has lived out of the country for years) and begging the rebels to drop their "absurd demand" that Carlos Salinas be removed from office.

The Sup dashed off letters to historians Enrique Krauze and Lorenzo Meyer— having historians around helps to make history. He wrote Elena Poniatowska, the Polish noblewoman who is a key force in Mexican feminism, begging her "to place her rosy foot in Zapatista lands." He summoned the Uruguayan writer Eduardo Galeano, plus Nelson Mandela, Desmond Tutu, Noam Chomsky, the journalist Ryszard Kapuscinsky, Rigoberta Menchú, Alexander Solzhenitsyn, Nikita Khrushchev, Yassir Arafat, nymphet pop singer Gloria Trevi, and Miguel Mejía Barón, coach of the losing Mexican selection in the World Cup. Few RSVPed.

The convocation for the National Democratic Convention was issued July 10th. The CND would be held August 6th–9th, 12 days before the national election in the "Aguascalientes," a jungle convention center the Zapatistas were now building east of Guadalupe Tepeyac. State conventions must first be held to select delegates. Two conspicuous stipulations in the convocation sparked immediate fire. "Those who are not willing to try the electoral path are NOT CONVOKED," and "those who think that armed struggle is the only way to separate the PRI from power are NOT CONVOKED."

The non-convocations shook so-called "ultras," who rejected the electoral option, particularly the one masquerading as Cuauhtémoc Cárdenas. The Independent Proletarian Movement (MPI), one of the rebellion's earliest supporters, had taken to burning plastic campaign banners in public, sending choking black billows of smoke over the capital. Now, at the state convention in

Mexico City, the ultras stormed the stage, demanding a boycott of the presidential elections.

AMADO FOR GOVERNOR

From the first minute of his campaign, Amado Avendaño let voters know he was not some power-hungry party hack. The PRD was merely lending him its registration to campaign against old Absalon's protégé Eduardo Robledo for the governorship of his state. "Chiapas is ungovernable," Amado would tell audiences at rallies. The anti-politico politico's plan was to win, occupy the governor's mansion just long enough to write a new constitution and alter the state's system of systematic injustice, and go home—a real government of "transition."

Despite its eccentric underpinnings, Amado Avendaño's crusade was remarkably like the standard model. He kissed babies and made rousing speeches—although his venues were more exotic than his rival Robledo's. On July 14th, Amado became the first candidate to actively campaign in the Zapatista zone.

The Guadalupe Tepeyac meeting was opened by the usual military salute. Amado's stump speech was translated into Tzeltal and Tojolabal. Sharing the platform was PRD senatorial hopeful Irma Serrano, a former exotic dancer, ranchera singer, and mistress of the president who had all those students shot at Tlatelolco back in 1968. "La Tigresa," as she is known professionally, was born at La Soledad just down the road from Tepeyac. Politics really does make for weird bedfellows.

Early on the morning of July 25th, Avendaño, campaigning around Tapachula on the coast, set out for the state capitol at Tuxtla to attend a political breakfast with interim governor Javier López Moreno. Amado usually did not attend such seances, but he told his wife and co-editor Concepción Villanueva on the phone that the governor had sounded anxious.

Avendaño and five members of his campaign team piled into a rented Suburban and headed north on the coastal highway before dawn. At 5:40 a.m. a dozing crew member, Jaime Aguilar, opened his eyes just as a licenseless green Kenworth trailer-truck plowed into the Suburban on a straightway near the Rancho of the Seven Cigarettes. Two Avendaño cousins and Agustín Rubio, Amado's campaign manager, were killed instantly. Amado himself was cruelly injured, with a fractured skull and a crushed thorax. Both Avendaño and Rubio, a former farmworker organizer forced to leave Chiapas in 1988 because of threats on his life, had received repeated warnings to discontinue the campaign or face the consequences.

The murder weapon—the Kenworth—had been deadheading cargoless back towards the Guatemalan border. An expired driver's license found in the cab listed a fake Mexico City address. The driver had fled.

State and federal investigators seemed determined to erase all evidence of possible political assassination—the roadway where the accident took place was repaved the next day, recalls Amado Jr., who escaped the crash relatively unscathed. Rather than concerning themselves with locating the missing driver, police searched the victims' luggage.

Clinging to life, the candidate was helicoptered to a Mexico City hospital where he was visited by Attorney General Carpizo, Cuauhtémoc Cárdenas, Superbarrio, and, ultimately, Carlos Salinas himself—mercifully, Amado was still in a coma when Salinas came to his bedside.

But with just three weeks to go until election day, the Avendaño bandwagon had been cruelly derailed by the "accident." It had been no "accident," Marcos insisted. Now, just days before the Convention was to get underway, the EZLN went back on Red Alert.

THE LOCURA

Out beyond Guadalupe Tepeyac, in the natural amphitheater where he had received Cárdenas and Camacho and Don Samuel in May, Marcos's poetry was taking shape. 600 militia men and women hung their rifles on tree branches and picked up saws and hammers. Under the baton of Comandante Tacho, the diminutive leader of the Tojolabal zone, a theater seating 6,000 delegates, five "inns" ("Hiltons"), cookhouses, toilets, even a library, were being constructed. Electricity was contracted ($7,000 USD—the interim governor was said to have footed the bill).

The cutting and stripping of thousands of saplings to shape the amphitheaters' benches caused consternation among the protectors of the Lacandón rainforest, but Tacho's troops kept chopping and hammering. Mayor Moisés calculated the depths of the latrines. How many times a day might convention-goers defecate, and what might be the volume? Moy questioned Bellinghausen.

The rebels had somehow come by 4,000 meters of white nylon to roof the rural convention center. To Marcos, the huge swath was a great sail and the "Aguascalientes" an enormous pirate ship staffed by "stern sailors," its prow pointed into the jungle sea. Wags compared the Sup's *locura* (craziness) to that of Werner Herzog's deranged antihero Fitzcarraldo, whose mad dream was to bring the Great Caruso to the Amazon.

The National Democratic Convention was the ultimate ZapaTour, a voyage to the heart of the Zapatista experience that brought thousands of political tourists from Mexico and all over the planet to San Cristóbal, a city that had been largely bereft of paying visitors for months. "Marcos should have one of these every weekend," suggested a satisfied taxista.

At forums, or *mesas*, that preceded the descent to the jungle, the ultras unsuccessfully fought until they dropped to delete any reference to the impending election from Convention resolutions. The press was thankfully barred from witnessing such left hair-splitting. To compound this anti-democratic bent, a dozen media, led by Televisa, most of them critical of the Zapatista viewpoint, were banned from the National Democratic Convention. Le Monde's Bertrand de la Grange was so traumatized by the veto that he has carried on an obsessive vendetta against Marcos ever since.

The gargantuan 225-vehicle caravan lined up before dawn on August 7th for the dizzying plunge into the Lacandón. Despite the acute discomforts of transit, the trip was first-class locura every millimeter of the way. All along the side of the road, families gathered to cheer the convention-goers on. In Comitán, cops raised V's of Victory and soldiers boarded the buses, not to brusquely search the occupants but to wish them "a safe trip." "Marcos! Marcos!" gleefully screamed a tyke running alongside our bus in Las Margaritas.

After the Immigration checkpoint at the mouth of the cañada, the pace slowed to a bellycrawl. Buses mired in the mud or fell into ravines, transmissions gave up the ghost. Zapatista *milicianos* climbed aboard and checked luggage for contraband. As the hours passed, each bus became its own circle of conspiration, and the jungle light came up in live vermilion dawn soon enough on Monday morning.

At the gate to the rustic coliseum, long lines of delegates keeled over in the blazing sun as first Zapatista troops, then student volunteers, frisked each entrant one by one, confiscating six-packs (no drugs or alcohol) and Swiss Army knives (ditto weapons). Once inside the perimeter, the ambiance pulsed the way it does before a long-anticipated rock concert. Marcos's sail shimmied under the jungle rays. Thousands of little high-tech tents dotted the hillsides and hammocks were slung up in the "Hiltons." The urban safari-goers hauled backpacks and sleeping bags and water purification systems and every tin of tuna fish in Mexico's southeast. The campesinos, equipped only with their *cobijas* (blankets) brought tortillas.

As evening fell, the multitudes gathered under the great sail and the Zapatistas gave voice to the Convention. Tacho presented the EZLN's bases of support, "those who kept our secret, who bought us *pinole* and tostadas in the mountain." 300 men and women, most masked by paliacates, marched past the flag-bedecked podium, their measured tread stroking the earth as if it were the rebels' collective heartbeat. Then the distinguished members of the presidium were welcomed, each name read out, sometimes with difficulty, by the comandantes: writers and professors, actresses and statesmen, poets and politicos and defenders of human rights, prominent members of the civil society. "Ramona! Ramona!" the feminists chanted, but the tiny comandante was absent, said to be deathly ill in the highlands.

Suddenly, hundreds of Zapatista troops marched into the amphitheater. Each of their weapons had a white strip of cloth attached to the muzzle. "Welcome aboard!" Marcos took the helm, sounding a little like Captain Ahab: "Through my voice speaks the voice of the Zapatista Army of National Liberation." The Sup's discourse was directed at the soldiers with their muzzled guns: "The war will not come from us," he breathed, it was up to the government to give Mexico elections without fraud. "We have raised the tower of hope, and for a time, we have put aside our weapons and our rancor, our pain for our dead, our conviction as warriors, to hold this meeting, this first step towards a true peace…"

The Convention was "the celebration of broken fears. A Yes to the beginning of the end of this long nightmare that, grotesquely, we call the history of Mexico… We expect from this Convention a collective call to the nation to struggle for what belongs to us, for our place in history…" The delegates, the reporters, the dignitaries on the stage, were fixed on the Subcomandante, but the audience was all of Mexico, and it was in the palm of his hand. "For us, nothing! For everyone, everything!"

Then Marcos gave "Aguascalientes" to the Convention, announcing that the EZLN was retiring from the CND but would obey its dictates, whatever they might turn out to be. The flag of the nation Marcos presented to Rosario Ibarra, whose own guerrilla son had vanished in Monterrey at about the same time the leftist invasion of the jungle from that northern city had begun. And then, pale and trembling, Marcos, followed by Tacho and Moisés, disappeared into the increasingly turbulent jungle night.

The storm broke just as the Comandantes were making their exit. From the first drop of the downpour, it was evident that the sail would not hold water and that Marcos's great ship had no anchor. The tormentón (tempest) lifted the sail off its moorings, snapping the hawsers that held it in tension and sending 4,000 meters of soaking nylon cascading in soft billows over the trapped representatives of the civil society. The electricity went next, further panicking the delegates. Now the rain was drenching, unending, the worst aguacero (downpour) of the rainy season. Four times, the storm washed over the jungle clearing, turning the "Aguascalientes" into a hellish quagmire. The high-tech tents dissolved into the mud, and the lawn chairs floated off downstream. All the "old people" were gathered in the library—despite the slur, this reporter, a young senior citizen, followed his rescuers—the twins Pedro and Pablo Moctezuma—to shelter.

The sun's first rays and shared mugs of freshly brewed jungle coffee warmed up the morning after. Amidst the debris, Carlos Monsiváis, nursing a sprained ankle, ruminated on the Woodstock parallel—the CND had coincided with the 25th anniversary of that generationally charged craziness. One by one, the delegates hobbled back into the stripped amphitheater. Former UNAM rector Pablo Gonzalez Casanova encapsulated the moment: "This morning, we are without a roof, without food, without even a mirror in which to see our faces…this shows us that solidarity is not enough—now we know how it must be to wake up like this every day…"

To escape a second killer storm, the Convention would be curtailed after approval of the resolutions arrived at in the San Cristóbal mesas. No new constitution would be written at the National Democratic Convention, and no "government of transition" formed. Although the ultras kept the chants alive until the bitter end, the CND resolved that everyone go home and disassemble the state party, encouraging a big vote for the candidate who would support the CND resolutions—four days later, Cárdenas did just that.

Despite the harrowing night and the pervasive mud, the Convention had been a huge success, the Sup rejoiced, "almost an orgasm…" Then he threatened striptease. Should he remove his ski mask? "NO-O-O-O!" lowed lingering supporters, one respondent blowing a loud *cacho*, the cow's-horn trumpet of Mayan villages. "We don't really want to know," one mud-caked *convencionista* bellowed back.

The National Democratic Convention was not over. Marcos reminded his people to now go home and make this "locura" live locally. Charged with energy for August 21st and beyond, the Nahuas and the Tlapanecos of La Montaña, the Purépecha Nation of Michoacán, the Mixtecs and the Mixes of Oaxaca, the Mayan Yucatecos of the peninsula, the widows of the Costa Chica, the Chile Frío banda de guerra, the Yaquis and the Yuppies and the Men of Corn, the University *históricos*, young unionists, old social warriors, troubadours, thespians, painters, campesinos, PRDistas, periodistas, and even the ultras, slowly returned to their ejidos and schools, jobs and fields and barrios, with a sense that history had just happened all around them. For many, August 21st would be a cruel anticlimax.

THE FIX IS IN

11 days later, even as the last splattered stragglers were climbing up the canyons from Tepeyac, Ernesto Zedillo was elected president of Mexico with 48% of the popular vote. Cuauhtémoc Cárdenas came in a dismal third, with a shade under 17%. His numbers were nearly doubled by the PAN's bewhiskered Fernández de Cevallos. Zedillo not only crushed Cárdenas by 10 million votes, he also won the majority of the nation's poor, a constituency Cuauhtémoc had to capture to come close. In addition to the presidency, the PRI took all but 15 out of the nation's 300 electoral districts, renewing the party's absolute dominion over the lower house of congress. The Institutionals also won the overwhelming majority of seats in the Senate and, purportedly, the governorship of Chiapas.

On August 24th, Bill Clinton tendered his congratulations to the new Mexican president, a man whose candidacy had been born in the blood of a baffling assassination.

One week after being swamped by Zedillo and the PRI, Cuauhtémoc Cárdenas summoned chastened supporters to the Zócalo to confirm that he had not won the election and would lead no post-electoral protest. Thank you and go home. It was a repeat performance—although with a weaker hand than in 1988.

Cárdenas's landslide defeat surprised few. The writing had been on the wall ever since the debate in May. The EZLN never seriously considered a PRD victory, Marcos said. But what the EZLN had anticipated was a modicum of opposition fight-back to massive PRI fraud. It was a costly miscalculation.

The PRI did not have to burn ballot boxes and crash computers, as it had done six years earlier when Cárdenas caught the ruling party napping. Now it had the "autonomous" Federal Electoral Institute (IFE), to smooth over the rough edges.

Under the first election-spending regulations ever applied to a Mexican presidential election, the PRI's top line was $42 million USD, but despite the IFE's vigilance, the official party probably outspent Cárdenas 400 to one if the sub rosa donations were factored in. Indeed, during a fund-raising orgy at the home of emeritus banker Antonio Ortiz Mena (Salinas's uncle by marriage), the nation's 24 billionaires coughed up $25 million USD apiece, to be earmarked for the 1994 campaign.

Among the contributors were fugitive bankers Carlos Cabal Peniche, who rolled depositors (at the two banks he had received for a pittance in Salinas's bank privatization) for $700 million USD, and Angel Isidoro Rodríguez, "El Divino," who clipped his account holders for $400 million. Both skams were written off in a 1998 Zedillo-sponsored bank bailout that dumped $80 billion USD on Mexican taxpayers. Writing from an Australian gaol, Cabal Peniche confessed that he had also bankrolled the campaigns of Roberto Madrazo, the PRI candidate for Tabasco governor, and Eduardo Robledo, Avendaño's rival.

Opportune government payouts to the PRI electoral clientele further stacked the deck against the opposition. The Procampo (agrarian subsidies) payment calendar had been drawn up by Ag Secretary Carlos Hank, Zedillo's main man, to coincide with the August 21st elections. June-to-August checks destined for 3.2 million Mexican farmers totaled $3 billion USD. The 360-peso-per-head bonus ($115 USD) was payable upon presentation of one's voter ID. The Procampo bonanza captured perhaps 10 million votes from the poorest farm families in Mexico—each family being calculated to yield up six votes. Cárdenas could only offer the campesinos democratic change.

¿PUEBLO PUTO?

Election morning broke sultry over the Zapatista zone. The jungle sun dissipated the valley fogs, and the flat iron slabs that pass for church bells in Zapatista hamlets like Patihuitz, San Miguel, La Realidad, and the Ejido Morelia rang out to beckon the electorate to vote.

Under an agreement signed off July 31st by the CCRI, 65 voting precincts would be set up in the conflict zone—few polling places had ever been installed in the jungle. Indians who sold their votes to the PRI were usually trucked to Ocosingo and other county seats to fill out ballots. In 1988, Salinas had supposedly won 89% of the votes in the region. Now a special election commission, chaired by Chiapas poet Juan Bañuelos and socially committed actress Ofelia Medina, would oversee the process. In compliance with its word, the EZLN dismantled its roadblocks in the jungle and withdrew to the mountains the night before the balloting. The rebels would not vote or interfere in the process in any way—an August 18th proclamation pledged that the Zapatistas would not even retaliate with arms if and when PRI fraud was uncovered.

María Lorenzo had never voted before, she said, warily eyeing the ballot as if it was some new kind of PRI trick. "I'm 60 years old and this is the first time I have ever had a ballot in my hand," testified a farmer standing behind María in the line at the polling booth in San Miguel. "Before, the PRI would say that a lot of votes came from here, but it was a trick—we never had a place to vote around here before."

The ballots ran out in San Miguel before noon. Some had walked three days from Montes Azules to cast a ballot. A list was drawn up, and those who had no ballot gave their preference. On the Ejido Morelia, the shortage of ballots was just as acute. The *casilla* (polling station) had received just 504 ballots, when it required 1,500 to accommodate 12 surrounding communities.

Medina arrived back in San Cristóbal with the Zapatista ballot boxes early on the morning of the 22nd. 19,000 out of 28,000 registered voters had exercised their right to suffrage—many more could not vote because the ballots had run out or the military had confiscated or destroyed their credentials back in January. 70% of the ballots in Zapatista land had been cast for Cárdenas, Amado Avendaño, and the other PRD candidates, 14,000 votes. The rest went to Zedillo, Robledo, and PRI congressional candidate Lázaro Hernández, once Don Samuel's chief deacon and a defector from the EZLN.

Outside of rebel territory, the voting process had not been so tranquil. In the special casilla set up in the San Cristóbal plaza, 600 frustrated voters threatened to burn the booth if they were not allowed to vote—the ballots allocated to the polling station had been dispensed early to soldiers from Rancho Nuevo, and now, after election officials had fled in terror, the Army took up positions to safeguard their votes. Down in Tuxtla, riot police unleashed tear gas to repel angry voters similarly denied suffrage, and across the state in Tapachula, the rocks and bottles were flying, too.

From one end of Mexico to the next, the special casillas turned into tinderboxes. In Ciudad Juárez, furious would-be voters blocked the international bridges and the U.S. Migra went on Red Alert. Civil unrest was afoot in Guadalajara, Cuernavaca, and Cancún. Mobs marched on the IFE bunker in the extreme south of Mexico City, tried to vault the high steel fence, and were driven off by police dogs.

Fraud was pervasive and methodical. A network of secret PRI computer centers was unmasked by the opposition in the state capitals of Puebla, Sonora, Veracruz, and Guerrero. The preliminary results system was halted with 8,000 polling places unrecorded in the sample after Jorge Carpizo charged the opposition had introduced a computer virus into the tally. The final figures stink of computer engineering. Whether located in the rural outback or downtown Mexico City, virtually every district comes in around 50% for Zedillo, 30% for the PAN, and 17% for Cárdenas.

The Chiapas results were just as skewed. In the end, Robledo was awarded 50% of the vote and Amado Avendaño 34%, with the rest to the PAN. With 350,000 official votes, Amado had scored the highest turnout in state history for an opposition candidate, but evidence of mischief abounded.

In the dusty Chalco plaza out in the misery belt east of Mexico City, where Salinas's Solidarity program was born, hundreds of voters, erased from voting lists in their local polling places, seethed in the heat. The housewives clustered all around me were frantic with anxiety. They had to have their voting cards punched or local PRI authorities would not allow them to enroll their children when school began. One aproned woman with tears in her eyes explained that her husband had just died, and she needed to vote for Zedillo so the chief of her barrio would give her the permit to bury him in the municipal cemetery.

The moment defined the 1994 election for me. There seemed to be no legal way to beat a state party that barters votes for school enrollment, free milk programs, a job, a wedge of waterproofed cardboard for your roof, even a square of dirt in which to bury your dead.

Cuauhtémoc Cárdenas had banked everything on winning the vote of the poor, but the poor, precisely because they are the weakest and most disprotected constituents in the Mexican construct, are the most susceptible to the pressures and manipulations of the then-PRI-government.

One day after the Zedillo landslide, a spray-painted scrawl appeared on a wall near the Coyoacán plaza in southern Mexico City that summed up the disillusionment that was rapidly spreading across the land. "¡Pueblo Puto!" it read. Roughly translated: "The People Are Whores!"

WHAT IS TO BE DONE?

By the morning after, the CCRI had declared a fresh Red Alert and gone into permanent session to mull the results slowly seeping into the jungle. Already, the savants up in Mexico City were pointing fingers at the EZLN for having nourished "the vote of fear" that was supposed to have sunk Cárdenas.

The Zedillo campaign had cleverly played upon the national insecurities that followed the Zapatista rebellion and the assassination of the PRI's own candidate. "Better an old evil that you know than a new one you can't trust," became the tacit slogan. Marcos's rhetorical excesses—"The PRI must die by suicide or firing squad!"—did not help to dispel the taste of imminent violence. A few hundred million USD in foreign investment fled the country in the days before the election, and Roberto Hernández, Harp Helú's confederate at Banamex, predicted economic collapse if Cárdenas and his Zapatistas were to win the presidency. Economic collapse would of course come—scant days after Ernesto Zedillo assumed that office.

Marcos counters that the "vote of fear" was a PRI invention and that, if anything, the CND strengthened the civil society's commitment to vote. But now the "vote of fear" was on the Zapatista side of the barricades. Zedillo's landslide raised the specter of early invasion. With the election out of the way, Salinas now had the option of clearing the decks for his successor.

Down the canyons, beyond the checkpoints now closed to reporters, the EZLN was once again listening, straining to hear the sounds of protest and outrage on the streets of the cities. The rebels were not listening only for words. The possibility of fresh uprising was latent in the land. The ultras of the PROCUP had responded to the EZLN's January offensive with bombs. On August 23rd, a pair of suspected PROCUP operatives were arrested in Nezahualcóyotl, outside Mexico City, with a list of bombing targets allegedly in their pocket.

Guerrero seemed a likely geography for armed eruption. According to the scuttlebutt, the Harp Helú ransom had been invested in a huge arms cache— 20,000 AK-47s, which the U.S. Bureau of Alcohol, Tobacco, and Firearms told El Financiero was en route to that powderkeg state just in time for the post-electoral season.

The Zapatistas held their breath. And nothing happened. Cárdenas went home. There was no gunfire. The press lost all interest in what the Zapatistas might do now. The post-electoral struggle story was finished. Or was it?

INTO THE STREETS

Mass resistance to alleged electoral fraud in the Chiapas gubernatorial elections blew up in earnest September 4th as 20,000 citizens all over the state took to the streets, blocked highways, and invaded radio stations, demanding that Eduardo Robledo's victory be annulled. Marcos sent communiqués labeling the governor-elect a "usurper" and promised to send him cigarettes when he went to jail. The protests were spurred by the CEOIC—which had split into Zapatista and PRI wings during the election—and the newly created Chiapas State Assembly of Indians and Campesinos (AEDPCH). The AEDPCH (whose constituency was almost identical with the CEOIC-Zapatista) had taken to calling

Amado Avendaño "governor" and would soon become the vehicle for the crusading editor's "government-in-rebellion."

In the final days of Summer, Marcos created a master text that put bewildering punctuation to the electoral season. Dedicated to "Señor Ik" (the Mayan god of the wind but in real life Comandante "Hugo" [Francisco Gomez], a senior officer killed in Ocosingo), the tour de force entitled "The Long Journey From Pain to Hope" includes poetry by Paul Eluard, León Felipe, and Miguel Hernández; lists both the 24 Mexican billionaires created by Salinas privatization deals and the 24 poorest geographical regions in the nation; contains the Sup's most colorful condemnation of neo-liberalism yet; and offers an amazingly charitable analysis of the electoral battering the Mexican Left had just suffered.

According to Marcos's particular way of counting the results, the opposition had won the election 29 million to Zedillo's 17 million—that is, if you combined PRD, PAN and the tiny "satellite" parties' totals and factored in annulled ballots and those who didn't vote. The PAN was not so bad after all, Subcomandante Marcos suggested: "You can't deny that the PAN has always been a party of struggle." Vicente Fox (the party's chief, who would be the right-wingers' presidential candidate in 2000) was "combative and consequential." Cuauhtémoc Cárden, who had so disappointed the rebels by calling off post-electoral hijinks, was "the best hope for a peaceful, just, and democratic change for millions who live in Mexico's basement." The CND was "the new left, a tender craziness." Only Zedillo was "on the fade out in this tragicomedy that has lasted 65 years…"

The Sup's colorful ecstasy did not much match the inflexible march of events into a dull, gray, Zedillo-dominated future.

AUTUMN 1994

DEAD AGAIN

Autumn 1994 began much the way Spring had—with Mexico bathed in the blood of the PRI. On September 28th, on a central Mexico City side street near the domed Monument of the Revolution, where so many of the nation's heroes are entombed, the new secretary-general of the PRI, José Francisco "Pepe" Ruiz Massieu, was taken out by a single shot unleashed by an inept hitman whose .9 mm automatic pistol immediately jammed and dropped to the sidewalk—Daniel Aguilar was casually captured by a passing bank guard.

Until 1993 Ruiz Massieu had been the governor of Guerrero state, where his public security forces had mauled Cárdenas supporters for six years. "Pepe" was also the ex-husband of Carlos Salinas's sister Adriana, who (chisme had it) divorced him because of his penchant for the un-opposite sex. Politically, Ruiz Massieu seemed to signify continuance of Salinas influence in the incoming regime. Such influence, purportedly designed to return the family to the presidency in the year 2000, was obliquely referred to as "the Salinas Project."

Unlike the Colosio killing, the case drew few accusing fingers pointed at the EZLN. Whacking Ruiz Massieu went right to the heart and the head of the PRI. Aguilar, the pencil-thin gunman, became quite garrulous after a few jolts of juice—standard police investigative procedure. He had been hired for $16,000 USD to hit Ruiz Massieu by the muscle man for a deputy from his home state of Tamaulipas, Rep. Manuel Muñoz Rocha (PRI).

Carlos Salinas quickly appointed an unlikely special prosecutor: the dead man's brother, Mario Ruiz Massieu, then the czar of Mexico's War on Drugs. Mario rounded up 15 suspects, tortured them (one woman was raped), and came up with some answers. Fernando Rodríguez González, Muñoz Rocha's aide-de-camp, suddenly remembered that his boss had set up the hit. But by then, Manuel Muñoz Rocha was missing in action and would never be seen again—his wife had him declared legally defunct a year later.

Frustrated by the stonewalling of PRI officials who, he avowed, knew more than they would tell, Mario Ruiz Massieu quit as prosecutor and resigned from the PRI in late 1994. His successor, a shady Mexico City D.A., Pablo Chapa, wasted no time in forcing a half-million-dollar bribe on Fernando Rodríguez, whereupon Muñoz Rocha's man let it be known that his boss had been acting at the behest of an old compadre, Raúl Salinas de Gortari, because Ruiz Massieu was deemed a liability to the "Salinas Project." Rodríguez testified that he had given this same testimony to Mario who, apparently under Carlos's direction, systematically deleted every reference to Raúl in the depositions that had been tortured from those who were suspected of murdering his own brother. The mal gobierno often works in such callous and elliptical ways.

In early 1995, after Raúl Salinas was jailed for masterminding the assassination, a panicked Mario Ruiz Massieu flew off to Europe via Newark, at which international airport he was busted by U.S. Customs for not declaring $40,000 USD in cash money in his pocket. Placed under house arrest in New Jersey, he successfully fought off Zedillo administration attempts to extradite him five times, but the discovery of $7 million USD under his name in a Houston bank set him up for a federal money-laundering indictment. On the eve of Mexican Independence Day, 1999, Mario Ruiz Massieu allegedly washed down 100 antidepressant pills with a jug of vodka and never woke up. He left a note accusing Ernesto Zedillo of covering up his brother's murder.

At this writing, Raúl Salinas is serving a 50-year sentence for ordering up the execution of his ex-brother-in-law, Mario Ruiz Massieu is still dead (although he might be a beneficiary of the U.S. Witness Protection Program), Manuel Muñoz Rocha remains unfound, and the PRI is on the brink of losing power.

This new crime of state in the center of the country forced the EZLN even further towards the periphery in the national drama. It also ended all possibilities of renewed negotiations in what remained of the Salinas regime. "How can we convince our people that the government will respect our lives when it doesn't even respect the lives of its own?" Marcos asked Bellinghausen in early October.

"The group in power reiterates its inability to resolve internal differences. All the lies about clean elections and the vote for peace are shown up by this new crime," Marcos told a public assembly October 8th, the Day of the Heroic Guerrilla (the day in 1967 that the CIA's Bolivian proxies murdered El Che), accusing Carlos Salinas of the Ruiz Massieu murder (he was one brother off). You could not dialogue with these people, the Subcomandante personally instructed a few thousand armed rebels gathered at the ex–convention site of Aguascalientes, hoping that the government would notice that "our arms are no longer draped in white."

"ESTE NO VA A TERMINAR"

The military was on the prowl in the jungle. The Army occupied Tonina, the Mayan ruins outside of Ocosingo, where a new military zone would soon be under construction. The EZLN was back on Red Alert—its fifth since Spring. The roads would be re-mined (little signs, decorated with skull & crossbones logos, were actually posted on the shoulders). Rebel "anti-aircraft batteries" would be emplaced, presumably to knock down low-flying military reconnaissance aircraft.

October 12th is a significant day on the Zapatista calendar. On October 12th, 1992, to mark a half millennium of indigenous resistance to the European conquest, the EZLN, then masquerading as a peaceful campesino association, had taken San Cristóbal and pulled down the statue of the conquistador Mazariegos. Now, two years later to the day, Zapatista civil bases returned to the scene of the crime, 25,000 strong, and the coletos hastily locked their doors and slammed down their shutters.

The Indians were led by the new campesino-indígena alliance, the AEDPCH, which proclaimed nine autonomous regions (RAPs) in the jungle and the highlands and swore allegiance to Amado Avendaño's newly proclaimed "government-in-rebellion." The RAPs would boycott federal electricity bills and no longer pay taxes to the state government.

The military countered such impertinence October 13th, marching into the zona franca right past the Ejido Morelia, an unprecedented violation of the neutrality of the free zones. On the 14th, the EZLN troops gathered at the Aguascalientes ("I've never seen so many at one time," remembers Bellinghausen), lifted their weapons, aimed them at the heavens, and let loose with a collective volley that was heard as far away as Mexico City.

"Este no va a terminar / La mecha sigue encendida / Puede volver a estallar / Al Sub Marcos se lo puede preguntar," yodeled a corrido on the tapes being sold outside Chiapas bus stations: "This is not going to end / the fuse continues to be lit / it could explode again / if you want to know, you should ask Sub Marcos."

THE SECOND CONVENTION

The National Democratic Convention was giving Marcos migraines. By October, with both President Zedillo's and Governor Robledo's inaugurations just weeks away, the rebels' friends in the center of the country were disturbingly silent. Although civil insurgency was afoot in Chiapas, the CND, rather than organize similar resistance in the rest of the land, was quarreling over local control.

An evaluation of the first convention was programmed for San Cristóbal October 10th–12th, and the Subcomandante peppered the convencionistas with communiqués urging them to set aside differences between ultras and Cardenistas and go to work. Although the EZLN had promised to step back from the CND, the comandantes forwarded a suggested plan of action. In an October 6th note, Marcos complained that the CNDers had all become comandantes. A few days later, he sent along a tale told by his late comrade Old Antonio about how the first gods, the ones who made the world, all wanted to be stars in the heavens and left no one to tend the earth. Old Antonio himself, dead since June, put in a brief posthumous appearance with his own version of a CND action program that called for "a certain dose of tenderness," but if that did not work, he advocated "a certain dose of lead."

Nothing worked. The thousand or so delegates to the planning session adjourned without even agreeing upon a structure for the CND. The Second National Democratic Convention was set for San Luis Potosí in the north—but mounting civil unrest in Chiapas would force the venue to be shifted to Tuxtla Gutiérrez November 4th–6th.

Marcos resumed his letter-writing campaign, posting a suggested structural schema for the convention and new Old Antonio stories. Just before the CND was called into session in November (the second convention was being hosted by the AEDPCH), the Subcomandante disclosed that the urban group that had run the Spring Consulta and which was led by the ultra-like Independent Proletarian Movement (MPI), would no longer be the legal representative of the EZLN, a commission the rebel command had bestowed upon the MPI people even before the rebellion began.

The message was self-evident. The Zapatistas only wanted delegates in the presidium of the CND whose interests would be subordinated to those of the convention. But even with his people in place, the Sup still expressed skepticism about the CND's future. In fact, the Zapatistas were hedging their bet.

On November 9th, Cuauhtémoc Cárdenas, his second son Cuauhtémoc Jr., and Rosario Ibarra (now a federal congressmember-elect who more represented the Zapatistas than the PRD which had selected her) paid a mysterious visit to the jungle. Those who were on hand agree the atmosphere was more relaxed than in May, the villagers' chants less hostile. "Cárdenas is the one who returns!" the masked villagers shouted, and "Long live our musicians!"

The group talked all day in the safehouse up on the hill at Aguascalientes, and when they had done, Marcos designated Cuauhtémoc as the EZLN's "interlocutor" in the building of a National Opposition Front into which he presumably wanted to blend the faltering CND.

By the time the Second Convention was gaveled to order, the EZLN's situation was growing more stressful by the day. The Comandantes warned that if Robledo took office December 8th, the cease-fire was dead. The 4,000 CND delegates in Tuxtla would organize national mobilizations to challenge both the Robledo and Zedillo inaugurations. Three camps of civil volunteers—the first "peace" camps—would be installed in the zonas francas to observe military intrusions.

The Second Convention was attended by a number of sub-conventions: the women's convention, the workers', the Indians', the students', and a *clica* of Chicano activists who were already distributing Marcos's communiqués north of the border. Cecilia Rodríguez, a sweatshop organizer from El Paso, was chosen by Marcos as the EZLN's U.S. rep.

DAYS OF THE LIVING DEAD

Rooted in Aztec and Christian ritual, the Days of the Dead (Nov 1st–2nd), a time when Mexicans journey out to the graveyards to remember those who have gone on before, is not a mournful fiesta. Down in the jungle "our dead are always dancing," the Sup observed. But the truth is that both the dead and the quick are addicted to the *baile* (dancing) in the lowland Tzeltal and Tojolabal villages of the cañadas. Herky-jerky cumbias are the dance mode—in the first year of the rebellion, *El Sapito* (The Little Frog) was a favorite. On the Días de los Muertos, pretty young Zapatista women, their dark hair plaited with many silver barrettes to advertise their availability, stood by the muddy Aguascalientes *pista* (dance floor) waiting for the militiamen to ask them to dance.

Up in Mexico City, another Day of the Dead ritual was unfolding: Carlos Salinas's final *Informe* or State of the Union message. The lame-duck president actually gave the Zapatistas 20 minutes of his time, mostly to congratulate himself for not having annihilated the Indians. He sorted through old garbage, blaming the EZLN for "creating the conditions of violence" that killed Colosio, and labeled the Zapatista autonomy demands "secessionist," a line Ernesto Zedillo would parrot for the next six years.

Outside the Congress of the country, participants in "The March of Marches," jointly assembled by the PRD and the CND, were ridden into the pavement by the mounted police.

November 17th is the zenith of the Zapatista year: the anniversary of the day in 1983 when the six founders (three Indians, three mestizos) of the Zapatista Army of National Liberation established their first encampment in the jungle near Lake Miramar. Once again, 3,000 rebels from three infantry units massed on the Aguascalientes parade grounds. Marcos spoke from a stage decorated with the fruits of the harvest—corn, bananas, squash, sugar cane. His speech was kind of a summing up of the EZLN's first year on public exhibition, a report to the stockholders, full of pungent self-criticism ("we made many stupid blunders").

There was little doubt about the military tone of the event. Tacho invested Marcos with the seven staffs of military command (*bastones de mando*), each from a distinct Zapatista fighting force—the Tojolabal, the Tzeltal, the Tzotzil, the Chol, the Mam, the Zoque, and the Mestizo. Marcos received the staffs gravely: The Mexican and Zapatista flags: The Staff of Dignity. The Arms of Peace. The Bullet of Justice. The Blood of Truth. The Corn of Obeying the Will of the People. The Soil of the Living Dead.

There were only two weeks until Zedillo's inauguration and three until Robledo's. If Robledo took office, war was inevitable. Time was running out.

On November 20th, the day marking the declaration of the 1910 Mexican Revolution, thousands of Indians visited San Cristóbal once again. Their mood was not tranquil. Violence flared throughout the city and tear gas choked the autumn air. Soldiers crouched down behind sandbags in front of the Palacio Municipal. The scene was repeated in Palenque to the north, where a farmers' group called the Xi'Nich ("The Ant" in Chol) took the streets, in Marqués de Comillas on the Guatemalan border, where mestizo campesinos in a group called MOCRI marched, and out on the coast, where a dozen municipal palaces were taken and nine farmers wounded.

The drift towards war alarmed Don Samuel. Back in October, he had exerted his influence as mediator and formed a blue-ribbon "National Commission of Intermediation"—the CONAI by its Spanish acronym—to open up channels of communication between the incoming administration and the EZLN. Among the CONAI members were poets Juan Bañuelos and Oscar Oliva as well as leftist raconteur Eraclio Zepeda, one of the "Three Kings" Salinas had sent in to coopt the CEOIC back in January. Although the Zapatistas recognized Don Samuel's continuing role in settling the conflict, Zedillo had not yet given his blessing to the CONAI. Don Samuel urged that the new president act quickly. "Chiapas is fast becoming the Titanic," he preached from the wheelhouse of his cathedral. "The house is burning down and no one wants to put it out."

ZEDILLO'S TURD

The electoral calendar bonded Ernesto Zedillo and Eduardo Robledo like Siamese twins. Both had been elected the same day, and their inaugurations were programmed one week apart (December 1st and 8th). Although post-electoral protest also simmered in neighboring Tabasco, where the PRD populist Andrés Manuel López Obrador challenged the legitimacy of PRI governor-elect Roberto Madrazo's victory, Zedillo could see no further than Chiapas. The conflict welcomed him to office like a nasty turd left by some stray dog. Chiapas would be the first item on his presidential agenda, his most immediate test, and, though he would try to sweep it away time and again, the turd would still be there when he left Los Pinos.

Ernesto Zedillo had tried to make contact with the EZLN since the National Democratic Convention—Raymundo Rivapalacios, a journalist with deep inside sources, reported that the then-candidate had dispatched his own personal representative, most probably a member of the Moctezuma clan, to the Convention in August to open back channels with the rebels. According to Zedillo's own word, he sent a series of six messages to the EZLN before taking office (September 21st, October 11th, and November 7th were some of the dates). Most were never made public, and Marcos has only released his response to an October request for "secret and direct negotiations," in which he decried continuing Mexican military operations in the conflict zone and chastised the president-elect for thinking the EZLN would ever negotiate "in secret."

The EZLN's reluctance to respond to the president-elect also extended to Camacho's successor as the Commissioner of Peace & Reconciliation, Jorge Madrazo Cuellar. As ombudsman of the National Human Rights Commission, Madrazo had failed to condemn army atrocities in Ocosingo and the Ejido Morelia in the first days of the shooting war. When Madrazo resigned as commissioner November 28th, after five months in Chiapas (he would soon become attorney general and prosecute Zapatistas), the dozen messages he claimed to have forwarded to the CCRI remained unanswered—save for one, in which Marcos says sure, the rebels will talk to him if he will promise that the PRI will-stop killing its own, a condition over which the Commissioner said he had little control.

¡ZEDILLO PRESIDENTE!

On the morning of December 1st, before a select audience of the elite, legislators, and visiting dignitaries, Carlos Salinas removed the presidential sash from his narrow shoulders and draped it over the taller, vastly less experienced Ernesto Zedillo. After six years that seemed like they would never end, King Carlos was history at last. His successor would govern by rote, fumbling through several years in office before he picked up the tricks of the trade.

In his inaugural remarks, as expected, Ernesto Zedillo called for new negotiations with the EZLN (he would always use the initials, because pronouncing the word "army" in this context could be deemed insulting to the generals) and pledged that his military would unilaterally respect the cease-fire imposed by Salinas January 12th.

Marcos hovered over his radio down in the jungle and did not mince words in reply. The solemn changing of the guard had been more like "a funeral for peaceful change." "We don't believe you," he wrote. "If you were a man of honor you would renounce the presidency right away." "It's nothing personal—you are not you. Now you represent an unjust system.

"We are your other, your contrary. We will only disappear when you do," Subcomandante Marcos warned darkly.

To celebrate Zedillo's taking of power, on December 1st, police and military invaded the Organization of Small Coffee-growers (ORCAO) in Ocosingo, arresting and torturing its leaders. Up in the central Sierra, the German owners of the Liquidámbar and Prussia coffee plantations sent pistoleros to take back their fincas from the Francisco Villa Popular Campesino Union, which had been occupying them for months—one farmer was killed. The week previous in Palenque, the ranchers had sicced their guardias blancas on the Xi'Nich. Such one-sided violence made Zedillo's peace initiative ring hollow in Zapatista ears.

The rebels' injunction to the CND not to allow the inauguration to transpire without a show of resistance generated scattered street fighting in the center of Mexico City. One team of ski-masked anarchists shouted Zapatista slogans and burnt up a police car, but the cops, armed with dogs, horses, clubs, and tear gas, quickly quelled the malcontents. At the end of the day, Ernesto Zedillo was still the new president of Mexico. The next *sexenio* (six-year term) had begun.

COUNTDOWN TO THE WAR

Chiapas flavored the rookie president's cabinet. As his Defense Secretary, Zedillo chose Enrique Cervantes, the Washington embassy military attaché who had won his medals battling Lucio Cabañas's Party of the Poor guerrilla in Guerrero in the 1970s. On the 3rd, five days before Robledo's swearing in, Cervantes met with his commander-in-chief to review their options in the event of a fresh outbreak of the shooting war.

The new president's civilian point man on Chiapas would be his callow young Interior Secretary, Esteban Moctezuma, the brother of Pedro and Pablo Moctezuma, who had rescued this reporter from the biblical deluge at the Aguascalientes. On December 4th and again on the 5th, Moctezuma huddled with Amado Avendaño up in Mexico City and an odd agreement was hammered out: Amado would be permitted to hold an outdoor swearing-in ceremony in the center of Tuxtla Gutiérrez on the same day as Robledo took the oath in a nearby theater—but Avendaño must vacate the state capital immediately thereafter for San Cristóbal, where the Interior Secretary even offered his government-in-rebellion rent-free offices.

Moctezuma's proposed resolution did not sit well in the belly of the Chiapas section of the PRI. It stank of the kind of backroom deals Salinas had cooked up with the opposition to get rid of governors whose fraudulent election had generated protest in the streets. "If Eduardo Robledo does not take office December 8th, Chiapas is going to look like Central America. There will be death squads," affirmed state PRI chairman Plácido Humberto Morales.

Who had actually won the Chiapas election? The final tally, confirmed by the state electoral commission in September, had given Robledo a 16-point advantage over Amado Avendaño. Amado's supporters did not believe a word of it. Ofelia Medina was chosen as a sort of peoples' electoral prosecutor, and the AED-PCH established a truth commission. Irregularities had been reported in a third of the state's 3,000 polling places, and in her final report the actress wrote that she had discovered 177 distinct ways of committing fraud in the Chiapas election, a finding stoutly ignored by the state electoral commission.

Eduardo Robledo served his PRI masters loyally. He had been Secretary of State under Absalón's gore-splattered governorship, state PRI party boss when Patrocinio González ruled the roost, and head of Salinas's Solidarity program under Colosio. Now he drew gasps by announcing that he would be taking a temporary leave of absence from the ruling party to better constitute a "pluralistic" government. Among those fingered to participate were Jorge Enrique Hernández Aguilar, an ex–political prisoner under the Absalón-Robledo regime, who, as the state's new attorney general, would jail many new political prisoners himself. Another member of Robledo's cabinet was Jacinto Arias, director of the "Indian Attention" office—a Tzotzil scholar from Chenalhó, Arias would head a bumbling administration that allowed his relatives free rein to organize the 1997 Acteal massacre. But the star of the show was none other then the increasingly rotund Eraclio Zepeda, the Left writer and purportedly onetime Fidel Castro bodyguard, who signed on as Robledo's second in command. The onetime PRD deputy's collaboration so infuriated Cárdenas that Zepeda was ignominiously drummed out of the party. The appointment also outraged the CONAI, which x'd his name off its freshly printed letterhead.

On the eve of his inauguration, Eduardo Robledo made a startling offer: as a final gesture to peace in Chiapas, he would decline to take office if the EZLN laid down its arms. No deal, Marcos shot back. Robledo for our guns? It's not worth it. The Sup tendered one final warning: if the PRIista was sworn in as governor, then the war would come again.

On December 6th, Marcos summoned reporters down to the Aguascalientes to thank them for "all they had done" and wish them farewell (not for the first time). Despite being surrounded on three sides by "enough troops to invade Central America" (he estimated 40,000), the EZLN was ready for renewed hostilities. The cease-fire ended the moment that Eduardo Robledo took office.

Which, of course, he did two days later in a brief eight-minute ceremony in Tuxtla. With Ernesto Zedillo at his side, Robledo thrust out his stiff right arm in Hitlerian fashion (the Mexican way of swearing the oath of office), reiterated his willingness to resign if the rebels would give up their weapons, and then plagiarized the Zapatistas' 11-word program as his own. Zedillo and Robledo embraced, and then the new Mexican president flew off to meet U.S. president Bill Clinton at the Miami Summit of the Americas, a junta designed to spread NAFTA from Nome, Alaska, to Tierra del Fuego, Argentina.

"Zedillo's appearance at the inauguration was the sign he would never listen to us," Marcos told Le Bot, so "that's when the committee took the decision."

The swearing-in ceremony had been conducted under extreme security precautions: metal detectors, bomb-sniffing dogs, 2,000 heavily armed troops, and an indeterminate number of police guarded the precinct. Wild rumors flew that 600 Zapatistas were marching on the state capital.

Outside in the central plaza, under a broiling sun, Amado Avendaño assumed the other governorship of Chiapas in distinct fashion. With Indian drums flailing and fragrant copal fumes enveloping the stage, Amado was presented the bastones de mando before 7,000 bedraggled Indian and mestizo farmers who had trudged into Tuxtla from every corner of the state. "The PRI has no right of conquest here—Chiapas is not a rancho for which they can name an overseer from Mexico City," observed the governor-in-rebellion, whose eye was still opaqued from the attempted assassination.

Then he jumped in his car and careened up to San Cristóbal to claim the abandoned buildings of the National Indigenous Institute down beyond the market as his new state house. The lights and the telephones in the offices of the Chiapas government-in-rebellion had just been cut off, and there was no treasury to pay for the services anyway. The military was already setting up bunkers on the surrounding streets.

WELCOME TO THE NIGHTMARE

In its December 12th edition, much as in the rebellion's first weeks, *Proceso* featured Subcomandante Marcos's ski-masked mug on its cover. The difference was noticeable. The Sup's eyes seemed weary, tinged with yellow, fretful. In the war that was coming, the EZLN had lost its only advantage—surprise. To take on the military after giving so much warning seemed like slow-motion suicide.

The army was everywhere. Robledo's new Secretary of Government ordered stepped-up patrols in the highlands and the jungle—in one day, Zepeda had gone from peacemonger to counterinsurgency warrior. Marcos told reporters that the dread Guatemalan Kaibiles (special forces) were operating in the Cañadas and an unconfirmed report put Argentinean trainers at Rancho Nuevo. New army checkpoints had been set up along the state's highways, some of them strung with Christmas lights. The Air Force ruled the skies.

December 12th is the day all Mexico venerates the Virgin of Guadalupe, a national icon. The EZLN, normally not religiously inclined, honored the Dark Madonna by declaring that the first Zapatista autonomous municipality, "San Pedro de Michoacán," would have as its county seat Guadalupe Tepeyac (Tepeyac is the hill where the Virgin first revealed herself to the Indian Juan Diego). Tacho did the honors, and there was still time for tamales and cumbias before the war began again.

Marcos seemed abstracted. He handed out war correspondents' credentials (stamped with a red star) to the reporters and apologized about not answering his mail, but the CCRI had decided to burn it all so that there would be no return addresses for the military to investigate. The kids of the villages were already packed—when the war came again, the communities would seek sanctuary in the neighboring mountains. Heriberto clutched his beloved wooden truck. Eva carried her new white shoes because she didn't want to get them muddy on the trek into the hills. Tonita wouldn't kiss the Sup good-bye because his beard scratched.

On the 13th, Cuauhtémoc Cárdenas unexpectedly returned to the jungle, accompanied by Rosario Ibarra and "defeated" Tabasco gubernatorial candidate

Andrés Manuel López Obrador—López Obrador's appearance raised speculation of alliance with Avendaño and the establishment of rebel governments in two contiguous entities on the Mexican map. No reporters were present and the nature of the conversations was never disclosed. Subsequently, Cárdenas and Andrés Manuel met with Don Samuel and Amado up in San Cristóbal, but discretion ruled. Zedillo hinted that Cuauhtémoc was in Chiapas to talk some sense into the rebels. Marcos would only comment that the PRD leader remained the EZLN's "interlocutor."

Now the short, cool days grew eerily quiet in the Cañadas. Something was going on inside but no one could say quite what. A soldier standing duty at Gabino Vázquez, near Las Margaritas on the track to Guadalupe Tepeyac, told Bellinghausen that even the *chuchos* had stopped barking.

"I have been waiting 24 hours a day, seven days a week" for a sign from the EZLN to restart negotiations, President Zedillo told reporters at Los Pinos on December 14th. The correspondents held their breath, anticipating an announcement that military activity had been resumed, but no, the President said he was prepared to wait out the rebels. On national television that night, Zedillo announced the creation of a five-party legislative commission to explore dialogue with the EZLN. The proposed commission would replace Bishop Ruiz and the CONAI as peacemakers.

But the offer came too late. The EZLN had already gone on the offensive. By the 11th, Zapatista fighters had replaced the civilian militia at the Nuevo Momón checkpoint, about halfway to Margaritas. EZLN troops had set up a new checkpoint at Patate, 20 kilometers closer to Ocosingo than the old boundary of San Miguel. The move-up meant that the zona franca had been erased (the military had been violating it for months). Up in the highlands, farmers near San Andrés spotted Zapatista troops and federal army patrols not 200 yards apart. All of a sudden, the military situation in the jungles and the Altos looked no different than it had at the beginning of January. Although not a shot had yet been fired, the region was crackling with high-voltage tension, and the traditional Christmas season *posadas* (festive processions) that wended their way through the villages seemed a feeble voice for peace.

Then, on December 18th, reporters bunking at San Cristóbal's posh Casa Vieja Inn got the call for an Agusacalientes press conference. Under a full moon at 3:30 the next morning, Subcomandante Marcos, as military leader of the rebel forces, declared that two EZLN units had slipped through Mexican army lines between December 11th and the 14th and now held positions in 38 municipalities in eastern Chiapas, about half the state's land area. 30 new autonomous municipalities with names like "Che Guevara" and "Tierra y Libertad" would be carved out of the counties the Zapatistas had invaded, all of which would recognize Amado Avendaño as their governor. Rebel forces participating in the

"Peace, Justice, and Dignity for the Indian Peoples" campaign were under orders to avoid contact with the enemy.

From the lowlands to the mountains to the volatile north of the state, shadowy figures emerged from the early morning mists on the edges of towns as far away as Yajalón and San Andrés (rechristened Sakamchién de los Pobres). Mostly the insurgents had taken the roads, building barricades from felled trees, rocks, and town trash. The conflict zone had become impenetrable overnight. What was gong on in there? "The rebellion is inside now," Bellinghausen noted.

And inside, the villagers marched out to the roadblocks with atole and tamales and banners that welcomed the EZLN to their towns. Only in Simojovel, a strategic gate to the north of Chiapas, was there a reprise of January 1st, as masked Zapatistas set the public justice ministry ablaze.

State and federal authorities simply refused to acknowledge that anything remotely resembling what Marcos was describing had transpired. 17 roads and highways were reported blocked by an estimate 600 farmers "who covered their faces." The New York Times failed to even recognize the EZLN's role in the offense: "Peasants Block Highways in Troubled Southern Mexican State," read the page seven headline—below the fold.

By the time the military was able to dismantle the barricades and reach the villages, the Zapatistas had long since vanished. Some had fled to makeshift camps in the surrounding hills and others just took off their pasamontañas and paliacates and returned to working the fields. Cynics wondered whether this celebrated nonconfrontation was all a Marcosian hoax. Had the EZLN really broken through the Mexican military encirclement? Or had the CCRI merely called for the locals to take matters into their own hands? In the final analysis, both prospects were equally troublesome for Ernesto Zedillo.

"Welcome to the Nightmare," the EZLN had warned the new president on the day he took office.

Chiapas Municipalities

1. ACACOYAGUA
2. ACALA
3. ACAPETAHUA
4. ALTAMIRANO
5. AMATAN
6. AMATENANGO DE LA FRONTERA
7. AMATENANGO DEL VALLE
8. ANGEL ALBINO CORZO
9. ARRIAGA
10. BEJUCAL DE OCAMPO
11. BELUViSTA
12. BERRIOZABAL
13. BOCHIL
14. BOSQUE. EL
15. CACAHOATAN
16. CATAWA
17. CHALCHIHUITAN
18. CHAMULA
19. CHANAL
20. CkWULTENANGO
21. CHENALHO
22. CHWA DE CORZO
23. CHWILU
24. CHICOASEN
25. CHICOMUSELO
26. CHILON
27. CINTAWA
28. COAPILLA
29. COMITAN DE DOMINGUEZ
30. CONCORDIA, LA

31. COPAINALA
32. ESCUINTLA
33. FRANCI SCO LEON
34. FRONTERA COMALAPA
35. F RONTERA HIDALGO
36. GRANDEZA' LA
37. HUEHUETAN
38. HUITIUPAN
39. HUIXTAN
40. HUIXTLA
41. INDEPENDENCIA, LA
42. IXHUATAN
43. IXTACOMITAN
44. IXTAPA
45. IXTAPANG^IOYA
46. JIOUIPILAS
47. JITOTOL
48. JUAREZ
49. LARRAINZAR
50. LIBERTAD, LA
51. MAPASTE PEC
52. MARGARITAS. LAS
53. MAZAPA DE MADERO
54. MAZATAN
55. METAPA
56. MITONTIC
57. MOTOZINTLA
58. NICOLAS RUIZ
59. OCOSINGO
60. OCOTEPEC
61. OCOSOCOAUTLA DE ESPINOSA

62. OSTUACAN
63. OSUMACINTA
64. OXCHUC
65. PALENOUE
66. PANTELHO
67. PANTEPEC
68. PICHUCALCO
69. PIJIJAPAN
70. PORVENIR, EL
71. PUEBLO NUEVO SOLISTAHUACAN
72. RAYON
73. REFORMA
74. ROSAS, LAS
75. SABANILLA
76. SALTO DE AGUA
77. SAN CRISTOBAL DE LAS CASAS
78. SAN FERNANDO
79. SAN JUAN CANCUC
80. SAN LUCAS
81. SILTEPEC
82. SIMOJOVEL
83. SITALA
84. SOCOLTENANGO
85. SOLOSUCHWA
86. SOYALO
87. SUCHWA
88. SUCHIATE
89. SUNUAPA
90. TAPACHULA

91. TAPALAPA
92. TAPILULA
93. TECPATAN
94. TENEJAPA
95. TEOPISCA
96. TILA
97. TONALA
98. TOTOWA
99. TRINITARIA, LA
100. TUMBALA
101. TUXTLA CHICO
102. TUXTLA GUTIERREZ
103. TUZANTAN
104. TZIMOL
105. UNION JUAREZ
108. VENUSTIANO CARRANZA
107. VILLA COMALTITLAN
106. VILLA CORZO
109. VILLAFLORES
110. YAJALON
111. ZINACANTAN

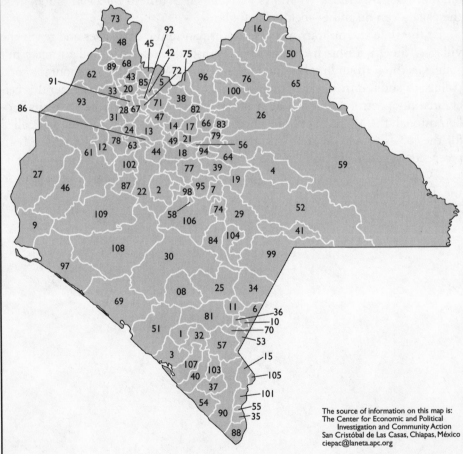

The source of information on this map is:
The Center for Economic and Political
Investigation and Community Action
San Cristóbal de Las Casas, Chiapas, México
ciepac@laneta.apc.org

WINTER 1994–1995

THE NIGHTMARE FOR REAL

It was just after noon on December 20th in the smog-choked capital of the country. Jaime Serra Puche, Zedillo's new Finance Minister, an intimate colleague, and fellow Ivy Leaguer, planted himself before a nest of TV cameras to deliver the bad news. The Zapatista offensive, which yesterday Zedillo had disparaged as a handful of peasant Indian blockades, had, in fact, so roiled money markets that "in order to confront uncertainties that have been generated by the conflict in Chiapas," the Mexican peso would have to be devalued by 15 percent.

The President's decision to devalue in the wake of the "Peace With Justice and Dignity for the Indian Peoples" offensive seemed to cede exceptional weight in determining the fate of the nation's economic policies to the Zapatista Army of National Liberation. Peso devaluation would soon trigger a nightmare slide into Mexico's deepest depression since 1932, a toboggan ride that unmasked the authoritarian nature of the PRI-run state every bit as much as had the Zapatista uprising just 12 months earlier.

48 hours after the initial devaluation, the new government was forced to let the weakened peso float freely on world markets. It promptly lost half its value, and the bottom fell out of the Mexican economy. The ensuing chaos was truly global, sinking markets up and down the Western Hemisphere in "the first crisis of the 21st century," as IMF director Michel Camdessus baptized the Mexican collapse.

What really prompted the crash? A collision of causes, some of them uniquely Mexican, nudged the economy into free fall. Salinas, obsessed with his niche in history, had refused to devalue a peso that was way out of whack with its true worth. The debut year of NAFTA had gifted Mexico with a huge commercial deficit, and hefty foreign debt payments plunged the current accounts balance into a $28 billion USD shortfall. $24 billion in foreign reserves dwindled to zero as investors, led by Mexican moguls, moved multiple billions out of the country. To keep his house of cards from crashing, Salinas had borrowed $33 billion on short-term bonds (*tesobonos*), $17 billion of which would come due in January. Default was in the wind.

The collapse could not be contained. At the nadir of "the first crisis of the 21st century," 10,000,000 Mexicans were left without any means of sustaining their families except by hawking latex masks of the now-reviled Carlos Salinas in urban traffic jams. Interest rates sailed over 100% and the banks hired off-duty cops to foreclose on helpless debtors. The future got very dim very quickly. Subway service in the Mexico City metro was slowed almost daily as a record number of suicides threw themselves before the bright orange trains.

According to the Zedillo theory, the EZLN and its flimsy barricades of stones and sticks out on the lonely country roads of a southern state no one had ever cared much about, had been the cause of all this calamity. The heavy hitters at Banco Interacciones (a Hank enterprise) counseled the new president to "put on his pantalones" and take charge of the deteriorating dynamic in Chiapas.

Outside Mexico, skepticism was pervasive. The head of the Banque de France marveled that international finance was skating on such thin ice that a handful of Indians could bring it down (Le Bot). Alan Galibert of the British Warburg investment group was more direct: "Investors have lost all confidence in an economy that can be wrecked by one little troop movement in the jungle." "The situation in Chiapas may not be the major fracture point, but the success of the government in quelling unrest there will be critical to solving the economic crisis," warned Joyce Chang at Saloman Brothers. Similarly, Riordan Roett, then emerging markets advisor for Chase Manhattan, was doubtful that the Chiapas conflict was at the root of the collapse but also advised Zedillo to put his pantalones on and obliterate the rebels anyway, for the health of the economy.

Subcomandante Marcos seemed perfectly willing to take the rap for the whole rotten enchilada. The collapse had been "larvating" for a long time, Marcos told Le Bot, but "we were like the pinprick that opened up the hole and let the air out of their balloon."

PEACE ON EARTH

Long trains of armored vehicles snaked down the canyons, their weapons trained upon the economy-wrecking villagers. Up in the highlands, San Andrés and Simojovel were occupied by hundreds of troops, but the Zapatistas had become an army of evaporating ghosts. Tucked away in high mountain camps, the rebels lay low and the "Peace With Justice and Dignity for the Indian Peoples" offensive became the "Guardian of the Heart of the People" campaign.

Although not one shot had yet been fired in this ethereal showdown, drastic steps needed to be taken to head off all-out war. Seated in the Cathedral of Peace, Don Samuel declared himself on an indefinite hunger strike, not a salubrious gesture for a diabetic septuagenarian. The Bishop's sacrifice touched hearts in a season of Christian peace, and dozens flocked to the cathedral from all over Mexico and the Americas not to eat too. The idea caught on. Up in Mexico City, Ofelia Medina gathered fasters under the gilded Angel of Independence statue on Reforma. PRD deputies in the congress of the country stopped eating in solidarity. Hunger became fashionable, a sort of graveside cackle in a nation where 40% of the population suffers from some degree of malnutrition.

Day after day, Don Samuel, wrapped in thick robes, prayed for peace in the freezing church. On Christmas Eve, Zedillo, who had steadfastly refused to recognize Samuel's CONAI as the mediational mechanism in any future dialogue with the rebels, at last relented. "A star of peace has appeared," the Bishop exulted but would not yet eat. The two armies had to be separated before the combatants got too trigger-happy. A delegation from the Bishops Council came and pleaded with Samuel to end the fast. "Laco" Zepeda and "Yayo" Robledo brought their act to the cathedral, but Bishop Ruiz was too weak to speak with them.

On the 28th, Zedillo ordered 4,000 troops to pull back from the deep jungle around Monte Libano and San Quintín. But then December 28th is the feast of the Holy Innocents, Catholicism's equivalent of April Fool's Day.

FIRST ANNIVERSARY, THIRD DECLARATION

The old year was dying in a blast of bad gas. Just outside of Mexico City, Popacatépetl, the smoking mountain, blew its top, expelling tons of debris and lethal vapors that seemed a metaphor for a year that had begun with an Indian uprising, featured the Colosio and Ruiz Massieu assassinations, seen a dubious presidential election, and ended in economic collapse.

Down in the jungle, a jagged cease-fire held for the holidays. Thinned out by heavy military patrols, the gathering out at the Aguascalientes was not exactly Times Square South. Governor Amado and maybe a thousand troops, militia, and villagers gathered on the parade grounds to commemorate the first anniversary of the uprising. "We have fulfilled our mission to show the world that poverty exists in Mexico," Comandante Tacho said in summing up the year: "We have not surrendered. We have not sold out."

The Sup attended on tape. "Today, and for a year now, to have Indian blood is not a disgrace in Mexico. It is an honor," the mestizo Marcos asserted. Then the Subcomandante Insurgente pronounced the Third Declaration of the Lacandón Jungle, which, as his huddles with Cárdenas had telegraphed, called for the creation of a broad front of the opposition—a "National Liberation Movement" (MLN), the Third Declaration called it. Now was the time—the economic collapse had fostered propitious conditions for a cross-class coalition of all opposing currents. The MLN—Cárdenas was asked to lead it—would battle for Indian autonomy, electoral reform, a government of transition, and a new Constitution.

Almost as an afterthought, the Zapatista leader announced a tentative seven-day truce.

The New Year's Eve pause convinced Don Samuel to abandon his hunger strike, and the post-holiday lull in hostilities took hold in most quarters. The temporary truce was extended to January 12th and then again to the 18th. Things got so quiet in the jungle that the Tuxtla papers reported Marcos was in Switzerland, preparing for the annual Davos World Economic Summit.

MOCTEZUMA OF THE JUNGLE

Zedillo's recognition of the CONAI fulfilled one of the conditions the EZLN had set after the December advance for entabling new talks—cleaning up PRI fraud in neighboring Tabasco and recognizing Amado Avendaño as governor of Chiapas were the other two. The Zapatista demands were politically astute. Zedillo, gravely wounded by the deepening crisis, desperately needed a "national political accord" to temper party differences during the long, dark tunnel of economic downturn ahead, and young Esteban Moctezuma was charged with brokering the deal. But the PRD's price for joining the accord was a steep one—the head of PRI governor-elect Roberto Madrazo in Tabasco and (with less fervor), that of Eduardo Robledo in Chiapas. The coincidence between EZLN and PRD demands was hardly an accident. Andrés Manuel López Obrador had met with Marcos during Cárdenas's December visit.

By the first week of January, the shattered economy was in free fall, floating aimlessly without anyone willing to throw it a life preserver. The Bolsa de Valores dropped a whopping 11% on January 10th when, at last, Bill Clinton woke up from his stupor and realized that Mexico was about to go under. The White House offered a $30 billion rescue package, but Clinton needed time to work out the fine print with his Congress.

Four days later, Interior Secretary Esteban Moctezuma, a branch of whose family claims descendance from the first Moctezuma, helicoptered into the Lacandón jungle to meet with the Zapatista Army of National Liberation. It was a spectacular turnaround for the Zedillo regime. Just three weeks ago, the President had accused the Indians of bringing down the economy. Now the second most powerful political officer in the land was shmoozing with Subcomandante Marcos in what could legitimately be called liberated territory.

Mocetzuma—"El Chamaco" (the boy wonder)—was seconded by the stern PRI matriarch Beatriz Paredes, a special commissioner for Indian affairs. The meeting was the first fruit of Samuel's fast, and he had come along for the ride, accompanied by the poet Juan Bañuelos. Marcos was flanked by Mayor Moy and Comandante Tacho. The conversation was "dense, intense, fecund, and cordial," the Bishop reported to the press. What was actually discussed was never divulged.

The Moctezuma-Marcos tête-à-tête sent new peace waves wafting over the conflict zone. On the 16th, the CCRI extended the truce indefinitely. The Mexican Army pulled out of Simojovel and San Andrés after a 27-day occupation. When we visited with Moisés and Tacho on the 18th, we sat on a log in the forest across the road from the Aguascalientes, I presented them with the newly published *Rebellion From the Roots*, and they expressed uncharacteristic optimism that the "dialogue" would soon begin again.

TABASCO BURNING

Esteban Moctezuma's pipe dream of a national political accord and peace in Chiapas blew up in Villahermosa, Tabasco, on January 19th when local PRI caciques got wind of Madrazo's arranged "resignation." A riot was quickly organized. For hours, drunken PRIistas rampaged through that tropical city above the wide Grijalba river, looting stores, tossing Molotov cocktails, torching cars and beating PRD militants to a pulp while the police stood by, occasionally teargassing the press. Madrazo was carried into the government palace on the shoulders of the loutish mob. There would be no deal for his resignation. There would be no national political accord. Negotiations with the EZLN were dead and stinking. El Chamaco's career as a political broker—the job description for Interior Secretary—was wrecked.

Ernesto Zedillo was in the hot seat. The U.S. Congress had suddenly grown testy about the loan, attaching conditions that would require Mexico to privatize PEMEX, capture select narcolords, and find a peaceful solution in Chiapas. Meanwhile, the coffers had run dry. By January 30th, Zedillo had just $2.4 billion on hand in foreign reserves, with $3 billion in tesobono pay-outs due the next morning. Clinton finally got the picture after a few hundred phone calls and withdrew the package from the slow-moving Congress, vowing to go it alone with discretionary White House funds. The rescue had been rescued. ¡VIVA CLINTON! the Mexico City afternoon headlines shouted. Zedillo breathed deeply. It had been a very close call.

QUERETARO

The Third Declaration of the Lacandón Jungle had called for the integration of the National Democratic Convention into a broad opposition front that cut across class lines in a moment—some would say a window of opportunity—of economic crisis. "The economic farce with which Salinas swindled the world and the nation has exploded," Marcos argued. The crisis had awakened Mexicans from the sweet seductive dream of the first world. Now many more Mexicans were just as poor as the Indians. The time was ripe to throw neo-liberalism on the garbage heap of history, the Third Declaration commanded.

The engine for accomplishing this heroic deed would be the National Liberation Movement (MLN) with Cárdenas at the helm—Cuauhtémoc himself was already preaching a government of "national salvation." The two projects dovetailed. With the crisis k.o.-ing the workers and farmers of the country, the Zapatistas were no longer the only force the PRI-gobierno feared. The Indians and their supporters had to forge alliances with a middle class that had been crushed by the peso collapse. Indeed, El Barzón, a debtors' union originally of small farmers damaged by spiraling interest rates, was spreading exponentially into the cities and would soon organize a moratorium on payments that brought the banking system to its knees. El Financiero reported one U.S. intelligence agency considered the Barzón even more dangerous to Mexico's stability than the Zapatistas. Now, as Clinton and Zedillo closed ranks around a rescue package that would force Mexico to deposit its oil export revenues in the Federal Reserve Bank at the foot of Wall Street as collateral on a "bailout" that all but annexed Mexico to the U.S., national sovereignty was at peril. Construction of a national liberation movement could not wait.

The third Convention met in the Central Mexico city of Querétaro February 3rd–5th, the latter date being the anniversary of the signing of the Mexican Constitution of 1917 in this colonial capital. The dates guaranteed that Ernesto Zedillo would be in town.

4,000 delegates came to Querétaro as divided as ever. Many convencionistas were fearful that the CND would drown in the wider waters of the MLN. Ultras battled stridently for the class line. How could the Convention align with class enemies like bankers and industrialists, even if these sectors had been devastated by the crisis? Ideological cat fights broke out in the mesas. When the "Plan of Querétaro," which would have officialized the birth of the MLN, was brought to a vote, it was greeted by whistles and rhythmic foot-stomping and the mindless chanting of *"Frente de Masas!"* (Front of the Masses!)

Just then, Cárdenas and a pride of party cronies strode into the auditorium. Had the CND franchise been sold to the PRD? The jeers (and a few tossed paper cups) drove Cuauhtémoc from the stage before he could even assume command of the MLN. And thus the Zapatistas' latest scheme for mobilizing the civil society died stillborn in a single afternoon of leftist hectoring. With it collapsed the CND, which divided into separate conventions and would never meet again as a single body.

Another death mourned at Querétaro was that of Comandante Ramona, "the smallest of the small" and leader of the Zapatista women who, newspapers reported, had died in Mexico City of uterine cancer. The National Women's Convention held a memorial meeting . She was 32. RIP.

On February 5th, across town at the rococo theater where the Revolution had been constitutionalized 68 years previous, Ernesto Zedillo addressed the nation's governors. He looked vexed on the small screen in the CND press room. His voice was unduly severe. The EZLN had to agree to talk right away or he was going to turn the matter over to the PRI-controlled Congress for "resolution." It sounded very much like an ultimatum. On the small screen, you could not see behind the podium, but it seemed clear Ernesto Zedillo had at last put on his pantalones.

The morning after Querétaro, the initial $7.7 billion USD installment on the rescue loan was deposited in the vaults of the Bank of Mexico but did not bring immediate relief. On February 8th, stock market prices closed at their lowest level in 18 months and the peso hit an all-time, rock-bottom low against the Almighty Dollar.

THE FRAME-UP

The President seemed even more vexed when he returned to the tube with an urgent late-afternoon address to the nation February 9th. Zedillo had just learned that the EZLN General Command was "not Indian, not from Chiapas, and did not struggle in the 'popular' interest." Yes, they were Mexicans, but bad Mexicans, who were plotting "terrorist" attacks on the nation. Rebel "arsenals" had just been discovered at two EZLN "safehouses" in Mexico City and Yanga, Veracruz, and the President had ordered arrest warrants for Comandantes (sic) "Vicente," "Elisa," "Germán," "Jacobo," and "Marcos." The last-named, he of the florid pen, was unmasked as an unemployed philosophy professor named Rafael Sebastián Guillén Vicente. An assistant kept flicking a mock-up of a ski mask over an old photo of Guillén to reinforce the likeness.

40 judicial police officers would be sent into the jungle to capture these desperate criminals and restore the state of law in that leafy enclave. Invoking Article 89 of the Mexican Constitution, under which the military can be deployed to quell civil violence, 4,000 federal army troops would accompany the cops on their "judicial" quest. The generals pledged that the operation would take out the EZLN leadership in five days max.

Zedillo had breakfasted with the leaders of the armed forces just that morning at the commemoration of the "March of Loyalty," an annual ritual at which the military reiterates its undying loyalty to the Commander-in-Chief. February is a month stippled with such military fetes, and the President, increasingly isolated because of the economic crisis, utilized these martial celebrations to woo the generals whose support he craved. Moreover, turning the military loose in the Lacandón was a way of making amends to an army brass that had been sorely offended when Zedillo, then Salinas's Education Secretary, issued grade-school history textbooks suggesting military culpability in the 1968 Tlatelolco student massacre (the textbooks were hurriedly withdrawn).

The February 9th charade was backed up with spurious dossiers of the criminal Zapatista leaders, generously distributed to the foreign press by the Interior

Ministry. The Attorney General's office, under the command of the PANista Antonio Lozano, the first opposition party member ever appointed to a presidential cabinet, obligingly displayed the rebel "arsenals"—a third cache had been discovered late on the 9th, after a two-hour shoot-out at Cacalomacán, near Toluca, in the state of Mexico. In all, 23 suspects had been rounded up, including "Comandante Jacobo," aka José Santiago Santiago, an old comrade of Don Samuel's; 13 warrants remained outstanding. The suspects were found to be holding a total of 16 weapons, most of them handguns (at least two starter pistols)—not really a Baghdad-sized bunker. In addition to the weapons, a batch of Zapatista propaganda was laid out on the AG's tables, including such incendiary rags as The New York Times, plus a couple of quickie books on the conflict in Chiapas. *Rebellion From the Roots*, my award-winning chronicle, was absent from the displays, and the next time I visited Lozano's offices, I left him a copy to be included in any future presentation.

"RIOT, SEDITION, TERRORISM, TREASON"

The first wave of paratrooper-fusiliers dropped onto the Aguascalientes fairgrounds around 10:30 a.m. on the morning of the 10th. 2,500 ground troops were already rolling down the cañada from Comitán. Only Televisa and Azteca, the two-headed TV monopoly, were permitted to accompany the troops into the jungle—for the next five days, the rest of the press was bottled up at a military checkpoint installed at Nuevo Momón.

No one was home at the Aguascalientes. In downtown Guadalupe Tepeyac, chickens and a few peacocks gabbled in the empty streets. The comandantes had long since fled, the villagers right after them. A few stragglers (including two U.S. writers from Transition magazine whom Amado's government-in-rebellion had accredited) were gathered in the Emiliano Zapata–Che Guevara Solidarity hospital under the protection of the International Red Cross. Accused by General Ramón Arrieta of having counseled the villagers to flee, the IRC pulled out of Tepeyac too.

For Subcomandante Marcos, Guadalupe Tepeyac had the smell of Chinameca. Days earlier, the Sup had been holed up in his cabin above Prado Pacayal down the canyon from Garrucha when word came that Moctezuma would be in contact with him February 8th at the Aguascalientes. The quixotic Zapatista leader hopped on his horse and crossed the sierra of Corralchén. Independent TV correspondent Epigmenio Ibarra and his assistant Javier Elorriaga were already waiting at the rebel camp. Both contend they were not the messengers.

The sealed message from the Interior Secretary was in response to a February 2nd "secret and confidential" note the Sup had dropped on Moctezuma, accusing the government of buying time to prepare a military invasion. "Perhaps the (rescue) agreement Zedillo has signed with the White House includes a clause that calls for our annihilation."

Moctezuma's response did not please Marcos. Nor did the news coming in over the EZLN's radio communication system. 300 police agents had hit the Yanga bicycle-repair shop—seven had been taken. In Mexico City, Elorriaga's apartment had been raided; his wife Elisa ("Comandante Elisa") was missing and presumed to be in custody.

The Comandantes had cleared out of Guadalupe by eight the next morning, eight hours before Zedillo would appear on television to signal the military advance. Elorriaga and Ibarra headed back to civilization and got as far as the checkpoint at Gabino Vázquez, where they were taken into "protective custody" and helicoptered to Tuxtla Gutiérrez. The President had issued no warrant for Epigmenio and he was released. As Javier was hustled into the judicial police interrogation room, he heard Zedillo pronounce his name (incorrectly) on an office TV. He was accused of being "Comandante Vicente" and charged with riot, sedition, terrorism, and treason.

ESCAPE TO THE BLUE MOUNTAINS

"They must have thought we weren't ready for this," Marcos muttered to Bellinghausen just before he moved his men out of Tepeyac early on the morning of the 9th. "We're going to win," the Sup shouted over his shoulder and then disappeared into the bush. Rather than take up positions above the villages, the Comandancia would split up and regroup to the northeast in the real jungle, the Montes Azules biosphere, where the EZLN had set up its first camps a decade earlier and into which the Mexican Army would have a problem pursuing them, because the Blue Mountains are a United Nations–sponsored environmental reserve. From there, the EZLN could launch a counterattack, the "guerra of the guerrilla," sucking the army into a treacherous terrain where one savvy guerrillero was worth 50 frightened federal soldiers.

As Marcos ran for the Blue Mountains, he left behind a trail of defiant notes. To Moctezuma: "You failed, Esteban Guajardo Moctezuma. Guadalupe Tepeyac was not Chinameca."

To Zedillo: "The value of Indian blood has been raised. Yesterday, it wasn't worth a chicken in the corral—today it is a condition of the most ignominious loan in world history...this loan will be paid off in Indian blood."

To his pursuers: "I have 300 bullets left, enough for 299 cops and soldiers. The last is reserved for your (humble) servant."

The Sup's full-day lead on the soldiers was narrowing. On February 10th, he scaled the heights of the sierra. The next morning the troops were already spreading out below him, using dogs to track his scent. At one point, they were just 15 meters away: "My finger was on the trigger like I had seen this movie before." But he did not fire. Marcos jotted down his thoughts in "a notebook no one will ever read." His body hurt—life had not been so strenuous since a year ago January. Now he was sleeping in the rough again "with only the helicopters and Orion's Belt for cover." His young comrade Camilo roared with laughter when the Subcomandante bellyslid into an enormous deposit of cowflop and Marcos had to shush him up. By February 15th, they were eating snakes and drinking their own urine.

THE EXODUS

"This is the war," General Arrieta told Televisa as paratroopers plummeted into the Aguascalientes. "No way you can call this a war," Esteban Moctezuma insisted up in his plush Mexico City offices. But it sure looked like war down on the ground.

The villages by the side of the road were in the direct line of fire and the comandantes' flight was designed to draw that fire away from the civilian population. Air Force bombings were reported in the Corralchén above Garrucha on the 10th, but the press was kept out of the zone until the 14th and could never locate the alleged blast sites.

As the military stormed the Zapatista base communities, the Indians packed up and fled into the jungle mountains. Most families had cleared out of Tepeyac after Zedillo's speech and walked for days in the hills looking for a new place for their village. They hauled with them on their shoulders a marimba to make music when they got there. Tepeyac had been the scene of "bailes, muchos bailes," Bellinghausen reminisced wistfully as the displaced villagers wandered through the wilderness.

Down the road on the Zapatista ejido with the surreal name of La Realidad, the Tojolabales encamped on the mountain above their settlement. Ofelia Medina, who seemed to be everywhere during these hectic days, camped out with them. "Its better to die with dignity here than get run over by a taxi on Reforma," she deadpanned later.

Hundreds of campesinos tried to escape the advance of the Mexican army by crossing into Guatemala, but the Kaibiles were moved up from the Petén to keep them out. Indeed, in the dark weeks that followed, movement in the river canyons of southeastern Chiapas much resembled the Guatemalan exodus of the early 1980s, when Kaibil terror forced tens of thousands of Mayan Indians to flee into Mexico. Perhaps 20,000 villagers were in transit in the conflict zone in February 1995, either running to the nearby county seats for sanctuary or searching for safe ground up in the hills.

Out at the Ejido Morelia, the community was organized for exodus. The terrible events of January '94 had prepared them for the worst. At dawn on the 10th, the villagers packed up their corn, their comales, their machetes, and their hammocks and headed down the cañada for safety. Michael McCaughan, the intrepid Irish Times correspondent, accompanied the Diaspora and noticed that one villager hauled on his back the boxed-up computer that a U.S. solidarity group had donated to the Indians. For months, the townsfolks had been logging in the oral histories of their elders. It was all inside the machine and they were not going to leave it behind for the soldiers.

Cloaked in the mountain mists near San Andrés in the highlands, Mayor Ana María lamented to La Jornada's Elio Henriques that the children were sick and dying of diarrhea: "They are killing our babies with their invasion." The dangers were deadly: the dread nauriaca snakes underfoot and the black flies that caused Leishmaniasis or Mountain Leprosy. In the Cathedral of Peace on the first Sunday of the military advance, Don Samuel wept publicly for the "suffering of the communities" who were now living out "under the trees."

The soldiers were pissed off, frustrated by the fleeing villagers and the jungle heat. The few Indians that ventured out on the roads were grabbed for "questioning."—"Where is Marcos, cabrón?" A score were beaten and jailed. In the empty villages, the soldiers rampaged through the flimsy little houses, pissing in the grain, shitting on the floor, and looting what little there was of value. In Prado, they poisoned the corn and slashed the necks of the chickens. "We want Marcos dead or alive!" they spray-painted on the ejido house, an allusion to the village's most celebrated resident. At the Sup's cabin, the soldiers seized Sherlock Holmes pipes and tobacco and books as evidence of sedition before they trashed the premises. Despite the damage, the army carefully numbered each house as if mapping the settlement for future genocide. In Germany, they would be marking Juden, observed Bellinghausen.

The ultimate work of destruction was the Aguascalientes, where the Zapatista story had been written largest. The Hiltons and the benches and the library were reduced to ashes. Then the entire space was plowed under and reseeded with fast-growing pine and eucalyptus. "Reforestation," the general in command explained, as if the army were out on an environmental expedition, payback for the ecological crimes that Tacho and his carpenters had committed in preparation for the National Democratic Convention.

The whereabouts of Marcos's great sail were never satisfactorily established, although a delusional Sup, stumbling through the deep jungle on the sixth day of the Zapatista retreat, claims he saw a ghost ship slide by, its sails a-billow and the pirates up on the deck declaiming Federico García Lorca.

GUILLÉN

Ernesto Zedillo's unmasking of Marcos was designed to strip the Subcomandante of his power and his mystique, as if the conflict in Chiapas was some national "lucha libre" (wrestling) championship in which he who loses his mask first, loses the contest. The President's disclosures had been culled from a 13-page declaration made to authorities by one Salvador Morales Garibay, aka "Comandante Daniel," and signed February 8th, although the information appears to have been logged in much earlier. Morales Garibay is purportedly an ex–teaching colleague of Rafael Guillén who followed him into the jungle but had a falling out with the Subcomandante many years later over the Zapatistas' decision to go to war. The Zapatista General Command says it never heard of Comandante Daniel.

For his efforts, Morales Garibay was commissioned as a second captain in the Mexican military intelligence's Second Section. The Second Section and the Center of Investigation and National Security (CISEN) had long entertained suspicions about Marcos's true identity. Fingerprints had been lifted from the Cathedral after the February 1994 peace talks and reportedly fed to the U.S. FBI, but no match was found on file. The search for the Sup's real identity had been narrowed down to a handful of suspects, among them Samuel Orozco, a radical from Chihuahua who for years had run Radio Bilingüe in Fresno, California. But until "Daniel" was turned, the agents were barking up the wrong tree

The Rafael Sebastián Guillén Vicente cited by Ernesto Zedillo is a native of Tampico, Tamaulipas, the son of a part-time poet and full-time furniture store impresario. One of seven siblings, he has a sister who has long dabbled in PRI politics and, at this writing, is speaker of the Tamaulipas state Congress. Rafael and his four brothers attended Jesuit schools—the senior Guillén claims the supposed Sup won a scholarship to the Sorbonne, but the official bio has the man who would be Marcos at the UNAM, where he took his doctorate in the early 1980s with a thesis championing the thought of Louis Althusser, a French existentialist most noted for strangling his wife. Guillén's thesis writing bears an uncanny resemblance to the mocking tone and colorful epithets of the Subcomandante's communiqués.

Rafael Guillén's last known place of employment was as a professor of communication philosophy at the Autonomous Metropolitan University's Xochimilco campus in the far south of the capital. Like many other international supporters, he was sighted in Nicaragua soon after the triumph of the Sandinista revolution in 1979. The government alleges that Guillén came to Chiapas in the early 1980s as a member of a ragtag band of big-city radicals, the Forces of National Liberation (FLN), which, after years of pamphleteering, manipulated the Indians into rebellion in January 1994.

Just about everyone who remembers Rafael Sebastián—like PRD deputy Carlos Heredia, who grew up next door to the Guilléns—has only good things to say about him. The suspect was "a brilliant orator," a person of great solidarity, "congenial," with "a good sense of humor," and a way with the "chavas." Rafael Sebastián Guillén Vicente would not be a bad person for Marcos to be, but the Sup vigorously denies the whole story. "I've only been in Tamaulipas one time," he disclaimed, "and that was when I had a job as a bouncer (*cazaborracho*) in a whorehouse near Ciudad Victoria."

Marcos has his own version of who he really is: "I'm gay in San Francisco…a Black in South Africa…an Asian in Europe…a Chicano in San Ysidro…an anarchist in Spain…a pacifist in Bosnia…a Palestinian in Israel…a *chava banda* (gang member) in Nezahualcóyotl…a woman alone in the metro after 10 p.m.…an Indian in San Cristóbal…" (with apologies to Joaquín Sabina). "'Marcos of the Jungle' is the son of Old Antonio and Doña Juanita. He was born in the jungle camp of Agua Fría in August 1984. He was born again January 1st, 1994 and has been re-born again and again ever since…"

Zedillo had accused the EZLN leaders of not being Indians, which must have surprised the all-Indian General Command. Marcos had never made any bones about being a mestizo and the CCRI rose to his defense. "Subcomandante Marcos has been with us on the side of the people for the past 11 years. He has suffered with us…he has eaten the same food we have eaten," the comandantes remonstrated with the President.

TODOS SOMOS MARCOS

I was balanced precariously on the back of Don Aurelio Monroy's tractor as his son toured me around Matlazinca Indian land stolen by PRI boss dinosaur Carlos Hank out in Mexico state, when the old man came running down the street yelling for me: "Juanito! They got Marcos!" One of the elders had been with us the night before, and we had never turned on the TV. Now we huddled over the radio for fresh news. Contrary to Aurelio's perceptions, Marcos was still loose, but the military was closing in fast. We dashed for the bus to Mexico City and were downtown by mid-afternoon.

A crowd had already gathered around the Angel of Independence trying to sort out response to the military offensive. Zedillo's unmasking of the Zapatista leader did not have a lot of support. Reforma reported that 50% of those polled did not buy Zedillo's identification, and of the half that did, 22% didn't think the Sup had done anything wrong.

The base of the Angel is a series of ascending circles, and we stood on the top step and looked out on the gathering. Way back on the edges, the students were shouting something but I couldn't make out the words. As the chant rolled in from the periphery it became clearer: "*¡Todos Somos Marcos!*" "We are all Marcos!"

During the weeks that followed, the cry of "¡Todos Somos Marcos!" became the inspiration for murals and songs, poetry and fiery speeches, and many marches. Three times between the 11th and the 18th the civil society thundered up Reforma boulevard, filling the Zócalo to capacity, 100,000 at each showing.

Those who marched were not just the usual Zapatista rabble. "I've never been to a march before," an elderly orange-haired woman stopped me: "What do I do?"

On February 15th, the Presidential palace was attacked—by toy soldiers, battery-powered tanks, and the foot soldiers of the Assembly of Barrios bearing plastic bazookas.

The mobilizations in Mexico City rippled out into provincial capitals, south and north, leaped over the border into a dozen U.S. cities and across the ocean too, where French sympathizers chorused "On est tous Marcos!" in the lobby of Mexico's Paris embassy. Demonstrations were held in Barcelona and Berlin, Switzerland, Chile, Madrid, all over Italy. Umberto Eco sent a message of solidarity. So did Noam Chomsky. So did Nobel laureates Adolfo Esquival Pérez and Rigoberta Menchú. So did Willie Nelson. In his conversations with Le Bot, Marcos dates the internationalization of the Zapatista movement to February 1995.

On the seventh day of the Zapatista retreat, Subcomandante Marcos and Camilo reached a clearing in the jungle mountains and the Sup climbed a tree to survey the surrounding terrain. Down below, his young sidekick had an urgent question: Why were they running? When were they going to stop and fight? Shhh, Marcos cautioned, I'm listening to the drums of peace. He could hear them out there all over the world, the feet beating against the pavement, the chants of "¡Todos Somos Marcos!" The civil society had reawakened and was again demanding peace.

At least that is the literary explanation for the EZLN's refusal to confront the Mexican army in February 1995. But the reasons were clearly more pragmatic. Going to the gun would have brought the sky down on the Zapatista villages. The images of Vietnam with its flaming shards of napalm falling upon the civilian population, of Guatemala, the butchered Indians burnt alive in the churches, are powerful deterrents to guerrilla gung-ho. The EZLN's decision to retreat without firing a single shot revealed a soft-heartedness that betrayed the Zapatistas' military pretensions.

Despite the quiescence of Zapatista guns, there were reported battles in the jungle throughout February, but only one fatality was ever confirmed in the war of the Cañadas: Colonel Hugo Montorola, who, the military says, was shot by a sniper at Nuevo Momón February 10th. Mayor Ana María claims that Montorola, who was married into the family of Marcelino García Barragán, the Secretary of Defense thought responsible for the 1968 massacre at Tlatelolco, was fragged by his own men.

ROBLEDO'S HEAD

Besieged by daily marches, bad press, jittery investors, and international consternation, Zedillo called off the dogs of war 120 hours into the offensive.

Although the President had achieved his short-term military objectives and taken the jungle back from the rebels, the operation had failed to capture Marcos and the comandantes—some claim they were allowed to escape—nor did it divert public attention from an economy that was stuck in the toilet. In Washington, Clinton's generous bailout had run into ever stiffer opposition in congress. Alfonse D'Amato flashed documents that proved the administration had known about an impending Mexican meltdown for months.

The White House had also received an advance copy of Zedillo's TV speech and quickly endorsed the military's incursion into the Lacandón jungle—"the Mexican government had every right "to deal with domestic terrorism." Military attachés were dispatched by the embassy to reconnoiter the conflict zone for an on-the-ground appraisal of the situation. "John Kord" and "Alan Hassen" (not their real names, an embassy report obtained by the National Security Archives indicated) were turned back by Mexican troops at the Nuevo Momón checkpoint on February 11th. Ironically, the commanding officer at Nuevo Momón, General Manuel García, was a graduate of the U.S. School of the Americas.

The military invasion activated human rights concerns beyond Mexico's borders. Robert Torricelli (Dem, NJ) called for hearings on human rights violations in Chiapas in the House of Representatives. Pastors for Peace, Doctors Without Borders, and a group of Catalans were already canvassing the Cañadas for military abuses, and delegations of North American Indians and Spanish leftists were about to touch down.

Nonetheless, Zedillo had won the military to his side, and as the nation tumbled into an economic abyss, the generals would be an invaluable asset. Sure, Marcos was still loose and taunting the mal gobierno from deep inside his reduced swatch of rain forest, but it was to be hoped that the rebels' weakened military position would temper their demands. Now was the moment to sit them down at the bargaining table.

On February 14th, the "Day of Love and Friendship" in Mexico, the President ordered the military to halt in place and avoid any confrontation with the insurgents. The troops did not immediately get the message. On February 16th they took La Grandeza, and a Zapatista sympathizer was killed under cloudy circumstances. The military now controlled all the chokepoints in and out of the canyons, and both Guadalupe Tepeyac and San Quintín, deeper inside yet, had become sprawling bases of operation. After February 1995, the army would never leave the jungle.

Speaking to a group of Solidarity program Indians trucked in from Puebla state, Zedillo also renewed the amnesty offer that the Zapatistas had rejected a year earlier ("Why should we ask for pardon?") when it was proffered by Salinas. The proposed amnesty law was sent on to Congress, where, a month later, it was transformed into the "Law for Dialogue, Reconciliation, and a Dignified Peace in Chiapas."

But the big offer on Zedillo's platter was the head of Eduardo Robledo, who "voluntarily" resigned after 66 agonizing days in office and was shuttled off to Argentina as the new ambassador. The new (interim) governor was no-name Julio Ruiz Ferro, once a collaborator of Raúl Salinas's in the government's corrupt grain-distribution bureaucracy. "Are you really a Chiapaneco?" rancher Sinar Corzo hooted at the sweating Ruiz, a Tapachula native but long a denizen of Mexico City power circles, as he was ushered into the state Congress. Ruiz Ferro was Chiapas's fifth governor in six years.

In his letter of resignation, a bitter Robledo extended invitations to Amado Avendaño and Bishop Ruiz to do likewise so that, once again, peace could reign in Chiapas. Robledo's leave-taking considerably weakened Amado's threadbare government-in-rebellion which had been constructed solely to counter the now ex-governor. With Robledo gone, Avendaño had lost the backbone of his mandate.

AUTO-DA-FE

The bellicose ballet between Zedillo and the Zapatistas was shadowed by an ugly war over land for the Spring planting. The AEDPCH-CEOIC coalition was fast losing control of the campesino movement, and a fresh wave of occupations gave the ranchers pretext to re-arm their white guards. On January 10th, guardias blancas killed seven Emiliano Zapata Campesino Organization (OCEZ) members in Chicomuselo near the Guatemalan border. New state attorney general Jorge Enrique Hernández helicoptered in for the clean up and threatened to imprison his old newspaper-reporting crony Amado Avendaño for provoking the bloodshed.

Don Samuel also faced blistering attack during the Winter of '95. Two arson attempts were made on the diocese's historical archives, and the cathedral in Tila in the north of the state was firebombed January 27th. On February 15th, San Jacinto in Ocosingo was once again raided by authorities. Marcos-Guillén's Jesuit background made the Church complicit—30 armed men broke into a Jesuit seminary in Palenque looking for Father Xjel, Jerónimo Hernández, whom Televisa had once identified as the Sup. The ties between the diocese and the jailed Jorge Santiago Santiago, "Comandante Jacobo," established that Don Samuel was a co-conspirator—Morales Garibay declared that the Bishop had foreknowledge of the rebellion (as did about half the population of Chiapas).

Down in Tuxtla, a poster in the window of the state ranchers' association accused Don Samuel of being "the Minister of Foreign Relations—for Sendero Luminoso" and labeled him "a corrupter of nuns." Federal deputy Walter Leon, lunatic fringer Lyndon Larouche's main man in Chiapas, called for Samuel's imprisonment, and there is evidence that an actual arrest warrant was drawn up in the Bishop's name. According to La Jornada's José Ureña, the Tatic was summoned to Los Pinos February 11th in the company of Cardinals Juan Sandoval Iñíguez and Mexico City's Corripio Ahumada, and Attorney General Lozano exhibited the order. Zedillo, calculating Samuel's value in extracting him from the Chiapas morass, instructed the AG to set the order aside.

Robledo's forced resignation and the renewed amnesty offer further exasperated the ranchers. On Armed Forces Day (February 19th), a mob of ranchers, authentic coletos, and anti-Zapatista Chamula Indians held a noisy pro-army rally in back of the San Cristóbal Government Palace. A block away, I watched a city truck dump dozens of wooden folding chairs right in front of the rectory. Suddenly, the mob behind the palace charged into the Cathedral square and made a beeline for the chairs, which they broke up into throwable slabs of timber. The windows of the rectory were smashed out. Elderly Indian women who had linked hands around the Cathedral, armed only with white lilies, were pelted to the ground. Fires were set and Molotov cocktails tossed. Reporters and photographers who had lined up in front of the women were jostled and punched.

Then gunshots rang out and everyone dove for cover. Evangelicals from Chamula under the direction of their roughneck leader, Domingo López Angel, had come to rescue Don Samuel from the authentic coletos. The mob scattered. The Bishop, who had not even been home to receive his visitors, was unscathed.

THE PRISONERS

Even with Marcos's arrest in abeyance, 23 prisoners had been taken in a half-dozen raids between February 8th and the 10th. In addition to the order for the Subcomandante's arrest 12 warrants were temporarily frozen—including one for the alleged Grand Dragon of the EZLN-FLN, "Comandante Germán," aka Fernando Yañez, a childhood pal of Rosario Ibarra's.

The 15 suspects taken at Yanga, Veracruz, and Cacalomacán were arraigned behind bars, their faces and bodies covered with welts from repeated beatings. Fernando Paredes, a shoemaker from Torreón, confessed through bruised lips that he had been assigned to teach the rebels the art of shoe repair. In Orizaba, near Yanga, Alejandro García, accused of toppling electricity pylons in Puebla and Veracruz, tried to escape arrest by forcing a pet nauriaca snake to bite him, but he survived—García later "confessed" to being an intimate of "Marcos," "Daniel," and "Germán." After García's detention, military patrols were sent into the nearby Zongolica sierra and rousted Nahua Indian villages as if they were in Chiapas.

Up in Mexico City, Elorriaga's compañera, "Comandante Elisa" (María Gloria Benavides) was captured while her infant son Vic was at day care and compelled to sign prepared documents corroborating Morales Garibay's account of the EZLN inner workings, under threats that the child would be killed.

Lozano's dragnet rounded up other unlikely suspects: Padre Nacho, an eccentric Mexico City priest to the poor who was charged with distributing Zapatista literature; Alberto Hijar, an art critic who in his activist days had been an FLN member; Sylvia Hernández, apparently one of Guillén's long-ago lovers. The PRD's Carlos Heredia was implicated by virtue of having grown up next door to the Guilléns in Tampico. PRD Senator Mario Saucedo, once an urban guerrillero in Guadalajara, was falsely accused of having old Jesuit school ties to Guillén-Marcos. Ricardo Barco, "advisor" to the Ruta 100 bus drivers, was fingered for having supplied funds and old uniforms to the rebels.

After a brief stay in the Alcatraz-like Almoloya outside the capital, the three Chiapas prisoners —Elorriaga, Santiago Santiago, and an 18-year-old Tzeltal, Sebastián Entzín—were returned to Cerro Hueco, the rotting lock-up above Tuxtla. Elorriaga was brought to court under heavy guard and Garibay's statement read to him. A date was set for "Comandante Daniel" to come in from the cold and ratify his declaration. He never would. Although he had a Ciudad Nezahualcóyotl address, Second Captain Morales Garibay was not at home—he is said to be stationed in the Los Angeles area. The court would wait for Salvador Morales Garibay to show up for the next year and a half. Locked down in the Cerro Hueco infirmary, the debonair Elorriaga, the scion of wealthy Acapulco hotel owners and the brains behind the EZLN's internet operation, would use the time to write columns for La Jornada and a book describing in abundant detail the subhuman conditions of life inside Cerro Hueco.

Sebastián Entzín, a teenage Tzeltal, had been picked up a month before Elorriaga in Altamirano, allegedly in possession of an UZI—his case was attached to Elorriaga's to demonstrate that the EZLN was armed. The third Chiapas prisoner, Jorge Santiago Santiago, "Comandante Jacobo," was the longtime director of a social program associated with the San Cristóbal diocese that seeds agricultural and artesian projects. Santiago Santiago was charged with being the rebel bagman, transferring funds from European NGOs into Zapatista accounts.

The Zapatista Army of National Liberation would never recognize any of the prisoners as being theirs. Nonetheless, those unfortunate souls locked up in the February raids were now Zedillo's hostages against any further negotiations with the EZLN.

Another prisoner eclipsed the notoriety of the accused Zapatistas. On February 28th, Zedillo green-lighted the arrest of Raúl Salinas for masterminding the Ruiz Massieu hit. The jailing of Carlos's incommodious brother put the coffin nail in the "Salinas Project," although it has sought to rise from the grave like a pesky ghost ever since. Complaining loudly of persecution, the ex-president found sanctuary in a run-down Solidarity colony in Monterrey and staged a short-lived hunger strike. 24 hours later, arrangements were made with his onetime protégé Ernesto Zedillo. Salinas was flown out of Mexico and has wandered the globe ever since.

In the interim, he has become part of Mexican folklore, blamed for every ill that afflicts the nation. During Zedillo's six years in office Salinas, became his most conspicuous if inadvertent ally, allowing the successor to pin all his failings on the ex-president whenever the going got rough, which it often did in the first years of his mandate. The famous Salinas masks sold briskly throughout Zedillo's six years in office, but the day Zedillo masks hit the street, they were confiscated by the police.

TOÑITA'S TEACUP

As Congress cautiously crafted the law that would create conditions for dialogue, the villagers drifted back to their ejidos. Many were sick. Outbreaks of cholera and hemorrhaging dengue and bonebreak fever were recorded in the conflict zone and epidemic was feared. The jungle doctor Marcos Arana told me he diagnosed 118 cases of Leishmaniasis among the returnees. Although three old men had died in the mountains, "we lost only one child in our group," a thankful villager told Bellinghausen in Prado Pacayal. The refugees' homes had been sacked. Clothes were strewn everywhere and the cooking pots were all smashed. The lamentations of the women filled the village.

Down the cañada at La Sultana, the ejido council had prepared a list of missing articles for the Jornada reporter: 170 machetes, 87 comales (clay skillets), ten saddles, two tons of rice, two trucks, 40,000 pesos from the cooperative offices. The soldiers were encamped in the schoolhouse, and Hermann asked them if they knew what happened to the abstracted items. "The dogs and the pigs must have gotten hungry and broken into the houses," the commanding officer conjectured.

Over in the Tojolabal cañada, the denizens of Guadalupe Tepeyac were nowhere to be found. "The Clinic of The Poor" had been cleaned out in San José del Río. In Vicente Guerrero, soldiers had escorted back to the ejido a handful of PRI families who had fled in January 1994, and then set up camp to make sure they would stay.

All over the conflict zone, many of the 17,000 registered refugees who had fled the Zapatista zone in the first weeks of the rebellion were trucked back to their villages by the military. 5,000 troops were assigned to perform "social labor" in the cañadas, cutting hair, pulling teeth, repairing household appliances, and protecting the newly returned informers.

When finally he came back on line, Marcos mourned the destruction of the Zapatista villages. He was most appalled that the soldiers had smashed Toñita's teacup, "the one she had been saving to have tea with the March Hare and the Mad Hatter." The little girl had spent all morning pasting the pieces back together with mud. So the Zapatistas themselves would resurrect their villages. They would survive.

Another survivor (barely) was Comandante Ramona, who was not dead after all. On February 25th, up in the highlands, Mayor Ana María passed on a videotape of the leader of the Zapatista women. She was ill, yes, and she might soon die, because there were few doctors in Los Altos. She wanted the soldiers out of the towns, and she asked for protection for Tatic Samuel, "who knows our suffering so well." *"No nos dejen solos,"* she signed off softly: "Do not abandon us...."

THE LAW OF THE DIALOGUE

The legislative commission that would conduct the "dialogue" once the kinks in the law were worked out—the *Comisión de Concordia y Pacificación*, or COCO-PA—was composed of representatives of the five parties that held seats in Congress, with a rotating chairmanship. Senator Heberto Castillo, the veteran Left leader and guiding spirit behind the commission, arrived in San Cristóbal on February 26th and was told that conditions were not yet ripe for face-to-face talks. Instead, Marcos proposed an "epistolary" dialogue.

"Hey ho, how are things out there?" the Subcomandante Insurgente asked in his first communiqué after a two-week blackout. Pretty soon, he was the same old Sup, quoting Shakespeare and Antonio Machado and thumbing his nose at the mal gobierno. Although the CCRI objected to the new law because it made them sound like "delinquents," they saluted its spirit.

The main snafu in fashioning the "Law for Dialogue, Reconciliation, and a Dignified Peace in Chiapas" was how to treat a group the President labeled "criminals" and "terrorists." In the end though, it became a matter of redefinition: The EZLN was now "a group of citizens, mostly Indians, who, for diverse reasons, had joined the armed insurrection." The law cleared congress March 11th. The rebels were given 30 days in which to begin negotiations or face reinstatement of the arrest warrants for Marcos and the comandantes.

On March 14th, Zedillo ordered the military to pull out of the towns in which they were encamped, but the troops just moved to the edges of the villages and set up new camps. The soldiers trampled the fields and dirtied the rivers, and the women had no privacy to bathe there anymore. The army's garbage was everywhere, lots of meals-ready-to-eat packaging ("beef mash," "potatoes au gratin"). The first truckloads of prostitutes had already begun to trickle down the canyons. Entrepreneurs from Ocosingo and Comitán trucked in the alcohol and the marijuana. Such worldly vices had long since disappeared from the Zapatista zone.

The military presence inhibited the Indian farmers from preparing the soil for the Spring planting. Many tools were missing, and plow animals had strayed or been rustled. Often when the villagers went out into the fields for the traditional roza y quema, the soldiers interrogated them roughly: "Where's Marcos, *cabrón*? Where do you hide the guns?" "The time for the planting is passing," a campesino in La Sultana fretted. Many communities, in fact, did not plant during the Spring of 1995 and had no harvest in the Fall.

The peace camps were set up in response to the plight of the villages. They would be "neutral spaces of observation between the people and the military" explained Pablo Romo of the Fray Bartolomé diocesan human rights center— Fray Bart and the San Cristóbal NGO called CONPAZ would coordinate nine camps to start off with, in Prado and Patihuitz, Roberto Barrios, La Garrucha, San Juan, Rosario Ibarra (the ejido, not the doña), Morelia, San José, and La Realidad. They would be staffed both by Mexican nationals and by international volunteers who would stay on for 30-day stints. The peace camps were a beacon for growing international involvement in the Zapatista movement. People of like mind from all over the world came to man and woman these lonely outposts—to the Mexican government's immense displeasure. Subcomandante Marcos recognized the internationals' contributions to halting the military advance in a March 17th letter that compares them to the "San Patricios," the Irish volunteers who had fought the Yanquis during the 1846–1848 war of annexation. For their heroic efforts, the St. Patricks had been hanged.

BOOK TWO

THE TIME OF THE ARMED WORD

"...and if after our weapons talk, we take
up the word—well, that's good, too..."
—*Comandante Tacho to Yvon Le Bot*

SPRING 1995

THE ROAD TO SAN MIGUEL

The second Spring of the rebellion unfurled over the highlands and the jungle, half Winter and half Summer—the leaves turned brown in some places, a curious mix of hope and foreboding.

The promise of the new season clashed with the bad vibes of the military. On March 29th, Rosario Ibarra brought her half of the CND down to Guadalupe Tepeyac in a spirited push to reclaim the Aguascalientes, which the comandantes had given to the Convention in August '94—but military police, equipped with army dogs, drove the demonstrators off when they tried to crash the gates of the recently constructed command base.

Holy Week came next, and the twin resurrections of the martyr-deities Jesus Christ and Votan-Zapata took precedence over politics. Those communities that could, dug their *coas* (planting sticks) deep into the exceedingly dry ground and dropped in the seed.

The Law mandated that peace talks be entabled within 30 days, but where to set up the table became a matter of public acrimony. The CCRI, under Marcos's pen, proposed four sites in Mexico City—including the Basilica of the Virgin of Guadalupe and the United Nations offices in the swank Polanco district. The Zedillo administration blanched at the thought of Marcos and his ski-masked minions strolling up the Paseo de la Reforma. The talks had to be held in Chiapas to avoid contaminating the rest of the country. Palenque, Ocosingo, Comitán, and even the hamlets of La Trinataria and Teopisca were floated, all of them inside the conflict zone to further reduce the Zapatista rebellion to its proper dimensions.

The stand-off raced against an April 10th deadline. Compromise voices urged that the negotiations be moved next door to Belize—but the Zedillo administration would brook no further internationalization of the conflict.

Finally, with 48 hours to put the pieces together, in a communiqué sent April 5th but published on the 8th, the CCRI proposed that the first session be scheduled for the San Miguel ejido at the mouth of the Ocosingo cañada, where the

EZLN had concentrated its forces in preparation for the New Year's Eve takeover of that county seat. San Miguel, which had formed one sector of the zona franca in 1994, was also located within the new Zapatista autonomous municipality of Francisco Gómez, which had been declared during the EZLN's December offensive.

THE TABLE

All four sides of the table—the government, the COCOPA, Don Samuel's CONAI, and the rebels, had to scurry to get their act together. The delegation fielded by the Interior Secretary would be led by Gustavo Iruegas, a diplomat who served in Nicaragua and El Salvador during crucial moments in the 1980s and became a facilitator of the peace process in both countries. Jorge del Valle, a beefy former Trotskyist and PRI hack, and Javier Zenteno, an Interior Ministry legal beagle, would round out the team. Tacho and the highland leader David would head the hastily-thrown-together seven-member EZLN representation. Because of military considerations ("the olive factor") and the bounty on his head, Subcomandante Marcos would not be in attendance—his physical absence throughout 18 subsequent months of on-and-off negotiations would encourage a whole new echelon of public spokespersons to rise from the ranks of civil Zapatismo.

The COCOPA would also be on hand at San Miguel as a sort of institutional buffer zone for the government men. Chaired by Chiapas PRI senator Pablo Salazar, the Commission was an eccentric mix-up of legislators ranging from venerables (Heberto Castillo and the PAN's moral authority, Luis H. Alvarez) to freshmen like Oscar López Velarde (PRI) and César Chávez (PRD), both enormous men who would dwarf the rebel representatives for the next two years.

Finally, Don Samuel's mediation body would be in place throughout the interchange. With Pablo Romo and poet Juan Bañuelos as his lieutenants, the Bishop's task was to keep the Zapatistas at the table.

Where exactly that table would be placed was much ruminated. Finally, it was plunked down on the grounds of San Miguel's hermitage, and a sort of outsized wood-plank, tin-roofed bungalow was thrown up around it. The talks were convened therein on April 9th, Palm Sunday on the Christian calendar, and the eve of the annual rebirth of Votan-Zapata.

DOMINGO DE RAMOS

There were but two items on the San Miguel agenda: a set of protocols to govern the negotiations that had been drawn up by the CONAI, and the setting of a date and a place for a more substantial second session to focus on easing the tensions between the two armies. The EZLN urged that Mexican troops be returned to pre–February 9th positions if the talks were to prosper. Instead, the Army was digging in all over the jungle and the highlands.

The tensions crackled around the quadrisided table, the angry words of the Zapatista delegation sometimes escaping the leaky meeting house and breaking against the tropical Palm Sunday air. "You do not listen to us," Comandante Tacho remonstrated in his shrill Tojolabal tones. "We are farmers—we want to stay being farmers," David tried to explain to the diplomat Iruegas, who later confessed he had a hard time deciphering the Indians' peculiar Spanish. The government delegation grew testy when the rebels would call for a caucus, which they did seven times. Each time the Zapatistas abandoned the bungalow to huddle in the nearby hermitage, a thousand members of civil society who had arrived to form the peace cordons chanted "vivas" to Marcos and "mueras" to the mal gobierno. "These are chingaderas," grumbled Senator Salazar to little avail—this was a home-team crowd and he was on the visiting side.

A few hundred representatives of the press stood watch long into the velvet night. A joint statement was issued by the parties to the process near midnight. The San Miguel accord would guarantee mutual respect, civility, reciprocity, continuity—no incident would be permitted to derail the talks. All sides would provide reliable information about the progress of the negotiations. The government men, who would promptly break every single one of the protocols, hailed this first encounter as a great success and agreed that the arrest orders would be frozen until such time as the negotiations were terminated by mutual consent. The Dialogue for Peace and Reconciliation in Chiapas would resume 10 days hence on April 20th in Los Altos, at San Andrés in the scarred, snaggle-toothed mountains above San Cristóbal.

THE CLIMB TO SAN ANDRES

It is a steep climb from San Miguel to San Andrés, about 150 kilometers and 3,000 feet. Like the jungle ejido, the new meeting site is a Zapatista autonomous municipality to which the EZLN has restored its ancestral name of Sakamchién—adding quite accurately "de los Pobres" (the town is the 40th poorest municipality in all of Mexico). For the Tzotziles, the People of the Bat (Tzotz), Sakamchién ("the White Cave") is where their history begins. Here in this rocky perpendicular topography, Vaxakaman, a sort of Tzotzil Hercules, sustains the eight pillars that support the Indian world.

For Zedillo's negotiators, on the other hand, San Andrés Larráinzar (Larráinzar was a geographer whose name was attached to the Saint's during government secularization in the 1930s) was a PRI-controlled administrative county seat, conveniently situated inside the conflict zone, to which they had been assigned to limit the Zapatista contagion. These two distinct worldviews would color and confuse the negotiations for the next year and a half.

Both the Zapatista and the government delegations remade themselves for the second round of talks. Because the Dialogue would be held in the highlands, the EZLN representation would be weighted with delegates from the surrounding mountains. On the government side, Iruegas, who was ill-at-ease bargaining with unschooled Mayans, was demoted to second fiddle. Added to the team was General Tomás Angeles Duharc, a confederate of Defense Secretary Cervantes.

The new chief negotiator was Marco Antonio Bernal, a onetime associate of the Marxist-Leninist "23rd of September League" in the 1970s, who, after a liberal dose of secret police torture, came over to the PRI. Long a ruling party diehard, the new chief negotiator had been the PRI representative to the Federal Electoral Commission during the fraud-riddled 1988 presidential elections, and vigorously defended Carlos Salinas's theft of Cárdenas's victory. An early Colosio man in the Solidarity boondoggle, Bernal challenged the Zapatistas to reach a quick agreement so that they wouldn't miss out on the government's crumb-distributing programs.

SAKAMCHÍEN DE LOS POBRES

By April 20th, the stage was set in San Andrés Sakamchíen de los Pobres. A perfectly decent basketball court on one side of the disheveled market plaza had been sacrificed, and now a red-tiled chalet stood on the site, whitewashed and ready to house the talks. Satellite dishes were hauled up the mountainside so that Televisa would have an instant feed, metal detectors were installed, a sort of press room was assembled. There would be three cordons of protection around the meeting house—the Mexican Red Cross and the civil society would form two of those rings and unarmed military police the third. 600 troops remained encamped on a hill above town and could quickly be mobilized to retain logistical control if trouble should arise.

But despite the byzantine security precautions, the government, in its monstrous arrogance, had failed to correctly appraise the importance of Sakamchíen in the Tzotzil cosmography. With a population of 20,000 Indians distributed in 46 strongly Zapatista communities around this municipal seat, the town has an exemplary reputation for rebellion. As late as 1974, the *cajitas parlantes* ("talking boxes"—instruments of Tzotzil prophecy) had spoken to the shamans and the Tzotziles rose up and drove the mestizo landowners from the region. Steeped in deep syncretic traditions, Don Samuel's church has a strong following in Sakamchíen—the priest at the time of the talks was Padre Lalo, a Nicaraguan liberationist.

Throughout the long months of the Dialogue, one religious celebration after another would come spilling out of Padre Lalo's powder-blue house of worship, the revelers garbed in mirrored clothing, playing drums and flutes and distributing great clouds of copal and *tragos* of potent *posh* (sugar cane alcohol). Post-modern chaos became general as the procession reeled around the plaza through the peace cordons, the MPs, the satellite-dish cables, and market fruit stands.

THE DIALOGUE—AT RISK

The pageant on the plaza thrummed with Indian energies. 7,000 Zapatista supporters in their beribboned ceremonial hats, short black chujs, and embroidered *huipiles* (blouse cloths) had poured out of every seam in the mountains and descended upon Sakamchién to stand with the EZLN on the opening morning of the talks. They had come from Chenalhó, Zinacantán, Chamula, Magdalena, Simojovel, El Bosque, Oventic, Vayalemo, Tibo, Bochil—you could identify the towns if you recognized the embroidered patterns of the huipiles. The brigades had come carrying banners that read "Todos Somos Marcos" and "I Am Ramona" and they chanted "vivas" and "mueras" that were not always "respectful of the government," Bernal wrote in his chronicle of the Dialogue.

The gathering in Sakamchién was the largest in memory in these remote mountains, and it mightily displeased both the government delegation and their COCOPA adjutants. "We came to negotiate with eight Indians, and there are maybe 15,000 of them here," one legislator was overheard barking into his cell phone.

Down in San Cristóbal, Bernal & Company refused to budge from their five-star hotel rooms. Despite the presence of hundreds of troops on the scene, the wild Indians of San Andrés Larráinzar constituted "a threat to (the government men's) personal safety." In early afternoon, the delegation issued a press bulletin accusing the EZLN of bringing *acarreados* to disrupt the Dialogue—*el acarreo* (trucking in non-local supporters) is a traditional PRI device for augmenting crowd size. Bernal had orchestrated acarreos for Zedillo during the 1994 campaign. Don Samuel was summoned to a dressing-down at the Flamboyans hotel, where the CONAI was accused of being a willing accomplice to the EZLN "aggression." Police agents showed footage from San Andrés that zoomed in on Indians utilizing walkie talkies, clear proof of the CONAI's connivance. Walkie-talkies are common paraphernalia at non-Indian demonstrations, but not at Indian ones, the government men reasoned, once again exhibiting the racist vision that would pervert the talks for the next two years. The walkie-talkie video was subsequently passed on to Televisa and TV Azteca to incite a fresh wave of calumnies against the beleaguered bishop.

All day the Zapatista delegation sat alone in the meeting house in their new clothes, watching the paint dry. Finally, in late afternoon, Tacho spoke with the multitudes outside. "We lament that the government has taken your presence here as a pretext to avoid the Dialogue," he sighed, and he thanked the bases and asked them to return to their homes. Silently, as the night fogs drifted into Sakamchién de los Pobres, the People of the Bat packed up their meager supplies and melted into the mountains. But they would be back. They would always be back.

The Dialogue began on this sour note, and matters only deteriorated from there. In the view of the government men, the Indians spoke poor Spanish or none at all and did not make much sense. The sessions, which often had to be translated and re-translated, moved excruciatingly slowly for the impatient bureaucrats. Iruegas grew frustrated when he tried to outline his plan for defusing the military situation.

The government proposed that EZLN fighters be concentrated in three sectors (the highlands, the jungle, and in between), where they would be housed and fed until such time as agreement was reached, after which disarmament could begin. The scheme had been devised by the diplomat Iruegas based on Central American models—in the Nicaragua stand-off, the Contras had regrouped in *bolzones* (pockets) and in Salvador, the FMLN was assigned to "enclaves."

The EZLN delegation would buy none of it. An indignant Tacho snorted that the government was asking for the Zapatistas' surrender. "First the government makes fun of us, and then they want to put us in the pig pen with a rope around our necks," David resonated. Both insisted that discussion of Zapatista disarmament should come at the end of the talks—"they have the procedure upside down," David complained. Tensions could only be tamped down if the military retreated to pre–February 9th positions. High-decibel recriminations rang out at press conferences.

And at midday April 23rd, the rebels stomped out of Sakamchién, halfheartedly pledging to bring the government's enclave proposal to the communities for consultation. The next round of talks was calendared for May 12th, but observers wondered if either side would ever voluntarily return to the table.

MAY DAY! MAY DAY!

During the Spring quarter of 1995, the Mexican nosedive touched rock bottom. A thousand businesses went bust a month and home mortgage rates jumped 120%. The debtors' union El Barzón had taken to disrobing in public in protest—up in Chihuahua, Barzonistas tarred and feathered a bank official. Half the banks' outstanding loans were deemed unpayable, and many appeared in imminent danger of collapse.

March unemployment rates were the highest since the government began collecting such data. Although the National Geographic and Statistics Institute deploys measurements designed to minimize real unemployment, Zedillo could not camouflage the ocular evidence. In the spring of 1995, about a third of the 36-million-person Mexican workforce was not working.

The macroeconomic picture was all gloom, with Mexico registering minus 10% growth in 1995. A more palpable parameter of suffering was the increasing hunger of those at the bottom of the food chain. In May, a mob descended upon the Monterrey freight yard and emptied the boxcars of tons of imported corn in a scene that stirred memories of the Mexican Revolution.

The fallout from the continuing crisis was so acute that Fidel Velázquez, the mummified czar of Mexican labor, was prompted to call off the traditional May 1st International Workers' Day march, fearing mayhem if the members of his PRI-affiliated unions were allowed to get too close to a president who had caused them so much grief.

Velázquez's retreat from the Zócalo opened the great plaza to an independent union movement which each year had staged May 1st marches that often blew up in mêlées with the mounted police. But on International Worker's Day 1995, uncounted thousands of independent unionists and their families lined up on the Paseo de Reforma all the way from Chapultepec park to the Old Quarter of the city, and it took a continuous stream of marchers four hours to fill the great square. Many marched because the treacherous economic conditions had cost them their livelihood, among them the Ruta-100 bus drivers who had been locked out by the Mexico City mayor in a putsch to privatize public transport in the capital. Every day, the Ruta-100 drivers marched, snarling big-city traffic beyond repair. Marcos, the government claims, was once a Ruta-100 driver.

The rebels sent one unlikely delegate to the magnum event: Don Durito de la Selva, the Sup's pet jungle beetle (La Realidad is always crawling with *duritos*), who had purportedly borrowed Marcos's shoelace to use as reins for his trusty steed Pegaso, a turtle, and galloped off to Mexico City to joust with old Fidel Velázquez. Marcos, whom Don Durito had appointed as his Sancho Panza, received a postal card from the errant knight describing the May 1st turnout— Durito had marched past the U.S. embassy on Reforma with his feelers clenched into a fist, chanting "¡Yanquis No! ¡Dodgers Sí!" Now the beetle was hanging around the Zócalo, refining his thesis on the ills of neo-liberalism, which he soon would submit to the national autonomous university.

RETURN TO SAKAMCHÍEN

By the second round of the Dialogue, San Andrés-Sakamchíen was adjusting to the routine. Hundreds of reporters who pounced upon the highland town when the talks began again were met with bemused indifference by the locals. Oscar, the good vibes man, re-installed himself on a corner of the plaza, chanting and fanning his ceremonial fire, offering a pipe of peace and focusing the energy of his crystals upon the meeting house to stimulate the peace waves. Down the street, a new restaurant, "El Diálogo," which featured "Bifstek Zapatista" (garnished with ski-masked radishes) was doing standing-room-only business (granted there were only two chairs in the house).

The EZLN delegation had been expanded for the third edition of the negotiations—the Tojolabal grandmother Trinidad came up from the jungle with Tacho. "Abuela Trini" (Grandma Trini) provided fresh firepower for the rebel representation. During the heated discussion May 13th, after Bernal and del Valle suggested that the EZLN was "pretending not to understand" the government's offer, Abuela Trini launched into an animated discourse, entirely in Tojolabal. When she had done, the old woman glared over her paliacate at Bernal and inquired in halting Spanish if he had understood what she had just said. The government's chief negotiator had not caught the drift. "Now you know how we feel," shot back Grandma Trini.

The Zapatistas responded to the government's enclave scheme with maximum distrust. Instead, the rebels had come with their own proposal for separating the hostile forces. The Mexican Army would retreat to pre–February 9th positions and the EZLN would hold its positions in the mountains and not reoccupy the zone evacuated by the federal military. But the government was not about to relinquish its military advantage—what the EZLN had not won in the war, they would not win in the peace. Iruegas countered with a new scheme: the Army would remain the authority in the areas it now held, as would the EZLN in its own base communities—the military would, however, continue to patrol the roads in eight "corridors" or "routes" transecting the Cañadas.

The corridor plan was to be imposed upon a very convoluted geography, and the rebels did not reject it out of hand. The routes could give the EZLN's autonomous municipalities in the Cañadas some breathing space.

Bernal and his colleagues demanded an immediate yes or no. "They do not understand our time," Tacho later lamented—the rebels were, of course, obligated to consult with their bases before responding. Bernal was convinced that the rebels were stalling, and after an afternoon drumming his knuckles on the wooden negotiation table, he called their bluff. Abruptly, half of the military police outside were withdrawn. Troop movement on the hill above town was noticed by reporters. Then the metal detectors were dismantled. Vehicles were revved up to ferry the government delegation back down the hill to San Cris. Bellinghausen reported a dark cloud scudded across the face of the full moon.

But by the next morning, the two sides were back at the table as if nothing had happened, even issuing conciliatory press bulletins. Who had called whose bluff?

On the 14th, the Zedillo government and the Zapatista Army of National Liberation inked a "minimum agreement," the first signed document to evolve from the talks at San Andrés. Under its terms, the Zapatistas pledged to consult with their bases and return June 7th, having selected a test route. Because the government men were suspicious that the rebels were utilizing the *consultas* to prolong negotiations, the CCRI cordially invited them to hump it through the jungles and the highlands out to the villages to witness the assemblies, an offer

Zedillo's representatives, whose job descriptions did not include jungle treks, refused.

Down in San Cristóbal, in the patio of the Mazariegos hotel on the concluding night of the May dialogue, Gustavo Iruegas was irate. "How can you negotiate with people who are always running off to the jungle to consult?" he asked reporters, swirling the brandy in his snifter petulantly.

CHIAPAS BRONCO

While the Dialogue up at San Andrés groaned on in fits and starts, the rest of Chiapas was coming unglued. In late March, masked bandits blocked the highway near Oxchuc, shot out the tires and the windshield of a Pastors for Peace bus, and relieved the men and women of the cloth of 10,000 pesos—similar heists were experienced by commercial bus lines.

Fresh land occupations by campesino groups numbered in the hundreds—nine militants were slain in the first two weeks of April, with the violence spreading from Tapachula on the Pacific to Yajalón and Tumbalá near the Tabasco line. As far off as Naja, in the heart of the jungle, tranquil Lacandones were challenged by Tzeltal farmers pushed east by the conflict. Laco and Jorge Enrique sent in state police "to prevent violence" and only triggered it. The Francisco Villistas ("Panchos") were evicted twice from the German-owned fincas Liquidámbar and Prussia in the central sierra. When the Panchos began a march towards Tuxtla, they were tear-gassed on the highway and one farmer was shot dead.

As the spring planting wars reached crescendo, the Zedillo administration moved to undercut the vitality of the campesino movement. Dante Delgado, ex-governor of Veracruz (he would soon go to jail for purloining state funds), was delegated to buy off the campesinos of the CEOIC-AEDPCH and get rid of Amado Avendaño forever. One by one the farmers' groups succumbed to the lure of Delgado's lucre. The EZLN turned irate at this treachery. In early June, Marcos tongue-lashed so-called allies who thought the struggle was "just a photo-op." I caught up with Tacho in the candlelit schoolhouse at La Realidad. "We know these people," the onetime Tojolabal agrarian leader snapped—"we know they are for sale."

By June 1995, the conflict zone exhibited telltale signs of textbook low-intensity conflict: helicopters and fixed-wing reconnaissance aircraft relentlessly criss-crossed the seamless sky just to remind the Indians on the ground who was on top now; troops were dug into every nook and cranny of the Cañadas; bandits and paramilitary groups terrorized the towns and the roads; offers they could not refuse were being tendered to former rebel allies. It wasn't Chechnya, but it had its moments. CONPAZ reported that troops opened fire at Beteatón, near La Sultana, on May 26th, and on June 3rd the military paid a "courtesy visit" to the civil peace camp at La Garrucha and ransacked the volunteers' luggage. The troop movements in the jungle were merely "administrative," explained General Mario Renán Castillo, a military intelligence expert who had replaced Godínez as commander of the seventh region. As a graduate of the Center for Special Forces in Fort Bragg, North Carolina, Renán Castillo knew by heart the Pentagon manuals on low-intensity conflict.

AT LAST, THE RAINS

The EZLN came back to Sakamchién armed with one additional woman delegate—Andrea—and a pair of lengthy Marquesian documents.

"The Story of Mirrors" was so fat that La Jornada took three days to publish it all. The opus contains multiple Old Antonio stories ("everyone must have an Old Antonio in their life") and the full text of Don Durito's thesis on neo-liberalism. "The Story of Mirrors" is an insightful reconfiguration of Mexican politics in the bankrupt Spring of 1995: in one mirror a civil society is driven to suicide by the economic crisis. In another, the reader is invited to reflect upon his or her own image and decide what to do next.

The second communiqué was just as heavy: a call for a summertime national and international "consultation" to decide the Zapatistas' future—it would ask if the EZLN should transform itself into a political organization. "We thought we should listen to those who support us," the CCRI explained.

The two sides squared off for round four on June 7th, and from the opening bell it was evident that there would be no movement. The EZLN complied with the minimum agreement by selecting a test corridor—Las Margaritas to San Quintín to Ocosingo, the longest and most traveled route, around which 15,000 to 20,000 troops were now clustered (Guadalupe Tepeyac was right in the middle). The military would be allowed to control both ends of the corridor, but the EZLN would rule in between. The proposal was flagrantly unacceptable. Defense Secretary Cervantes had made it very clear that the Army would never surrender Guadalupe Tepeyac.

Outside the embattled meeting house, darkly furrowed rain clouds loomed over the mountains, ushering in the rains in spectacular fashion. Throughout the torrential downpour, the Indians, who had returned to Sakamchién, but in smaller numbers, stood impassively on the peace lines, pelted by the rain and soaked to the bone.

Marco Antonio Bernal was not pleased by the Indians' return. One group of youngsters who had brought flowers to the vigilers drew the government negotiators' fire. "They are being used for propaganda purposes," Bernal fumed, demanding that the children be taken away.

Finally, on June 9th, the CONAI called a halt to the ceaseless bickering over troop separation, and the issue was shelved, to be resuscitated when the two sides were ready. The negotiations now turned directly to the heart of the matter—the Zapatista demands and methods for resolving them.

The EZLN had made a mistake by presenting their demands as a package (the pliego petitorio) in February 1994, Tacho admitted. Now the delegates proposed a series of mesas or sections that would hash out themes of Democracy and Justice, Indian Rights and Culture, Woman's Rights, Agrarian Rights and Economic Welfare, and corresponding regional issues. The mesas would be scheduled consecutively and would proceed from dialogue to negotiation to agreement. They would be flexible enough to include other constituencies that shared Zapatistas' concerns in these areas.

The inclusion of national issues in the EZLN formulary drew a gasp from the diplomat Iruegas. "This is not possible—they don't represent everyone." Moreover, the mesas would take years to accomplish at the Zapatista rate. The whole thing was a devious rebel scheme to exhaust the federal government. The talks broke off once again on the 12th without any agreement except to return to the table July 4th—but even that date was problematic. Little progress was expected until after the EZLN's August consulta, when the rebels' mandate to negotiate national issues at San Andrés-Sakamchién would be tested.

By mid-June it was raining so hard that just getting in and out of the mountains had become a problem. Down in the jungle, the rain enclosed the tangled green landscape. Decay, mud, shit, infection were everywhere. "In this season, the selva takes its revenge on man for trying to tame it," Bellinghausen wrote. Hermann had just turned down the National Press Award, doled out by the President each June. The cronista had spent much of 1995 documenting the military occupation after the February offensive. No, he shrugged after the award was announced, no, he could not accept this questionable distinction from Zedillo so long as the president's troops continued to vex the villages of which he wrote.

SUMMER 1995

JESUS OUT OF CHIAPAS

Just a few ticks on the far side of the vernal equinox, the Zedillo regime began summer with a bang by expelling three of Don Samuel's non-Mexican priests from Mexico. The padres all had served parishes in the north of Chiapas where land takeovers, paramilitary formations, and clashes between PRIistas and groups identified with the PRD and the EZLN were escalating day by day. Avendaño had won 60% of the votes in the region the previous fall, and with municipal elections coming up in October, the PRI was apprehensive.

On the morning of June 22nd, Father Loren Reibe, a southern California native who had spent the last 19 years of his life in Yajalón, a Tzeltal-Chol parish north of Ocosingo, was contemplating arrangements for the coming feast of Santiago Apóstol, the town patron, when he heard that the church pick-up had been detained at a police barricade on the edge of town. When Padre Loren, a robust man, marched out to the roadblock to straighten the matter out, state police hogtied and blindfolded him, threw him up in the back of a police truck, and delivered him to Tuxtla Gutiérrez immigration offices, where he was joined by two other victims of the coordinated snatch—Jorge Barón, an Argentinean priest who had spent many years in Tumbalá on the Tabasco border, and a young Spaniard, Rodolfo Izel, who served in Sabanilla. The operation would be the first of many such deportations of nosy non-Mexicans to be carried out by the National Immigration Institute, the Mexican Migra, in Chiapas.

The three priests were flown under heavy guard up to Mexico City, held in an immigration jail at the airport overnight, and, without ever being told what the charges against them were, put on the first plane to Miami the next morning, with only the clothes on their backs to show for decades of work with the poor of Mexico. The three priests were expelled for life under Article 33 of the Constitution, which gives the President draconian power to boot out any foreigner whose continuing presence on Mexican soil is deemed "inconvenient." Two other non-Mexican diocesan priests who were out of the country in June were never permitted to return to Mexico.

"These expulsions will contribute to restoring an atmosphere of order, stability, and concord in the region," a bare-bones Interior Secretariat press bulletin explained.

During 30-plus years at the wheel of the San Cristóbal diocese, Don Samuel had never suffered a more stunning blow.

Days after the priests had been shipped home, Interior revealed that the expulsions were provoked by anonymous allegations that the padres preached politics from the pulpit and led local land invasions (the PRI mayor of Yajalón told me that there were no land invasions in the municipality). Loren Reibe was also accused of selling protection from kidnapping to a local rancher for $130 USD (!) and inciting Indians "to take the money of the rich and divide it among themselves." In addition, Father Reibe was purported to have met with "PRD and EZLN sympathizers," urging them "to rob cattle and buy guns."

Following Mass two Sundays after Loren was kidnapped and deported, 5,000 parishioners carrying white roses and wild gladiolas circled the tiny plaza of Yajalón all morning—similar services were conducted in 42 diocesan parishes. "If Jesus Christ were alive and in Chiapas today, the government would throw him out, too," testified Father Heriberto Cruz out in the dangerous north state town of Tila.

THE HOLY FATHER MAKES A MOVE

Many of the actors in the Chiapas drama were barnstorming European stages during the Summer of '95. Don Samuel himself was saying Mass in Madrid on the day of the deportations. Foreign Secretary Angel Gurria flitted from capital to capital, arguing that there was no war in Chiapas and declaring the conflict to be merely one of "ink and the Internet." Amado Avendaño was also playing the continent, opening embassies of his government-in-rebellion in Barcelona and Paris. So was PRI deputy Walter Leon, Lyndon Larouche's agent in Chiapas, whose spiel at the Schiller Institute in Paris was disrupted by masked *Zapatistes*. Leon subsequently camped out at the Vatican, demanding Don Samuel's immediate removal as bishop of San Cristóbal.

Rather than removing him, in August the Vatican would appoint a coadjutor or associate bishop to nudge Samuel out of the diocese. Assigning coadjutors has been the Church's modus operandi in ridding southern Mexico of troublesome liberationist bishops, such as the late Bernabé Carrasco and Arturo Lona in Oaxaca. Raúl Vera López was hand-picked by the *Papa* (pope) at the behest of papal nuncio Prigione to be the coadjutor and probable successor to Don Samuel when he would be forced into mandatory retirement at 75, in the year 2000.

But the Holy Father is really not as infallible as he is cracked up to be. Although the appointment of a Prigione boy as Samuel's coadjutor sent the authentic coletos into paroxysms of joy, the matter was hardly settled. Raúl Vera had been bishop of a dirt-poor, narco-ridden diocese in the hot lands of Guerrero, a region that has produced guerrilla priests like José María Morelos y Pavón, who led the liberation struggle against Spain. Raúl Vera himself was not unfamiliar with the dread liberation theology, having gone to school with Ruiz devotee Pablo Romo and Vicar Ituarte, and in a matter of months, Raúl would fall under Don Samuel's enchantment and be transformed—much as Ruiz and Bartolomé de las Casas both had been transformed—by the vibrant and combative spiritual life of his new Indian parishioners, into a serious defender of the indígenas of Chiapas.

AGUAS BLANCAS

As resumption of the Dialogue approached, the feel of the land was as ugly as the scowling clouds massing over San Andrés Sakamchíen de los Pobres.

On the morning of June 28th, far off on Guerrero's volatile Costa Grande just north of Acapulco, a truckful of farmers, some of them members of the Campesino Organization of the Southern Sierra (OCSS), but others simply hauling corn and avocados down to market in Coyuca de Benítez, were ambushed by state motorized police at a mountain wash known locally as Aguas Blancas. 17 were killed and 23 wounded, some crippled for life. Governor Rubén Figueroa argued the "preventive" attack was justified because the OCSS farmers were a bunch of "radical troublemakers" whom he suspected of having ties to the long-dead Lucio Cabañas's Party of the Poor. Once upon a time, Cabañas kidnapped Figueroa's father, also the governor and also named Rubén—the Figueroas have frequently been governors of Guerrero. The OCSS, which was constituted just 13 days after the Zapatista uprising, had been skirmishing with the younger Figueroa for months over the control of community forests the governor's cronies were merrily chainsawing down.

Although the Aguas Blancas massacre is only one on a long list of mass killings in Guerrero—15 new victims in three separate incidents would be registered in the next 11 days—the circumstances of the butchery were particularly grotesque. Five of the farmers had been given the coup de grace as they writhed in their own blood. Figueroa's agents descended upon the Acapulco hospital to which the victims had been rushed, offering them money in exchange for silence. A doctored video prepared by the governor's press office to justify Figueroa's version of the massacre was rushed over to Televisa for an early afternoon showing. A year later, after the unadulterated video had been leaked to the press, Figueroa was forced from office.

The bloodbath at Aguas Blancas tripwired immediate retaliation. Quick-tempered locals lost little time in burning out the Coyuca city hall—the mayor, an ex–Lucio guerrillero who had come over to Figueroa, fled in panic and never returned. Five police agents were gunned down by unknowns near Olinalá across the state in La Montaña.

Allegations of OCSS ties to the Party of the Poor and its notorious confederate, the PROCUP, brought the Mexican Army storming into the state. Leaked military intelligence documents, reported by Nacho Ramírez in Proceso, affirmed that seven distinct guerrilla formations were moving in Guerrero. The whereabouts of the 20,000 AK-47s allegedly purchased with the Harp Helú ransom became of acute concern to the military. Whether or not such wild tales were tainted by the truth, the massacre at Aguas Blancas had opened a second counterinsurgency front for the Zedillo regime.

Although he denied any ties between the EZLN and the Campesino Organization of the Southern Sierra, Subcomandante Marcos "lamented the murders of our brothers." The connections were clear: "Aguas Blancas tenders a bridge of brown blood towards the indígenas of Chiapas."

SAN ANDRES IV & V

On June 28th, the same day that the barbarities at Aguas Blancas bathed Guerrero in blood, Interior Secretary Esteban Moctezuma snapped shut his attaché case on Bucareli Street in the old center of the city and went home for good. Dissed by the Zapatistas as a traitorous Guajardo and shrugged off by veteran politicos as a lightweight, Moctezuma had never been able to bring the parties together in the national accord which Ernesto Zedillo demanded. In his stead, the President tapped Mexico state governor Emilio Chuayffet, a political fixer who had been the first director of the Federal Electoral Institute.

The switch begged the question: with just whom was the EZLN negotiating? "We do not know this man's thought," Tacho wondered on the eve of the fourth Dialogue at San Andrés.

The inauguration of the session was delayed while military police searched the meeting house for time bombs. San Andrés IV (the meetings had now achieved Roman numeral status) seemed earmarked for disaster. The EZLN delegation had come to the table to propose procedural rules, a format, and the themes for settling their demands. When they offered 16 theme groups that would include national issues, the government men leaped out of their seats. "No! You have no representation to discuss national issues," Iruegas shook his finger. "This will take three years to settle under your proposal," the often undiplomatic diplomat added, demanding an end to the rebels' dillydallying tactics ("They just want to gain time to tell more lies").

Bernal's sidekick, Jorge del Valle, an ex–Party of Revolutionary Workers (PRT) comrade of Rosario Ibarra, tried to mollify Iruegas: "The Indians' cosmovision is distinct from the Western Christian world. What is disrespectful for them, is ordinary for us..." To the government men's left, members of the COCOPA nodded in silent agreement.

"Your silence makes you accomplices!" Tacho exploded at the legislators. A stiff rain beat down upon the red-tiled roof.

The inclusion of national issues and the number and sequential order of the mesas (the government insisted upon simultaneous "tables") were steep hurdles to conciliation. "We have to examine the issues carefully, one by one, not like the deputies do, in a package," Tacho insisted, casting a sidelong glance at the congressional representatives around the table. The EZLN wanted to invite a team of advisors and experts to the mesas. Iruegas recalculated and suggested that the experts would add two more years to the three years he had already calculated for the negotiations. "Things go slowly. It takes time for the government to learn," David sagely counseled the few representatives of the fourth estate who were still paying any attention by July 5th.

The fourth Dialogue recessed abruptly the next day. The EZLN proposals were complicated—for instance, under the theme of agrarian reform, the EZLN wanted to discuss not just land claims but questions of production and the environment as well. The government men needed a little time to analyze the proposals. The two sides would reconvene on the 24th.

San Andrés V got off to a late start. A posse from the Bishops conference, Raúl Vera among them, had came up the mountain to hear the rebels' side of the story, leaving the government delegation with little to do except watch *telenovelas* in their deluxe hotel suites.

When the Dialogue finally got under way on the 25th, Bernal cast the first monkey wrench, threatening to inundate the Cañadas with government money and steal the Zapatista base if the rebels did not start talking reasonably. A huge boodle was already promised to the state's ragged Indian farmers—one billion pesos in the 1995–2000 Chiapas development plan, 360 million in immediate relief for the conflict zone, and a *cañonazo* (cannon shot) of 250 million for poor coffee-growers, many of whom were Zapatista supporters.

"You have the face of a good man but the heart of a hypocrite," Tacho challenged Marco Bernal, and the flak was flying again. "They think they are like the Conquistadores. They are trying to humiliate us. Bernal never tires of trying to buy us off—but he doesn't even offer money. It's all words."

When the CONAI was finally able to redirect attention to the agenda items of rules, format, and themes of the real negotiations, differences over negotiating national themes re-ignited. Although the government delegation stubbornly refused to touch the matter, the PRD and PT (Party of Labor) members of the COCOPA had been tenderized by the rebel name-calling and began to see the light. "The EZLN did not rise up against Chiapas but against the federal government," Cocopo Juan Guerra (once a guerrillero himself) reasoned. Moreover, the law that governed the Dialogue instructed the parties to resolve the issues that had caused the conflict, most of which were national ones.

The Zapatista mandate to raise national issues could not be resolved until after the scheduled August 27th Consulta for Democracy and Peace in Chiapas, a date that mooted further discussion. Both sides agreed to submit their final proposals on the themes and procedural points to the CONAI by August 20th, and the documents would be reconciled for presentation at San Andrés on September 5th. There would be no dialogue until after the consulta results were counted. By the 27th, the embattled parties retreated, under umbrellas, to their respective encampments. Outside, the bone-chilling rain drilled down on the muddy streets of Sakamchién de los Pobres.

THE PRISONERS

From his crowded cell in the infirmary of Cerro Hueco, Javier Elorriaga wrote often of his desperation: "Today another session has ended in San Andrés, and it only generates more pessimism—nothing will come of this until the government realizes what country it lives in…"

Javier's court appearances had turned into frustrated spiritualist sessions in which the prosecution could never quite raise the ghost of Salvador Morales Garibay, no matter how many times he was summoned to appear to ratify his rat-out declaration. Elorriaga fretted he would be trapped in this Kafkaesque conundrum forever. "I must be guilty. The president said it on TV. How could he be wrong?" he shrugged one gray summer day, chewing on the stem of a pipe which, like Marcos, he never lets alone, as we scrunched down against a scraped jailhouse wall.

Although they were unnamed at San Andrés, the prisoners were always present at the table. The lack of tangible progress had become a real concern for them, because it meant that they would be hostages of the state indefinitely.

Of the 21 prisoners taken February 8th–9th, 19 remained behind bars. Jorge Santiago Santiago had been released in April for lack of evidence. On July 14th, the more insidious charges against Elorriaga's then-wife, "Comandante Elisa," were dropped and Epigmenio Ibarra posted 72,000 pesos in bail. Her release, like Santiago Santiago's, put the lie to the President's charges of treasonous conspiracy against the nation and made him look like a gullible rookie who had swallowed whole the egregious untruths of his hard-line advisors.

But for the Cacalomacán Eight, isolated in Almoloya prison, there was no movement. Ditto for the Yanga Seven, now segregated in Mexico City's Northern Penitentiary despite the ratification by the government's National Human Rights Commission of their claims of torture. The electric shocks—*toques*—and near drowning in a feces-filled tank—*el tambo*—administered at

Military Camp #1 in the hours after the raid should have nullified their forced confessions.

THE CONSULTA

In its June call for "The Consulta for Democracy and Peace in Chiapas," the CCRI petitioned the Alianza Cívica ("Civil Alliance"), a watchdog group that fought fraud in post-1988 elections, to organize the vote throughout Mexico. The Alianza had recently expanded into running citizens' referendums as a new way of doing nonpartisan politics, and, despite the sordid fact that the group received funds from the U.S. National Endowment for Democracy, AC was an expeditious mechanism for managing the technical concerns of the consulta.

The CND was assigned to promote the national and international balloting— a kids' consulta would be organized by a separate commission. Marcos personally hand-picked the compañeros responsible for the promotion, selecting ideologues like political scientist Octavio Araujo and Ruta-100 lawyer Benito Mirón from both factions and instructing them to get along—the operating theory being that *chamba* (work) and not *rollo* (words) tends to dissolve differences. The promoters were asked to set up consulta committees in all of Mexico's 2,400 municipalities, the U.S., and Europe.

The consulta would ask the patria five fundamental questions:

(1) Did the respondent support the EZLN'S 11 demands (Democracy, Justice, Housing, et al.)?

(2) Should the democratic forces in the country work together to achieve these demands?

(3) Did the Mexican state require a profound reform to achieve democracy?

(4) Should the Zapatista Army of National Liberation transform itself into a political force?

(5) Should the Zapatista Army of National Liberation join with other democratic forces to form a new opposition alliance?

A sixth question, asking if women should be integrated on an equal basis into the nation's developing democratic culture, was later added on by the CND, and it was indeed women who took the lead in promoting and voting in what was really "the women's consulta."

Not all the questions asked were loaded ones. Four and five sparked genuine debate, and Marcos was repeatedly called upon to interpret what was really being asked. Transforming the EZ into a political force did not mean that the rebels were laying down their arms, the Sup underscored—that question was not on the ballot, disarming would only come when the Zapatistas' 11 demands were met, and maybe not even then. Once more, a yes answer on questions four and five did not mean that the Zapatistas intended to form their own political party, much less join up with the PRD. The EZLN sought a new way.

The public convocation for the August consulta coincided with the first anniversary of the founding of the National Democratic Convention at the now-disappeared Aguascalientes. In Mexico City, there were, of course, two public convocations. The ultras—Ruta-100, the Independent Proletariats, and the Francisco Villa Popular Front—took the Zócalo, where the Subcomandante was displayed upon a giant screen in a Marcos-made "infomercial" in which the Sup and a flimsy Durito do battle with a neo-liberal spider (it looks more like a sock). In a separate communiqué, Marcos apologized to the Ruta-100 drivers for EZLN silence about their struggle with the city—Zapatista solidarity might have boomeranged, the Sup reasoned, because the government was charging that the driver-run company had diverted union funds to the EZLN.

Across town at the Cine Opera, Rosario Ibarra's CND showed the uncut hour-and-a-half-long edition of the video. In that version, Subcomandante Marcos shows off an R-15 and reiterates that the consulta does not mean that the EZLN is disarming.

Both CNDs invited Comandante Tacho to tour the land and give visibility to the consulta. Although the Dialogue law gave the comandantes safe conduct outside of the conflict zone, Chuayffet, Moctezuma's successor as Interior Secretary, would hear none of it and threatened arrest.

The consulta was a real "war of the Internet," heavily promoted on the world-wide web by solidarity groups both in and outside of Mexico, an exercise that demonstrated the Zapatistas' growing electronic range—one could even vote electronically.

10,000 polling places in 24 out of 31 Mexican states would be coordinated by Alianza Cívica, and the growing solidarity networks carried the vote to the rest of the world. Early returns looked promising. The vote in Chiapas had been hefty—1,307 communal assemblies were held in Indian communities, where the vote was taken by voice under traditional "uses and customs" procedures. 7,000 AEDPCH farmers, encamped in front of the government palace in Tuxtla, also voted out loud. Up in Mexico City, ballot boxes were set up in public plazas, outside metro stations, and inside prisons. The PRD, meeting in congress in Morelos state, broke to cast ballots in the consulta.

In Hollywood, California, such heartthrobs as Antonio Banderas, Melanie Griffith, Oliver Stone, Susan Sarandon, Laura Dern, Quentin Tarantino, and Salma Hayek filled out their ballots. Across the water in Milan, 50,000 sympathizers voted en masse during a monster rally.

The internationalization of the consulta stuck like a bone in the government's throat. Nearly 100,000 votes were tabulated in the International Consulta for Democracy and Peace in Chiapas, the bulk of them in Europe—the EZLN's support had grown solid on the continent since the February offensive. Meeting in Brescia, Italy, September 1st, delegates from all over the continent cobbled together a European solidarity network that would become increasingly useful to the rebels. In return, Marcos offered the European compañeros an international conference to tackle the neo-liberal scourge before the year was out.

Totaled together, the national, international, and juvenile (200,000 votes) consultations topped 1.3 million ballots cast. The most votes ever tallied previously in such a citizens' plebiscite, a call for the indictment of the universally reviled Carlos Salinas, was 600,000 votes. Questions one, two, three, and six received over 90% "*sí*" responses. Questions four and five muddied the waters. 56% voted that the EZLN should transform itself into a political force, not an overwhelming mandate, but a slim majority turned thumbs down at joining up with any other political formation.

Oracles like Harvard scholar John Womack took this to mean that "the civil society wanted the Zapatistas to drop their disguises, stow their guns, and come out from inside." The Mexican government's reading was not dissimilar: despite Marcos's repeated disclaimers that the rebels were not disarming, Interior Secretary Chuayffet insisted that "the EZLN refuses to disarm even though the civil society has demanded that they do so."

I saw the numbers distinctly: the civil society (if that is who voted) was telling the Zapatistas to do politics but not to lay down their guns—and more emphatically, not to enroll in the PRD.

The final results of the Consulta for Democracy and Peace in Chiapas were presented to the comandancia in Los Altos, under the brooding clouds around the mountain from San Andrés, at the Oventic ejido. The rain beat down in buckets. Marcos had sent a congratulatory note, encouraging the formation of local "civil committees of dialogue" and applauding the CND for not having permitted personal differences to tear them apart during the consultation. Which they did immediately. Although Rosario Ibarra was designated to make the closing speech, ultras jumped on the stage one after another to offer their own closing remarks. Octavio Araujo publicly resigned from the CND on the pages of La Jornada. The chasm between the factions of the CND had grown fathomless.

SAN ANDRES VI

On the eve of Ernesto Zedillo's first Informe, September 1st, the Subcomandante put the kibosh on the modest optimism that had been lit by the consulta when he declared that the Dialogue at San Andrés was *agotado*. The use of the descriptive "agotado" which usually means "tired, worn-out, drained, running on empty," was not judicious. The correspondents misinterpreted "agotado" to mean that the talks had broken off, and filed dispatches to that effect.

The August 30th epistle may have reflected Marcos's frustrations with jungle living—where he was under incessant assault from *zancudos, chaquistes, garrapatas,* and other household pests, and there was only thin *pozol* (corn gruel) for dinner (August is like Ramadan in the Lacandón)—as much as with the glacial pace of the negotiation process. Comandante David would later have to explain that what the Sup had intended to say was that the table at San Andrés was too limited and that it had to be made larger to accommodate national issues.

Zedillo's Informe was streamlined and muted—and his tone apologetic: he had inherited a nasty pot of beans—but the economic gloom would soon be lifting, and in the meantime, let's all pull together for the good of Mexico. The line on Chiapas was the soft one—the Zapatistas' "inconformity" had enormous support in the land, but Mexicans rejected the rebels' use of violence. In the coming year, Zedillo promised he would send congress an Indian Rights law. The indígenas of Mexico would have a voice in the National Dialogue.

In a surprise September 2nd meeting with the 16 members of the COCOPA at Los Pinos, the President welcomed the EZLN's proposed transformation into a political force and told the legislators he would not be opposed to the rebels' inclusion in "a national dialogue"—so long as they did so from Chiapas. Whether or not the invitation was extended on the condition that the EZLN first lay down its arms was open to interpretation.

The interchange around the table up at San Andrés Sakamchién September 5th was less hostile than at pre-Consulta sessions, but it was not exactly peaches and cream. "The EZLN rejects the decision of its sympathizers and refuses to disarm," taunted Bernal, whose understanding of the President's overture was that the rebels could only participate in the "national dialogue" once they had turned in their weapons.

"We didn't come here to be subservient to anyone. We don't have a patron now. That's why we rose up in arms," an exasperated Tacho contested. The COCOPA intervened before the testiness became generalized, inviting the EZLN delegation to caucus on the national issue.

For 48 hours, the two factions consulted behind locked doors, hammering out a 12-point agreement that would allow the Zapatistas' voice to be heard in the now much abused concept of "national dialogue." Just exactly what this "national dialogue" was, was pretty fuzzy. Two separate sets of discussions on "the reform of the state" (actually focused on reforms to the electoral code in anticipation of 1997 midterms) were ongoing in Mexico City—the mesa of Chapultepec Castle, where the opposition parties had huddled for months, and the mesa of Barcelona Street, where Interior Secretary Chuayffet and the PRI met with the opposition parties.

The EZLN, not an advocate of the party system, really did not want any part of these two ongoing "national dialogues." Their goal, as always, was a wider table. That table could be set up in Chiapas, but it would have to speak to the nation. The agreement worked out between the Zapatistas and the COCOPA provided for "special" forums on national issues, the conclusions of which would be carried to the congress for transformation into laws of the land by the legislators.

The COCOPA-EZLN honeymoon pitted three sides of the table against the government when the plenary convened September 8th to hash out the rules, format, and themes of the negotiation on Zapatista demands. The 16 mesas proposed by the EZ had been condensed to four in the CONAI's reconciliation of government-rebel positions: Indian rights and culture; democracy and justice; development and welfare; and the rights of women. The EZLN, very aware of the reform talks up in Mexico City, wanted first to discuss issues relating to democracy and justice. The government men, considering that Indian rights would have less "national" content, pushed for the latter as the first area to be negotiated.

Compromises gradually became reachable, and on the 12th, after six days of intense give and take, a sigh of relief went up from the big house on the corner of the inundated plaza. The first mesa would begin October 1st and would zero in on Indian rights and culture. The two sides to the hostilities were encouraged to invite experts to the sessions, which would be both public and private. The EZLN would be allowed to recruit a corps of advisors to counsel them on legal intricacies. Once installed, the mesa would break up into working groups on such thorny sub-themes as indigenous autonomy, cultural rights, and access to communication.

The marathon negotiations had generated 20 distinct documents and lasted almost a full week, but both sides were reserved about success. "A draw" was how the government laconically described San Andrés VI. "There's no reason for a fiesta," Tacho warned. "Things have their times. This is the experience of our ancestors, of the first Zapatistas, and now us…"

Both delegations got out of town as quickly as they could, stepping briskly around the great puddles that swamped the plaza of San Andrés Sakamchién de los Pobres. It had been a long, wet summer.

AUTUMN 1995

ELECTORAL CONTUSIONS

Just when Chiapas needed it least, fresh electoral conflict brewed October 15th, on which date voters were to select presidents of the state's 112 municipalities and local representatives from 21 congressional districts. The forthcoming elections had cast a pall over the state political agenda for months. A third of the entity's municipal presidents had resigned or been run off by irate citizens since the rebellion had exploded in 1994, and discontent was universal down at the grassroots.

Although a more liberal-looking electoral law had been invented for the occasion, the PRI still controlled every aspect of the voting apparatus. The Procampo checks and the sacks of Maseca tortilla mix continued to rain down like manna on the municipalities from the great God PRI in the sky.

"The PRD-EZLN alliance," working through Don Samuel's priests and catechists, were hell-bent on "destabilizing" Chiapas on election day, a military intelligence analysis obtained by Proceso revealed. Troops were ordered to stand on early alert.

By fall, PRI violence was ubiquitous in the north of the state where, in 1994, Amado Avendaño had won Tila, Sabanilla, Salto de Agua, Tumbalá, and Yajalón—all townships from which Bishop Ruiz's foreign priests had been excommunicated by federal immigration authorities. Now the PRI goons of the euphemistically tagged "Peace & Justice" were out of the closet, training openly at El Crucero, a paramilitary stronghold—the group, like others in the conflict zone, had been instigated by an army counterinsurgency plan that called for the formation of groups of "patriotic" citizens in the 38 municipalities in which the EZLN had influence. In the four months preceding the October elections, 19 Indians were murdered in Tila. Confrontations in El Limar and Usipá took 10 lives on both sides of the political aisle. Meanwhile, Peace & Justice founder Samuel Sánchez's campaign for a state Congress slot was flourishing.

Another *foco rojo* (red light) on the electoral map was the central sierra around Angel Albino Corso, where the Francisco Villa Popular Campesino

Union continued to challenge the German coffee planters at Liquidámbar and Prussia. In mid-September, the PRD candidate for municipal president, a local tailor, was assassinated in broad daylight by unknowns—similar killings were recorded after the '94 election. In retaliation, the PRI candidate, Ansul Sánchez, was "disappeared" along with a doctor friend.

For the now-coadjutored bishop of San Cristóbal, the coming elections had an unsanitary flavor. Predicting from the pulpit that October 15th would be a "bloody Sunday," Samuel pleaded with Governor Ruiz Ferro to call off the balloting. Don Samuel's dire prognosis was treated as practically treasonous by the political parties. Even the PRD, which was positive it would win big (Cárdenas had campaigned in state), opposed canceling the October 15th exercise in futility. Only in Ocosingo were elections suspended when the pro-Zapatista and PRI factions of the ARIC, both with extensive constituencies in the Cañadas, clashed on that jungle city's streets, and Indians set up roadblocks to prevent election materials from getting to town.

The EZLN's position vis-à-vis the 1995 election was pragmatic—and ambivalent. The experience of Amado Avendaño's gubernatorial bid had embittered the insurgents to the electoral process. But in October 1995, the CCRI left the decision about voting up to the local communities, and the results were not always clear.

Unlike August 1994, there was no special arrangement between the EZLN and the state election commission. In the district of the Cañadas that pertains to Las Margaritas, soldiers accompanied election workers into the communities and Zapatista supporters prevented between seven and ten precincts from being installed. But in Altamirano, the hometown of Jorge Constantino Kanter and his Ku Klux Klan–like ranchers, Zapatista bases from the Ejido Morelia cast ballots in considerable number and community militant Rogerio Santiz, running on the PRD ticket, won the municipal presidency—there was even talk of moving the government palace out to the ejido.

In Los Altos, the outcome was distinct. Some of the "autonomous municipalities" declared in the December offensive took advantage of the electoral period to hold communal assemblies and select their new authorities by traditional means. In San Andrés Sakamchién de los Pobres, for example, partisans of the "PRD-EZLN alliance" assembled on the plaza in July to reach consensus in the old way, and on October 14th—the eve of statewide balloting—they invested their new officials with the bastones de mando amidst clouds of incense in the blue church on the corner of the plaza. The next day, the PRIs voted 2,000 to 34 by paper ballot for their own municipal president. Although the autónomos would continue to control municipal offices here at the heart of the peace talks, the conflict between parallel authorities would never be resolved.

This same process repeated itself over the mountain in Chenalhó where the Zapatistas selected their own officials by voice vote, and the PRI took 100% of all the paper ballots. Only in Nicolás Ruiz, near Simojovel, was there equanimity—the "100% rebel" farmers voted both by uses and customs and at the ballot box for their authorities, giving their *autonomía* double-barreled legitimacy.

In the north state, where the PRD thought it had the elections won, most of the voters just stayed home. Those who tried to vote, such as at Panchuc near Tila, were forced to mark their ballots for the PRI at gunpoint. "My heart is sad that the compañeros did not vote," the PRD candidate in Yajalón moaned to the press.

According to the PRD, the Zapatista sit-out had cost the Party of the Aztec sun between 14 and 20 municipalities. The EZLN was certainly not the only culprit responsible for 67% absenteeism—Amado and the AEDPCH had also refused to participate. But whoever was to blame, the results were the same: a PRI landslide, 84 out of the 109 municipalities that voted on "Bloody Sunday," and all 21 local congressional districts. Samuel Sánchez won his seat with a near-unanimous plurality, and Ansul Sánchez became the first "disappeared" candidate ever to win a municipal presidency (his moldering corpse turned up a few days later). Only in Tuxtla, where the PAN unexpectedly won the state capital, was there any good news for the opposition.

Porfirio Muñoz Ledo, the prickly, eloquent then-president of the PRD, lashed out furiously at Subcomandante Marcos for supposedly ordering his people not to vote at the last minute. "Marcos knows he has hurt us more than any of the other parties," Porfirio rued. "It was us who saved the Zapatistas from being ground up into little pieces!" The ingrates!

"We didn't rise up in arms just so the PRD could win political office," Marcos retorted. Besides, the huge absenteeism proved that the EZLN was the dominant political power in the state.

"We're not the political arm of the EZLN," Porfirio nah-nahed back, seemingly cementing the divorce. "The EZLN has picked a fight with the only party that has ever shown any sympathy for their cause," gloated Marco Antonio Bernal.

Post-electoral trauma set in right away. PRD militants took 25 town halls and the roads were blocked yet again. Laco and Jorge Enrique sent in the troopers, and the fragrance of tear gas wafted over southeastern Mexico. Although the turmoil would torment Chiapas for the rest of 1995, President Zedillo, as usual, saw the events through a rosier lens, congratulating the citizens of Chiapas for holding such an equitable election.

MARCOS IN THE FLESH

Communiqués had peppered the Internet with machine-gun frequency and a big-screen Marcos had been projected in the Zócalo in August, but few had seen the Subcomandante in the flesh for seven months. Now, at the very end of

September, a gaunt horseman, flanked by a hundred armed troops, thundered in from the dark mountain under a hangnail moon and entered the hamlet of La Realidad, 15 kilometers east of Guadalupe Tepeyac, where the locals were building a new Aguascalientes to welcome their leaders in from the cold.

The Sup's familiar figure, equipped with trademark bandoliers and Sherlock Homes pipe, seemed so thin and pale that he had to convince the onlookers that he really was who he said he was. "Pardon my sad physique—the months have been difficult ones—but I really am Marcos," he told the crowd that had turned out to greet him. Besides the Tojolabal women in their neon ribbons and skirts, a few hundred members of the civil society had journeyed to the jungle for the rumored reappearance. So had Don Samuel, who escorted Comandante David and other highland *jefes* to La Realidad for the re-emergence.

And so had the COCOPA, on its first trip into the rebels' Lacandón lair and its first-ever encounter with the legendary Marcos. The get-together, on the eve of the initial October round of talks in San Andrés, would smooth the way for substantive talks on Indian Rights and Culture and reaffirm EZLN participation in the "national dialogue."

Unsure of what the lodgings might be like, the Cocopos had brought with them portable toilets, useless cell phones, tents and picnic tables, and even their own chef, who whipped up a lunch of chicken breasts in Hollandaise sauce.

As usual, Marcos's greeting was perverse. Reading a 22-page diatribe, the short-winded Subcomandante reiterated that the rebels wanted no part of the "national dialogues" in which the government and the political parties were engaged up in capital. The Zapatistas' "national dialogue" excluded the government and the political parties—theirs would be with the usual suspects: El Barzón, Ruta 100, the combative Nahua townspeople of Tepoztlán, Morelos, who had just turned back a neo-liberal golf course,—in short, the civil society. The COCOPA, an early experiment in multi-party legislative harmony, was called upon to coordinate this anti-party "national dialogue."

Despite the bumpy road to love, the Cocopos had come a long way and the honeymoon held. The new Aguascalientes, the first of many the EZLN had called for (Aguascalientes were also inaugurated in Tijuana and Chapultepec park), filled up with fiesta-goers. The rainy season was on the run, and the nightly storms had taken a breather. Marcos gazed at the new moon and mused, "Something good could happen here tonight."

It was not a bad moment for the Zapatistas. Communities that had been hidden in the hills for months trekked down to La Realidad. Cousins out of touch since February, hugged and conviviated. The ponging of the marimbas was heard again, and the baile began. The local band, now sardonically redubbed "The 9th of February" (the day of the army offensive) tootled the Sup's favorites: *"Cartas Marcadas"* and the narco-corrido *"Pacas de a Kilo."* The Cocopos barbecued and the party mood was epidemic. Bellinghausen spotted Comandante Trini, a

Chicago Bulls' cap pulled down over her ears, chatting with a bishop, two poets, deputies, senators, armed Zapatistas, and a passel of grandchildren.

The comandantes and the Cocopos met in a tent the legislators had packed in, and the interchange was easy—for once, Tacho and David were not fending off Bernal's invective. "We know now that the Cocopos won't sell us out," Marcos chimed. Agreement for setting up a "national dialogue" outside of the government and the political parties was quickly reached. The lawmakers pulled out their Kodaks and snapped pictures with the comandantes. Then three sides of the table bedded down for the night together in the same jungle.

The next morning, the love fest translated itself up the Cañadas towards Los Altos. Before the delegation pulled out of La Realidad, the tall, spindly, and increasingly fragile Heberto Castillo bent to shake hands with the villagers and worried for their safety because they had hosted the meeting.

INDIAN RIGHTS & CULTURE

San Andrés VII (October 1st) was the briefest since the first get-together in San Miguel. The rules of engagement for the first mesa on Indian Rights and Culture were resolved. There would be six sub-mesas, five of them to be held at a former convent in San Cristóbal, and what was shaping up as the main event on Indigenous Autonomy to be entabled behind the barricades in San Andrés.

The government contingent would be largely limited to Chiapas: officials of the National Indigenous Institute, the PRI-run National Farmers Confederation (CNC) and government Indians with whom the EZLN had quarreled for a decade. The Tzotzil scholar Jacinto Arias, Ruiz Ferro's director of state Indian Affairs, would speak for the "authentic" Indians. The government delegation would show that the EZLN had no monopoly on the indígenas of Chiapas.

The Zapatistas invited all of Mexico to the shindig. Ancient savants and Indianist venerables would form a front line of ideological defense A team of younger hotshots—Luis Hernández Navarro, an advisor to Indian coffee growers, anthropologist Gilberto López y Rivas, and agrarian historian Julio Moguel— would hover over the rebel delegates' shoulders, dispensing advice. Half of civil society was on the guest list. So were the three deported priests. General Renán Castillo was invited to take his place at the table. So were 17 purportedly Zapatista prisoners (Elorriaga wondered if they would be brought to the table in handcuffs). So was still governor-in-rebellion Amado Avendaño. So were Las Abejas, the honey- and coffee-producing civil society from Chenalhó, who stood on the peace lines at San Andrés. And so were the representatives of 22 *Pueblos Indios* (Indian Peoples), who probably had the most at stake in the negotiations on Indian Rights and Culture that began October 18th.

The "Indigenous Question" is a half-millennium-long subtext to the post-Conquest history of Mexico. It is an issue that touches national nerve centers of sovereignty and separation, racism and white guilt, the class and cultural fabric of this conflictive society. For the government, the combination of forced integration and the patronizing policies of "Indigenismo" (conserving culture, forgetting about Indian people) would take care of the problem.

For the Left, the "Indigenous Question" (indígenas call it the "Mestizo Question" since that's mostly who asks it) has too often been reduced to the missionary position. During the 1970s and '80s, Indians lost their cultural identity and became "campesinos," and whether or not they were members of the rural proletariat was a crucial quandary—cultural issues being irrelevant to the class-driven Left (Marcos is an exception). But the 1992 500 Years of Resistance movement put Indian Rights back on the Left's map. Rigoberta Menchú's Nobel Peace Prize focused worldwide attention on the role of Latin America's 50-million-strong Indian underclass. The Zapatista rebellion strengthened the global resonance of Indian resistance, and by the Fall–Winter of 1995–96, indigenous peoples were in the vanguard of social change in Mexico.

The talks at San Andrés would define a new relationship between the Pueblos Indios and the national state, and expectations were buoyant. In June, the Oaxaca state constitution had been modified to allow the entity's 400-plus majority Indian municipalities to vote by uses and customs, and the ANIPA (the National Assembly of Indian Peoples for Autonomy) was drawing up a blueprint for declaring "Autonomous Pluri-ethnic Regions" (RAPS) from one end of the country to the next.

On the eve of San Andrés VIII, Marcos rode back into La Realidad with his hundred horsemen behind him. The cow-horn trumpets sounded and the *cohetes* (fireworks) boomed above the Aguascalientes. The Cocopos were back, and so was the New York Times. But the guests of honor were the corps of EZLN advisors who would guide the rebels through these intricate, historic talks.

THE POWWOW

The six-day powwow numbered San Andrés VIII was a jubilant outpouring of many streams and currents of thinking on the "Indigenous Question." While the experts pondered autonomy up in the hills, five sub-mesas flourished at the convent El Carmen in San Cristóbal. Eager participants packed debates on Indian justice, the defense of indigenous culture, access to communication, and political participation (where "uses and customs" was a pivotal issue). The sub-mesa on Indian Women's Rights was an "uncontainable torrent" in which Comandante Trini blasted the government women in nonstop Tojolabal, and even Tacho caught an earful. "It's good that he is here, because now he will hear that the men are still beating up women in the communities," snapped Comandante Sebastiana.

During the six days of effervescent give and take, 496 invitees presented 131 *ponencias* (papers) for consultation. 20 Zapatista comandantes sat in on the six sessions while Bernal and del Valle prowled from table to table supervising their delegates, profoundly uneasy because their Indians were dialoguing with the EZLN Indians in Indian languages beyond their comprehension.

Even when, on October 20th, the director of the National Indigenous Institute, Carlos Tello, announced that the Mexican government would hold its own series of regional indigenous forums to find out What Indians Really Wanted, the energies at San Andrés VIII remained stoked. A curious transformation was taking place around the tables that confirmed Bernal's worst fears: government and Zapatista guests were agreeing on solutions—"low-intensity familiarity," the invitees labeled this rapprochement. Some of Bernal's experts would even jump to the other side—the INI's Magda Gómez was one such defector. Moreover, everyone concurred that you could not fence off local solutions from national ones. There would be no solution for Chiapas if there was not a seismic reform of the Mexican state from the bottom up.

The COCOPA and the CONAI called a temporary time-out on the 23rd. The conclusions of the sub-mesas would become consensus talking-points for the next round, to begin November 13th. All four sides offered optimistic evaluations of progress made at San Andrés VIII, and the government men even suggested that a final agreement could be signed as early as February. "We have taken the first little step," pronounced David, sounding a little like an astronaut who had just set down on the moon. "For us, the national dialogue has begun…"

EL COMPA GERMAN

The comandantes had barely risen from their seats when word reached San Andrés that federal police in Mexico City had detained Fernando Yañez, who back in February had been fingered by Zedillo as "Comandante Germán," the supposed supreme leader of the Zapatista Army of National Liberation. Arrest warrants for "Germán" and other alleged Zapatista leaders had been suspended under the terms of the March 11th dialogue law.

The blocky, avuncular architect had been picked up after visiting with friends of Rosario Ibarra in the north of the city and was accused of possession of two illicit weapons and 1.4 grams of cocaine—the drug charge would disappear by the time "Germán" was arraigned. Yañez testifies he was surrounded by seven police cars near the Basilica of the Virgin of Guadalupe, blindfolded, and taken to a location he surmised was Military Camp #1, where he says he was interrogated by a "General Diego." Unlike those detained at Yanga and Cacalomacán, he was not physically tortured at the camp. Yañez was removed from the military installation on October 22nd, a few hours before then–U.S. Defense Secretary William Perry was scheduled to review troops on the parade ground there and deliver his landmark "third link" speech, which called for virtual integration of the Mexican and U.S. armed forces.

All of these extraordinary events transpired while Ernesto Zedillo was out of the country, in New York City for the 50th anniversary of the United Nations. Who had ordered "Germán'"s detention? Was the military making its move?

The comandantes beat a swift retreat from San Cristóbal. No, they did not know this "Germán," but all those accused by the President on February 9th were at risk of arrest, including Marcos. Moreover, if the government could break its own dialogue law by capturing "Germán," what were they to expect of any agreement reached with Zedillo's reps at San Andrés? On the 25th, Mayor Moisés rode into La Realidad on a black mule and told reporters that the Comandancia feared government betrayal "just like in February." The EZLN had declared a new Red Alert.

Attorney General Antonio Lozano tried to explain that the dialogue law did not exempt those accused by Zedillo of crimes committed after it was passed. Doña Rosario, who had known Yañez all his life, stormed into the PANista's office and pounded on his desk. The COCOPA appealed to the president not to let this absurd glitch disrupt the San Andrés dynamic. Heberto Castillo, declaring the bust to have been cooked up by "dark forces" opposed to the negotiations with the Zapatistas, threatened to quit the legislative commission. It dawned on Lozano that keeping Yañez was going to cost him a lot more than he was worth. The charges were dropped on the slippery grounds that Yañez had been confused about his immunity under the dialogue law. Uh-huh.

Fernando Yañez walked out of prison with his fist in the air. Flashbulbs popped. The alleged EZLN supreme commander pronounced a few half-baked words of support for Marcos, offered to go to Chiapas at his own expense to help the COCOPA find a solution to the conflict, and immediately dropped from sight. He has not been heard from since.

On October 29th, the EZLN called off the Red Alert, the briefest alarm the rebels had ever sounded. "The police ought to be awarded the National Agronomy Prize" for planting the phony evidence on "Germán," the Sup chuckled.

Who was this white fly in the ointment of Indian Rights negotiations? First of all, he was not "Germán"—"Germán" had been the nom de guerre of his brother, César Yañez, a founder of the Forces of National Liberation, who vanished in Chiapas in 1976 after the military ambushed an FLN encampment. The younger Yañez says he spent several fruitless years searching for César in the Lacandón jungle, which is where he bumped into María Gloria Benavides, aka "Comandante Elisa."

Fernando Yañez was almost certainly a member of the FLN high command, whose time had long since passed. In a 1993 meeting at La Sultana reported by Carlos Tello Díaz, son of the INI director, in his dubious volume, *The Rebellion of the Cañadas*, Marcos is supposed to have dismayed the FLN *históricos* with the news that the communities were preparing for the war. Yañez, along with other old-timers, objected strenuously, but what could they do? They had no army to back them up. Indeed, Marcos had their army, which by now was an independent Indian army. "Germán" was put out to pasture. He was long out of the picture, but "dark forces" had tried to pin on him the sin of the EZLN's genesis and remind the Mexican people that the Zapatistas, although they waved the flag of Indian Rights, were not really Indians.

SAN ANDRES IX

Both sides returned to the subject of "Indian Rights and Culture" on November 13th as if "Germán" had never existed. The government delegation had undergone significant adjustment: its untrustworthy Indian representation had been replaced by state bureaucrats who made it clear they were not there to debate the passionate issues at hand. Uriel Jarquín, another ex-Trot and Eraclio Zepeda's second-in-command, was anointed coordinator of the government's "Chiapanization" strategy and the dialogue became a monologue—or rather a lively back-and-forth between the EZLN's advisors and experts with little input from the gray men across the table. It was as if it did not much matter what was being advanced, because in the end the government would do whatever it wanted to do. Let the Indians and their white friends disgorge their anguish. They would feel better for it.

Nonetheless, the cocktail being prepared around the sub-tables was a heady one. Autonomy did not mean secession from the patria, Luis Hernández Navarro advised—it was a new way of finally integrating Indian Peoples into Mexico on their own terms. The government men grunted mindlessly. Furthermore, autonomy must be defined by "territoriality," that is, a place in the world. The territoriality of native peoples was one stanza in Resolution 169, drawn up by the Organization of International Labor (OIT in Spanish), the universal norm in defining indigenous populations. Although Mexico had ratified OIT 169 in 1990, no one had ever taken the time to find out what it really meant. Now OIT 169's most salient points—autonomy and the concept of territoriality—would become a cornerstone of a promised Law of Indian Rights and Culture.

In theory, the government men did not object. But they had distinct parameters. Whereas the Zapatistas and their colleagues spoke of "Pueblos Indios" (Indian Peoples or Nations), Bernal, Jarquín, and their underlings kept referring to Indian "*Pobladores*" (townspeople). Indian Pueblos had territoriality in the Zapatista schema, a homeland. The pobladores of Indian "communities" had land too, but only that which was defined by town titles, maintained the government men. At every level of the autonomy debate, they were tasked with shrinking the "Indigenous Question" down to the smallest possible size.

Surprisingly, this complicated polemic on Indian Rights produced 57 points of consensus between Bernal's boys and the EZLN, some of them quite significant. For example, both parties to the hostilities agreed that constitutional changes were needed "to establish and assure the autonomies of the Pueblos Indios." Among other remedies, autonomy would "guarantee the Indian Peoples exercise of their own forms of sociocultural and political organization." The Pueblos Indios would have "dominion over their natural resources" (except those over which the State had dominion).

On the other hand, literally hundreds of Zapatista proposals, ranging from representation in state and federal legislatures to the revocation of the changes to Article 27, were not accepted by the government and appear in the final document inside brackets, making it look more like a multiple-choice exam than a working paper for further negotiation.

After an all-night session on the 19th, the four factions and their guests packed it in. The next stop would be a "special" COCOPA-sponsored "Magna Forum on Indian Rights and Culture" to which representatives of 10,000,000 Mexican Indians would be summoned, to take place January 3rd–8th in San Cristóbal. There would be no December session at San Andrés—the Mexican government traditionally shuts down between December 16th and January 6th. San Andrés X would begin January 10th and would be a "resolutive plenary" during which the final shape of an accord would be hacked out.

Dawn was already breaking on the plaza at Sakamchién, strands of the 6 a.m. Mass seeping through the big wooden church doors. Military police peeled off like Power Rangers and accompanied the government men to their cars. The peace cordon had grown thin and hungry by November. Many farmers had to tend to their crops. The Indians stood there shivering in the clear, cold dawn, in their short chujs that make them seem, as Hermann noticed, like farmers out of the Iliad. The comandantes thanked them once again. Inside the church, the worshippers were dressing San Andrés in freshly laundered robes for his feast day. The season of the saints had begun. Soon it would be the fiesta of the Dark Virgin and then the celebration of the birth of the baby Jesus on the floor of a stable in a town not unlike this one. Another year had come round.

The comandantes' leave-taking that November morning was garnished with irony. Fighting had broken out between PRI Indians and armed evangelicals in neighboring San Juan Chamula, through which the caravan returning the EZLN delegates to the jungle had to pass. Six Chamulans had been killed in an all-day gun battle, and the natives were torching cars out on the road. The comandantes descended from Sakamchién de los Pobres with a Mexican Army escort riding shotgun to cover their backs.

LIC

No chapter ever ends cleanly in Chiapas. The dis-tension at the table (*distención* in Spanish) translated to tension in the jungle and the highlands. The brawl in Chamula was one of several around the state as the fall harvest kicked in. One Tzotzil had been killed and seven wounded during a violent police eviction on the periphery of San Cristóbal the day before the bloody shoot-out in San Juan. A Tzeltal farmer was beaten to death by police in Cancuc, and when a team from CONPAZ sought to investigate the circumstances, they were taken hostage by local PRIistas and held for two days. "Force & Power," Laco and Jorge Enrique's elite state police unit, broke up an AEDPCH road blockade out on the coast, arresting 20 and beating and tear-gassing dozens. Rubicel Ruiz, an AEDPCH spokesperson, reported that 40 members of his group had lost their lives in 1995, 860 had been arrested, and the year wasn't over (Ruiz would later be assassinated).

As the talks on Indian Rights and Culture drifted off into the abstractions of autonomy, the violence out in the real world was painfully concrete.

In the jungle, the military overflights had been incessant ever since Marcos's reappearance in October. In November, the army started flying nighttime reconnaissance missions, keeping the villagers of La Realidad awake until the cocks began to crow. Now each day, twice a day, a convoy of U.S.-supplied Hummers and light tanks moved slowly through La Realidad, cannons trained upon the new Aguascalientes, the flak-jacketed troops always filming the Tojolabal villagers with handheld camcorders. In December, the patrols were stepped up to four a day. 36,000 soldiers were then encamped in the Cañadas, according to a census complied by La Jornada.

The military pressure was so intense that a December 4th sit-down with the COCOPA had to be waved off. Although there had been no open confrontations, everyone in the jungle was spooked—one goal of low-intensity conflict is to crank up the tension, ratchet up the paranoia, and rattle the enemy into losing its cool and making costly mistakes.

Behind the army were the paramilitaries. Peace & Justice had shown its face in the north of Chiapas, but other armed groups were moving in the shadows. And then there were the rapes. In early October, three nurses returning from a vaccination campaign in rebel base communities around San Andrés were gang-raped by ski-masked thugs trying to pass themselves off as Zapatistas. On October 26th, Cecilia Rodriguez, the EZLN rep in the United States and the spiritual leader of the U.S. National Commission for Democracy in Mexico, was raped by three masked men during an outing at Lake Montebello, south of Comitán. "I'm a victim of low-intensity warfare," Cecilia would tell a Los Angeles press conference, leveling blame for the conditions in Chiapas at the U.S. government.

WINTER 1995–1996

CHRISTMAS CRUNCH

The convoy bumped down the wretched dirt road bordering the Ejido Oventic, parting the high mountain fog like so many Darth Vaders, the cannons of the light U.S.-built tanks trained upon the men and women of the Bat as they labored on the outbuildings of the new Aguascalientes that was taking shape below. It was the first day of Winter, and the military patrols had been coming back for a week. Now the exasperated Tzotziles threw down their hoes and their shovels and advanced chanting epithets at the implacable intruders, most of whom appeared to be of similar Indian blood. A few stones glanced off the armor-plating of the vehicles, and the Zapatistas supporters pressed in around the itchy-fingered soldiers.

In this war of nerves and wild mood swings, whenever peace seemed just around the corner, as at San Andrés (literally just around the corner of the mountain from Oventic), the monkey wrenches inevitably starting flying...

By the 27th, the daily confrontations had become a kind of Tzotzil intifada, with the villagers, led by the women, barraging the recruits with big rocks and running them off when they tried to install a camp 500 meters from the new Aguascalientes. As the stones flew around their heads, 150 soldiers dismounted from the tanks and crouched down in attack formation, but before they could unleash the first volley, the Indians backed off. It had been a narrow call, admitted Comandante David, who was supervising the construction, warning that he might not be able to control his people if the convoys kept coming.

The "crisis of the Oventics" was careening perilously close to the brink.

To celebrate the second anniversary of the uprising, the EZLN had undertaken the construction of three more "Aguascalientes" convention centers—at Oventic, on the Ejido Morelia, and at Garrucha—in addition to the Aguascalientes inaugurated in La Realidad in October. The military was obsessed with the projects. Weapons could be stockpiled in the covered buildings, the rebels training under the new roofs for a fresh assault January 1st. Overflights soon blotted out the sky, the fixed-wing aircraft reportedly equipped with infrared capabilities. Comandante David watched in wonder as a plane swooped soundlessly over Oventic quiet as a Stealth bomber, reconnoitering the thousand or so volunteers on the ground for weapons as they threw up grandstands and dug latrines for the coming celebrations—but communalism was the Zapatistas' only weapon.

"Our tradition is one of collective toil. By building this Aguascalientes, we are showing that we can make things without the government's help. We are building a house for everyone here, a house of peace on our own land, and we do not need the permission of the president to do so," David explains on a videotape passed out to the press.

36,000 troops were now on alert throughout the state, braced for a new Zapatista offensive. The troop movements were routine and corresponded to the military's social labor mission, fibbed General Renán Castillo.

On Christmas Eve, substitute governor Ruiz Ferro was flown into Guadalupe Tepeyac under heavy security, putting down at the once-upon-a-time first Aguascalientes to distribute Batman dolls, badminton paddles, and beach pails to the nonexistent Indian children there—the villagers of Guadalupe Tepeyac had fled before the February offensive and never returned.

Now, under the rubric of "Operation Happiness," the army trucked in PRI families to receive the governor's largesse of plastic, the troops nervously strung out in the underbrush, on the alert for Zapatista grinches. The Christmas crunch had rolled round again.

The five days of Zapatista festivities were scheduled to get under way on the 28th, and the EZLN, poised between fiesta and Red Alert, prevailed upon the COCOPA and the CONAI to intercede on their behalf. But at Los Pinos, Zedillo was less than conciliatory: "We're not going to permit any infringement of the law," he told the Cocopos. "We don't know what's in those buildings."

The Zapatistas had not asked government permission to build the Aguascalientes warned Interior Secretary Chuayffet, a violation of the agreement reached at San Miguel not to disrupt the Dialogue by staging "propaganda events." The government had already given in on Germán's release and had allowed the "transgressors" to meet 11 times alone with the COCOPA and the CONAI, he whined to reporters. In spite of these multiple olive branches, the Zapatistas were still intent on "rupturing the public order."

Juan Bañuelos, who was privy to closed-door negotiations with the burly minister (Chuayffet was said to be imbibing heavily), looked down into the abyss and reported, "We have never been so close to a resumption of the war." It was a striking place to be, with the dialogue seemingly headed in the direction of peace.

Just a few hours before the festivities were to be opened on the 28th, a bargain was struck: the celebrations would be permitted on the condition that the rebels did not display their weapons in public. As a result, the only EZLN arms to be seen during the second anniversary commemoration were strapped to

Subcomandante Marcos in a handcrafted video ("Durito Productions") during which the Sup first appears as an ersatz anchorman reporting the sighting of masked rebels in "Quito, Guashington, and Timbuctoo" and then gets serious enough to pronounce the Fourth Declaration of the Lacandón Jungle.

The video was viewed New Year's Eve by hundreds of well-wishers gathered in La Realidad, many of them of European persuasion—in particular, a delegation of Italians who fashioned New Year's Eve pizzas for the Tojolabales on their cookstoves. Getting in and out of La Realidad was a harrowing undertaking for foreigners that New Year's, and many opted to attend festivities at Oventic, considerably closer to San Cristóbal. New checkpoints had blossomed all over the Cañadas, and the military was pressuring the peace camps. Immigration agents fanned out into the hotels, checking registries for outside agitators.

The big party took place on schedule at the besieged Oventic ejido. "The government can destroy our Aguascalientes, but we will build more until the whole country is covered with places of encounter and hope," Comandante Guillermo told the camera—Japanese, German, and Peruvian TV crews were filming the celebrations.

On New Year's Eve, the icy winds whipping off the hillside ripped the stage to shreds and carried off the big red five-pointed star that had been affixed to the proscenium. But there was the baile and even some boogie-woogie (bluesista Memo Briseño) and "The Liberating Army of the South" showed up armed with heavy guitars to sing "Las Mañanitas."

Long after the New Year had come tippling in, Mayor Ana María read the Fourth Declaration, and hours after that, the comandantes wished the frozen revelers, "Feliz Año Nuevo, compañeras y compañeros. Now you can embrace."

THE CUARTA

The "Cuarta" or Fourth Declaration of the Lacandón Jungle, stirred more controversy than its two immediate predecessors. With its invocation to Votan-Zapata's struggle for la tierra and its hypnotic refrains, the cant of the Cuarta is reminiscent of the 18th-century Mayan warrior Jacinto Canek, whom Marcos is fond of citing. To insure equal access to the document, the Fourth Declaration was disseminated in Nahuatl, the language of the descendants of the Aztecs.

From a literary standpoint, La Cuarta has a nocturnal, even batlike feel, to it—"We were born in the night," it says of the birth of the Tzotzil people. The Fourth Declaration includes a lovely Old Antonio tale, "The Story of Dreams," in which the first gods give "each woman mother a moon in her breast to nourish the dreams of the new men and women."

But the Cuarta is focused on a more pragmatic theme: building a mass civil base so that the EZLN could fulfill its consulta-driven pledge to transform itself into a political formation.

Three structures are proposed: the convocation of an international forum against neo-liberalism to consolidate non-Mexican support, the resurrection of the National Liberation Movement, and the construction of the Zapatista National Liberation Front or FZLN. "We need new forms, because as it stands now, the people can only sympathize with us and not participate in our work," Marcos later elucidated.

The FZLN would be an organization of like-minded individuals, civil and unarmed, who did not aspire to elected office and would not accept public posts. The FZLN would not covet state power, even by peaceful means, and would certainly not become a political party like certain nearby "f" groups—notably the Nicaraguan FSLN and Salvador's FMLN. The FZLN would direct itself to the *sin-partidos* (partyless) and "organize the demands" of those who stood outside the party system.

The Zedillo government lauded the Cuarta as an avenue towards disarming the rebels. The stock market even had a bonanza day in appreciation. But the Old Left was uneasy. The FZLN posed an oblique threat to the PRD, whose rank and file not only shared the Zapatistas' belief system but were also increasingly disillusioned with their party's PRI-like behavior.

"I don't understand—isn't taking state power the whole purpose of political participation?" PRD old guarder Pablo Gómez sneered. But others in his party saw the light—deputy Carla Botay avowed that she would resign from Congress if membership in the FZLN required her to do so. Indeed, the EZLN's congressional delegation—Botay, Rosario Ibarra, Edgar Sánchez, and Tojolabal leader Antonio Hernández, all Zapatista supporters who had been elected on the PRD ticket—considered resignation.

For the EZLN, the creation of the FZLN, and the strings that were attached to membership in it, were nothing new. The rebels had always rejected political office or state power. They trusted in the old ways of selecting their authorities by communal assembly, of leaders who would mandar obediciendo and assume the *carga* (charge) of serving the community. "We have invented nothing new," Marcos argued. "We did not invent the word and the struggle."

The constituency for the FZLN was ready-made. A promotion commission headed by the historian Antonio García de León was constituted. García de León had been active in the consulta and the committees of dialogue that sprang from it and was in the thick of things, in his hometown of Tepoztlán, when the Jack Nicklaus Golden Bear Corporation wanted to build a golf course on communal lands—the so-called "golf war." He conceived of the FZLN as being the historical descendant of the thousands of liberal clubs formulated on the eve of the Mexican Revolution to overthrow the regime of Porfirio Díaz. But despite a healthy prospective membership of non-ideological sin-partidos, the Zapatista National Liberation Front was not to be formally constituted for almost two years. The EZLN's political metabolism is distinct.

Recognizing that the old denizens of the CND could never really work with each other, Marcos devised a clever division of labor in the Fourth Declaration, urging separate structures to get the job done. Whereas the FZLN would sign up high-minded sin-partidos, the National Liberation Movement (MLN) would be turned over to the Hard Left to build an alliance of already existent organizations—a superbly ironic gesture in that it had been those same ultras who had thwarted the formation of the MLN in Querétaro the previous February.

The MLN was called to order in Acapulco at the end of January. Over 300 organizations (mostly the letterhead Left) were on hand. Cuauhtémoc Cárdenas and Andrés Manuel López Obrador were in the house but not particularly welcome—the ultras were already charging ideological admission. Guerrero state hard-liners dominated the podium—Benigno Guzmán of the Campesino Organization of the Southern Sierra (the OCSS, which had lost so many at Aguas Blancas), firebrand local deputy Ramferi Hernández (now in exile in Paris), PRD wild man (then senator) Félix Salgado, and the Independent Proletarian Movement's Benito Mirón. Fistfights broke out when Mirón refused to read a paragraph from a letter of encouragement forwarded by Subcomandante Marcos which urged a meeting to settle ancient differences. In the end, not the MLN but the FAC-MLN ("Broad Front in the Construction of the National Liberation Movement") was birthed in Acapulco. Months later, the FAC-MLN would become the cover under which a new guerrilla army announced itself to the nation.

INDIAN NUTS

San Cristóbal had become the Indian capital of the Western world by the first days of January. Delegates from all over the country poured into town for "The Special Forum on Indian Rights & Culture": Totonacos, Zapotecos, Yaquis, Huicholes, O'odhumes, Nnanhus, Kikapoos, Purépechas, Raramuris, Nahuas from the Zongolica and the Huasteca, Mixtec day laborers from the Baja California tomato fields, new voices like Chontal poet Auldarico Hernández and Mixe lawyer Adelfo Regino. Not to mention the Mayans.

Since the Zapatistas had emerged from the shadows, many mestizos had become Indians too, and distinctions were blurring so fast that you couldn't tell the indígenas without a scorecard. 27 Mexican Indian nations were represented at the forum by a total of 359 representatives, 152 of whom were from Chiapas. Bernal made an issue of the 56 "foreigners" in attendance, but many of these outlanders were Indians—Quichés and Kakchiqueles from the other side of the jungle in Guatemala, Apaches, Dinés, Seminoles, AIM representatives from across the northern border. The EZLN advisor corps was there, of course, in force—Luis Hernández, Gilberto López y Rivas, the Jesuit Ricardo Robles, the ex-Jesuit Jan de Vos, amongst other distinguished white Indians. Bartola Martínez, the wise woman of the Chinantecas, conspired with Padre Pato, the Mattachine-dancing priest from the Tarahumara. Government spies hovered on all the street corners surrounding the ex-convent El Carmen.

The event was hosted by the COCOPA—the legislators would forward the conclusions to Congress in preparation for Zedillo's promised new Indian laws. But what happened at the forum would set the tone for the resolutive round at San Andrés January 10th. The "Special Forum" would also give birth to another EZLN love child—the National Indigenous Congress, one more mass structure in the Zapatista dream house.

The government challenged the legitimacy of the Special Forum on Indian Rights and Culture to speak for all of the Indian people. In a speech delivered January 6th at the Totonaco pyramids of Tajín in northern Veracruz, Ernesto Zedillo warned, "No one holds the exclusive answer to the Indian Problem." The government had held its own forums with its own Indians and would draw its own conclusions about their problems. Zedillo's insistence put the "Indian Problem" at the forefront of the nation's political agenda.

After centuries of denial, Mexico had gone Indian nuts.

The theme of autonomy was pervasive, permeating all the other topics in San Cristóbal. Some, like Carlos Manso, said to be a Nahua, argued against governmental legitimization of "indigenous autonomy"—"Autonomy is our business, not theirs," he exhorted his colleagues. The deeply spiritual Huichol delegation shared this "Zion is within us" train of thought. The radicals of the ANIPA did not: Margarito Ruiz remonstrated that the Indian Peoples were Autonomous Nations with territory that included the sky above that land and the minerals in the ground beneath it—a veiled reference to much-talked-about Chiapas oil wealth and a position far to the left of the EZLN, which was willing to cede Lacandón petroleum deposits to the federal government. Other Indians argued against the inclusion of any mention of "human rights" in the final documents on the grounds that it was a "Western concept."

This "flowering of the word" (*flor de palabra*) was declared open January 3rd by Comandantes Tacho and David, speaking for the 24-member EZLN delegation. The blind troubadour Don Luz crooned "*Carabina 30-30*," and mariachis sawed away on "*Son del Negro*." Later that night, I began hemorrhaging from an undiagnosed ulcer and woke up in the spartan Civil Hospital a few blocks from El Carmen. The doctor in attendance had played *bajo sexto* in the mariachi band that welcomed the Zapatistas.

On January 7th, the doctors removed the IVs and I stumbled into my shoes. The rockets were already booming above the old city to announce the third coming of Subcomandante Marcos to San Cristóbal.

Marcos was coming to close the flowering of the word before it got out of hand. Difficult negotiations with a very hung-over Chuayffet guaranteed his safe passage, but some were leery. When Don Samuel and Juan Bañuelos helicoptered down to Guadalupe Tepeyac to make ground contact with the Sup, they collided with a large vulture and almost crashed, not a propitious omen.

In La Realidad, Marcos stripped off his weapons and his bandoleros and handed them to Mayor Moisés—the President's office would distribute copies of the photographs to the foreign press corps to promote the illusion that Zedillo had convinced the rebels to disarm.

The weather had been stormy for days, and now, as the caravan climbed towards San Cris, each time Marcos would call for a *parada técnica* (pit stop) to relieve himself, he would see a new rainbow; there were six of them in all, multiple signs of hope—and bladder trouble.

Serendipitously, up at El Carmen the Sup told Viejo Antonio's "Story of the Seven Rainbows"—the multicolored bridges of light to the future (the seventh was the forum). It was a moment of calm in the Indian Tower of Babel that the flowering of the word had loosed.

The forum on Indian Rights & Culture had almost shipwrecked on the rhetoric of the many orators. Ultras and Mods clashed by proxy in the plenaries and old Efrén Capiz, the Purépecha agrarian agitator, never tired of shouting "*la lucha sigue y sigue y sigue y sigue*" (the struggle goes on and on and on) ad infinitum, as he had at the first convention. One almost hoped for a new deluge to dampen the relentless debate. But Marcos and his crew took the rudder to guide the ship back to port. "We have to know when to plant and when to harvest," he told the closing session on the 9th, sounding awfully like Chance the Gardener. "Now it is time to work our own *milpas* (corn fields). The stones in the land that we plow will not be soft ones..."

SAN ANDRES X

Friction was afoot in San Andrés when the four sides reconvened for the 10th and crucial resolutive round in the big meeting house on the corner of the plaza. Rumors ran rife that the Zapatista autonomous authorities would kidnap the statue of the patron saint, and the PRIs were in a snit. Police were poised to take back city hall from the EZLN supporters who had seized it at the end of December. The autónomos sent out to the villages for reinforcements and the crowd around the plaza got so unruly that the Dialogue seemed imperiled.

The government had arrived in San Andrés with what Bernal hailed as "a generous offer." The EZ and its associates were preparing for reductionist schemes, Bernal gloated, but instead had to deal with substantive proposals. The government positions were, in fact, mildly conciliatory, conceding the national nature of the negotiations and a measure of "judicial plurality," i.e., the recognition of an Indian justice system (albeit with severely constricted jurisdiction). Local authorities would now be elected by the "localities" rather than appointed from the county seat or the statehouse by the political parties.

But the holes in the government's "generous offer" were gaping enough to drive a mule train through. Autonomy would be recognized only on the community level—not on the municipal and regional ones. Municipal autonomy was critical to the EZLN proposal—of nearly 2,500 municipal entities in Mexico, 800 have Indian populations of 40% or more. The government also nixed "territoriality," on the grounds that such status would set the stage for Indian secession and balkanize the nation, a Bosnia in Chiapas.

The Zapatista corps of advisors brainstormed back. By recognizing the communities' traditional "public rights" (*derechos públicos*) and the principle of "free determination" (*libre determinación*), the "localities" would be able to freely associate into autonomous municipalities and the municipalities into whole autonomous regions.

The Bernal boys did not reject this counterproposal right away. Such language as "libre determinación" and "derechos públicos" were open to multiple interpretations, and the ultimate test of how much autonomy might be achieved at San Andrés depended entirely upon how the legislation was to be written.

The Zapatista delegates were understandably wary of Bernal's "generous" offer. They had been in meetings for weeks now, sleeping on cold concrete floors and eating store-bought food while their adversaries curled up on soft beds in San Cristóbal's more expensive inns. Now the Indians huddled with their advisors in all-night sessions, going over the language of the various proposals—a misplaced comma could cause crisis, Don Samuel would later recall. But in the mornings, when the rebels submitted their revisions, the government delegation would refuse to read them or, more disconcertingly, wave them through without review, decidedly suspicious behavior. Was Bernal really interested in reaching an agreement? Would the government really honor what it signed at San Andrés? Was this Dialogue just another facade of low-intensity conflict?

Some advisors, Bernal affirms in his chronicle of the negotiations, had begun "to recognize the value" of the government's positions—the names of two venerables, philosopher Luis Villoro and social organizer Gustavo Esteva, were floated. At least some of the advisors were arguing that what was on the table was the best deal the Zapatistas were going to get—the accord would be the most complete autonomy agreement ever signed by indigenous peoples in the Americas, advised Gilberto López y Rivas, who had been a party to the 1987 negotiations that brought a modicum of autonomy to Nicaragua's Atlantic coast. Another of López y Riva's claims to fame: he was a self-confessed Soviet spy while teaching at U.S. universities in the 1970's.

The proposed accords would define a new relationship between the Indian Peoples and the State. The talks had put the "Indian Problem" squarely in the center of the national debate, Luis Hernández wrote. The rebels' insistence on addressing national issues had indeed prevailed.

Finally, on the 18th, the Zapatista delegation, outnumbered by the advisors 45 to 19, opted to take the final proposals back to their communities for consultation. If the "*sí*" vote carried, they would return February 12th to ink the accords. "It is shameful that the Mexican government has waited until the last decade of the 20th century to finally recognize that Indians have rights," Tacho sighed.

Approval of the Indian Rights agreement was anything but automatic—the last time that the EZLN had taken government pledges back to the communities, they had been overwhelmingly rejected. "Tell the PRI not to kill any more of its leaders until we have finished with the consulta," Subcomandante Marcos pleaded.

CONSULTA IN CHIAPAS, TROUBLE IN TABASCO

Would the military give the rebels enough space to conduct the consulta in the villages? Troop movements suddenly intensified at the end of January, with the army taking the Chol ejido of Roberto Barrios, near Palenque, on the 26th and searching the village hut by hut—Renán Castillo said his men were looking for narcos, not Marcos. Meanwhile, the Migra notched up the ethnic cleansing, tossing Colorado small coffee importer Kerry Appel and Global Exchange activist Eva Schulte out of the country for purportedly meddling in Mexican affairs.

Bellinghausen viewed the consultations from the site the exiled villagers of Guadalupe Tepeyac had chosen to re-establish their settlement. Between January 20th and February 1st, the community studied the proposals in separate groups of men and women. Voting took place between February 1st and 10th. Many thought the agreement to be "nothing." How could you trust this government's word? Consensus took days to reach.

While the villagers caucused, national attention was diverted to neighboring Tabasco, where López Obrador and the Chontal actor and poet Auldarico Hernández were inciting the local Indians to occupy 59 PEMEX oil-drilling platforms in that oil-drenched jurisdiction, home to Mexico's largest land-based deposits. For decades, Chontal land had been poisoned by acid rain, pipeline leaks, blowouts, and deadly explosions. The PRI government denied them compensation for the damage because the Chontales sided with the PRD. Now, contaminated by Zapatista autonomy fever, the Chontales were talking about taking their land back from PEMEX.

The prospect of two adjacent oil-rich states falling to advocates of indigenous autonomy was frightening not only to the Zedillo government but to Washington as well—the Clinton bailout had required Mexico to deposit its export oil revenues in the U.S. Federal Reserve as collateral for the loan, and Tabasco was where a good deal of that export revenue was generated. The State Department sent investigators south to find out what the Indians wanted.

In the first days of February, army troops and state police brusquely evicted the Chontales from PEMEX installations. Andrés Manuel and Hernández were beaten so badly during a bloody battle on a bridge near Nacajuca February 8th that they required stitching. Over a hundred Chontales were arrested and charged with "sabotage" of the nation's oil wealth. At a press conference in Mexico City, López Obrador answered this reporter's question: the possible signing of an Indian rights agreement between the Zedillo administration and the Zapatista Army of National Liberation would not be helpful to the Chontales' struggle at this time.

THE DOTTED LINE

When the rebels returned to Sakamchién February 13th, again a day late, the results of their consulta were still veiled, and the appeal from Tabasco not to sign had Bernal worried. "It would be an error of historic proportions" if the rebels were to reject his "generous offer," the government's chief negotiator fretted. Bernal was sweating another deadline: Sakamchién de los Pobres was to begin its traditional Carnival February 18th, an annual riot of unbridled drunkenness and bloodletting definitely not conducive to serious negotiation or personal safety. Now, as usual, the EZLN had been slow in returning to the table. Could an arrangement be wrapped up before the fireworks exploded, the town drowned itself in a sea of *posh*, and the general joy got so intense that you could get permanently maimed by it?

The EZLN divulged the consulta results on the 14th, and as their return to Sakamchién hinted, they did not reject the accord. 97% had voted to accept the package, but 100% rejected the government's rejection of municipal autonomy, regional autonomy, and nullification of the revisions to Article 27. The women's rights provisions were inadequate, and the agreement made no mention of the Indians' demand for time on the Morelos satellite. The language of the proposed agreement ceded control of petroleum deposits on Indian land to the State, and there was no mention of the political prisoners, who had just completed their first year in jail.

The accords were really nothing more than a shopping list of good intentions, a symbol of a new relationship whose transformation into the law of the land was a dubious proposition. Nonetheless, the EZLN would sign on the dotted line.

The accords on Indian Rights and Culture reached at San Andrés Sakamchién de los Pobres February 16th, 1996, are really four separate documents. The first is a joint statement of agreement on a broad range of points. The second document commits the federal government to making concrete changes in existing legislation and fashioning new laws to make the agreement a reality. The third commits the state of Chiapas to do likewise. The fourth is a kind of addendum listing all the Zapatista demands rejected by the government. The four documents together would alter 12 federal constitutional articles and hundreds of secondary laws on communication, health, education, culture, and the electoral process, in addition to giving the Chiapas state Congress enough legislative business for the next 10 years.

Although the San Andrés accords have become holy writ for the Zapatista, the documents themselves were withheld from public view for months, and the actual signing at San Andrés (Tacho, David, and Zebedeo for the EZLN; Bernal, del Valle, and Uriel Jarquín for the state and federal governments) went unwitnessed, because the Zapatistas flat-out refused to be photographed in the act. "The government has wounded us, and that wound has not healed," Comandante David explained, righteously anticipating new treachery. "This is just a piece of paper," Tacho snorted to the inevitable press conference, confessing that the EZLN had received an urgent message from the embattled Chontales asking the comandantes not to sign the agreement while they remained under attack in Tabasco.

Both sides concurred that the agreement was less than it had been cracked up to be, a "minimal" accord, as its official title attests. Despite their sacred screed status, the four documents are hardly a blueprint for revolution. One reason for their exalted spot on the Zapatista dial may be the valued input of the advisors, who have fought tenaciously to place the agreement in its proper niche in history.

MEXICAN MYSTERY

Why Ernesto Zedillo instructed his personal representatives to sign the San Andrés agreements when he never had the slenderest intention of abiding by them has always been something of a Mexican mystery. Was the signing premeditated trickery or weak-kneed incompetence on the President's part? One has to savor the macroeconomic moment—the only measure of national well-being by which Zedillo, a glorified accountant, governed—to understand the skam.

The great 1994–1995 plunge had been declared officially over and done with at the annual IMF–World Bank junta in October 1995, and the next move was to convince the world that recovery was real, that Mexico was a safe haven for speculator investment, and you could make a lot of money south of the border.

Europe was a particular target of this gambit. The North American Free Trade Agreement was so heavily weighted to Washington that Mexico needed a commercial counterbalance to survive in a world that was globalizing at breakneck speed. Now, with macroeconomic recovery on the horizon, Zedillo was about to apply for associate membership in the European Union, and the illusion of an agreement with the Indians was an essential building block of this strategy. The Zapatistas had name recognition on the continent. A support network thrived in Spain and Italy, France and Germany, which held votes in the European Parliament.

The February 16th signing of the San Andrés accords was to be a photo op for Zedillo to display to world leaders as he touched down around the globe during the winter of 1996 selling the Mexican recovery—indeed, on the day of the sign-ing, the President was in Costa Rica reassuring his Central American neighbors that their Mexican big brother was in full economic recovery. He could have used the photo—just as he could have used it a few weeks earlier when he visited Spain to preach the Mexican bounce-back and Zapatista supporters chased him around old Barcelona all afternoon. And certainly, the President would have appreciated a photo of the rebels putting their Juan Hancocks on the accords dur-ing an upcoming free-trade junket to France, where the solidarity movement was preparing to ambush him.

Ernesto Zedillo would never forgive the Zapatistas for denying him his Kodak moment.

Nonetheless, the administration would make as much of the secret signing as it could. European ambassadors in Mexico were encouraged to extend written congratulations. Bernal and del Valle winged to Brussels to extol Zedillo's hon-orable intentions before the European Parliament. State Department spokesper-son Nicholas Burns patted both the Mexican government and the EZLN on the back. But that damned Kodak moment would always be a missing piece in this picture.

DEMOCRACY & JUSTICE NEXT

With the negotiations on Indian Rights and Culture concluded and its codi-fication into law in the pipeline, the second phase of the Dialogue—"Democracy and Justice"—was set for San Andrés March 5th. The theme "exposed the regime's Achilles heel" (Carlos Monsiváis), because it put the EZLN smack dab in the middle of the national debate on "the reform of the state." Bernal was entrusted with the thankless duty of steering San Andrés away from the nation-al debate. Such reform was "the property of the political parties," he posited, and he would brook no EZLN invasion of this proprietary turf.

The EZLN offered a complex schema for the new round of talks. There would be eight sub-mesas and 61 points of discussion, many of which—such as the use of referendum and plebiscite and the registration of coalition candidates—were already being debated in Mexico City. In return, the government offered five sub-mesas and 14 talking points.

The EZLN summoned hundreds of notables to back them up at the second mesa: historians like Enrique Semo and Carlos Montemayor, agrarian economist José Luis Calva (two of his titles were discovered by the military on the Sup's bookshelves in Prado Pacayal), as well as Superbarrio, Cárdenas, López Obrador, the PANista Vicente Fox, and select dissident PRIistas. The prisoners were invit-ed back, as was Rosario Ibarra's long-disappeared son, Jesús. So were Mexico's version of the Gray Panthers and rebel oil workers and the Tepito Free Shoe Clinic. So were the iconoclastic artists El Fisgón and Alberto Gironella and the writers Paco Taibo I and II. The traffic between Mexico City and San Cristóbal got so thick that Octavio Araujo published a guide in La Jornada that listed plane schedules and fares, taxi services, and helpful hints about hotels and restaurants in San Cristóbal.

For its part, the government announced that it was inviting no advisors or experts to the second mesa: zero, zilch. Instead, it would sit back and listen.

As this fresh impasse loomed, the COCOPA and the CONAI switched the subject to unfinished business. Now the formation of the Commission of Oversight and Follow-up (COSEVER), which would oversee the implementation of the Indian Rights accord, became the bone of contention. The EZLN wanted all four parties to the agreement to sit on the commission, plus a handful of distinguished personages like Carlos Fuentes and Amalia Solórzano, Lázaro Cárdenas's widow and Cuauhtémoc's mom. The government, fearful that the rebels' inclusion on the commission would allow EZLN leaders to travel freely around the country, wanted only neutrals.

The deadlock was symptomatic of where the Democracy & Justice mesa would head in the months to come as Zedillo's interest in achieving any new agreement, or even the implementation of the old one, faded. Indeed, no Oversight and Follow-up commission would ever be needed, because there was no agreement to oversee. Zedillo and his boys had gone for the photo op and that moment had passed. "The policy of the morgue," of starving the talks to death until the corpse dried up and blew away, was now the government's negotiating strategy.

SPRING 1996

EL FINIQUITO

The President shook each callused hand gravely as the farmers in their new store-bought clothes, or freshly laundered chujs and short kilts, passed before him. Zedillo had asked the directors of 60 campesino organizations up to Los Pinos on March 19th to celebrate "the end of the dispute for the land in Chiapas." The End: El Fin. This spring, instead of the traditional bloodshed, "dialogue and reason would bring tranquillity" to the Chiapas countryside.

"El Finiquito" was the culmination of negotiations with farmers' groups that had sputtered on since the rebellion went public and was actually the sum total of 2,400 separate settlements of land claims that would distribute 300,000 hectares (750,000 acres) among 58,000 Chiapas farmers, about five hectares a head. The campesinos had been represented by just about every agrarian pressure group in the state and nation—most of AEDPCH's member organizations were inside the Finiquito, the long-lived CIOAC, the farmworkers' group founded by the Communist party back in the 1970s, being the last to sign up—only Xi'Nich "Democrático" (the Xi'Nichs had split into two factions) and the hardscrabble militants of the Francisco Villa Popular Campesino Union in the Sierra Maestra stayed outside the agreement.

The deal, engineered by old Agrarian Reform warhorse Arturo Warman, extended important credits to the farmers, one-time-only handouts to purchase the land. In return, each community and ejido would hold an assembly at which the settlement would be irrevocably ratified and an end to land occupations pledged.

To jigsaw together the Finiquito, the government shelled out about $120 million USD to ranchers who wanted to divest themselves of land that was either too troublesome or too unproductive to be profitable. Land invasions became a growth industry, with the ranching oligarchies paying off "leaders" to usher land-hungry peons onto properties the owners wanted to dump, which the government would then snap up at a pretty penny to round out its last offer, the Finiquito. It was a tidy deal for everyone concerned: the landless got a little wedge of land, the "leaders" picked up a payday, the ranchers realized respectable profits, and agrarian officials socked away creamy kickbacks.

Zedillo's was not the first Finiquito to have been hammered out between Chiapas farmers' organizations and those who governed them. In 1989, Governor Patrocinio González had decreed another "end to the dispute for the land in Chiapas," and campesinos from around the state were called up to Los Pinos to shake another president's hand. Reportedly, Carlos Salinas pressed flesh with one Humberto Trejo, leader of Tojolabal farmers in the Lacandón jungle, better known today as Comandante Tacho.

For the Zedillo–Ruiz Ferro axis, the Finiquito was another photo op—but with real teeth that made the rebellious Indians of Chiapas liable for serious punishment if they disobeyed the terms of the agreement. Some 200 plots long in the hands of local farmers had ultimately not been included in the settlements, mostly because their owners would not sell. Their exclusion from the pact gave Laco Zepeda and Attorney General Jorge Enrique Hernández the pretext to go kick some Indian booty.

One owner who had refused to part with his land was fugitive banker Carlos Cabal Peniche. On March 20th, the day after the "finiquitos" visited Los Pinos, state police hit Cabal Peniche's San Luis ranch near Pichucalco, in the central north of the state, where the CIOAC had set up housekeeping. Two farmers and a cop fell in the interchange, daubing the vernal equinox with its annual quota of blood. 52 Indians were arrested at San Luis "with etiquette and professionalism," Laco quacked. "We are not going to permit one more occupation of land that is not in the Finiquito," snarled Jorge Enrique.

The next morning, the first official day of spring, Laco's goons hit the Gran Poder hacienda, adjacent to the pro-Zapatista municipal seat of Nicolás Ruiz in the northern valleys, for which local Indians held land grants dating back to 1734. Warman claimed the Gran Poder was removed from the Finiquito because Nicolás Ruiz had been given 2,000 hectares elsewhere. The fine points of agrarian covenants aside, the state police were just following orders. Alfonso Gómez was sipping pozol in the doorway of his shack when his chest was perforated by a brace of bullets. The troopers surrounded the field and laid down a dense blanket of tear gas, an alien scent in the Spring mountain air.

The tear gas ignited grass fires and the farmers were driven from the field into the arms of the police. Two more were killed and 124 arrested—on the same morning, other state police units evicted Indians from six sites around nearby Venustiano Carranza, driving 500 villagers into the mountains. Shell casings found at the Gran Poder bore U.S. and European markings, prompting the EZLN to demand that the European Parliament embargo arms sales to Mexico.

In its first 48 hours, the Finiquito had meant the end for five Chiapas Indian farmers, 20 had been wounded, and 178 new prisoners joined Elorriaga and Entzín in Cerro Hueco.

VOTAN ZAPATA COMES BACK

The news of the attack at Nicolás Ruiz spread wings. Up in San Cristóbal and San Andrés, where the first round of the Democracy & Justice mesa was in session, Comandante Tacho, almost in tears, asked how the rebels could continue to negotiate with criminals? Looking dead ahead at the mute government men, he pronounced sentence: "They are closed down like sepulchers, because they accompany death." The government delegation walked out.

Would the EZLN stay at the table? "The people are dead and we don't know how many more will be killed tomorrow—this is the cause of our rebellion!" Comandante David said mournfully as Zapatista advisors and invitees rose to their feet chanting "¡Dignidad! ¡Dignidad!"

The March session of the Democracy & Justice mesa was perhaps the most pluralistic meeting of the Mexican Left since the formation of the PRD in 1989, and the killings at Nicolás Ruiz galvanized the assembled radicals. Writers in attendance—Monsiváis, Sergio Pitol, Federico Campbell, among others—condemned their ex-colleague Eraclio Zepeda for his callousness: "Now he writes his stories with bloody hands."

The evictions and the resistance would go on for weeks—Luis Hernández Navarro catalogued 18 distinct incidents. On April 9th, the eve of the 77th anniversary of the betrayal of Emiliano Zapata at Chinameca, Governor Ruiz Ferro flew around the state dispensing the first installment of the Finiquito— 71,000 hectares to 16,000 farmers, not even the promised five hectares each.

The next day 40,000 marchers flooded the streets and highways to once again mark Votan-Zapata's death and resurrection. "¡Zapata Vive y la Lucha Sigue!" (Zapata lives, the struggle goes on) thousands sang, "y sigue y sigue y sigue..." The dispute for land was not over. It would go on and on and on. But the Finiquito was dead and stinking.

Up in the Zapata country of Morelos state that April 10th, the defenders of Tepoztlán sought to deliver a letter to Ernesto Zedillo, once again demanding the cancellation of the golf course Jack Nicklaus wanted to install on their communal lands. But the President was otherwise occupied, proposing a new finiquito to another set of farmers that morning, and police beat and arrested upwards of 40 women and children. One old Nahua campesino, Marcos Olmedo, was murdered in cold blood and his corpse tossed to rot in a vacant lot. Shaken by the violence, Nicklaus's people pulled out of the deal. The finiquito had finished off their golf course.

THE STARS FALL ON CHIAPAS

The stars fell on Chiapas in the spring of 1996. The parade of Hollywood celebrities and European luminaries began in March with Oliver Stone (Natural Born Killers, JFK, Nixon). Next came Edward James Olmos (Miami Vice, Zoot

Suit, The Ballad of Gregorio Cortez), followed by Régis Debray (starred with Che in "Bolivia"), the recently widowed Danielle Mitterrand, former first lady of France, and the Mothers of the Plaza de Mayo from Argentina. Background music was provided by the Basque punkers Negro Goriak (expelled from Mexico) and the veteran *chilango* (Mexico City) rockers Botellita de Jerez. Jodie Foster and Susan Sarandon were supposed to be en route to meet the Sup at the forthcoming Continental Forum for Humanity and Against Neo-liberalism. Purists accused Marcos of catering to radical chic.

Actually, the spurt of celebrity visits had more to do with agricultural necessities in the Spring of 1996. Because the 1995 planting season had been offset by military invasion, there was little to eat in La Realidad and other Cañada hamlets that Spring, and there would be less if the military kept the farmers out of the fields to prepare the ground for planting. With the soldiers breathing down their necks, the villagers had been unable to perform the traditional roza y quema—keeping the enemy hungry is a vital element of any self-respecting low-intensity conflict.

Now, with the spotlight on the exalted personages descending the canyons to hobnob with their pipe-smoking idol, there would be more room for farmers in this corner of the Lacandón to work their fields. "There is nothing in the *champa* (pantry)," Marcos wrote, making his intentions explicit. The Sup was "risking his reputation to save the communities from starvation," the usually skeptical political commentator Jorge G. Castañeda noted.

Oliver Stone arrived in San Cristóbal on March 24th and was welcomed by Tacho and the mariachis at El Carmen, where "Democracy & Justice" was in full bloom. The director was red-eyed and teary—his aides explained that he was "allergic to plants," not a salubrious prognosis for a trip to the jungle.

The next day—Oscar night in Hollywood (Stone's *Nixon* was up for four of them)—the movie man's caravan passed through the Gabino Vázquez immigration checkpoint with a minimum of inconvenience, although word had it that Stone was hauling in a satellite phone. If indeed *Nixon* won him an Oscar, he would encourage Marcos to accept it for him via the wonders of the satellite, endowing the EZLN with a sky-high platform from which to pitch their revolution. But *Nixon* did not win an Oscar (*Braveheart* and Nicholas Cage led the honors).

Subcomandante Marcos presented the movie maker with a pipe as compensation. The groggy Stone donned a ski mask (the summertime satin model) and rode out with the comandancia to a secret camp. "It was wild," Stone later told Blanche Petrich—the scene had reminded him of one from *Viva Zapata*. The mogul insisted he was not scouting locations for a film.

Oliver Stone understood his role very well. Guided through the script by a team of 18 assistants, Stone promised Marcos he would use his "moral authority" to raise money to keep La Realidad and other EZLN communities in corn until the new harvest was in.

Even if "Oliver" was not entertaining notions of doing The Zapatista Movie, plenty of screenplays were floating around Tinseltown. Luis Manduki (*White Palace, Gaby*) had one, and Kevin Costner was whispered to be looking at another. If Harrison Ford wasn't available to play the Sup, maybe Mel Gibson would be. The flicks had discovered the jungle by 1996—John Sayles, the earnest independent, had shot *Men With Guns* in PRI-controlled villages near Palenque the previous fall, and a bunch of documentaries were in the works: Saul Landau was editing *The Sixth Sun* and Nettie Wild had just arrived to shoot *A Place Called Chiapas*.

Out on Sunset and Vine, magazine writer Anne Moore was shopping around *El Ultimo Hombre* (The Last Man) in collaboration with Catherine Ryan, a winsome L.A. journalist who was then frequenting La Realidad. When Moore sent Ryan a fax in San Cristóbal suggesting that a Jimmy Carter character play a role in *El Ultimo Hombre*, it was intercepted by the coletos and Carter's impending arrival was leaked to the national media. Impact magazine fingered Ryan as the EZLN's gun-running moll. The script was allegedly purloined by an agent whose business card reads "Avarice & Greed Productions," and *The Last Man* fell into terminal *fracaso* (ruin). It's a down and dirty business.

Nonetheless, the Zapatistas remain true-blue movie fans. Videos do a brisk trade in the Zapatista zone, the VCRs hooked up to car batteries for showings of everything from *Bambi* to Bogart.

The ham is definitely in the Sup too. Marcos is an avid amateur cineaste who shoots his own home movies, and his communiqués are peppered with film references—once, he accused the government of behaving like a band of rich delinquents in an unspecified Peter Fonda movie. Eddie Olmos told me that Marcos told him that he had attended the actor's film workshops in East Los Angeles in the late 1970s.

Olmos was the next in the chute to come down the canyon. Accompanied by veteran producer-director Robert Young (*Nothing But a Man, Alambrista, Gregorio Cortez*), Edward James Olmos sat in the first row at the opening of the Continental Forum for Humanity & Against Neo-liberalism as the Sup connected the dots between Simón Bolívar and Che Guevara and Gregorio Cortez, the border legend who battled the *rinches* (rangers) all up and down the Texas line in the teens of the century. "Trying to catch him was like trying to catch a star," Marcos told.

Edward James Olmos is a disciple of César Chávez and a self-anointed role model for Chicano youth (the Mexican Mafia put out a contract on him after *American Me*), who cleaned up Los Angeles with a big broom following the Rodney King riots. Now he brought his big broom of nonviolence to La Realidad.

"It hurts me to tell Marcos this, but violence only brings more violence," he argued during a break in the Continental. "The EZLN has to be convinced to put aside its guns, right Brian?" he asked, turning to Brian Wilson, the Vietnam vet who lost his legs to a train trying to block arms shipments to Nicaragua at the end of the '80s. Olmos intended to bring over the Chontales from Tabasco, who were alleged to be Gandhian adepts (untrue), to teach the Zapatistas a thing or two about nonviolence.

FRANCOPHILE

The next shift of marquee attractions was plucked from the altar of the French intelligensia, a drift that delighted the Francophile Sup.

The French left dailies Libération and L'Humanité were sometimes guests in La Realidad in 1996, and the fashionable satirical review Charlie Hebdo devoted a whole issue to the struggle in Chiapas. Later in the summer, the eminent French Latin Americanist Yvon Le Bot would get a book-sized interview with Marcos. Even ex–Le Monde correspondent Bertrand de la Grange's snide send-up of Marcos, *The Genial Impostor*, enhanced the Zapatista mystique in gay Paree. Chiapas was getting so much media exposure in France that the venerable Le Canard Enchaîné needled "¡*Ya Basta, Zapata!*"

Subcomandante Marcos is more fluent in French than he is in English, and Paris reporters always got interviews before their Anglo colleagues. One explanation for the Subcomandante's galloping Francophilia: Alfonso Guillén, Rafael's father, brags that his son studied at the Sorbonne and even fathered a child during his academic years there.

Régis Debray voyaged to Cuba early in the revolution, where he hooked up with Che and wrote *Revolution Within the Revolution*, a volume that advanced the "foco" or small group theory of Latin guerrilla war. Accompanying Guevara on his impossible Bolivian dream, Debray was captured before Che was executed by an elite Bolivian-CIA team in October 1967, and eventually made his way across the border to Chile, where he became a member of Salvador Allende's inner circle. By the mid-90s, though, Régis Debray was writing novels and tell-all books and had become a kind of parody of himself.

In late March, Che's onetime comrade-in-arms motored down to La Realidad, where he hung his hammock in the ejido house and marched door to door asking the villagers batteries of pertinent questions. He wasn't allergic to plants. He sat under the giant ceiba tree and smoked a pipe with Marcos. The secret camp reminded Debray of Nancahuazo, where Che was ambushed. He proclaimed the EZLN "an antidote to Sendero Luminoso" and the Subcomandante "a new Guevara for the Americas." "This is the real revolution in the revolution."

The dread Migra pounced on the way back up to San Cristóbal. Agents seized Debray's tourist visa and grilled him for hours. Although the distinguished revolutionist was not tossed bodily from the country, the Mexican government addressed a diplomatic protest to its French counterpart, objecting to the guerrilla-author's "interjection" in domestic politics while under cover of a tourist visa.

Now it was Danielle's turn. Madame Mitterrand's Libertades foundation bankrolled CONPAZ projects, and she had legitimate business in the region.

During her days in La Realidad, Compañera Danielle, the still-youthful "pathological utopian" (as François had tagged her), met so often with Marcos that my colleagues considered them an item. Danielle compared her new companion to the Dalai Lama. "Our time together was very beautiful, very intimate, very profound," she gushed to Proceso's Ann-Marie Mergier.

The Subcomandante entrusted Danielle with an important mission: she would accompany Tacho back up to San Andrés for the April 19th session of the Democracy & Justice mesa and inform Bernal that Europe was watching the negotiations closely. "I was scared to death. I thought I would be thrown out of the country," she confessed to Mergier.

Nonetheless, at the plenary that morning, Danielle looked the government man in the eye, coughed, and began softly: "Today the world has grown very small. Maybe the people of just one country cannot solve their own problems…we are here to encourage your work and offer our assistance…"

To the government men, Danielle's tiny spiel at San Andrés resounded like a new French invasion. Bernal and del Valle, who had just been to Europe to boast about the Indian rights accords and lobby for a free trade treaty with Europe, were stunned. Their worst fears of foreign intervention in Chiapas had just been confirmed by Danielle's feckless performance.

THE CONTINENTAL

The Continental Forum for Humanity & Against Neo-Liberalism ("The Continental") was the first leg of a protracted "Zapa-tour" that brought thousands of non-Mexican "revolutionary tourists" to the rebels' lair in the Spring and Summer of 1996, to the intense irritation of the immigration authorities and those who paid their salaries.

The Continental was set in motion by the first Declaration of La Realidad (January 30th), in which the EZLN postulates that, under the name of "globalization," "a new world war has been unleashed against humanity" that aims to concentrate "power in the powerful" and "misery in the miserable." Those who are "excluded" must band together to expose "the lie of the defeat of hope, the lie of the victory of neo-liberalism." Continental Forums in Defense of Humanity & Against Neo-Liberalism would be held in Europe (Berlin), Asia (Tokyo), and Oceania (Sydney). Africa was to be announced. The conclusions would be gathered together and presented at the midsummer Intercontinental Forum for

Humanity & etc., an event Marcos was already referring to as "The Intergaláctica."

The Americas converged on La Realidad during Holy Week (April 3rd-8th). It was scorpion season and the sun was on high broil, and immersing oneself in the cool river seemed more inviting than the mesas condemning the neo-liberal beast. To complete the mood, "neo-liberal" breakfasts (cornflakes) were served at the Zapatista restaurant under the ceiba tree.

Non-Mexican Americans in attendance were mostly of the northern sub-species, but trade unionists, students, and left intellectuals from Argentina, Chile, Brazil, Peru, Ecuador, Uruguay, Costa Rica, Guatemala, and Puerto Rico filled out the mesas. Chickens pecked around the toes of the participants gathered in the available shade, sweating the weighty problems of the globalization of practically everything. The discussions, anchored in mutual geographies, were more centered than they would be in a few months at an Intergaláctica that sometimes seemed to be taking place in outer space.

"I know it is not easy to get to La Realidad, but reality is never easy," Marcos welcomed the Americans to the jungle. He spoke first of Elorriaga and the other Zapatista prisoners, who had hardly rated a mention in months. Switching to the business at hand, the Subcomandante defined neo-liberalism: "Theft and corruption are its principal industries...the lie is its supreme god...neo-liberalism is the Internationale of Death." To give the struggle against neo-liberalism in the Americas immediate context, he recapped the last 48 hours of resistance throughout Latin America: street venders vs police in Lima, schoolteachers in Argentina, Bolivian miners on the march...

On the third day of the Continental, Marcos offered a position paper written by Don Durito of the Lacandón, a talking beetle, entitled "Promising Elements for an International Analysis As the First Basis for an Original Approximation of the Primogenic Considerations in Respect to the Supra-Historic and Overwhelming Spread of Neo-liberalism in the Decisive Conjunction of April 6th, 1996, at 11:30 Southeast Time With a Moon That Looks Like It Is the Pocket of a Worker in the Time of the Augmentation of Privatization, Monetary Adjustments, and Other Economic Measures That Are So Effective They Produce Encounters Such As That of La Realidad."

Critiqued for poking fun at those who were trying to conduct serious business in the mesas, the Sup was not contrite: "This making of a new world is a serious business. If we can't laugh, the world we make will be square, and we won't be able to turn it."

Village life continued unabated despite the odd strangers that prowled the community. Indian farmers sat with their backs against the trees, smoking cigarettes and fingering their bags of seeds. A surprise April shower had brought out clouds of gnats but softened the soil. Now the campesinos had to decide when was the best time to plant.

In the clapboard church on Easter Sunday morning, the Tojolabales sang and prayed in soft voices for the resurrection of Christ and Votan-Zapata and the new corn.

On Sunday night, the Subcomandante concluded the encounter. The conclusions, which roundly condemned neo-liberalism's multiple crimes against the planet, would be forwarded to the Intergaláctica. Through his voice, Old Antonio told the history of the roads and those who traveled upon them. "In the before, there was no after..." In the end, one had to reach back to the beginning to get to the after.

Before dawn, the travelers broke camp and climbed up on the trucks and microbuses for the return to San Cristóbal. As the Americans moved out of La Realidad in the early light, the smoke from adjacent fields was already dense. The roza and the quema had at last begun, and now shadowy men and women moved through the milpa, poking holes in the blackened ground with their coas and dropping in the seed.

WAR ON DRUGS

Early on April 13th, a North American visitor in the Oventic civil peace camp, the pacifist David Hartzo, sounded the alarm—dozens of soldiers had taken the hill above the ejido and were about to attack. The villagers slipped on their ski masks and readied themselves for the long-awaited confrontation. But the sodiers receded into the trees and did not invade the Aguascalientes.

Later that day, the seventh military region issued a bulletin claiming that 11 marijuana patches had been located and destroyed on the ejido. The raids would be ongoing, and in the following weeks, the army uprooted dozens of patches, mostly on Zapatista lands.

Marijuana is part of the agricultural cycle for the dirt-poor farmers of the highlands of Chiapas, who realize far greater remuneration from the evil weed than they do from their coffee—the illicitness of the product and the risk-taking involved act as a sort of price-support system.

Bushels of *mota* are ripe for the picking as the dry season matures in the mountains and jungle of southeastern Chiapas—San Andrés, right around the mountain from Oventic, is a traditional collection point for the crop, which is mostly destined for sale to the hippified tourist crowd down in San Cristóbal.

It is doubtful, however, that the dread cannabis being tracked on Zapatista ejidos by the military was really being grown by Zapatistas. The EZLN wages its own war on drugs, destroying all patches found on their lands and punishing those who grow the *yerba*—"sometimes we tie them to boards" (Capitán Noé). A more likely scenario is that the dope is grown by PRI farmers or the soldiers themselves—the Mexican army, since the days of Pancho Villa's *cucarachas*, has traditionally smoked marijuana *para caminar*.

Now the Zapatista farmers draped banners by the just-planted milpas that read "Soldiers and Drugs ¡No! Corn and Peace ¡Sí!" which the soldiers would rip down and proceed to trample through the newly seeded fields on search-and-destroy missions that only upped the daily quotient of bad blood.

DEMOCRACY & JUSTICE, CONT.

With 500 lively Zapatista invitees on hand, San Andrés XII (March 19th–24th) had been a blast, another flowering of the word, the conclusions of which were gathered and sorted for presentation at the second round of Democracy & Justice talks (San Andrés XIII), convened April 18th even as the drug warriors were vamping through the surrounding hills.

The government men across the table appeared to be slumbering until the Zapatistas presented their proposals for a new constitutional convention. No, a new constitution was not going to be discussed at San Andrés, argued Alan Arias, an Interior Secretary apparatchik, and that goes for a government of transition too. Limiting the powers of the almighty President was not a fit topic for Indians, or their advisors either. His delegation proposed instead to discuss a new federalism to better define the relations between federal, state, and municipal authorities.

By now, both sides were flagrantly debating "national" issues, often duplicating the Mexico City mesas, which were floundering, the PAN having walked away from the table after high-handed PRI fraud in a Huejotzingo, Puebla, election.

As the session wound down April 25th, Bernal boasted to the press that at least 17 points of consensus had been reached at San Andrés XIII, including "a new equilibrium between the powers of the state," new rules for the relationship of the parties to the state, and the constitutionalization of the use of referendum and plebiscite to decide vital national matters. The EZLN, for its part, calculated that not one consensus had been reached, that, in fact, the government had rejected 18 of their proposals aside from a new constitution—among them a second round in elections and civilian control of the military. The credibility gap between the sides of the table was widening exponentially.

Because the Cocopos' "special" forum on Democracy & Justice, a copycat of the Indian Rights & Culture conclave, was scheduled for May 28th–June 3rd, the next negotiating session was circled for June 5th, a date so far in the future that Bernal considered it a violation of the San Miguel agreement to keep the talks moving continuously from month to month. It was also a date the EZLN would not keep.

THE SENTENCING

18 alleged Zapatistas arrested after the February 1995 military incursion were still imprisoned: the 15 men and women taken at Yanga and Cacalomacán, Javier Elorriaga and Sebastián Entzín in Cerro Hueco, and Alejandro García, charged with toppling electricity pylons in Veracruz—the 19th prisoner, a Tehuacán, Puebla, schoolteacher, had been cut loose with little fanfare at the end of 1995.

Elorriaga was the poster boy of the campaign to win the prisoners' freedom, his matinee-idol good looks omnipresent in the literature and numerous newspaper ads (placed by his colleague Epigmenio Ibarra) to lobby for their release. During the 15 months Javier had been locked up, he had become a star Jornada columnist, his slim volume *Ecos of Cerrohueco* had sold out its first printing, and lately he had acquired the title of editor of a new monthly, Espejo, an organ of the nascent FZLN.

This busy literary life emanated from a narrow cell in the Cerro Hueco infirmary (he was not ill), considerably more cramped than the lodgings of the rare Quetzal bird in the Tuxtla zoo just below the penitentiary. Biologists at the zoo complained that raw sewage generated by Elorriaga and his fellow inmates was fouling their charge's drinking water and slowly killing the nearly extinct Quetzal, a bird whose iridescent feathers were much treasured by Mayan and Aztec emperors.

Although Javier Elorriaga and Sebastián Entzín had been irrevocably chained together by legal proceedings, their cases had precious little in common. Elorriaga was captured February 9th, 1995 after he and Epigmenio had split Guadalupe Tepeyac in the hours before the military assault. Entzín had been arrested January 7th near Chanal with an AK-47 in his pack. "I did badly. I got caught," he would later confess. But both were charged identically with terrorism, rebellion, and conspiracy.

While the case against the young Tzeltal (he was only 17 at the time of his arrest—too young to be prosecuted as an adult) seemed substantial, the tissue of untruths the government was knitting around Elorriaga was too flimsy to hold feathers. Salvador Morales Garibay had been summoned to court eight times to ratify his declaration but had failed to materialize. The prosecution bolstered the record by including portions of Javier's own wife's forced confession, already deemed unacceptable by the judge in "Comandante Elisa"'s case.

Nonetheless, AG Antonio Lozano Gracia was still asking a 40-year sentence for terrorism. Elorriaga's attorneys, Miguel Angel de los Santos and Pilar Noriega, countered that Javier was merely a messenger between Zedillo and Marcos who was seeking to promote a just peace. Whether Elorriaga was even the messenger has never been righteously established—the suspicion that Javier, a stand-up guy in the Cosa Nostra definition of the word, took the fall for the far more influential Ibarra, is a persistent one.

On May 2nd, Elorriaga and Entzín were escorted into the sentencing cell at Cerro Hueco to hear federal judge Juan Manuel Alcántara dictate their fate: 13 years for Javier, six for Sebastián (the court scurried to find him a translator to communicate the bad news). An immediate appeal was filed—de los Santos told reporters that both Moctezuma and Zedillo would be subpoenaed to testify to Javier's messenger service.

The sentence was absurd. No credible crumb of evidence establishing that Elorriaga had participated in terrorist activities had ever been presented in court. Javier had been convicted of terrorism only because the President had said the Zapatistas were terrorists on television.

The judge's decision had far-ranging implications: By negotiating with terrorists at San Andrés, were not Bernal and his boys guilty of what Mexican law labels "delictive association?" By utilizing Javier as a conduit, were not Moctezuma and Zedillo immersed up to their necks in a terrorist conspiracy? What about the role of the COCOPA and the CONAI and the advisors in this terrorist plot? The press was implicated too—Elorriaga had been an accredited journalist at the time of his terrorism. So was anyone who had ever visited an Aguascalientes or marched for peace.

The Interior Secretary applauded Judge Alcántara's decision as proof of the effectiveness of "the division of powers." An "independent judiciary" had made its own decision. The sentence had not been ordered from Los Pinos, as is usually the case in most high-profile political prosecutions in Mexico. What a ridiculous assumption!

So are the Zapatistas terrorists or what? Emilio Chuayffet was asked. "The Zapatistas are what the dialogue law says they are," the Interior Secretary responded obliquely. (The Dialogue law says they are "an organization of Mexican citizens, mostly indigenous, who did not agree with the government for diverse causes and were involved in the armed conflict of January 1st, 1994 in the state of Chiapas.")

Attorney General Lozano's position was even less tenable. Although he had asked 40 years for terrorism, a week previous, at an international antiterrorism conference in Lima, Peru, Lozano explicitly told delegates that the Zapatistas were not terrorists.

Was the sentence really the work of an "independent judiciary"? Of course not. Was the conviction ordered by Zedillo? Probably not. Was it imposed, then, to pull the rug out from under the negotiations and the Zedillo administration's "peace" efforts? Sounds right to me, agreed de los Santos, Javier's stick-thin lawyer.

The response of the General Command was to be expected—a "maximum" Red Alert was ordered. The sentence was "a deadly blow to the Dialogue," the CCRI communicated. How could the EZLN "dialogue" with one arm of the government when another was trying "to kill and jail us"? Four conditions were demanded for the continuation of the peace talks: leading the list was the immediate release of Elorriaga, Entzín and the 16 remaining alleged Zapatistas.

The Interior Secretary's reaction to the new demands was ominous—the EZLN's failure to show up at San Andrés Sakamchién on June 5th would be taken as evidence that the rebels had unilaterally broken off the dialogue, and arrest orders for Marcos et al. would be forthwith reinstated.

In the cities, the Zapatistas' supporters took to the streets. Superbarrio and 250 members of the Assembly of Barrios chained themselves to Lozano's offices and pled guilty to "terrorism." The international network kicked in and demonstrators in New York, Frankfurt, Montreal, Rome, Amsterdam, and Buenos Aires (where ex-governor Eduardo Robledo watched pensively from an office window) stood in front of Mexican embassies and consulates and screamed for Elorriaga's freedom. In San Francisco, protesters built a jail in the street and Greenpeace flung a major banner from the roof of the consulate. 162 notables from 22 countries (Mario Benedetti, Desmond Tutu, Oliver Stone, Earth First!) signed newspaper ads to protest the sentence.

Elorriaga's and Entzín's appeal would not be heard until sometime during the first week in June, and the EZLN had a fatal date in San Andrés June 5th. Whether they would be there pretty much depended on what happened with the appeal. The trains were on the tracks and a showdown seemed unretractable.

FREE AT LAST!

On June 2nd, a jumpy Marcos met with reporters for the first time since the sentencing had come down. The hurried huddle was held under cover of darkness at the provisional camp where, earlier that spring, Marcos had entertained "Oliver" and Régis Debray and Danielle Mitterrand. The heavy patrols and overflights preyed on his paranoia. "We're all terrorists now," he said grimly, cradling his weapon. The Sup was convinced that one part of the government was testing the rebels to see how far they would move in "the military direction." The EZLN had become a *botín* (trophy) for various ruling-circle factions. "For us, there are no distinctions between *duros* (hards) and *blandos* (softs). They both desire our extinction."

The countdown to June 5th now stood at 72 hours, and although Chuayffet was volunteering that there were no real "fatal dates," the memory of many Chinamecas had the EZLN on the edge of its seat.

From a legal standpoint, the sentencing of Elorriaga and Entzín had certain benefits. Under Mexico's twisted justice system, where suspects are condemned as guilty until they can either establish their innocence or buy off the judge, most prisoners festering in the nation's jails are unsentenced. Once sentencing comes down, it automatically triggers an appeal, which, unlike in U.S. courts, can bring quick release.

On June 6th, not 24 hours after the San Andrés talks had been scheduled to resume and had not, a judge at the next level of the federal judiciary reversed the terrorism sentences and ordered Elorriaga's and Entzín's immediate release from Cerro Hueco. Javier was brought up to the warden's office and given his papers to sign—he was still described as "Comandante Vicente" in the documents. Guards came and told him good-bye and not to forget them. The prisoners around him were happy that he was going but sad that they would stay. "*¡Pa' fuera!*" (out of here) they shouted as he walked out of the old prison. "*¡Pa' fuera!*"

Suddenly, Javier was outside in the free air and the reporters were hurling stupid questions at him like "How do you feel?" and "What will you do now?" "One doesn't make plans in prison," he responded—but, of course, Elorriaga had plenty of plans. He would join the EZLN delegation at San Andrés as an advisor and soon was coordinating the day-to-day work of the FZLN.

Reporters had to wait around for Sebastián Entzín, for whom the judge's decision had to be translated into Tzeltal before he was set free. He would go back to his community, El Naranjal near Chanal, and make amends for being caught. "I want to work in the corn and the coffee for now." Sebastián told reporters proudly that he had been a Zapatista since he was 13.

The EZLN issued no statement in respect to the release of Elorriaga and Entzín.

WHAT EVER BECAME OF INDIAN RIGHTS?

Yet another crisis in this unsettling skein had been surmounted, but would the Dialogue survive the shock? The Elorriaga sentence had almost torpedoed the talks, and they were listing badly. Bernal would write that Javier's release demonstrated "the spirit of justice that invigorates the Mexican state," but Elorriaga's 16 months in prison did not exactly prove this axiom or promote much confidence in San Andrés's future.

President Zedillo was stalling on the implementation of the Indian Rights accords. First he had promised to submit the accords to Congress by March 15th, but that deadline melted into April with no explanation. When, on April 16th, the COCOPA presented him with the pertinent documents, the President pledged that the legislature would take up the matter the moment electoral reform was settled—in other words, not any time soon.

Now the Interior Secretary was sifting through "11,000 proposals" made by its own Indians during the government-sponsored forums, the conclusions of which were presented May 22nd at the National Anthropology Museum. Actually, the conclusions of the government Indians did not vary wildly from those reached at San Andrés or the special forum—"free determination" and "collective rights" were mentioned repeatedly—"autonomy" less so. No new date was set for the submission of the San Andrés accords to Congress.

While the federal government sat on its hands, the Chiapas state legislature acted with exemplary alacrity. A re-municipalization bill was introduced in the local congress, and other modifications in state law were crafted to complete the Chiapas government's obligations to the accords. The speed with which the Ruiz Ferro regime acted was part of the master plan to shrink the Zapatista rebellion down to its proper size.

The government's mixed bag of messages did not put a happy face on immediate resumption of the Democracy & Justice mesa. Elorriaga's and Entzín's release meant only that the EZLN had 16 more prisoners for whom they had to deal. There was no Indian Rights law and no Commission of Oversight & Follow-up to oversee it. A new formula needed to be found if peace talks were to resume.

EL NORTE

The pain in the north of Chiapas had been palpable since the 1995 electoral turmoil divided the population into two camps—the PRIs and the PRDs-Zapatistas-catechists.

A wild riot in March at a Palenque baseball game between the Tabasco Olmecs and the hometown Mayans left one dead and City Hall in ashes. On March 14th, PRIistas shuttered Our Lady of Tila chapel in Tzaquil because it was a nest of PRDs-Zapatistas-catechists. On the 27th, the PRD stormed the PRI-controlled Sabanilla City Hall. On April 6th, two PRDers were gunned down near that north state county seat, and on the 10th, Zapata's day, one Chol farmer was killed and five more wounded in Sabanilla by the PRI-controlled paramilitary group Peace & Justice.

Closer to Ocosingo, in Chilón, which the PRD had won two to one the previous October, PRIistas under the direction of Gerónimo Gómez Guzmán, aka *El Chinchulín*, kidnapped and beat PRD officials. Los Chinchulines, legally known as the Luis Donaldo Colosio Civic Front, were not a noble fraternity: Gómez Guzmán, a local cacique, ordered expulsions and liquidations when the spirit moved him and ruled the ejido San Jerónimo in neighboring Bachejón with an iron claw. When he imposed his own candidate as the ejido commissioner upon a resistant assembly May 5th, enraged campesinos went to his house and burnt El Chinchulín alive.

Rioting continued all that day—six were killed, three on each side, and 28 homes were burnt to the ground. The Chinchulín mob threatened to torch a local nunnery and Padre Mardonio Morales's Jesuit center. Laco's police didn't arrive in the smoldering town until long after dark, when most residents had fled to safety elsewhere.

The Chinchulín uprising spurred military and police occupation of the region. Roadblocks were established, sometimes in conjunction with local Paz y Justicia chapters. In Tila, the army encamped in the courtyard of the cathedral, intimidating worshippers and doing their "necessities" right there, an irate Father Heriberto Cruz testified.

In May, as Peace & Justice continued closing down country churches in Tila and Sabanilla, coadjutor bishop Raúl Vera paid his first visit to the tense region. Walking on foot between outlying villages wearing only floppies and shorts (a style Don Samuel eschewed) and washing the mud from his surplice in country streams along with the Chol villagers, Raúl defiantly said Mass in the chapels that had been closed up by the PRI paramilitaries. "We expected a bishop for the rich, but instead we received a bishop for the poor. Raúl is learning how to be Samuel," Father Heriberto marveled.

But the Bishop's vibes could not stem the bloody tide washing over the north of Chiapas. On May 9th, presumed Chinchulines murder a farmer with the highly suspect name of Rafael Guillén. On May 24th, two more are killed at Usipá— Peace & Justice stood accused. On June 14th, two teenagers are shot down at Los Moyos in Sabanilla—Paz y Justicia is again named. In the mountains near Simojovel another PRDer is executed, also on the 14th. On the 17th, Peace & Justice kills again at Corrazal Nuevo. On the 18th, two more Chol campesinos are cut down on the Jesús Carranza ejido (Sabanilla)—one is a catechist. On the same day, two Indians described as members of the Party of Labor (PT) are murdered in Simojovel, allegedly by catechists. On the 21st, three more die at El Guacal, and the next day, two more killings are reported on the Carranza ejido.

The totals are grotesque. 11 corpses in eight days. Since January 1st, 34 Chol and Tzeltal farmers had died violently in the north. It seemed like Chiapas had its own *chupacabras* (goat sucker, a recurrent Latin American folk vampire) and now it was on the land, lapping up the blood of the lambs.

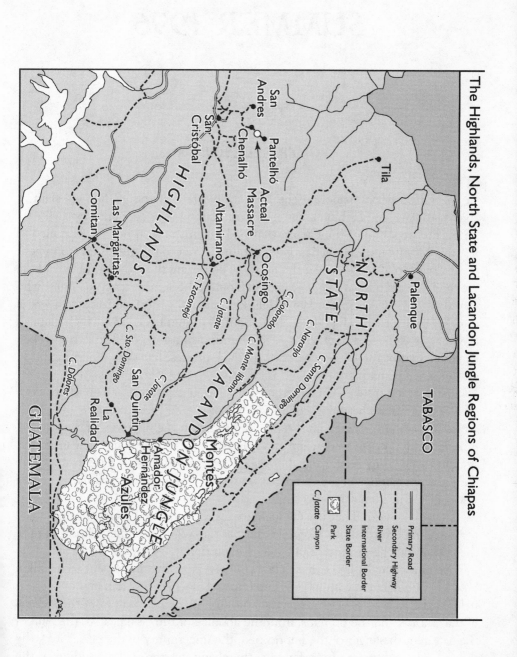

The Highlands, North State and Lacandon Jungle Regions of Chiapas

TABASCO

Palenque

Tila

NORTH STATE

San Andrés
San Cristóbal
Chenalhó
Pantelhó
Acteal Massacre

HIGHLANDS

Altamirano

Ocosingo

Comitán

Las Margaritas

C. Tzaconejó

C. Jatate

C. Colorado

C. Naranjo

C. Santo Domingo

C. Monte Libano

LACANDON JUNGLE

Montes Azules

C. Sto. Domingo

San Quintin

La Realidad

C. Jatate

Amador Hernández

C. Dolores

GUATEMALA

Primary Road
Secondary Highway
River
International Border
State Border
Park
C. Jatate Canyon

SUMMER 1996

GUERRILLA REDUX

The rally to commemorate the first anniversary of the 17 farmers slain at Aguas Blancas June 28th on Guerrero's Costa Grande was convened by the FAC-MLN, the stepchild of the Cuarta that had taken shape in nearby Acapulco in January. Monitors in yellow hats guided militants out to the mildewed monument planted with plastic flowers in the meadow bordering the mountain wash where the men had been killed. Padre Máximo Gómez, the skinny, renegade priest who served as go-between in the Harp Helú kidnapping, performed Mass. Leaders of the Organization of Campesinos of the Southern Sierra (OCSS), which claimed the martyrs, delivered fiery oaths of retribution against deposed governor Rubén Figueroa. Ten of the widows perched in black dresses, like dark mourning birds, on the wood-plank platform.

The featured speaker, Cuauhtémoc Cárdenas, had just finished up when, a few ticks after 1:30 at the most scorching hour of the day, four columns of heavily armed and uniformed men and women appeared on the ridgetops of the tropical hills above and began to descend at a slow trot. With their brand-new uniforms, standard-issue army boots, and their heads swathed in loose red cloth that gave them the appearance of sad-faced penitents, the 79 fighters looked like they had just checked in from central casting.

"Don't be afraid! They are compañeros!" OCSS leader Hilario Mesino urged the recoiling crowd. Then Comandante Santiago took the microphone to raise the curtain on the just-arrived Popular Revolutionary Army (EPR in Spanish).

The new guerrilla had come to lay wildflowers on the monument to its fallen brothers. It had come with its own flag (crossed machete and hammer on a green field) and it had come with its own manifesto: "We have risen from the sadness of the widows and the orphans, from the absence of the disappeared, the pain of the tortured, the anger of the imprisoned, the uncertainty of the persecuted, the illness and the hunger of the farmers, the abandonment of the children of the street..." The comandante's words were translated from the podium into Nahuatl, although that language is not spoken in coastal Guerrero.

The new rebels laid their flowers by the marker and retreated back to the ridgetops, pausing to fire off 17 volleys, one for each of the slain farmers, before disappearing into the trees.

Cárdenas was appalled. He had been set up by the FAC-MLN, the victim of ultra-left opportunism. The abrupt appearance of the EPR had been "a grotesque pantomime," he said, probably arranged by Rubén Figueroa. He had to get out of there—just being at the rally made him liable to investigation and arrest.

Not all the witnesses to this strange apparition were so negative. "At least there are still some real men in Guerrero," Doña Paulina Mendoza, one of the black-clad widows, said admiringly.

THE EPR GOES TO WORK

The Popular Revolutionary Army was next heard from that evening about 100 kilometers to the southeast, near Zumpango off the Acapulco-Chilpancingo freeway, where rebels jackknifed a Corona beer truck, draped a banner on the trailer that called for "Death to Neo-liberalism!" and passed out the Manifesto of Aguas Blancas to dismayed motorists. When state judicial police agents rushed to the scene, the EPR opened fire, wounding four of them. The new guerrilla had drawn its first blood.

The fighters' retreat into the hills was covered by the season's first Pacific hurricane, Boris, which dumped two days of hard rain on the western Sierra Maestra. Nonetheless, military response was swift. Convoys swarmed over the Costa Grande, the Costa Chica south of Acapulco, Tierra Caliente up in La Montaña, all regions of this mountain-bound state where the guerrilla was spotted.

To a reporter humping the muddy, broken road between Coyuca and Tepetixtla after Guerrero erupted, the Bell 212s flashing over the hilltops and the long string of U.S.-built Hummers seemed like a frame from *Apocalypse Now.*

Or Chiapas January 1994 and February '95.

The military mobilization was the most ostentatious in the 20 years since Lucio Cabañas roamed these same hills. Back then, 25,000 troops had finally run Cabañas to ground in December 1974. Now, his nephews, sons, and grandsons had again picked up the gun.

The appearance of the new guerrilla at Aguas Blancas was "a lamentable incident," the President parsed, and indeed, for Zedillo, the unveiling of the EPR was not good for the vaunted miracle "recovery" he was seeking to sell the world.

Interior Secretary Chuayffet tried to dismiss the aberration as criminal *gavillas*, narco-gangs, protecting turf in the opium-saturated hills of Guerrero. But as hit-and-run attacks extended into the summer, causing (according to EPR estimates) 59 army and police casualties, the narco-gavillas soon became "terrorists."

There was no cause for alarm, Chuayffet assured reporters—there were only "50 or 60" of these *terroristas* loose in the land. The PROCUP was pinned as the brains of the gang, and 14 of the group's prisoners, including its spiritual godfather Felipe Martínez Soriano, an ex-rector of the Oaxaca state university, and David Cabañas, Lucio's half-brother, were buried deeper in the dungeons of maximum-security prisons.

Military Intelligence fingered the OCSS as an EPR front group, and Hilario Mesino, whose brother had been killed with Lucio in 1974, was jailed for flimflam crimes. A warrant was issued for OCSS founder Benigno Guzmán, and eight members of the campesino organization were swept up in the mountains above Coyuca, tortured, and forced to sign confessions that they had been paid 2,000 pesos to pose with shiny new AK-47s and AR-15s at Aguas Blancas. An arms cache was retrieved from the Hill of the Guajolote, exactly the same caves in which Lucio had once stashed his meager arsenal. The discovery numbered dozens of short and long guns, a portion of the 20,000 *cuernos de chivo* the EPR had purchased with the receipts of the Harp Helú kidnapping, Comandante José Arturo would later semi-confirm.

The EPR's June 28th curtain-raiser triggered a crackdown on suspect indigenous communities in Guerrero, Oaxaca, up in Puebla, and to the east into the Huasteca mountains, where a second arms cache was discovered along the Hidalgo-Veracruz border, and where the EPR would stage its first press conference in early August. Round-ups of radical campesino leaders were ordered, and the FAC-MLN soon counted over a hundred political prisoners. 23,000 troops, about the same number that came for Lucio, were now deployed throughout the newly militarized zone.

PUBLIC RELATIONS

Dubbed a pantomime from its inaugural performance, the EPR battled for legitimacy all the summer of 1996. The Huasteca press conference was their idea of public relations.

Proceso reporters were approached in Chiapas, rendezvoused with unknowns in Mexico City, then rendezvoused again in Pachuca, Hildalgo, where they began a three-day at-night-only trek into a hill camp so steep they had to pull themselves up on ropes.

The EPR camp was no Aguascalientes. 40 highly disciplined troops, masked in the red face cloths that had become the EPR's trademark, marched and sang the national anthem. More manifestos were read—the Manifesto of the Eastern Sierra Maestra made 45 demands, many similar to the Zapatistas' goals. Comandante José Arturo's cant exhibited a Marxist-Leninist twang, but he avoided buzz phrases such as "dictatorship of the proletariat." Like the EZLN, the EPR wanted a new constitution, the rollback of the revisions to Article 27, and indigenous autonomy (although the EPR would never flex its Indian muscle, preferring to identify its base as "workers and campesinos").

Unlike the EZLN, the EPR endorsed elections as being one arm of the strug-gle for "revolutionary democracy." The EPR also did not smoke—Marcos's pipe was a dead giveaway to the enemy in combat situations, José Arturo sniffed. The EPR didn't think you could make a revolution with poetry either—"poetry is no excuse for politics," the comandante cruelly swiped at Marcos. Nonetheless, the EPR supported the Zapatistas' efforts to negotiate a just peace in Chiapas. The EPR and the EZLN were not rivals, the commander maintained, and they were not the only armed options around. Yes, the EPR had its heart set on taking state power, but the struggle for socialism was no longer paramount.

The Popular Revolutionary Army, explained the guerrillero, was a concentra-tion of 14 armed focos, among them the PROCUP and an old Cabañas spin-off, the Campesino Adjustment Commando, but most of the groups listed by José Arturo were unknown. All 14 groups had forged a political party as well as an army—the Party of the Democratic Popular Revolution. Both the party and the army were financed by "expropriations" from the elite and the kidnapping of members of "the banking oligarchy" like Harp Helú.

The EPR also kidnapped the spotlight. By midsummer 1996, the press had turned its high beams on Guerrero. The New York Times, the Washington Post, and Newsweek all ran front-pagers, and the Wall Street Journal fretted about col-lateral damage to the stock market.

The appearance of the Popular Revolutionary Army irrevocably altered the equation for both the Zapatista Army of National Liberation and the Mexican government. Now Zedillo was battling armed options on at least two fronts (the Huasteca conference hinted at more). While the EZLN seemed more than ever to be fighting a war of "ink and Internet," the EPR was rampaging through the land, drawing real red blood.

YADATA YADATA

On the afternoon the EPR fired off its guns on a hillside above Aguas Blancas, the Zapatista Army of National Liberation was about to inaugurate the "Special Forum for the Reform of the State and the Transition to Democracy," a gabfest of frightening proportions, at the ex-convent in downtown San Cristóbal. Postponed once by the squabble over Elorriaga and Entzín, the special forum was important enough to once again bring Marcos in from the jungle.

Down in La Realidad, Marcos stripped off his snub-nosed weapon and hand-ed it to the faithful Moisés even as the EPR were strapping on theirs in Guerrero. The gesture crystallized the distinction between the directions of the two guer-rillas.

Relations had never been cozy with the PROCUP, whom the Sup had pub-licly chastised after Martínez Soriano's boys presumably hit a soldier near Tuxtla on April 15th 1994—the incident signaled a Zapatista Red Alert. And the EZLN had rejected the PROCUP bombings in the first days of the war.

At the opening session of the special forum, in a packed San Cristóbal theater that the Zapatistas themselves had tried to torch in January 1994, Marcos directed his gaze to the EPR. "How many guerrilla groups would have to appear, in how many places," before the mal gobierno woke up and smelled the coffee? Who the EPR was and why it had shown its face mask just when the EZLN was weighing a transformation to peaceful political activism, was to be seen. The EPR would first have to "establish its legitimacy," and not just with guns, the Sup advised. Finally, the EZLN's commitment to such a transformation remained unshaken.

Despite the Sup's efforts to dismiss the EPR, their aura clung to the special forum like malignant Velcro.

Marcos tried to keep himself busy, presented fanciful position papers (in collaboration with Don Durito of the Lacandón and a certain B. Brecht), gave long interviews to the European press, and entertained a steady stream of political courtesans, even strolling arm-in-arm in the ex-convent garden with Andrés Manuel López Obrador, Muñoz Ledo's replacement as president of the PRD. On July 3rd, the EZLN and the PRD announced a pact of mutual respect, the first of several Zapatista "concrete alliances" with mass opposition organizations.

The Sup tried hard to make it appear that the EZLN had not been stung by the EPR's sudden show-up. But the truth was other—the new guerrilla had exposed the old one's glaring lack of firepower, and the special forum was proof. While the EPR was considered armed and dangerous, the EZLN could only back up its words with more words.

The Zapatistas' skepticism irritated the EPR. When Marcos demanded they prove their legitimacy, Comandante José Arturo retaliated by borrowing the Sup's celebrated "pardon" riff: "Why do we have to ask pardon for the fact that we are not disposed to let the government kill us? Must we ask the EZLN's pardon for taking this decision?"

Marcos struck back by citing the EPR's position that poetry did not make revolutions, sneering that such orthodoxy reminded him of the "revolutionary" faction that had executed Salvadoran bard Roque Dalton for deviating from the Marxist-Leninist line by writing poetry.

But for all the literary repartee, the future was writ large. The way it worked was this: the Zapatistas' option for dialogue made them the good guerrilla on the government's books while the EPR were just a bunch of common criminals. This was not a comfortable place for the Zapatistas to be.

It is the tension between violence and nonviolence that is the Zapatistas' best weapon (Le Bot), but the EZLN had been effectively disarmed since the February 5th offensive. Now a curious paradox held sway: if the cards came up right, the EPR had given the EZLN its firepower back without the Chiapanecos ever having to fire a single shot.

DEMOCRACY & JUSTICE: THE FINAL CHAPTERS

In late June, the COCOPA managed to broker a deal for a revised dialogue format, and the protagonists convened on July 6th for the first time since May to ratify the new rules. The most significant revision delegated to the legislative commission the exclusive power to declare the talks dead when an impasse like the Elorriaga snafu provoked rupture. This definition neutralized the Interior Secretary's threats of reinstating the arrest orders should the EZLN not show up at San Andrés and has protected the Zapatistas ever since, whether they were negotiating or not. A solution was also reached for the constitution of the oversight commission, the COSEVER, that allowed the EZLN to participate in the commission. Yet, despite the agreements, the shadow of the EPR sat like a bad black bird above the meeting house at San Andrés Sakamchíen.

During five days of negotiation on the new rules, the rebels and the government men met only twice head to head—at the opening and closing sessions. The CONAI and the COCOPA, striving to keep the combatants in their respective corners, ferried the documents between camps. Tentative agreement on the new rules was reached on the 12th.

Like arm-weary pugilists, the combatants took a three-day breather and returned to San Andrés for the grudge match July 15th. This contest was billed as the second plenary of Mesa II, "Democracy & Justice." San Andrés XV (if you are keeping count) had been set aside to consolidate a final document that would be ratified at the following session in August and then returned to the communities for consultation.

As its contribution to this prolonged process, the government presented a thin eight-page offer that essentially obligated the Zedillo administration to honor the electoral reforms being drawn up in equally protracted negotiations between the political parties in Mexico City. For its part, the EZLN offered a 37-page master plan for the nation's transition to democracy.

The feathers flew right away. Bernal accused the EZLN of clinging to ingenuous demands like a new constitution and re-negotiation of NAFTA. The rebels called the government offer "miserable." Whereas the government viewed electoral reform as being the penthouse of the transition to democracy, the EZLN saw it as the basement from which to build. The negotiations spiraled into accusations. Bernal was a racist. He was the obstacle to "democracy and justice." He had to be removed if the talks were to continue.

San Andrés XV broke off without a conclusion July 16th, to be renewed August 6th when the final agreements would be forged. It was a fantasy timetable—there were no preliminary agreements, just two documents and no inclination to find common ground between them.

On July 16th, the day the talks recessed in bewilderment, the EPR attacked an army convoy at Chilapa in the Montaña of Guerrero, inflicting either no or eight casualties, depending on whom you choose to believe.

The government offer was a hollow exercise, advisor Luis Hernández warned—the EZLN had not taken up the gun to achieve the legal recognition of non-government organizations, one of Bernal's generous offers. San Andrés XVI would produce no resolution either.

"A dense and ominous phase of the oft-interrupted Dialogue had begun," Monsiváis writes in the third volume of EZLN documents. Negotiations at the Democracy & Justice table had begun in March, and six months later the two sides weren't even making eye contact anymore.

The *chingaderas* began again on August 6th. The government was just using San Andrés to "*chingarnos*" (screw us), David and Tacho groused. Bernal had to go if there was to be any advancement at the table. Moreover, the EZLN was tired of being bottled up in the conflict zone. They wanted to travel and meet the people. Bernal's response was succinct: the EZLN could only travel between San Andrés and San Cristóbal and their home communities.

While the government and the rebels hawed and haggled around the table, the EPR stepped up its attacks on military and police targets. Guerrilleros opened up on an army encampment August 7th near Yerba Santa, above Coyuca—the military says an army cook was killed; the EPR says it caused 30 casualties. On August 10th, both sides concur, two soldiers were ambushed near Zumpango.

As Luis Hernández anticipated, San Andrés XVI went nowhere. Finally, Tacho told Bernal that the EZLN would take his "miserable" offer back to the communities for consultation—the EZLN's 37-page document would also be put to a vote, and there was little confusion about which proposal would carry. Rejection of the government's offer would almost certainly lead to a new break in the Dialogue, and cooler heads in the CONAI and COCOPA sought to defer the consulta, suggesting instead that the Democracy & Justice mesa be suspended until conditions for resolution germinated. The motion was made to move on to the third phase of the peace process, "Welfare & Development," but the trains were on the tracks again.

On August 12th, the Indians and the government men stalked off to await the results of the consultations in the communities. In the plaza of Sakamchién, Comandante Zebedeo tried to explain what had transpired but was drowned out by the intense squealing of an about-to-be-butchered pig.

So ended the peace talks at San Andrés Sakamchién de los Pobres, more with a porcine whimper than the big bang of peace. The two sides would never again gather there.

ALL THE WORLDS...

In the midst of this cataract of events, the EZLN celebrated its long-antici-pated Intergaláctica (July 27th–August 4th) in the jungles and mountains of southeastern Chiapas at the zenith of an unusually moist and muddy rainy sea-son.

The magnum international conclave was the EZLN's tribute to diversity, a celebration of otherness, of "all the worlds the world needs to really be the world," as Marcos had grown fond of declaiming.

The first others to arrive in La Realidad (July 23rd) were the Barzonistas, del-egates to the debtors' group congress, which this year would be held at the near-by Aguascalientes rustic convention center—"our Aguascalientes are open to all social activists who want to use them," Tacho greeted these very other visitors.

Otherness is an eminently two-way street. The others from the outside came to meet these others from the inside—the embattled Mayans of the region—and they, in turn, came to know these other others from a world that suddenly opened wide for the Indians.

The Barzonistas are middle-class farmers and ranchers, ruddy, burly folks from the center and the north of the nation in Stetsons and cowboy boots, who stand twice as tall as the Zapatistas. The Barzón usually conducts its congresses in air-conditioned hotels in provincial cities like Morelia, where the beer is cold and the cell phones work. Now these very other others had trekked down to La Realidad to plot the next step in their war against the banks and sign a "mutual defense" pact with the Zapatistas, the latest "concrete alliance." "We are both on the same train," Barzón director Juan José Quirinos assured Sub Marcos.

Meanwhile, up in San Cristóbal, outlanders were streaming into Chiapas for "the global happening." Nearly 3,000 mostly European, mostly young activists registered for the Intergaláctica. In all, delegates from 55 nation states (counting Indian ones) would be on board the buses to embark for the Intergaláctica. Some had weathered hardships just getting to San Cris. For example, four busloads of FZLN recruits from Mexico City had been stalled for two days at a roadblock on the Tehuantepec isthmus mounted by that other offspring of the Cuarta, the FAC-MLN.

The Mexican Migra beefed up to battalion strength to deal with the influx of outsiders, creating monumental jam-ups at checkpoints in and around the con-flict zone as agents insisted upon filming, interrogating, and sometimes strip-searching each and every one of the visitors.

The immigration dragnet was not a useful tool for achieving a trade pact with the European Union. As the Euros endured hours of Mexican Migra harassment just to debate the failings of neo-liberalism in the middle of a jungle, they resolved to return home and redouble their efforts to thwart Zedillo's European ambitions.

The Intergaláctica opened for business at the Oventic Aguascalientes in the highlands, "a place of resistance against stupidity" (Mayor Ana María), on the evening of July 27th. Oventic had been gussied up for the strangers, and the display of folding chairs set up at this rustic convention center was impressive. So was the New Fire ceremony, a kind of Zapatista floor show that thrilled the rain-drenched visitors into deep silence.

The Intergaláctica was not a not-for-profit event. Each Intergaláctico & -galáctica had shelled out $100 USD to cover seven days of food, lodging, and transportation (press credentials went for $15). The gross gate for the Intergaláctica had to be 2,000,000 pesos plus ($300,000 Yanqui dollars)—the receipts from the "restaurants" alone would keep La Realidad afloat for the next year.

From Oventic, the Interglláctica/os spread out into a topography that ranges from Alpine to Amazon basin, to cogitate the disasters of neo-liberalism in separate mesas at the five Aguascalientes scattered throughout the territory. "The Economy—A Horror Story" was installed at a new Aguascalientes on the Roberto Barrios ejido, 40 kilometers from Palenque in the troubled north of the state. The military was encamped on the other side of the river and frisked the travelers as they arrived. The rain was dense, churning up Mississippis of mud. Cars got stuck. The mosquitos got testy. The *economistas* bogged down in heavy polemic and dwelt more on net war than Marxian thesis. The position papers got soggy and hard to read. Harry Cleaver, a red-bearded guru out of Austin, proposed "a cyberspace mosaic of local struggle." The local strugglers, the Choles of Roberto Barrios, did not much mix in the muddy debate.

At La Garrucha, the theme was Indigenous Peoples and Neo-liberalism. Bill Means from AIM tried to convince me that what the EZLN needed was Indian bingo. A diminutive woman from Brittany kept insisting that "we-are-all-Indians." Meanwhile, the gorgeously beribboned and silver-plaited Tzeltaleras of Garrucha danced cumbias far across the muddy compound.

Up in the highlands at Oventic, "What Society Is Not Civil?" was being asked. Things got uncivil quick. Intergalactical feminists were enraged when relegated to a sub-mesa. More nastiness ensued after the insensitive males' caucus called for an end to men-women conflict because, after all, are we not all mammals? Oventic Zapatistas, by now quite used to crazy foreigners, dozed under their ski masks as the argument boiled.

"All the Cultures for Everyone" was celebrated out on the Ejido Morelia in the Altamirano cañada. A German duo tootled Irish jigs for the Tzeltal children as they stood pressed against a wall mural that depicted the deadly military incursion on the ejido in January 1994. Participants in the culture mesa slurped cans of warm Coca Cola, globalization's number one culture killer.

The political end of neo-liberalism was put under the glass at bug-ridden La Realidad. Distinctions between European Intergalactics and their Mexican and

Latin American counterparts soon developed. Whereas Berlin anarchos championed autonomy as an *autonom* or squat—alternative spaces on the fringes of global bourgeois society—the Americans (mostly southern ones) wanted to confront capitalism and fight for inclusion.

Many kinds of political tables were laid at La Realidad. Ideologues from the European left parties—the Italian "Communist Refoundation," Spanish trade unionists, Basque independence fighters, Greens, German anarchist posses—intermeshed with the Brazilian Party of Labor, retired guerrilla leaders like Douglas Bravo (Venezuela) and Hugo Blanco (Peru), the Sem Terras (sometimes called Brazil's Zapatistas), even a very formal Cuban delegation.

In the candlelit schoolhouse, a special table was set for the Illuminati: Uruguayan writer Eduardo Galeano; Alain Touraine and Yvon Le Bot, distinguished French Latin Americanists; Danielle on the rebound with Gisèle Halimi, the Mitterrands' favorite feminist; Russian filmmaker Pavel Lugan, all crouched over the lamplit tables like figures in a Georges de la Tour painting.

What did this mishmash of Romance and Teutonic language speakers, Greeks, Turks, Kurds, South Africans, Japanese, Congolese, Swedes, and Mayan Indians have in common? Not very much, thought Le Bot: "Each has come with his or her own notion of what Zapatismo should be." This indefinition was helpful to the Zapatistas. It made Zapatismo very plug-in-able all over the globe to fight local struggles. In a globalized world, where international opinion is far more important than national, this adaptability gave the EZLN many allies who protected them from annihilation.

The otherness of the Intergaláctica was intractable. In its rush to a snap judgment, Reuters snidely reduced the multi-hued hordes to "a few thousand hippies, punks, and middle-aged leftists" but missed the fashion statement altogether. Men and women in green afros and Mohawks, dappled with tattoos or elaborately pierced, mingled with Mayans in ski masks. The hot L.A. cult band Rage Against the Machine was on hand to comfort generations x, y, and z.

The conclusions of the mesas, presented at the final plenary on August 3rd, stirred up a minor hornets' nest in the hosts' camp, the resolution supporting international same-sex marriage perhaps less so than the one calling for the legalization of all soft drugs, a measure that Marcos did not even want to talk about—"all drugs are prohibited in our communities," he steamed.

Other resolutions called for an international consultation (pledged but never held); the building of an international network against neo-liberalism was begun (but never finished). A second Intergaláctica was plotted for Europe a year hence (the Sup promised he would be there but wasn't).

In the end, what remained of the Intergaláctica was Marcos's incantation about all the worlds the world needed to really be the world. "Next Intergaláctica we'll have to invite the Martians," the Sup mused as the masses boogied in a sea of mud under a big orange moon to the lilt of a visiting Jarocha band. In his closing remarks, half as an aside to the EPR, a shadow that had not creased the event until now, Marcos demanded to know, "Who can now say that to dream is beautiful but useless?"

Actually, Comandante José Arturo was saying precisely that, far off in the wilds of the Huasteca, where the EPR conducted its first-ever press conference on the same weekend the EZLN was holding its fandango in the jungle.

As the final footsteps of the Intergalácticos faded into memory, crude reality returned to La Realidad. "They will never forgive the people here for this," wrote a rueful Adolfo Gilly in La Jornada. "I fear the sick craziness of a regime that never pardons. I feel it in my bones…"

THE NIGHT OF THE LONG GUNS

What struck terror in the hearts of Ernesto Zedillo and his closest associates was the synchronization of the EPR's multi-state August 28th rampage.

In Guerrero, elements of the Popular Revolutionary Army struck in three wildly divergent regions within an hour. At 22:35, 30 heavily armed guerrilleros laid siege to a motorized police barracks just south of Acapulco, tossing grenades and wounding four. A half hour later, up in the threadbare Montaña in Tixtla, two police were hit as the EPR stormed into the local government palace and slapped their manifestos on the walls. And within the hour, way across the state on the Michoacán border, seven police were wounded in a guerrilla drive-by shooting in Ciudad Altamirano.

Heading south into Oaxaca, the EPR had fired upon two army locations in the state capital, tried but failed to blow a military bank ATM, and momentarily taken over a radio station (the transmitter was down), all attacks timed to coincide with the Guerrero haps.

Also in Oaxaca: around 23:00 hours in the Mixtec Indian county seat of Tlaxtiaco, the EPR sprayed City Hall with machine-gun fire, killing three police. A half hour later, in the evening's deadliest assault, nine fell (two police, three sailors, two guerrilleros, and two civilians) in Huatulco, the luxury resort on the impoverished Oaxaca coast.

EPR attacks also occurred at four dams and power stations in Puebla and Mexico state—three police officers were wounded and a pair of possible EPRistas captured. An unconfirmed gun battle involving another guerrilla band was reported in the *bajío* (lowland) of Guanajuato, and a state radio station in Villahermosa, Tabasco was invaded by persons in trademark red face cloths, but no one could ever be located who actually heard the EPR read its manifestos.

Early on the morning of the 29th, near Tacámbaro, Michoacán, a drug-heavy region, uniformed fighters from an indistinct army opened fire on a military patrol, killing at least one soldier—the patrol was under the command of the general who had been in charge of Rancho Nuevo on the first night of the Zapatista rebellion.

The totals of the night of the long guns were chilling: 15 Mexican citizens had died and 23 more were wounded in the abrupt eight-state EPR offensive.

The eighth state was Chiapas.

At 23:25, not far beyond the timetable of activity to the north, the phone banged at the offices of Expreso, a progressive Tuxtla daily. A voice with an Indian accent read a prepared statement: "We are developing a national series of actions. In Chiapas, we are planning only acts of propaganda. We are not going to attack the Mexican Army because we don't want to interfere in the dialogue"—the EZLN was then in the throes of consultation on the government's "miserable" Democracy & Justice offer.

The EPR's propaganda acts had a familiar ring. Unpersoned roadblocks were thrown up around the state. The vital Tuxtla-to–San Cristóbal stretch of the Pan American highway was cut halfway in between. A banner fluttering on an adjacent hillside urged "¡Vivas!" for the EPR. The Pan-American was also cut between San Cristóbal and Comitán, as was the Ocosingo-Palenque link to the east and the coastal highway at two points in the west of Chiapas. The widespread action was an unmistakable challenge to the EZLN's influence in the region.

It had been a matter of long-standing conjecture that the PROCUP was loose in the state, mostly in the Sierra Maestra where the Francisco Villa Popular Campesino Union clustered—but few calculated that the PROCUPs, if that is who was at the bottom of the EPR, were this loose.

The EPR's brazen invasion of EZLN turf elicited measured rage from the Zapatista leadership. In a communiqué issued the next day, Marcos bluntly tells the EPR, "We did not ask for your help, we do not need your help, and we do not want your help..." The Sup accuses the Popular Revolutionary Army of placing the lives of civil Zapatistas in danger and lying about its true intentions. "Didn't you know our people were in the consultas?" Why would the EPR show up in Chiapas where the EZLN had the situation well in hand, when the new guerrilla had demonstrated its mobility to move freely around the country? There could be only one reason: "To brag that the EPR has cadre in Chiapas."

"The cost of the EPR attack will be paid by the Indian communities who have more than a thousand days in resistance with their arms and their poetry..." (notice the poetry). Marcos drew sharp distinctions between the EZLN and the EPR, even suggesting that the two could come to blows: "The difference between us is that our political perspectives are dramatically opposed. Thanks to your appearance, many now understand those differences. You fight to take power. We fight for democracy, liberty, and justice. It is not the same thing. Even if you have success and win power, we will keep fighting for democracy, liberty, and justice..."

INFORMES

The EPR's August 28th offensive did not come unannounced. Three days previous, reporters had been blindfolded and driven to a safehouse near Mexico City where Comandantes Oscar and Vicente peered attentively through their long red face cloths and advertised: "We have fresh forces in various parts of the country that will soon give a broader character to our struggle."

No, the EPR was not a pantomime. Suddenly, the new rebel army had become a national player, and the night of the long guns had been its Informe to the nation that all was not right. They delivered it just 72 hours before Ernesto Zedillo delivered his own annual state of the union address.

Zedillo's second Informe was to be upbeat. The nation had pulled itself up by its bootstraps and Mexico was in full recovery. Employment and growth were back on track and investment on the rebound. Moreover, the corner had been turned on democratic reforms, and barring any last-minute mishap, the nation would have a new set of electoral laws in place for the 1997 midterms. In Chiapas, the EZLN had been tamed and was about to transform itself into a peaceful political organization. Both the government and the Zapatistas were committed to the process of dialogue. Zedillo would soon send his long-promised Indian Rights law on to Congress.

On the other hand, the bad-boy EPR needed to be spanked. "Now that the country is on its feet once again, we Mexicans do not appreciate the appearance of groups that employ terrorism to murder, destroy, and intimidate. We will pursue every terrorist act with the full force of the state." The Prez was pounding on the rostrum to demonstrate that he truly had a hard hand (*mano dura*) to swat down this new terrorist scum whose name he dared not invoke. The gesture brought PRI members of Congress to their feet in a tumultuous roar of approval.

Other informes were being delivered that September 1st. The FAC-MLN organized a counterinforme under the Angel of Independence to protest the mounting militarization of southern and central Mexico. And back in the halls of Congress, a portly man in a Babe the Valiant Pig mask stood beneath Zedillo's elevated pulpit and unfurled jocose banners ("Long live the market economy! Love, the Rich") while the President droned on above. Inflamed PRIistas ultimately ripped the porker mask from PRD deputy Marco Rascón (the inventor of Superbarrio) and punched the pig-man's lights out.

The President's annual state of the union speech descended, like the nation he ruled, into tragicomedic spectacle.

The August 28th attacks touched the stock market for the first time since the EPR opened up, triggering sharp declines. J.P. Morgan (the brokerage house, not the defunct tycoon) even called from New York to probe this low-end reporter's evaluation of the havoc the EPR could wreak.

The tourist industry, Mexico's third generator of Yanqui dollars, seemed most vulnerable to the new guerrilla onslaught. The EPR had entered both Acapulco and Huatulco but refrained from attacking the hotel zones—the Huatulco assault took place less than a kilometer from Club Med. British and U.S. authorities posted travel advisories warning their citizens to stay away from Mexican beaches.

The Zedillo brain trust mopped its brow. An odd shoot-out at the home of Attorney General Lozano's private secretary heightened the sense of impending guerrilla attack in the capital. The PROCUPs had a jacket as bombers, and security was thickened around Federal Electricity Commission installations, PEMEX, TELMEX, Los Pinos. Backfiring cars had pedestrians ducking.

Not to worry, insisted Chuayffet. The EPR terrorists were a criminal band without any social base. At least the (formerly terrorist) Zapatistas represented a handful of disaffected Indians in the jungles and the mountains of Chiapas.

This argument didn't really hold much water. Tabulating FAC-MLN membership groups and factoring in such mass organizations as the Independent Proletarian Movement, Ruta 100, and the Francisco Villa Popular Front, which marched with the FACs, the EPR's social base might have been a respectable half-million very pissed-off Mexicans.

Zedillo's casting of the EZLN and the EPR as "good" and "bad" guerrillas was a political blunder that washed up any foreseeable restart of the Dialogue for Peace & Justice in Chiapas.

THE BREAKING POINT

In a communiqué dated the morning after the EPR attack but published September 3rd, the EZLN announced that, after weeks of consultation, the bases had overwhelmingly rejected the government's "miserable" offer and the comandantes were suspending their participation in the Dialogue at San Andrés Sakamchién de los Pobres indefinitely. The EZLN would not attend the programmed September 4th session but laid out five conditions for their eventual return

At the top of the list was the immediate release of the 16 remaining prisoners—the Yanga Seven had been dealt six-year sentences in August for firearms violations, and the Attorney General was asking 50-year terms for the Cacalomacán Eight. In addition, over a hundred pro-Zapatista prisoners taken in agrarian struggles around the state were now cooling their heels in Cerro Hueco.

The EZLN also demanded implementation of the Indian Rights accord and the activation of the COSEVER, an end to military and police harassment of Zapatista communities, a serious presentation at San Andrés, and the replacement of Marco Antonio Bernal. "Why don't you send him to negotiate with the

EPR? I know the EPR doesn't want to negotiate, but neither does Bernal," Marcos counseled Zedillo.

The new conditions suggested that it would be a long time before the two sides ever dialogued again. Up at San Andrés on September 4th, workmen dismantled the meeting house, hauling out xerox machines and computers. The metal detectors were stashed, the curtains drawn, and the big doors locked. They would never open again.

The rebels had calculated correctly that the break-off would bring the troops charging down the canyons, and General Renán Castillo responded with Pavlovian eagerness. By the 5th, his tanks surrounded La Garrucha, then pushed deeper into the jungle. By the 10th, fighters on both sides stood just a thousand meters apart, eyeball to eyeball through their rifle sights. Marcos wrote that he was not sure he could hold back his troops, most of whom were young, itching for action, and no doubt inflamed by the EPR's spectacular exploits.

The Sup fired off three letters to Señora Civil Society, asking plaintively if she still remembered him. The letters were now datelined Numancia, a Spanish town that had committed collective suicide rather than surrender to the Romans a hundred years before Christ.

But the truth was that no one was paying much attention anymore. The Zapatistas had cried wolf one time too often. "There is a rising tide of silence in the national and international press," Bellinghausen sweated. Attention had locked in on the EPR's next move.

But there was no next move, or if there was one it was so imperceptible that only a very few, with their ears planted firmly to ground, could detect it. By October it was time for local elections in Guerrero, and the EPR announced a temporary freeze on attacks against the Army and police. The Popular Revolutionary Army has never mounted a major offensive since.

Despite its classic guerrilla pose, exemplary weaponry, headline-grabbing attacks, hundreds of political prisoners (300 alone from the Loxichas in Oaxaca), and detailed reports of human rights atrocities committed against Indian villages, the EPR never galvanized much popular support. The new guerrilla had no Marcos to speak for it, and its rhetoric was clunky and lacked the poetry to reach the national heart. Although the EPR dispatched dozens of communiqués to the Mexican press, unlike those of the silver-tongued Zapatistas, they were never published.

BOOK THREE

A TIME OF SILENCE AND BLOOD

"Silence is an Indian weapon…"
—*Subcomandante Marcos*

AUTUMN–WINTER
1996–1997

THE SMALLEST OF THE SMALL

At the heart of the EZLN was a wedding of indigenous vision and the armed and not-so-armed Left. But the first fruit of this union—the San Andrés accords on Indian Rights and Culture—had been kidnapped by the mal gobierno, and the Zapatistas would have to pull together a strong enough coalition of indigenous peoples to wrest it from its captors.

The Special Forum on Indian Rights in January '96 had spawned a standing Indigenous Forum, which met at Oventic on April 10th and again in late July to plan a national congress October 8th–12th in Tenochtitlán—Mexico City, the 504th anniversary of Indian resistance to the European invasion of the Americas. The National Indigenous Congress (CNI) would be celebrated under the banner of ¡Nunca Más un México Sin Nosotros! (Never Again a Mexico Without Us).

The Zapatista Army of National Liberation was urged to attend. The invites were floated off the record all summer and formalized September 21st. Weary of being cooped up inside the conflict zone, the EZLN expressed keen interest. "We're coming," the comandancia signaled.

"It is impossible for them to travel," Bernal warned darkly. The exodus would constitute "a formal rupture" of the Dialogue law, and the government had an obligation to uphold the law—particularly now that the Dialogue was in suspension. The EZLN would be received "just like any other armed, clandestine army that has declared war on the government," i.e., as the government now received the EPR, with the full weight of the state.

"UUY!" (the Spanish-Mayan equivalent of "Oy!") replied Subcomandante Marcos in large type, a one-liner communiqué October 3rd. The dialogue law contained no travel restrictions, argued the late constitutionalist Emilio Krieger. On the contrary, the law defined the Zapatistas as Mexicans, and as Mexicans, they had a constitutional right to move about their country unhindered.

The mal gobierno's insistence that the EZLN was under house arrest in Chiapas was driven by a different engine. October was crucial to Zedillo's pet political reform project, now whittled down to a delicate consensus between the parties on changes to the electoral law, and Chuayffet did not want the rebels running amuck in Mexico City while the process came to a congressional vote. It was in the EZLN's interest to stay away and let the reforms take legal shape, the government men argued. Under the proposed reform, independent candidates would be allowed to run for public office. Who knows? Marcos might even be governor of Chiapas one day.

We're going, the rebels repeated, and tensions went to high voltage very quickly. Stepped-up patrols rattled down the Cañadas and new checkpoints were established on the Margaritas–La Realidad road to prevent the comandantes from being smuggled out in the trunks of cars. In Mexico City, the Judicial Police prepared for their capture. With the talks in limbo, the EZLN was in danger of losing its protected status. Overflights palpitated the night sky.

"We're going," the Zapatistas kept repeating. THEY'RE COMING! shouted the big black headlines of Mexico City's afternoon scandal sheets.

On October 3rd, Zedillo upped the ante when he flew directly into the conflict zone for the first time ever. Choles, Tzeltales, and even some rare Lacandones were assembled by the PRI at Nueva Palestina for the customary hand-outs. Although the visit was a benign one, this deep penetration of a portion of the jungle where the EZLN high command was holed up was a veiled warning of military missions to come.

Scant days before the comandantes' scheduled departure, the COCOPA finally moved to head off this two-way demolition derby. On October 6th, after a protracted session with Chuayffet, the legislators agreed to carry a "confidential" message to the EZLN—this period of sub-rosa negotiations was colored by such discreet communication—and on the 8th, the Cocopos and the comandancia were together again in La Realidad. The rebels were already packing. "We're going. We'll see you in Mexico City," Marcos waved to the reporters.

But the matter seemed more knotted than that. Negotiations extended for the next 24 hours. Periodically, the legislators would rush out of the Aguascalientes, jump into their cars, and race over to Guadalupe Tepeyac to call Chuayffet on the army's sat phone. Hermann thought the ambiance had a High Noon cast to it.

The deal came down midday on the 9th: Ten unarmed rebel delegates would be permitted to travel to Mexico City to attend the National Indigenous Congress. None of the delegates could have outstanding warrants pending against them, but they would be allowed to travel masked. Informal negotiations with the COCOPA and the CONAI on the EZLN's return to San Andrés would begin October 15th.

"We have decided to send a delegation that represents our most aggressive side, our most belligerent and intransigent part, and our greatest symbol of war," Marcos told startled reporters who were swarming over the ejido house. "Allow me…" The Sup strode over to a nearby hut and emerged with a tiny, fragile, ski-masked woman in tow, the smallest of all her compañeras, Comandante Ramona, la más pequeña.

The reporters were flabbergasted. Is that all there was? After days of "allegations, threats, and incendiary pronouncements" (Bernal) this was the whole Zapatista delegation? "Never again a Mexico City without us," Sub Marcos chortled and introduced Ramona to the press.

Bernal & company, blindsided by their own racism and misogyny, had always figured it was Marcos they were trying to keep away from Mexico City and never saw Ramona coming. What they failed to remember was that the EZLN was going to an Indian congress and Marcos is not even an Indian.

In her Tzotzil blouse and long serge skirt, the diminutive Ramona seemed a replica of the Ramona dolls the Chamula women sell in San Cristóbal—but thinner. She was sick, her kidneys were failing, and the Indian congress seemed a politically correct way of getting her to a hospital (the congress would be held in a medical center auditorium). Since she had first been secretly diagnosed during the conversations in the Cathedral back in   '94, Ramona had twice been declared dead or near death. The last time the outside world had seen her was on a video at the height of the February '95 military incursion, when she had pled for the soldiers to go home.

"Ramona is dying," Marcos somberly told the press. "It is her last wish to talk to other Indians and tell them what the EZLN is all about."

Sending Ramona to the congress was a measure of the EZLN's ingenuity. Not only did the move put them back on the front page, but the image of this tiny, terminally ill Indian woman traveling alone up to the capital when, for weeks, the mal gobierno had been painting the Zapatistas as war demons, handed the rebels the moral high ground yet again.

The villagers of La Realidad walked Ramona out to the cars. Marcos got down from his horse and bent to embrace her. "We didn't ask permission for Ramona to leave—she's just leaving," he reminded the press and presented her with three paper roses she would clutch all the way to Mexico City. "If they treat Ramona badly, the women will rise up!" the Tojolabales chanted as the engines revved for the climb to San Cris.

Up in the old city, Ramona hardly slept. Crowds gathered to glimpse her and the walls read "Todos Somos Ramona." On the trip down to Tuxtla the next morning, the comandante got sick twice riding the dizzying switchbacks, and unidentified vehicles kept trying to penetrate the motorcade. At the airport where the COCOPA had rented a private jet to fly her up to the big city, Ramona's first flight, two unknown "doctors," sporting stethoscopes around their necks, tried to push their way onto the flight but were repelled.

And then, at last, the jet lifted into the wild blue yonder and Ramona was airborne. She had broken out of the Mexican army's encirclement of her comrades, had—wrote Ramón Vera, who accompanied her on the flight—"broken the military, political, geographic, and judicial barriers" for the first time in the EZLN's nearly three-year public history.

NUNCA MAS UN MEXICO SIN NOSOTROS

Comandante Ramona touched down in Tenochtitlán on the final day of the National Indigenous Congress. Thousands went out to the airport to welcome her. At the medical center where the congress was coming to a close, mounted police and a bevy of nurses anticipated her arrival. Activists linked arms and formed a peace line to protect the tiny comandante. Roars of *"¡Ramona Salió y Zedillo Se Chingó!"* (Ramona Got Out and Zedillo Got Screwed!) and "Comandante Ramona! You are a *Chingona!*" filled the October night.

Inside the auditorium, there were Aztec dancers and clouds of copal. Purépecha, Nahua, Nnanhu, Totonaco, and Mixteco elders helped her to the stage, where she was nearly drowned in flowers. As she had years before in the Cathedral of Peace, Ramona extracted a folded flag from her pouch and presented it to the congress. "We must never forget that we are a part of Mexico," she said in a small, bird-like voice. "¡Nunca Más un México Sin Nosotros!" the congresistas roared back in unison.

Wrapping themselves in the Mexican flag was a way of underscoring that the autonomy that the EZLN—and the CNI—demanded, was a profoundly nationalist one.

On October 12th, 50,000 marchers streamed up Reforma, hurling epithets at the statue of Columbus adjacent to the Fiesta Americana hotel. Under an unrelenting Zócalo sun, the exhausted comandante read the words of the Zapatistas in halting Spanish. Here at the heart of the nation, "we are one small heart beating among many hearts." "I am only the first Zapatista to pass through here and all the places of Mexico…"

"Vaaaaaamos, vaaaaaaamos adelanteeeee!" the Zócalo sang back, the Zapatista hymn welling into the contaminated heavens. Just as they had promised back in January 1994, the Zapatista Army of National Liberation, in the fragile form of this lacerated Indian woman, had taken Mexico City.

Ramona was whisked off even before the last strains of the rebel anthem had died. Protected by students, she would rest at the university for a week and then move to the nuns of San José while the FZLN shook cans in the street to raise enough pesos to buy her a new kidney.

The founding of the National Indigenous Congress, the occasion for Ramona's visit, had promised a new dynamic in the Indian resistance movement. 600 delegates from 30 Indian peoples endorsed a familiar litany: the Indian Rights accords, Indian autonomy, a roll-back to the original Article 27, the dismemberment of the government's National Indigenous Institute—but delegates could not decide if they wanted a new constitution or just to patch up the old one.

The CNI was plagued by such indecision. It could never figure out if it was a national organization or a national network. Indian activists immersed in local struggles could not spare time to build a national movement, and caretakers with little political vision were left in charge. Although the National Indigenous Congress was perhaps the most consequential of the EZLN-inspired mass organizations in 1997 and '98, by 1999 attrition and internal squabbling had diminished it to a sentimental shell.

THE TRIPARTITES

The COCOPA's resolution of the Ramona Dilemma unplugged channels with the EZLN and reopened the possibility of a resumption of the Dialogue, suspended now since August. The legislators' scheme was to reconcile the EZLN's five conditions for getting them back to San Andrés. For the COCOPA, the road back led through San Cristóbal.

What became known as the Tripartite Talks—EZLN, COCOPA, CONAI—began at El Carmen on October 15th. The model had been utilized successfully once before, at the July new rules negotiations, when the government and the rebels were lodged in separate rooms so they wouldn't maul each other, and the Conais and the Cocopos shuttled the documents back and forth between camps. Now "the bureaucrats of war" were even farther off, in Mexico City—the Cocopos would be the carrier pigeons—and without Bernal's on-the-spot petulance, matters moved along on the *via rápida*, or fast track.

The one catch was confidentiality. All talks would be held behind locked doors. Communications between the protagonists would be kept from the press. Such an arrangement was a painful one for the EZLN, which does not like to bite its tongue. Moreover, it opened them to charges of bargaining secretly with the mal gobierno. But the tripartite talks were also an end-run around the detested Bernal, a ploy that so charmed Marcos that he volunteered to lead the rebels' 20-comandante delegation up to San Cristóbal.

Relations within the COCOPA-CONAI-Zapatista triad had permutated over the long months. The COCOPA was now the major mover, the CONAI sitting by like a gun-shy older brother that the government battered without remorse.

In September, Don Samuel had joined with hundreds of other civil organizations to formulate a sort of national CONAI (*Consejo Nacional de Paz*) because peace was "a national issue." The Peace Commission proposed that it intervene in other violent conflicts, such as Guerrero.

Bernal grew apoplectic at this "nationalization" of peace—it was his job, after all, to localize it—and accused Samuel of "provocations" and trying to bolster his standing for the Nobel Prize (another bishop, Carlos Bello of East Timor, took the laurels), even threatening to de-recognize the CONAI. "We're not Bernal's employees," Juan Bañuelos reminded the government negotiator. "The 'n' in CONAI stands for 'national,'" Bishop Tatic added. "Peace is not just a Chiapas issue."

The government pounded back, unsuccessfully trying to persuade the European Union to abandon its funding of Tatic's mediating body.

Meanwhile, the COCOPA had taken charge. An activist caucus of mostly opposition legislators—Heberto Castillo, Juan Guerra, César Chávez from the PRD, José Narro and Oscar González of the PT, plus the PRIista Jaime Martínez Velez and sometimes his party comrade Pablo Salazar and the old PANista Don Luis H. Alvarez—now functioned as the first truly non-partisan commission in Mexican legislative history. The Time of the Cocopos had come.

The first of the five conditions to be reconciled was release of purported Zapatista prisoners and construction of the oversight commission, the COSEVER. The prisoner issue was complicated by the more than 100 EZLN-related campesinos who were now on hunger strike in Cerro Hueco.

On the first day of the tripartite, eight PRD or EZLN prisoners (they were described as both), were released from Chiapas jails, a hopeful gesture. The Cacalomacán eight would gain their freedom during the first week in November, but the Yanga seven had to sit out a second Christmas in jail. They were freed in early January. Zedillo's big lie had cost the prisoners two years of their lives and countless hours of torture.

The shape of the COSEVER had been agreed upon at San Andrés in July—each side would have three representatives, two of whom had to be negotiators, and a joint secretariat would be formulated, with both the government and the rebels permitted five invitees. The Zapatistas invited Adelfo Regino from the CNI, writer Elena Poniatowska, anthropologist Rodolfo Stavenhagen, Archbishop emeritus Bernabé Carrasco of Oaxaca, and Doña Amalia Solórzano, mother of Cuauhtémoc.

The government invited four faceless bureaucrats and Emilio Rabasa, great-grandson of Porfirio Díaz's governor of Chiapas. Both sides deadlocked early on the issue of mobility—would the EZLN reps be allowed to move around the country to "oversee" compliance with the accords?

Finally, on November 7th, the COSEVER was formally installed during a ceremony in a San Cristóbal theater, a Pyrrhic victory if ever there was one—the commission would never have anything to oversee. It was stillborn, Gilberto López y Rivas comments—"no, it was assassinated by the government at birth."

The second tripartite began November 8th and addressed implementation of the Indian Rights accord. Now both the rebels and the government were invited to draw up their versions of what legislation would look like—Chuayffet insisted that the conclusion of the Government Indian forums be "homogenized" into the text. The tripartites became all-day work sessions. At night, there were press conferences that revealed nothing. Petitioners from all over the nation lined up for their minute with Marcos. Inside the white walls of the cold convent, the EZLN dined every night on pizza and the Sup joked about plastic surgery and retirement.

The optimism inside the old nunnery was not matched on the street. In early November, CONPAZ offices were firebombed and the peace group's accountant kidnapped and tortured by unknowns. On November 9th, Laco's state security troopers attacked campesinos who were blocking roads in demand of a better price for the corn they were harvesting. Three Indians were gunned down at Laja Tendida near Venustiano Carranza. The police shot to kill. "Maybe Chiapas is too dangerous for us to hold talks here," considered Comandante David.

On November 15th, the Zapatista delegates returned home, with drafts of the proposed legislation under their arms, to celebrate their 13th anniversary as a fighting force and consider what dirty tricks the future might have planned for them. They would return on the 24th to initiate a new installment of the tripartites.

But while the rebels were in fiesta mode, a tectonic shift was taking place inside the Zedillo brain trust. The consensus on electoral reform that the President so longed for, had fallen apart. Brought to Congress on the strength of a fragile pact between the parties, the PRI legislative majority rebelled at the giveaways Zedillo had offered in order to keep the PAN and the PRD interested in the agreement, and over the next month, ruling party deputies had systematically gutted it.

Now the opposition balked at voting up a reform that barred coalitions, had no provision for independent candidacies or the use of referendum and plebiscite, and, most of all, while it allotted enormous government subsidies to the parties, contained no oversight of PRI private campaign financing. In the end, the opposition—which would benefit considerably by the reforms in both the 1997 midterms and the 2000 presidential race—walked out of the Chamber of Deputies, and the PRI was forced to vote the legislation on its lonesome.

Though far removed from the scene of the crime, the loser in this fracaso was the EZLN. Now that the government no longer needed the opposition to pass electoral reform, it no longer needed to pretend that it supported the Indian Rights accord just to keep the PRD in the consensus. The key question now for Zedillo, Chuayffet, Bernal, and associates was how to worm out of their commitment to bring the Indian Rights accord to Congress.

SI OR NO

The villages of the Cañadas had begun the harvest, and it was abundant. The Sup's star-a-week cavalcade back in the Spring paid off with enough corn to get the ejidos through to the next planting. Full bellies ease tensions, and this moment in November was one of dis-tension—of both bellies and bellicose postures. General Renán Castillo spoke of one day withdrawing his troops and going home.

The 17th of November is usually a tribute to the EZLN fighting force, but the 1996 edition was rigorously unmilitary. Out on the Ejido Morelia, now an autonomous municipality renamed "17th of November," Zapatista hoopsters squared off in a rough-and-tumble basketball tournament, and European volunteers battled local Mayans in an international soccer match.

At the Aguascalientes in La Realidad, couples bounced to the cumbias and youth groups recited choral poetry. Bellinghausen noted star showers.

Marcos and the comandantes were back in business at El Carmen on the 24th. They had brought their final version of the proposed law, which the COCOPA would synthesize with the government's. The final COCOPA draft would then be presented to both parts for a *sí* or *no* response. No changes would be accepted. There would be no further haggling. The COCOPA laid down the law.

The legislators handed copies of the final version to the comandancia in San Cristóbal on November 29th and faxed off a set to Interior Secretary Chuayffet. The Zapatistas responded the next noon. They had reservations—the COCOPA had reduced the number of constitutional articles that needed to be amended—but the rebels would abide by their agreement to vote the version up or down, and they opted for up.

The COCOPA wording affirmed the right of Indian peoples to free determination, defined as "an expression of autonomy within the Mexican state." The document also mandated the "collective" use and enjoyment of natural resources and land. Territory was viewed as "the totality of the habitat of the Indian peoples" (the wording was borrowed from the Organization of International Labor's resolution 169, long since ratified by the Mexican Congress). The COCOPA draft also legislated the association of majority Indian municipalities into autonomous regions and allowed for Indian-owned and -administered communications media. The draft resolution was held close to the vest and not made public until January.

Government response to the COCOPA version was not immediate. Cocopos, Zapatistas, and the press sat around all day December 1st, Marcos playing peso-ante poker with the lawmakers and talking about going up to Mexico City to catch B.B. King. Everyone was waiting for the fax machine to kick in. Ashtrays filled. The legislative clock was running down—only 15 days remained before the end of the regular session of Congress, and a special one would have to be called to deal with the Indian Rights legislation at this late date.

Finally on the 2nd, a passel of Cocopos flew off to Mexico City to pry a response loose from Chuayffet. It was a bad moment—Attorney General Lozano had been fired and the President was winging in from Korea. *"Disculpa"* (beg pardon), offered the cherubic Interior Secretary. Ah yes, the Indian Rights agreement… Well, the government had a few observations, 33 of them in fact.

But the *sí* or *no* stipulation? protested the Cocopos. There must have been a bad understanding there, offered the Interior Secretary, maybe it was the 17 *chinchones* (excellent Spanish anise) that he had downed with dinner.

Back at El Carmen, Chuayffet's 33 "observations" did not play very well at all. The EZ went into deep caucus. Marcos did not want the whole comandancia rat-trapped in San Cristóbal if the shit started to fly again and sent 13 of the delegates home to reinforce the Zapatistas' positions in the mountains. Military aircraft buzzed El Carmen on the 6th and copters flashed over La Realidad and "17th of November." Luis H. Alvarez phoned from Mexico City urging the remaining comandantes to keep cool. We're cool, Marcos assured him, in fact, "we're bored…we've been bombed before…"

Later that afternoon (Dec. 6th), the lawmakers wrangled an emergency meeting at Los Pinos. According to one insider, the President already had his rejection written out but was convinced to consult one more time with constitutional experts. The COCOPA delivered another "confidential" message to Marcos on the 8th at El Carmen.

Zedillo's latest letter (which was immediately made public by the EZLN) pleaded for 15 days' time to consult his constitutionalists. He pledged careful consideration and no military activity while he did so.

After 22 months of negotiating an agreement his own representatives had long ago signed, the President wanted two weeks more to make up his mind about honoring it. Marcos warned that the EZLN would never re-open the negotiations or accept a Zedillo counterproposal. Debate on the legislation had ended. The ball was in the President's court now. The comandantes would go home to await his response.

The days were growing short and the nights cold. The holiday posadas were upon the land again. The government shut down for official business and would not re-open until January, but the Cocopos promised to stand holiday vigil. If anything happened, they would let the comandantes know.

HAVE A VERY RACIST CHRISTMAS!

During the 15 days the President was consulting with his constitutionalists, a number of prominent opinion makers, some of them the very constitutionalists with whom Zedillo was consulting, publicly assailed the Indian Rights accords in a suspiciously orchestrated campaign that reeked of racism. Constitutionalists like old Ignacio Burgoa, retrograde dean of the UNAM law school, labeled the San Andrés agreements "a dagger thrust to the magna carta," claiming that the accords created special laws for Indians. As had become standard operating procedure, Burgoa invoked the phantoms of balkanization and secession.

Indian justice was painted as being exclusionary and violative of human rights. The PRI's star intellecutal, Hector Camín, likened the proposed autonomías to North American Indian reservations and called the COCOPA legislation "demagogic and irresponsible." The EZLN and the COCOPA were trying to "legislate discrimination." Historian Enrique Krauze echoed the white rights commotion: "Who will protect the rights of the majority?" "This is not law, its anthropology," sniffed José Luis Soberanes, Zedillo's key constitutionalist.

Luis Pazos, Financiero columnist and darling of the crazy Right, exhorted Zedillo not to sign any pact with "Marxists pretending to be Indians who wear socks on their heads." TV Azteca pundit Sergio Sarmiento attacked the Zapatistas as bloody "Stalinists" because they wanted to "collectivize" the land, a process that had led to "30 million deaths" in the Soviet Union. The crusty Burgoa went one better: "uses and customs" would give Indians license to practice "human sacrifice," much as had their ancestors.

The fact that most of this racist woofing was emanating from Zedillo's trusted constitutional scholars did not breed glowing optimism about his response.

The COCOPA paid a surprise visit to La Realidad December 19th. The legislators brought with them Zedillo's "confidential" riposte. The interchange was entirely hush-hush. The EZLN would analyze the contents, consult with their advisors, and present its conclusions at the next scheduled tripartite, January 11th, 22 days hence. Christmas would be fraught with nagging suspense. Now the the bird was back in the Zapatistas' yard.

On December 29th, Ernesto Zedillo flew to Guatemala to witness the signing of the peace treaty between that government and its Mayan Indian guerrilla, the URNG—some of which had been negotiated in Mexico City. "Dialogue, not arms, must prevail," Zedillo advised. Just across the border, his own Mayan Indian guerrilla was putting his words to the test.

LA HORA FINAL

At dawn on the first day of 1997, across the jungle near Naja, the spiritual leader of the Lacandón people, Chan K'in Viejo, passed over to the other side. He was a century old and his scrawny little body was laid out in his favorite hammock and buried in the forest the next morning with his head facing east so that he would always accompany the rising sun.

The third anniversary of the rebellion was low-key. The Tojolabales of La Realidad acted out an almost real-time recreation of the New Year's 1994 taking of Las Margaritas and the kidnapping of General Absalón, a high point in La Realidad community history. The rebels carried wooden rifles and yelled "*¡Puta madre!*" a lot when imitating the soldiers and the police.

This year Marcos stayed up in the mountain and there was no new declaration of the Lacandón jungle. The CCRI's message was one of deep uncertainty: "Whether this year will be one of war or one of peace depends upon how the supreme power reads history…"

The clock was clicking towards the final hour. Some seers guessed that the EZLN's response to the President's response would be like Zedillo's—neither a yes nor a no. Under this schema, long-distance negotiations could continue, but the rebels would not return to San Andrés any time soon. On the other hand, if the rebels rejected the President's re-write out of hand, the COCOPA would be faced with the decision of taking its original legislation to Congress without Zedillo's endorsement, a suicide gesture, particularly so because constitutional amendment requires a two-thirds majority. Heberto Castillo, a career atheist, practically prayed that the EZLN would yield enough to accept Zedillo's modifications as a basis for further negotiations.

On January 8th, a delegation of advisors and CNI leaders, including Adelfo Regino and Luis Hernández, quietly slipped into La Realidad to work out the details of the Zapatista response. After nearly two years of compromising, the comandantes and those who advised them were not going to bend much further. The EZLN appeared adamant that the agreement not be re-opened for "adjustments." Luis Hernández had a hunch that the dialogue cycle had come to a dead end.

The Cocopos and the Conais came down to La Realidad on the 11th for the verdict. As Marcos rode in from the mountain, the notables joked nervously with the photographers. Years on this beat had drawn the press and the interlocutors close together—few on the outside spoke the same language or could follow the arcane twists and turns the Dialogue had taken since San Miguel. For the Cocopos, especially, San Andrés had become a full-time obsession—although many members would be leaving Congress after the July elections.

For all the players in this grueling drama—the COCOPA, Don Samuel, the EZLN, the villages, civil society, the mal gobierno—this promised to be a day of definition.

The Subcomandante presented two documents, both detailed rejections of Ernesto Zedillo's "counterproposal," which was "a joke on the Indians and a joke on the COCOPA…a grave negation of what had been agreed upon…every Indian right has been subjugated to local law…the only autonomy agreed upon is what we have already…the Nahuas, whose territory covers six states, would be reduced to a single municipality" under the President's parameters. The Zedillo document canceled association of majority Indian municipalities and eliminated the "collective" use of the land and natural resources. "This document is a moral,

historical, and judicial aberration...Zedillo's will for war has been made clear..."
Marcos grimly challenged the COCOPA to "honor and defend" its project.

After 22 months, the time of the word had at last run out. The dazed Cocopos
and the Conais walked woodenly back to the Suburbans, and Subcomandante
Marcos climbed up on his patient mount Lucerito and rode slowly off to the silent
mountains, half waiting for the sky to cave in upon him.

WINTER–SPRING 1997

AN INDIAN WEAPON

Silence fell upon the Zapatista inner circle like a curtain crashing down at intermission. The actors retired to their dressing rooms and were barely heard from for months. Between January and July 1997, only seven communiqués signed by either Subcomandante Marcos or the CCRI, one every 27 days, radiated from the jungles of Chiapas. And three of these were directed to the European solidarity movement, incisive x-rays of the neo-liberal project at work that contained little mention of the Mexican reality.

During the weeks and months of silence, military pressures would escalate to the stage where villagers were packed for escape to the mountains, yet the CCRI issued no urgent warnings to the Republic. Bill Clinton came and went to a Mexico City under U.S. military control for the first time since 1848 (Mexico ceded security precautions to Washington) with nary a peep from the Sup. Marcos was unavailable for interviews all Winter and Spring. No one in La Realidad had seen him for months. Rumors flew that he had flown the coop, was plying the canals of Venice and the cafés of Paris, and that the rebellion was through.

What little Zapatista news appeared in the media was all nostalgia, looking back upon the rebels' glory days. Le Bot's book came out and it was all old news. Outside of the conflict zone, supporters scratched their heads and wondered what to do next. Even Elorriaga was confused.

As a communications strategy, the EZLN's reticence stunk. The Zapatistas' visibility dried up and the civil society forgot about them as coming midterm elections dominated public debate. Some saw the shut-down as an under-the-table arrangement with Cuauhtémoc Cárdenas not to raise the rebel voice during the critical July elections and stimulate the "vote of fear" (see Summer 1994). Others, like Le Bot, saw the moment as one of reflection and maturation. Whichever, and it was probably a little bit of both, at a moment of national decision, the rebels were isolated on the fringe. They would never recover the momentum lost in this time of silence and blood.

"Silence is an Indian weapon," Marcos explained many months later. Indigenous people often clam up when confronted by outside authority. The stone faces keep the government guessing about what they are really thinking. Silence served the EZLN well for 10 years in the mountain. Now, more than the ski masks, the paliacates, their few arms, and their many words, their silence would speak for them again.

In its inimitably contrary fashion, the EZLN initiated this extended silence with a torrent of words. "Seven Questions About Neo-liberalism," a novella-sized epistle issued by Marcos January 24th "to whom it may concern," is larded with excerpts from Quijote and offers a panoramic vision of the nation in the first days of the new year: *niños de la calle* (street kids) living in the Mexico City sewers, garbage workers from Tabasco in the hundredth day of a hunger strike to the death on the doorstep of the National Human Rights Commission, Zedillo paying the gringos back 6 billion bucks on the Clinton bailout to sustain the lie that Mexico was in full recovery.

On the first anniversary of the San Andrés accords, February 16th, the Sup proffered a new Old Antonio tale that partially revealed where the Zapatistas were coming from now. The Story of the Noise and the Silence finds the first gods, the ones who birthed the earth, on the road again. They are surrounded by noise that they think is music but is not, and, because the first gods could only travel by dancing, they were stuck. But because they were gods, they were also wise, and they divided up and began to search for some silence. They looked everywhere and could find nothing until they looked in the last place, inside themselves. And only when they had found that inner silence did they regain the road. "Health, and may the noise help you to find the silence and the silence help you to find the road and the road help you to find us." Signed, the Sup.

But the sound of silence was meant exclusively for outside consumption. Behind the scenes (so to speak), the Zapatistas were talking and taking decisions amongst themselves. They had wasted too many words upon a government that would never keep its own word to make San Andrés the law of the land. Now the EZLN would quietly begin to implement the accords from the bottom up by consolidating and strengthening the autonomous structures in the jungle and the highlands.

THE REVOLT OF THE RATE PAYERS

While the CCRI was keeping its own counsel, the bases were busy as bees. Way back in 1994, during Robledo's brief regency, Amado Avendaño's alternative state assembly, the AEDPCH, had called for a rate-payers' strike against the Federal Electricity Commission (CFE) to pressure the PRI government into giving up the statehouse. The strike had sputtered along from month to month and year to year, energized by the soaring rates (150 pesos for a single 60-watt light bulb). The mood of the rate payers was not much improved by the fact that Chiapas accounts for half the nation's hydroelectricity supply. Preferential rates of a flat 10 pesos a month were demanded.

By 1997, according to CFE Chiapas chieftain Rey David Jiménez, 30% of the state was not paying its bills, and the commission threatened to cut the juice to some 70,000 deadbeats in 60 municipalities around the state. Such social flash-points as Simojovel and El Bosque were on the list.

It did not take long for the fireworks to blow up. In January, in Ixtapa, near Tuxtla, eight CFE workers were taken hostage when they tried to turn off the lights. Three others were wounded up in the northeastern corner of the state at Pueblo Nuevo Solistahuacán. When workers ventured into the marketplace of San Cristóbal in February and begin snipping wires, they were mauled by a mob of Tzotzil women. Out in La Independencia, *colonos* blocked the road to keep the cops out and hooked the municipality's lights back up. On the 21st on the coast, 20,000 residents of Tonalá stoned a dozen CFE employees and ran them out of town.

Because going into the communities to cut off the juice had gotten so dangerous, the CFE began shutting down regional substations, blacking out vast areas of the state and drastically increasing local irritation. Rural industry blinked and shut down. Clinics and hospitals went dark. Without refrigeration, restaurants shuttered, and there wasn't a cold beer in most of Chiapas. The tortilla mills did not even bother to open.

Although the rate-payers' strike had been carried out by PRD and Zapatista colonies, the blanket blackouts cut off PRIistas who had faithfully paid their electric bills for years. By mid-February, the state's key tourist corridors between San Cristóbal and the ruins at Palenque were being blocked daily. On February 18th, Laco's storm troopers collared 62 Indians and carted them off to Cerro Hueco. The blockades had united 28 ejidos in the region, some of them Zapatista-PRD enclaves, others firmly in the PRI trenches. The CFE had accomplished what not even the EZLN had been able to do: it had united all the political factions against the mal gobierno.

SPRING PLANTING

The great finiquito fiasco of '96 had left a lot of unfinished business, and the fourth agricultural cycle of the rebellion generated fresh invasions, incarcerations, and body counts.

For the EZLN, the 1997 planting season was fraught with the usual anguish. Military patrols were everywhere up and down the canyons, holding back the roza y quema. This year, with Marcos not receiving guests, the stars of stage, screen, and international politics stayed away in droves. Only the Indigo Girls (feminist folk rock) played the Aguascalientes at La Realidad (March 1st).

Solidarity caravans from the big cities trucked in the corn, but all over the conflict zone, there was never enough to meet the demand.

Chol villagers out in the mosquito-ridden scrublands that had once been the jungle east of Palenque occupied two sites owned by a local beer distributor. Although they were of little agricultural use to anyone, state troopers charged onto the plots March 7th, forcibly evicting the campesinos and setting fire to their hovels (the police claim that the Indians burnt their own homes down). Later, while they were breakfasting at the recovered sites, incoming sniper fire cut down two of the cops. A police dragnet snatched up dozens of suspects in surrounding communities.

Three days later, Father Jerónimo Hernández, Padre Xjel to his Tzeltal and Chol constituents, and young aide-de-camp Gonzalo Rojas pulled up before the downtown Palenque church where Xjel officiated and were pounced upon by state security agents. The priests and two Xi'Nich directors who accompanied them were charged with the cop killings.

Jerónimo Hernández is admired and despised in Palenque for his work with the Xi'Nich—in 1991, he led the "Ants" on a 1,200-kilometer hike up to Mexico City to denounce local caciques. During the first minutes of the war, Televisa fingered the Jesuit as Subcomandante Marcos; later, Xjel was named an EZLN advisor during the Indian Rights talks. Now the agitators were hogtied and blindfolded, taken down to Tuxtla, beaten, and held incommunicado for 20 hours.

The plot, as advanced by Jorge Enrique Hernández and Eraclio Zepeda, had some serious holes in it. Xjel and his aide had ironclad alibis—on the day of the killings, they had been at a diocesan meeting in San Cristóbal attended by virtually every cleric in the region. "I'm going to nominate Jerónimo and Gonzalo for canonization," Raúl Vera cracked to the New York Times. "They must be saints if they can be in two places at once…"

The state's case rested upon the "discovery" of a Star .38 pistol (serial # 5735977) in Xjel's pack. The padre had never seen the gun before. But others had. 11 years previous, this same Star .38 (serial #5735977) had been used by General Absalón Castellanos Domínguez to send seven Chiapas corn farmer leaders to Cerro Hueco. Among the seven was a then-newspaperman named Jorge Enrique Hernández.

The Padre Xjel frame-up tested the depths of Eraclio's depravity, and he would turn in his badge two weeks later. During 28 months as government secretary, Zepeda had presided over 56 police actions that had resulted in 111 deaths. Zepeda was subsequently appointed the PRI government's ambassador to UNESCO.

The arrest of Xjel was the most bruising body blow to Don Samuel's diocese since the 1995 deportations of the three priests (which had similarly occurred while Tatic was out of the country). In protest, the faithful pounded the pavement in Yajalón, where the memory of the forced removal of their priest, Loren

Reibe, was still fresh. Every other parish in the diocese held similar processions. Mass was said for the jailed padres in the Basilica of Guadalupe. Despite their differences, both the Mexican Bishops Conference and the Vatican expressed their displeasure at the dour turn of events. On the secular side, 10,000 students surrounded the UNAM rectory while a recovering Ramona demanded Xjel's release.

On March 11th, Jorge Enrique, insisting the two were only being held for "investigation," finally heard the prayers of the faithful and released the padres "under caution."

NICHTALACUM

On the same afternoon as Padre Xjel's release, far away in the Altos, in what the government calls the constitutional municipality of El Bosque and the Zapatistas the autonomous one of San Juan de la Libertad, down near the bottom of a rocky ravine in a dirt-poor cluster of huts known as San Pedro Nichtalacum, the caca was flying.

With the area already riven by PRI–Zapatista/PRD and religious rivalries, collision became unstoppable after two PRI cops were caught peeping at the Presbyterian pastor's wife as she bathed in a muddy mountain stream. When the Zapatista/PRDs retaliated by taking over what passed for the town's offices, shots were fired and six hostages taken. An exchange of prisoners was in the works when several hundred state security officers from the nearby county seat poured into the community, thoroughly drubbing the Zapatistas and hauling off four prisoners.

Minutes later, machete-wielding Zapatistas halted the cops' advance as they drove uphill out of town. Suddenly, a state police helicopter gunship roared in over the ridge and directed itself to the confrontation, unloading round after round on the helpless Tzotziles, killing six. The bullet-riddled pick-up was exhibit A in this latest travesty of justice. On board the death helicopter was, yes, you guessed it, state attorney general Jorge Enrique Hernández.

28 villagers were arrested and hundreds more driven into the nearby forests. Despite the fact that they had been attacked by the police helicopter, 13 Tzoztiles were charged with killing their own comrades. Pedro González González was accused of killing his brother (his son also died in the police attack).

Far from the public glare, the massacre at Nichtalacum took a while to sink into public consciousness. Towards the end of March, an independent team of human rights observers descended into the ravine and found Nichtalacum occupied by police and army troops. All the Zapatista/PRD homes had been sacked and defaced. A stench of rot clung to the hillside. The villagers were still missing.

When the refugees tried to return in early May, they were sent away by the police and the military. Weeks later, summoning Zapatista bases from Simojovel,

Chenalhó, Pantelhó, and San Andrés Sakamchién de los Pobres, 4,000 Tzoztiles accompanied the families to Nichtalacum, and they were allowed to stay. The police helicopters that had accompanied their march home hovered overhead, and Comandante Ramón had a hard time being heard. "Here is your land. This is where you were born. This is where you have to be," he told the weary villagers. "Don't ever ask anyone's pardon to stay here."

DEAD AS A DOORNAIL

The Dialogue was dead as a doornail, had been so ever since the silent Subcomandante rode off into the mountain without ever looking back. At first the government oozed confidence that the rebels would soon come in from the cold, but as the days and weeks ticked by without a word from the CCRI, hope biodegraded into consternation.

In the first two weeks of March, 15 Chiapanecos were slaughtered and 20 wounded (including 11 police) in ongoing agrarian disputes. Although the killings did not much differ from the customary Spring ritual of occupation and repression, 1997 was sort of uncharted territory. There was no dialogue between the forces in the field, no way to hold back the parties in the conflict. Now the restraints were out the window and the demons of war had been unleashed.

With the Zapatistas silenced and the CONAI marginalized, the COCOPA was of little use. As the July elections hovered on the horizon, the legislative commission which, in its best days, had achieved non-partisan unity, split apart along party lines.

In bidding adieu on January 11th, the comandantes had urged the Cocopos to defend their proposal with honor and bring it to the Congress to stand or fall on its own merits—if it went down to flaming defeat, as seemed likely, the rejection would show the whole world just how stacked the cards were against the Indians of Mexico. But the COCOPA didn't move a muscle for weeks. Meanwhile, Zedillo was circling the nation like a turkey buzzard picking at the bones of the COCOPA proposal. The lawmakers had written the law badly; their version was not a faithful interpretation of the accords at all, but rather one ghosted by radical EZLN advisors who did not have the Indians' well-being at heart. Zedillo did. "We won't permit this kind of discrimination and exclusion," Zedillo ranted to stone-faced Nahuas in San Luis Potosí. "The Indian communities do not want a legal reform that returns them to a past of exclusion or leads them to a future of paternalism and passivity," the President said to an impassive Indian audience in Hidalgo.

PRIistas in Congress roasted the COCOPA for overstepping its mandate, and Bernal berated the legislators for conniving with the rebels. Despite this alleged collusion, the Zapatistas refused to even communicate with their former interlocutors, even when convened by the Cocopos to an emergency meeting.

Finally, on March 4th, the badly wounded commission issued a new call for dialogue, publicly conceding that the language of their legislative proposal could be "perfected" (*perfeccionado*), a buzzword that in the Zapatista lexicon translated to "renegotiated." In private, the lawmakers considered that the *sí* or *no* option had been a big mistake.

The backtracking was immediately chastised as "an act of capitulation" (Gilberto López y Rivas). The National Indigenous Congress concluded that the COCOPA had destroyed its own proposal.

In only his fourth communiqué since January, a livid Marcos put the sealing wax on the COCOPA's death warrant. Rather than rescuing the Dialogue, "you have put us in danger of the final rupture: war…" The legislators' betrayal had made the EZLN vulnerable to military attack in the driest months of the year, a season when the troops had maximum mobility. "Understand that we have nothing to lose," the Sup spat at the lawmakers. No one had even seen a Zapatista for 60 days.

The COCOPA's cave-in landed the legislators in the enemy camp. Now when marchers took to the streets, be it 10,000 teachers in Tuxtla or protesters in 30 U.S. cities, they blamed the COCOPA as much as they did Zedillo for failing to come through with what had been agreed upon up at San Andrés. But not all the Cocopos were equally culpable. Heberto Castillo, who had wasted much of his fading breath on the Dialogue over the past 24 months, made it clear which side he was on: "We were witnesses to the signing of the accords, we gave our word," he told his fellow commissioners. "If there are some here who want to renegotiate them, they can do so, but at the cost of their own honor."

When, on April 7th, Heberto Castillo succumbed to his damaged heart, the COCOPA died with him. The stoop-shouldered, pale-faced old "Flaco" had been the bellwether of the commission, renouncing and returning to it as if tied to the idea of peace with justice in Chiapas by a bungee cord. Now his death became a metaphor for the demise of the Dialogue.

The funeral parlor in Mexico City was stuffy with memorial wreaths and memories. In one corner, Cuauhtémoc Cárdenas recalled the long years between the two old warriors—during the 1968 student strike, Cuauhtémoc's father had hidden Heberto from the police. Across the room, a handful of Indians brought red roses, a branch of wheat, a Zapatista doll, and a banner that read "Thank You for Your Example." It was whispered that they were emissaries of the Zapatistas, but the comandantes never sent formal condolences or even acknowledged Heberto's passing.

A communiqué April 10th, on the occasion of the 78th commemoration of the murder and resurrection of Votan-Zapata, made no mention of the old man. "*Aquí estamos,*" the letter repeated over and over again, here we are and here we will be, and mourned instead "all those years, all those seasons, all those deaths" the first Zapatistas had endured. "But you didn't die," Marcos wrote the old Liberator of the South: "You became us…"

The COCOPA twitched on for some months more after Heberto's departure, but its time was over. July 6th federal elections would mean a retrofitted commission in the next Congress.

With midterm elections brewing, the government, too, bailed out of the canoe. Bernal was sent home to Tamaulipas to train for a senate seat. On April 26th, Zedillo named a caretaker chief of the government delegation, Pedro Joaquín Coldwell, a former governor of Quintana Roo, who had been a subsecretary of Tourism and one of the innovators of the failed tourist sham "Mundo Maya," which was supposed to increase the flow of visitors' dollars to indigenous communities. Like San Andrés, Mundo Maya never came through. The new commissioner promised fresh proposals after he had time "to soak up the theme." In nine months in the slot, the Mundo Maya man would never ever meet a single member of the EZLN.

The dialogue was as dead as, well, the late Heberto Castillo.

BUILDING AUTONOMY

"The autonomous municipalities are where the real work of resistance takes place," Hermann Bellinghausen notes, a kind of low-intensity democracy in the midst of a low-intensity war. Although 38 autonomías had been proclaimed during the December 1995 break-out, the 32 that had survived differed widely in their levels of realization. Some had authorities, some not yet, some existed only on paper, and some, like Tierra y Libertad, whose municipal seat of Amparo Agua Tinta hugs the Guatemalan border, and Sakamchién de los Pobres in the highlands, were becoming viable realities.

In general, autonomy was more formal in Los Altos, where the autonomías were being built in the shells of constitutional municipalities with already defined boundaries, such as at San Andrés or El Bosque–San Juan de la Libertad. They were also the most conflictive, pitting parallel authorities against each other in communities like Sakamchién, Chenalhó, and Pantelhó, where the PRI had ruled since the advent of time.

In the jungle, the autonomías were carved out of enormous existing municipalities like Ocosingo and Las Margaritas, grouping together communities that were sometimes days away from the county seats. Generations of surviving in the deepest crannies of the jungle had already granted these communities de facto autonomy.

Delegated the job of co-opting and "Chiapanizing" the San Andrés accords, the state would legislate Indian uses and customs laws, invent an Indian justice system, and remunicipalize majority Indian sections to give the (PRI) indígenas greater voice in government. A state commission was constituted to consult with communities that were to be remunicipalized and come up with a consensus on the redistribution of political representation. But the EZLN refused to come in from the mountain until the Indian Rights accord had first been translated into federal law, and the rebels were no-shows at preliminary commission sessions. The PRI-controlled state legislature voted to go ahead with the consultations whether the EZLN liked it or not. They had had their opportunity to speak out.

One of the first consultations was set for a distant Margaritas outpost, Maravilla Tenajapa, but when 1,600 fuming Zapatistas appeared out of nowhere and took over the meeting, the PRI deputies dashed for their helicopter. To the east, at Damasco, an ejido endowed like so many others with a New Testament name, hundreds of EZLN backers crowded onto the rural runway, so that the deputies' helicopter could not even touch down.

On April 19th, the remunicipalization commission tried to hold a session in the PRIista community of El Edén, just off the Margaritas–La Realidad road near Nuevo Momón. On the Zapatista map, PRI-controlled or not, El Edén is part of the autonomous municipality of San Pedro de Michoacán, and the meeting had just gotten under way when hundreds of ski-masked autónomos from new Guadalupe Tepeyac, San José del Rio, and La Realidad, the San Pedro municipal seat, stomped in chanting ditties like *El fusil está guardado pero nunca abandonado*" ("The rifle is put away but never abandoned"). The PRI Indians jumped to their feet and cussed out the *pinche indios* of the EZLN. "The only reason you get everything you want from the government is because of our rebellion," a comandante preached from the seized stage. Chairs splintered. Blunt objects took wing. Once again, the frustrated deputies fled for the helicopter.

During the Spring of 1997, the EZLN autonomías selected their new authorities in communal assemblies by uses and customs consensus. Despite the multiple conflicts between the communities and the PRI government and the latent threat of violence in Las Cañadas and Los Altos, where military and paramilitary harassment was permanent, Bellinghausen, who was invited to witness the installation of new authorities in Tierra y Libertad and San Pedro de Michoacán, caught a whiff of intense animation in the Zapatista villages: "There is a state of excitement that I've never known before. The tension, the risks, the indignation seem to have strengthened their resolve to persist."

Both autonomías have functioning health and education commissions and rudimentary justice systems to resolve civil disputes (even in non-Zapatista communities), keep alcohol and marijuana out of the region, and lock up wife-beaters and drunks.

San Pedro de Michoacán, the most visited and visible of the EZLN municipalities, celebrated the renewal of its authorities May 18th at the Aguascalientes in La Realidad in a ceremony that exuded humility. "If we failed in our administration it is because we did not have enough capacity, but we were always willing to work," considered "Rubén," the outgoing headman, to his constituents. "We're just learning how not to commit *pendejadas* (stupidities)," "Manuel," another member of the old authority, told Bellinghausen. "Francisco," the new town official, was equally low-key: "We'll do our best, and let's see what happens..." The style was distinct from the obligatory bombast of Mexican politics.

"Rubén" presented "Francisco" with an inventory of San Pedro de Michoacán's assets: 21,000 pesos (about $2,000 USD), six houses, two jails with chains, 12 chairs, 10 wooden benches, two typewriters, three cots, two reams of white paper, plus numerous seals and cooking pots, and, of course, the community's Mexican flag.

The guest of honor, Mayor Moisés, delivered a brief keynote address: "It has been four years now that we have not let the government of the rich govern us. Now it is you who name your own authorities, the ones who will mandar obedeciendo—to our brothers and sisters who are not affiliated with the Zapatista Army of National Liberation, we ask you to stop believing that the government is going to do everything for you—it has not bettered your life in 504 years, has it? We ask you to join with us, because organizing small is a big job, but if we do our work right, one day all of Mexico will have an authority that governs by obeying the will of the people..."

As night fell and the big jungle moon ballooned over the clearing, "Rubén" performed his last official act, summoning the village to the baile.

HOT SPOTS

Autonomous and PRI municipalities faced off against each other with little give and take on either side in El Bosque–San Juan de Libertad and San Andrés Larráinzar–Sakamchíen de los Pobres and a dozen other hot spots in Los Altos. At Pantelhó, the autónomos were twice burnt out of their communities, in January and again in May when the Zapatista bases refused to work on a road being reconstructed by the PRI authorities.

Next door in Chenalhó, a murky May 24th gun battle near the hamlet of Yaxhemil left one Zapatista missing (the whereabouts of his body caused problems for months) and provoked the "Abejas" (The Bees)—the coffee- and honey-producing civil society that was aligned more with Don Samuel and the local priest Michel Chanteau than with the EZLN—to flee their homes. Some resettled at the autonomía of Polhó, where hundreds of displaced villagers were already gathering, or at nearby Acteal, where they found sanctuary on a muddy hillside.

Despite the government's persistent denials, up in the highlands, down in the jungle, and in the north of the state, Chiapas was bristling with paramilitaries. As the autonomías grew in authority, so did the paramilitary structures. Recruiting from a ready pool of unemployed, disenchanted young men, the shadowy squadrons were encouraged to accumulate arms, and military trainers were assigned to show the recruits how to use them.

In the north, Peace & Justice was feuding over government monies, and the skirmishing made the paramilitaries that much more unpredictable and dangerous.

Closer to Ocosingo, in Chilón and Bachejón, the paramilitary Chinchulines were reorganizing, and new house-burnings were recorded. In the Cañadas, the ejido of Tomás Mauser, a colony composed of ex-cops and PRI-affiliated bilingual teachers, was said to be armed to the teeth. The MIRA ("The Indigenous Revolutionary Anti-Zapatista Movement") patrolled the Taniperlas and Las Tazas cañadas, reportedly with the protection of soon-to-be PRI deputy Norberto Santiz.

There were others in the field. The *Degollados* ("throat-slashers") were reported at work in Venustiano Carranza, and pintas had appeared near Oventic advertising the existence of *Máscara Roja* ("Red Mask") in San Andrés and Chenalhó.

According to the Mexican Defense Secretary's "Manual of Irregular War," a knock-off of a more ample Pentagon volume, paramilitaries do the dirty work for the military, fight the *guerra sucia* (dirty war), sow terror in the civilian support communities, disappear witnesses, and make the Army look good.

But in Spring 1997, their activities were still muffled. Young men gathered each night down in Santa Marta, below Chenalhó, to smoke marijuana and watch pornographic movies with the soldiers, their wives and girlfriends complained to Bellinghausen. And in June, La Jornada's Elio Henriques reported a chilling taste of what was to come: after PRI toughs had roughed up Zapatista supporters in a row over electricity bills, municipal president Jacinto Arias was so gratified that he offered the boys beer all around. "Now we have to prepare ourselves for further action," he instructed the young men. "First let's put all our guns together and count how many weapons we have..."

SUMMER–AUTUMN 1997

DEMOCRACY'S FIESTA

Long after midnight, the Zócalo could not contain the jubilation of the tens of thousands of cheering chilangos who had descended spontaneously upon the great plaza to celebrate the victory of Cuauhtémoc Cárdenas as the first-ever elected mayor of Mexico City. Nine years previous on another July 6th, Cárdenas had won and lost the presidency of Mexico (he carried the capital by almost the same margin in '88), but this time his landslide 2-1 victory over the PRI and the PAN would be allowed to stand. Having swept both the local legislative assembly and 29 out of the city's 30 federal congressional districts, the PRD appeared to be in the driver's seat for the year 2000 presidential elections. Where it would drive the car was another story.

Although Cárdenas dedicated the victory to Heberto Castillo, the lopsided triumph must be credited to three other unlikely protagonists. Ernesto Zedillo's truncated electoral reforms, which Cuauhtémoc's own party had walked out on in December '96, had provided for the first election of what used to be an appointed "regent" of the federal district of Mexico City—behind Zedillo and the Interior Secretary, the third most significant political position in the land. The president's economic bellyflop had also pretty much assured that Cárdenas would get the slot.

Ironically, Carlos Salinas boosted Cárdenas to victory too. Cuauhtémoc's public refusal to even meet with the now-loathed Salinas burnished the new mayor's public image of incorruptibility (although, as it turned out, the two had met). Subcomandante Marcos also added his *granito de arena* (grain of sand) by keeping his lips locked tight as the fiesta unfolded.

"¡Cuauhtémoc! ¡Cuauhtémoc!" the mob yowled, the measured cadences of the name that had become a permanent fixture of electoral Mexico ricocheting off the Zócalo walls. "The city is ours!" the masses screamed at the darkened city buildings Cárdenas would soon inherit. One survivor circled the plaza reading out loud the names of the more than 500 PRDs slain since Cárdenas had first begun his crusade 10 years back. There were no ski masks in sight.

From a more global vista, the 1997 midterm turnaround was one tremor in a slight worldwide wobble to the left of center that saw socialist and labor governments elected in France and Great Britain and the victory of the former Farabundo Martí Liberation Front in 14 Salvadoran cities. But in a Mexico eternally ruled by the Institutional Party, this ever-so-slight shift leftward meant a momentous fiesta of democracy.

In addition to dropping the capital, the PRI lost control of the lower house of Congress for the first time in its seven-decade dossier. Although once the mists had cleared, the still-ruling party remained in possession of 239 seats, the PRI lost its absolute majority in the 500-seat house to the combined totals of the opposition PRD, PAN, PT, and the "Mexican Green Ecology Party" (PVEM). For the first time in three millennia, the Tlatuoani or Supreme Chief of the Mexican peoples would have to govern with an opposition Congress. That is, if the opposition could stop quarreling and get its act together.

To the PRI, the concept of an opposition Congress was an absurd one. The PRI was Mexico, always had been and always would be. Now, as the scattered opposition began to find common ground and even started calling itself a "bloc," the anguish of the Institutionals was painfully on display. When, on August 29th, the 261 members of the opposition bloc took over the Chamber of Deputies, installing themselves as the nation's 57th Congress and electing Porfirio Muñoz Ledo as its president, the PRIs condemned the new Congress as "spurious" and "illegitimate" and convoked its own, to be held the following day, a threat that would force constitutional crisis.

Everyone held their breath. Was there a coup d'état in the wings to thwart the seating of an opposition Congress? But Zedillo blinked first, and a deal was cut so that Muñoz Ledo would not swear in the new PRI deputies, a strophe perceived by the ruling party as the ultimate insult to its honor.

On September 1st, the President meekly took the congressional podium to deliver his third Informe. The date may well have marked the death of the Imperial Presidency. Zedillo was stripped of the cadets that had always accompanied a Mexican president to the Congress, and the protocol was revised so that the opposition would respond for the entire legislature. Once he had finished his remarkably abbreviated Informe, the President was forced to endure a lecture from Muñoz Ledo on, of all things, how Zedillo must learn to mandar obedeciendo (as if Porfirio ever had). Curiously, Zedillo's state of the union message never once mentioned the state called Chiapas.

THE AGUAFIESTA

Chiapas was the one spot on the nation's new political map where it had rained heavily (both physically and figuratively) upon Democracy's Fiesta. "Serious irregularities are being reported throughout the state," crackled the radio dial the morning after. Chiapas was also one of the few entities in which the PRI strengthened its chokehold on the populace, sweeping 10 out of 12 congressional districts. Unlike the capital with its eager voters, in some places absenteeism registered 100%. "Its not easy to understand that those who live in Chiapas did not participate in the election with the same enthusiasm as here in Mexico City," the respected analyst Carlos Montemayor marveled.

From January 24th through the first days of July, the Zapatista Army of National Liberation chose to remain in silence about its electoral preferences, although they were not very difficult to decipher. "Why can't they just send a little note, like they used to do back in 1995?" wondered the COCOPA's Oscar González—even the EPR had commented on the coming balloting. But even if the Zapatistas had spoken up early and often, no one really would have been listening. Mexicans could speak of nothing else but what would come down July 6th.

Then, in a communiqué dated July 1st, the day that by law political campaigns had to close down around the country, Subcomandante Marcos shed a ray of light on the Zapatistas' protracted mumness. "In these days, the men and women of the corn kept their silence and worked thinking. We have shut up to look inside ourselves and plant us all over again so that the heart and the word can encounter new places. Others want us to speak. They say to not do so is to cede the space we have won and that the powerful will then talk of our defeat.

"Others asked that we be humble, that we realize that this is the time of the political parties. They ask for humility from the always humble. They ask silence from the always muted...

"The military listened to our silence and thought they had gained the upper hand. The government took advantage of our silence and increased the pressure on our communities. Now we have come to the electoral hour, a time that serves as a thermometer to measure the terminal illness of the state party..."

The Sup offered electoral guidelines: Vote if it is an expression of rebellion. Do not vote if the ballot strengthens authoritarian structures. Actually, most communities had already made up their minds. In June, the autonomía of Sakamchién de los Pobres voted not to vote. Up towards the north of the state, voters in Pichucalco and Nicolás Ruiz notified the state electoral commission not to bother to set up precincts in the district.

Three districts were flashpoints on the Federal Electoral Institute's maps. District I, which extends from Palenque all the way to Salto de Agua in the Grand Guignol north of Chiapas, was a tinderbox of contentiousness. 4,000 refugees would have to fight their way back through Peace & Justice barricades to vote in their home communities, and even PRD candidate Manuel Pérez, a Chol leader regularly threatened with assassination, had asked the IFE to call off the election in the district for fear that people would be shot for casting a ballot in his name.

District III, which takes in Ocosingo, was equally explosive. 23,000 troops were suddenly everywhere in the Cañadas "to protect the electoral process." Most of the soldiers were old enough to vote in the federal election, and to insure a healthy turnout from the PRIs and the military, many of the 280 precincts in the jungle had been conveniently located near military installations, locations that PRD supporters were not likely to approach.

Up in Los Altos, District V was also booby-trapped. In San Juan Chamula, a municipality whose internal logic would require its own book to divine, the opposition had been barred from campaigning, thereby threatening the validity of the district outcome. In nearby Chenalhó and Pantelhó, violence between the political camps was building towards civil war status.

As the election loomed, Ernesto Zedillo winged into the highlands, handing out social development checks to PRI cadre in highland municipalities—like Pantelhó, June 30th, where not a month before, PRI paramilitaries had burnt out 40 Zapatista families.

One week later, on election morning, masked Indians, some purportedly armed, invaded precincts in the three flashpoint districts, dragged out the voting paraphernalia, and burnt it in the public thoroughfare for all to witness. Some polling stations were themselves torched and the election officials run off by rebels wielding big sticks. In Chenalhó, a Molotov cocktail was tossed into an IFE truck. At San Andrés, the PRI reversed the tables and attacked the Zapatista autonomous municipality with lead pipes and guns. Down in the jungle near La Realidad, the rebels blocked the road to El Edén to prevent ballots from being cast, and when they were, burnt the ballot boxes. When asked why, everywhere the rebels had one response: the mal gobierno should fulfill its obligation to the San Andrés accords.

According to state electoral commission stats, 610 precincts in the three districts were not able to receive voters July 6th—over 100 of them had been set afire. In the third district, 34% of the ballot boxes went uninstalled; electoral law requires a re-do if more than 20% of the precincts do not report. The PRD would appeal the District III results to the regional electoral tribunal and win annulment, although the decision was later reversed by the supreme tribunal, and the paramilitary Norberto Santiz was elevated to membership in the Mexican Congress.

The EZLN's display of bad humor July 6th did not do much for its weakened image. Civil society had endorsed the electoral option with a vengeance and now perceived that it had carried the day. The Zapatistas had lost the argument over the validity of the electoral option at the polls, and their bonfires were considered poor sportsmanship. Pundits obligingly credited January 1st, 1994, with setting the place for the July 6th Democracy Fiesta but the EZLN refused to take the blame. Their post-electoral lapse back into silence further depreciated the rebels' declining stock.

Now, while Cárdenas and his diehards danced in the Zócalo, the Zapatistas had gone far inside, jailed up in their jungle, the dark rain drilling down in buckets as they tried to figure out what to do next.

THE ZAPATISTAS' EUROPEAN VACATION

By July, negotiations between Mexico and the European Union on a free trade treaty were hanging in the balance, after Mexico rejected the EU's unique "Democracy Clause," which demanded a modicum of human rights compliance, as an illegal restraint of trade. The second Intercontinental Forum in Defense of Humanity and Against Neo-liberalism—Intergaláctica II—carried extracurricular leverage.

Given the high commercial stakes involved, it seems a miracle that "Dahlia" and "Felipe," residents of new Guadalupe Tepeyac, were able to unobtrusively leave Chiapas, travel up to Mexico City, obtain passports, and land in Madrid, Spain, July 25th. The first international Zapatistas, "Dahlia" and "Felipe" bore a Quijote-saturated note from Subcomandante Marcos that made no bones about tying the trip to the pending free trade pact.

The leitmotif of the second Intergaláctica was how to make the international network "in defense of humanity and against neo-liberalism" less virtual, i.e., more real. Mesas were to be held in four of Spain's designated autonomous regions. Madrid I would dissect the economic question and Madrid II "The Struggle Against the Patriarchy" (men were barred). "Dahlia" and "Felipe" climbed aboard the "Train for Humanity" and headed for the cultural mesa in Barcelona, where they strolled the Ramblas and worshipped at Gaudi's overwrought cathedral, after which okupas (anarchists) took them home to their squat. "Dahlia" also saw the sea for the first time, charging into the Mediterranean surf to discover that it was salty.

Next came the "marginalization" mesa at Ruesca, a ghost town on the old pilgrimage road to Santiago de Compostela. Driving south through La Mancha, the two masked rebels were taken to see the windmills made immortal by Cervantes. Bellinghausen reports that the literary message was lost on the travelers.

Near Granada, the Zapatistas attended a session that dealt with Drugs, Sex, T'ai Chi, "Dances of the World," and "other first world themes" (Hermann). The second Intergaláctica, despite the presence of Zapatistas, Sem Terras, Kurds, and the Tuaregs from the Sahara, was a distinctly first world shebang.

The Grand Finale was held at El Indiano, a farm near Seville that had long been occupied by Communist olive pickers. The Andalusian sun was on fire and the 10-hour sessions consumed with where the next Intergaláctica would be held the—Tuaregs of the venerable Polisario Liberation Front offered the Sahara and the Sem Terras Brazil. The few Mexicans in attendance timidly suggested a return to Mexico, but the Intergaláctica had gotten away from the Zapatistas. They were no longer the reason for the gathering, and although everyone faithfully sang the Zapatista hymn, when it came time to chant "¡Todos Somos Marcos!" radical feminists refused.

Undaunted by intercontinental travel, the CCRI dispatched two more representatives, "Macías" and "Maribel," from the Ejido Morelia to Venice for an international conclave against racism in August . With the grand doges of the European Left in attendance, the Zapatista couple were toasted with fine Italian wines and navigated the canals in a gondola to view the floating palaces, and the leftist Mayor of the city decorated them with the prestigious medal of the Golden Lion. Travel was good for the Zapatistas. It was broadening and gave them new horizons to conquer.

1,111

On August 10th, the EZLN disclosed fresh travel plans. "We are going to Mexico City, the site of the power. We are going to show this country that we are Mexicans." The rebels would be represented by a delegation of 1,111 unarmed but masked delegates, one for each EZLN-affiliated community in the jungle and highlands. The July 6th election had concentrated national attention in the capital of the country and now the EZLN must sally forth to win some of the limelight back.

The dates were significant ones. September is the month of the Fatherland in Mexico, celebrating not only liberation from Spain in 1821 but also popular resistance to the U.S. invasion and annexation of 1847–48. During the cluster of ceremonial dates from the 12th to the 16th, many flags would be waved.

Just as Comandante Ramona had wrapped herself in the flag one October ago, now 1,111 Zapatista delegates would wrap themselves in 1,111 red, white, and green mantles of the Patria. The world would be the rebels' witness that that they were not separating themselves from Mexico, but just wanted in the door.

The numbers were equally significant. In the Zapatista numerology, 1,111 equaled The One. From this standpoint, it did not much matter whether one or 1,111 Zapatistas set foot in Mexico City, but Marcos settled for the four-digit option, although an equally significant smaller number, say 666, would have considerably eased supporters' mad scramble to come up with enough buses to get so many Zapatistas up to Chilangolandia.

During their six-day stay in the big city, the 1,111 would be guests of honor at both a hastily arranged assembly of the National Indigenous Congress and the founding session of the Frente Zapatista de Liberación Nacional, whose time to be born had at long last come due—the success of the electoral option, which the Zapatistas profoundly distrusted, demanded the construction of a non-electoral left.

The march of the 1,111 would mark a year since the rupture of the Dialogue. 12 months later, only one of the five conditions for the EZLN's return to the table had been even vaguely met (Bernal's replacement by Coldwell). There was no Indian Rights and Culture Law, and even with a new majority opposition Congress, which the Zapatista pilgrimage was hoping to impress, there would not be enough non-PRI votes to pass constitutional reforms.

Although fulfillment of the San Andrés accords was its raison d'être, very political motives motored the march. Before actually taking office in early December, Cárdenas and the PRD had to be reminded that they did not have the Left locked up, that there were, in fact, other viable non-electoral options.

"We are going to Mexico City to congratulate the people for their valiant insurrection and remind them that today we have the possibility of tomorrow or the risk of yesterday," read the marching orders. Marcos declared the battle for the bases joined. "You are going to find Zapatistas everywhere, even in your soup," the Sup threatened amiably. "There's no other way. Your monopoly of the Left is through. What comes next, comes next. As someone always says, 'let the bases decide.'"

The jungle and the highlands were abuzz with anticipation at the journey of the 1,111. On August 23rd, Marcos appeared in the flesh for the first time in seven months to huddle with Elorriaga and other FZLN pooh-bahs in La Realidad. "Whatever the government is thinking, we are not abandoning our weapons," Marcos reiterated. From the outset of this adventure, the CCRI, speaking through Marcos's hand, left its participation in the FZLN deliberately up in the air. Nonetheless, it suited the Zedillo government to profess the belief that the 1,111 were coming up to Mexico City to transform themselves into an unarmed political organization.

Assemblies were convened to choose representatives from every autonomous region, municipality, community, settlement, and cluster of houses in the highlands and the jungle. Sessions were conducted at the Aguascalientes, where groups of trainee travelers were taught how to march on big-city streets. Security precluded accompaniment by any member of the CCRI–General Command, and a whole new line of young leaders—Claribel, Carlos, Hugo, Issac, Karina, Obed, Omar, and Brower (reporters could never get his name right)—were recruited to do the talking.

38 ancient buses were concentrated in San Cristóbal, some of them labeled "Gran Turismo"—the 1,111 were in fact tourists in this unknown land of theirs. Many had never set eyes on Tuxtla Gutiérrez, and now they would caravan through the states of Oaxaca, Puebla, and Morelos, all deeply Indian entities, before putting into Tenochtitlán.

On September 8th, 15,000 Zapatista bases crowded onto the cathedral plaza in San Cristóbal to wish their 1,111 caminantes godspeed. After the speeches and the handing over of the ceremonial bastones de mando to the travelers, the sisters and brothers of the corn climbed on board the flag-bedecked buses, each of which had been given a name corresponding to one of five historical leaders of the struggle for liberation from Spain: Miguel Hidalgo, José María Morelos y Pavón, Vicente Guerrero, Leona Vicario (one of the few heroines of the Patria), and Francisco Javier Mina (a Spaniard—read foreigner—who fought with Mexico against his home country).

"We are going to Mexico City to defend the heroes who gave us a Fatherland. We will recoup our national history from below, the one the government has kidnapped and buried under a pile of economic statistics," the tour guide instructed.

One other hero celebrated by the caravan-march: the Mayan God of the Wind, Ik. "We are like the Ik," a banner dangling from the lead bus announced.

AN INDIAN WIND

The Chiapas state police protectively escorted the Zapatista caravan to the Oaxaca line, an unnerving sensation for the passengers. The first stop would be Juchitán on the Tehuantepec isthmus. The longtime stronghold of the Zapotec Indian COCEI (Coalition of Farmers, Workers, & Students of the Isthmus), Juchitán is a must-see on any tour of Left Mexico. National Indigenous Congress runners sped ahead to prepare the welcome.

By late afternoon, several thousand women in their snazziest Tehuantepec finery lined the entrance to Juchitán, strewing rose petals in the Zapatistas' path. The 1,111 were paraded to the plaza and embraced by Huaves and Chontales, Zoques, Popolucas, Chinantecos, and, of course, Zapotecos, being that Juchitán is the seat of the coastal Zapotec empire. More bastones del mando were presented to the delegation. At every step of the march, the 1,111 were pushed by a profoundly Indian wind.

The buses wheezed uphill, puncturing tires and losing transmissions, and it took all day on the 10th to travel the 350 kilometers from the Isthmus to Oaxaca City. In Matatlán and Tlacolula, Zapotecs boarded with food and more embraces. Between the towns, the 1,111 men and woman of the corn climbed down from the buses and pissed in the corn tasseling up in the fields by the side of the road.

The caravan crawled into the darkened state capital near midnight, and at 3 a.m. the rebels and 6,000 red carnation–carrying sympathizers marched in a drenching downpour to the Plaza de la Danza where the Zapatistas were embraced by Mixtecos, Triquis, Mazatecos, Cuicatecos, and Chatinos. More bastones del mando were presented.

The caravan was considerably lengthened by rickety truckloads of new Indians when we hit the road the next morning, moving through the central valleys of Oaxaca under heavy police and military protection. The army cleared off the highways up ahead and the Condor helicopter group hovered overhead. Why had 20,000 troops and police been mobilized to protect a rebel band that had declared war on the Mexican government and, just a few months earlier, been so uncouth as to burn ballot boxes in a federal election?

Up ahead in the capital, the military, now in command of the police, had just butchered six young men in a botched raid over stolen auto parts in a popular colony. The youths' body parts were found distributed around the south of the city.

Were the 1,111 marching right into Military Camp #1, a new Chinameca?

The highway to Huahuapán was posted with maverick teachers and students from the militant normal schools, and many Indians. An old Mixtec woman and her grandson perched on the shoulder near Huahuapán and reached up to touch callused hands with the rebels through the bus window. "These are the Zapatistas," she told the child proudly, and they both smiled. Then the two padded across the highway to a clump of huts planted on the edge of a maguey cactus patch, where the Day the Zapatistas Passed By would no doubt soon become legend on their tongues.

From Huahuapán, the caravan crossed into Puebla. Feeder marches from the Montaña of Guerrero joined up, and the line of march grew to nearly a hundred vehicles. We reached Tepoztlán, Morelos, in Zapata country, where the towns-people had heroically beaten back Jack Nicklaus's golf course, in the middle of a torrential deluge around 1 a.m. When poor Amado Avendaño stepped from the bus, he plunged into a pitch-dark ravine and busted his pelvis.

On the morning of the 12th, the caravan-march, now 159 buses, minibuses, taxis, vans, private vehicles, dump trucks, pick-ups, motorcycles, bicycles, and horse-drawn carts long, snaked over the Sierra of Chichinautzín and began its descent into the capital, the same route that the first Zapata had taken to meet up with Francisco Villa in December 1914 at the apogee of the Mexican Revolution. In Milpa Alta, the villagers came out to the crossroads with tamales and atole and told how they were the grandchildren of those who had fed General Zapata's troops 80 years ago. History put its glaze on the march of the 1,111 wherever it went.

Xochimilco was the setting for the first Mexico City ceremony—with two million Indian residents, the capital is the most Indian city in the Americas, many living in the still-rural southern zones like Xochimilco, famed for its flow-ers and its floating gardens (chinampas). It was there that the Liberators of the North and South camped under an ahehuete tree and tried to puzzle out what to do with the Mexican Revolution back in 1914. "We are going to Mexico armed only with history," Marcos had boasted.

The 1,111 gathered for the final hike up the Paseo de la Reforma to the Zócalo at dusk. After 44 months and 12 days, the Zapatista Army of National Liberation was finally advancing on the heart of power.

Even in their own jungle, the Mayans are short people, but here in the urban one, they were positively dwarfed under the skyscraper hotels, the golden Angel of Independence, the blinding sheets of neon on the movie marquees, the bubble-domed stock market, and the rococo remains of the Palace of Bellas Artes. At the Alameda Park, a lone strand of green space in the center of the city, not a few of the 1,111 rushed to relieve themselves on real ground. Like travelers far from home everywhere, many were suffering intestinal evils.

The Zócalo was ablaze with the patriotic pictographs the government hangs each September during the month of the Patria—Hidalgo's huge head probably occupied more light bulbs than glow nightly in the entire conflict zone. The throng was so dense and excited that it took the 1,111 the better part of an hour to reach the rostrum. "This is the biggest anti-racist demonstration ever held in Mexico," Carlos Monsiváis shouted into my mini-recorder. "It's another January 1st!" exulted Luis Hernández. "*¡No Están Solos!*" the enormous gathering roared over and over again: "They Are Not Alone!"

TENOCHTITLAN TIME

The days and nights of the 1,111 in Gran Tenochtitlán flurried with activity. Although the rector had forbidden the use of campus facilities during the Zapatista visit, the rebels played soccer at the UNAM (12 to 2 for the visiting team) and danced cumbias with the Urban Popular Movement in the Plaza of Three Cultures at Tlatelolco, where they learned first-hand of the 1968 massacre of the students on that killing floor.

With 3,000 delegates on hand, the CNI convened its second national assembly at Cuicuilco, a southern Mexico City ceremonial site a millennium older than Teotihuacán. Today Cuicuilco is a green teardrop strangled by freeways and condo towers on all sides. Amongst the tower builders is Carlos Slim, the richest man in Latin America, who operates the Cuicuilco shopping mall on the northern boundary of the site and who planned to throw up a wall of skyscrapers that would plunge Cuicuilco into darkness. Anthropologists, Indians, and Cuicuilco's neighbors were appalled.

"We will defend the land of Cuicuilco with our lives," the old Purépecha troublemaker Efrén Capiz thundered to the visiting Indians as 1,111 masked Zapatistas marched in a slow spiral to the top of the ceremonial mound, adding their muscle to the struggle.

The centerpiece of the Zapatista journey was the founding convention of the FZLN, scheduled to pop out of the cake at an inner-city dance hall, El Salón Los Angeles ("Who doesn't know the Los Angeles, does not know Mexico") on September 14th, and in a gesture of great goodwill, Cuauhtémoc Cárdenas, about to be sworn in as mayor, showed up bright and early at the warp-floored dance palace to welcome the 1,111 to his city. Accompanied by his elderly if always solidarity-minded mother Doña Amalia, Cárdenas sat down to await the rebels' arrival. By mid-afternoon, exasperated at the EZLN's inexplicable no-show,

Cuauhtémoc and his mom left the Los Angeles, leaving behind a conciliatory speech welcoming the formation of the FZLN for the rebels when and if they ever arrived.

20 minutes later, 1,111 members of the Zapatista Army of National Liberation marched into the dance hall and the birthing of the FZLN could begin. To this reporter's knowledge, the snub has never been explained.

The message the 1,111 delivered that afternoon was not optimistic. "When we called for the formation of the FZLN, we thought peace was near and our rebellion would have to find other roads, but we were wrong—peace is far away," Marcos spoke through Obed's voice. Because of the mal gobierno's continuing military pressures, "the EZLN cannot be a part of the FZLN. We stand aside so that you can find your own face—the hour has come, sister and brother *frentistas*, you have to be born without us in your body…" The EZLN was not going to lay down its guns, was not going to transform itself into a political organization—at least not today, at least not until San Andrés was the law of the land. The best-laid plans of the Zedillo government to tame the EZLN would have to wait.

Almost 2,000 voting delegates were on hand to assist at the birth. 137 issues were on the dance floor, the most pressing of which was "double militancy," i.e., could an activist be both a member of the FZLN and a member of a political party (the PRD)? After days of debate, 72% of those voting cast ballots in favor of keeping the Frente pure and against "double militancy," which may explain why the FZLN has remained so small and cliquish in its three years of intermittent activity.

In addition to the veto on party membership, no professional politicians would be allowed in the door. In line with the Fourth Declaration of the Lacandón Jungle, no FZLNer could hold political office. FZLN leadership would be collective and would mandar obedeciendo. Javier Elorriaga would be at the day-to-day controls.

The FZLN would "not struggle to take state power or by the old methods of doing politics—we must not freeze ideas as immovable truths—our thought must be a continuing confrontation with reality." What this meant in practice was not spelled out. With a self-restricted constituency and unclear as to whether it was one more Zapatista support group or free to work on non-EZLN issues, the FZLN never sparked a prairie fire.

The men and women of the corn climbed back up onto their antique Gran Turismos and bid adieu to old Tenochtitlán September 18th, thanking everyone who had made their stay a memorable one, from the Francisco Villas (with whom they had been bunking at a housing project in the east of the city) to the Gays and Lesbians (for the first time at a political meeting here, ski-masked men had held hands during the FZ plenary), and two days later, with only one major fender bender, the 1,111 were back on the reservation, heroes in their hometowns, with enough tales of their travels to last a lifetime.

The impact of the odyssey upon the nation was not much measured. The New York Times' blasé correspondent Julia Preston wrote that the EZLN was "like a bad elbow," bothering the body politic but not endangering the nation's health. Had Ernesto Zedillo heard a word the Zapatistas had said? "Now we'll go back to our communities to see if the president listened to us or just doubled over his ears like a damned burro," Obed considered. "I don't think he's paying any attention," thought a young Zapatista named Juan. "We're going to have to keep fighting."

THE ANTI-CHRIST

The 1,111 voyagers came home to a darkening Chiapas. The Army was pressing right up against the Oventic Aguascalientes, and down in the jungle, troops took up new positions at the Euseba river, five Ks from La Realidad. The convoys passing through that community each day now stretched to 32 vehicles.

But the paramilitaries, the Frankenstein love-children of the Mexican Army and the PRI high command, were the most worrisome feature of the Autumn offensive against the Zapatista communities.

Having received the first installment of a $450,000 USD government grant (outgoing Seventh Region military chief Mario Renán Castillo signed as witness to the contract), Peace & Justice added "development" to its legal name and squabbled over the money. Leader Samuel Sánchez's brother was gunned down in late July as the paramilitaries split into armed factions.

With the backing of the military and public security, "Development, Peace & Justice" bullied the villages of the north into quiescence. 55 citizens had lost their lives there due to political violence since the first of the year, and 4,100 refugees had been driven from their homes.

The conflict was suffused with singular religious animosity. Evangelicals, traditional Catholics, and non-believers ganged up on Don Samuel's priests and catechists, padlocking 14 churches and chapels in four north state municipalities, an aggression that not only touched the diocese but reached all the way home to Rome. In early November, Don Samuel and Don Raúl scheduled a journey through the north of Chiapas to prepare the ground for a December visit by the new Papal Nuncio, the Spaniard Justo Mullor, who would report to the Vatican on the church closings.

The portents for the bishops' junket were not pleasant. Two weeks before the November 4th tour began, DP&J issued leaflets calling for the expulsion of all priests and catechists from Tila and Sabanilla. Heriberto Cruz, the oft targeted priest of Tila, was threatened with extinction should Samuel and Raúl manifest themselves in the region. Another pamphlet, "Diabolic Doctrine," advised locals "to arm themselves against Don Samuel's poison…"

During the run-up to the dangerous trek through the north, the diocese was blindsided from an unexpected quarter. In a blistering late October communiqué,

Marcos, who had relapsed into silence upon the return of the 1,111, attacked the high clergy for siding with Zedillo and the COCOPA in urging that San Andrés be renegotiated.

The Zapatista spokesperson also accused the Bishops Conference of seeking to supplant the CONAI as mediator in the evaporated talks with the government, and alleged an insidious plot to lure the 1,111 to the shrine of the Virgin of Guadalupe during their stay in the capital, where Pedro Joaquín Coldwell, Bernal's replacement, was said to be lurking to entrap the Zapatistas in new negotiations. The Apocalypse-quoting epistle claims that the hierarchy had cut a deal with Zedillo to "annihilate" the rebels—Justo Mullor would "exchange the head of Marcos" for revision of Constitutional Article 130, which defines Church jurisdiction. The Nuncio would be nominated for Samuel's Nobel Prize.

The Subcomandante's unwanted solidarity put Bishop Ruiz in a ticklish space—Mullor's visit would draw national and international attention to the cruel equation in the north and could mitigate Samuel's problems with the Vatican. In a rare display of unanimity, Don Samuel, Raúl, and their counterparts in Tuxtla and Tapachula assailed Marcos as an "ingrate." A shaken Mullor called the charges "all lies."

The gunfire flashed from the hillside above, two bursts from an AR-15 in the dusk, just as the bishops' convoy moved through El Crucero, a DP&J power spot. Samuel and Raúl had performed a Mass out in the countryside, and the caravan was steaming back up the hill to Heriberto's cathedral in Tila.

The van careened wildly across the road to evade the barrage, but it was too late: Two catechists and the keeper of the shrine of "The Señor of Tila," a black Jesus, had been hit, staining Heriberto's white surplice with blood.

Miraculously, Samuel and Raúl, having gone ahead to Tila 10 minutes earlier, were not among the van's passengers—Bishop Ruiz's longtime bodyguards did not even hear of the incident until a distraught Heriberto arrived an hour later. Whoever the bullets were intended for (Heriberto Cruz suggests he was the real target), the assassination attempt left the bishops shaking. A programmed Mass in Sabanilla was canceled, handing DP&J a big victory, and Raúl and Samuel retired to Chilón, where they were better protected.

The hit on the bishops' convoy stirred international indignation—the U.S. Bishops Conference and the Vatican Secretary of State faxed off protest notes to Ernesto Zedillo, demanding that the culprits be brought to justice. Although local authorities dutifully opened an investigation, as with nine other ambushes against Church and human rights caravans in the north of Chiapas, no blame was ever affixed. The local prosecutor spent months questioning the wounded men about their church duties and the diocese's strategies in the region.

Despite the lack of legal resolution, one message came through loud and clear: the paramilitaries were no longer taking orders from the government and the military that had so assiduously financed and trained them. They were, in fact, out of control.

A lot of bad shit can come down in a Mexican minute. The next day, November 5th, while Padre Heriberto was still sponging the blood off the van's upholstery, Miguel Méndez Toporek, a 23-year-old Tzotzil painter and Samuel's godson, rang the rectory buzzer in San Cristóbal and asked to see the Bishop. When told he wasn't in, Toporek settled for Samuel's sister and housekeeper, Doña Lucha. Left alone with the old woman, he pulled a hammer out of his clothing and smashed in her head, then calmly went home—later, remorse-ridden, he would return to the Cathedral and confess the deed. The television had told him that Samuel was the Anti-Christ and, as his godson, it was his obligation to destroy the demon. Toporek unsuccessfully slit his throat in jail.

Found unconscious by church workers, Lucha was rushed to Tuxtla with multiple skull fractures. Don Samuel turned a Christian cheek, forgiving the young man for the bizarre assault, explaining that his godson's mind had been contaminated by the venomous Chiapas press. Even as Tatic spoke, the Tuxtla daily *Cuarto Poder* was "reporting" that the Bishop had hired Toporek to bash in his sister's head so as to stimulate fresh sympathy for the diocese.

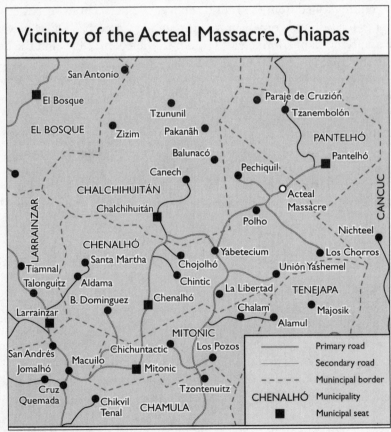

Vicinity of the Acteal Massacre, Chiapas

BLACK AUTUMN

The sky above Chiapas grew darker the higher one climbed during the Autumn of 1997. Up in Los Altos, the municipality of Chenalhó had become a black hole of violence. Up against the heavens in fog-shrouded, cave-encrusted, deep-green mountains, Chenalhó ("Cave of Water" in Tzotzil) is an impoverished hotbed of Indian millennialism where the saints sweat and *rayos lucentes* (lightning bolts) flash and sputter whenever the Indian world rises in rebellion.

Like neighboring municipalities San Andrés, El Bosque, and Pantelhó, Chenalhó had entertained parallel authorities since late 1994, with the PRI-gobierno established in the county seat at San Pedro Chenalhó and the autonomous government dug in at Polhó, 24 kilometers off in the northeast corner of the county, just up the road from the flourishing Majomut organic coffee cooperative that was then exporting 20,000 sacks of the aromatic to Europe yearly—many Majomut members were also pro-Zapatista, and profits were plowed back into Polhó to keep the autonomous municipality afloat.

Despite the co-op's success, coffee was at least part of the problem. Prices were good for once in 1997, and as the harvest drew near, gangs from PRI-affiliated hamlets began raiding patches controlled by the Majomut members. Perhaps the violence began there.

For three decades, Chenalhó politics had been dominated by bilingual teachers associated with the INI and the PRI, who had long ago deposed traditional authorities and become little caciques in this upland enclave. The current municipal president, Jacinto Arias, was the nephew of the Tzotzil scholar of the same name, now Chiapas governor Ruiz Ferro's Attention-to-the Indians Secretary. The younger Arias had replaced the old municipal president after the bodies of six young men, reportedly the sons of Zapatista supporters (others said they came from the PRI), were pulled from a garbage-strewn cave near Chixiltón in June 1995. Their testicles had been eaten by tarantulas. Perhaps the violence began then.

Down the road from the county seat, the autonomous municipality of Polhó grew out of the struggle to unseat Eduardo Robledo. It was first declared a "rebel" enclave in 1994, when Polhó swore allegiance to Amado Avendaño, who carried all of Chenalhó with a 62% majority that year. After the EZLN's December offensive, the "rebel" hamlet was designated an autonomía and its supporters boycotted the October 1995 municipal election (they had done so again in July during the Democracy Fiesta when 18 ballot boxes were burnt in the county).

Authorities of the new autonomous municipality were chosen in April 1996, and Domingo Pérez Paciencia was selected "principal" of the Polhó council. That June, Polhó declared that a sand and gravel bank located at the entrance to the Majomut co-op pertained to the autonomous municipality, a claim that inflamed Chenalhó's PRIistas and their confederates in the so-called "Party of the

Cardenista Front" (not the PRD), who had been awarded the concession by agrarian authorities. Maybe that's where the skein of murderous violence that now spasmed through Chenalhó was unchained.

Or maybe the homicides can be dated from the gunfight at Yexhemil, close by Majomut, on May 24th, 1997, when Professor Cristóbal Pérez, a member of the Polhó council, disappeared—the discovery of his skull months later in a burlap bag in the corner of a chapel where his wife was praying, sparked fresh violence.

The truth is that Chenalhó was just waiting to blow sky-high by the Autumn of 1997, and anything could have triggered violence: a stolen marimba, as in Tzabletum (two dead in June), or the blazing ballots in the July election, or the coming coffee harvest.

The house burnings first flared in June—the initial victims were members of Las Abejas, the deeply religious civil association organized by catechists and Chenalhó's rebel French priest, old Michel Chanteau. Abejas were forced to flee their homes in PRI-dominated communities like Los Chorros, Puebla, Chimix, and La Esperanza, all clustered around Polhó in that far north corner of the county.

By September, Chenalhó was on the brink of civil conflagration. On the day the 1,111 left Mexico City (September 18th), 60 families were burnt out of Los Chorros—six Abejas were allegedly taken hostage (hostages were used as porters to carry off the farm tools and domestic appliances from the looted homes and harvest the abandoned coffee patches). On September 21st, the two bands squared off in their first "official" firefight—two were killed on either side near Majomut. On September 23rd, when Zapatista bases marched in San Pedro Chenalhó to welcome their Mexico City delegation home, a sniper was flushed from the roof of the town hall.

Although both sides were furiously arming for the inevitable showdown, the PRIistas had state security forces and the military in their corner. In late October, for example, a military patrol under the command of Captain Germán Parra found 20 long guns stashed in an abandoned La Esperanza house and, rather than confiscating them, returned the weapons to their PRI owners, testified a Public Ministry agent who went along for the ride.

At ejido assemblies in Los Chorros and Puebla in mid-September, the decision was taken to form "self-defense" squads, *Pojwanej* in Tzotzil—as part of their "self-defense" responsibilities, the aggressive young men who joined the "Pojwanej" went out on "excursions," pillaging Zapatista and Abeja colonies, stealing their crops and their animals. Relations between the Pojwanej and local police and military detachments were very cordial.

"War taxes" were collected in the PRI hamlets to up the marauders' firepower. Those who contributed their hard-earned coins (the tax could be as high as 600 pesos) got their hovels painted with the PRI logo to ward off possible Pojwanej arson.

BUSINESS REPLY MAIL

FIRST-CLASS MAIL   PERMIT NO. 5   MONROE ME

POSTAGE WILL BE PAID BY ADDRESSEE

COMMON COURAGE PRESS
PO BOX 702
MONROE ME 04951-9987

Yes! Please Send Me Your Free Catalog!
Call 1-800-497-3207

Founded in 1991, Common Courage's goal is to turn pens into political swords in an effort to hack away at propaganda and injustice. Authors include:

- Noam Chomsky
- Gore Vidal
- Jennifer Harbury
- Edward Said

- Judi Bari
- Norman Solomon
- Margaret Randall
- and many others!

For more information:

Email: orders-info@commoncouragepress.com

Fax: (207) 525-3068   ...or mail in this postcard.

Name _____

Address _____

City _____ State _____ Zip _____

Send us your email address if you want email updates:

Email _____

Have you bought our books before?_____

How did you hear about this book?_____

www.commoncouragepress.com #DB

The go-between in the gun-running in and out of Chenalhó was Jacinto Arias, whom Polhó authorities accused of stockpiling 200 automatic weapons on his home ejido of Puebla. Arias, an evangelical Presbyterian (the National Presbyterian Church has been proselytizing in the Altos since the 1930s), invested the villagers' war taxes in guns and ammunition readily available in the evangelical barrio of San Cristóbal, La Hormiga. Domingo Pérez Paciencia, the Polhó headman and also an evangelical Presbyterian, claims Arias used a municipal ambulance to smuggle the guns back into the county.

On October 1st, Ernesto Zedillo popped up in San Cristóbal and lashed out against the Zapatista autonomías as "counties without law." After the speech, Jacinto Arias, in the name of the constitutional municipality of Chenalhó, handed the President a typed request to arm his law-abiding fellow PRIs against the depredations of the criminal autonomous gang at Polhó.

Bad blood flowed between Arias and Michel Chanteau, the 69-year-old disciple of Don Samuel who had been in charge of the Chenalhó parish for three decades, during which he had often run afoul of the PRI authorities, particularly after Padre Michel accused a PRI teacher of fondling his students, for which he was labeled "an agent of international communism."

By November, things had turned so sour between the mayor and the priest that Jacinto Arias swore before witnesses that he would burn down the priest's church, kill Chanteau, and burn his body, "so that the worms won't get sick."

The death warrant presumably extended to Michel's flock, Las Abejas. Now encamped in exile at Polhó, X'oyep, and Acteal, the Bees never stopped praying for peace. "Jacinto Arias wants us all dead," a white-clad farmer told Bellinghausen at Acteal one afternoon. "I am ashamed to admit that we are of the same race."

The future was written on the wall in San Andrés in late October: "We are Máscara Roja—if you want to know us, meet us in Hell."

All throughout the coffee and corn harvest that black autumn, farmers watched the houses go up in smoke. Bursts of automatic gunfire punctured the mountain silences, the two sides sometimes opening up on each other from opposite hillsides. Those who had been burnt out did not take the evictions on their knees. Between October 25th and 28th, the Zapatistas counterattacked, wounding 17 PRIists (13 in one truck) in three separate incidents—the Polhó council insisted that the PRIs had fired upon themselves.

By early December, 4,000 refugees were crowding into the makeshift camps around Polhó. Since the shoot-out at Yexhemil in the Spring, 29 had died in Chenalhó, the last four at Aurora Chica, where at least one of the bodies had been mutilated. Among the Tzotziles, the mutilation of the dead is thought a sign of cannibalism. Both sides stood accused of gnawing on the enemy dead, purportedly to steal their powers.

The carnival of death in the highlands had begun to attract international attention—Human Rights Watch planned an on-site investigation, and citizen observer caravans were on the road at the end of November. Despite the Mexican Migra checkpoint at the entrance of Chenalhó to keep out nosy foreigners, CNN showed up and filmed for international television.

On December 9th, Ricardo Rocha, then Televisa's only independent reporter, broadcast an hour-long documentary shot in and around Chenalhó, *Chiapas: Testimony of an Infamy*, that stunned a good share of the Sunday evening viewing audience. Choking back tears, Rocha interviewed refugees in the mountain (one woman gives birth on camera) and at Polhó, as they described the brutality and enforced hunger of their days. Michel Chanteau recounts Jacinto Arias's horrific death threat, and Samuel and Raúl cry out for someone, anyone, to stop the madness.

On December 11th, the NGOs, the CONAI, and the diocese's Fray Bartolomé Human Rights Center finally brought the two sides together at the schoolhouse in Las Limas, the midpoint between Polhó and the county seat. "They needed four tables, 70 chairs, 29 dead, almost 5,000 displaced, and an uncountable number of homes burnt, in order to realize this first negotiation," Hermann observed. Jacinto Arias and Domingo Pérez Paciencia stared each other down, and then Arias's cell phone binged with the news that the Zapatistas were burning down Chimix. A commission was hastily formed to investigate but could find no evidence of the new attack. Finally, the two headmen signed a tentative cease-fire. A joint verification committee would see if promises were kept.

The next morning, the Chiapas state government bought full pages in national newspapers to advertise that peace had been achieved in Chenalhó. The ad also listed the number of blankets handed out to the thousands who had been displaced from their communities.

The nuncio Mullor began his long-awaited visit in the north of Chiapas on December 14th. Under heavy security, with Raúl and Samuel on either wing, the white-haired Spaniard moved cautiously through the communities to inspect the shuttered chapels and hermitages. In Jolnextie, ski-masked Zapatistas welcomed the irritated nuncio with defiant chants. At El Limar, the prelate was menaced by a mob of DP&J loyalists. "Who closed this church?" the nuncio sputtered, staring at a crumpled portrait of the Señor of Tila underfoot. "It was a decision of the people," mumbled ex–military man Marco Albino. "But what authority do you have?" Mullor demanded. He was escorted back to the cars before the bullets began flying again.

The nuncio's visit did not bring peace to Chiapas. Up in Chenalhó on December 17th, a truckful of PRIistas was ambushed near Quextic just a few hundred meters north of Acteal. One man, Agustín Vázquez Secum, was killed and six others wounded. After months of preliminary bloodshed, it would be this 30th death that finally tipped the glass.

WINTER 1997–1998

FEAST OF BLOOD

The men from Quextic gathered at the elbow of the road above the Abejas' encampment at Acteal early on the second morning of Winter, their collective breath seeping into the chill mountain air through the red kerchiefs that masked all but their dark, angry eyes. The PRIistas were impatient to get the killing done, and the tardiness of their compañeros coming from Los Chorros did not improve their disposition.

Mondays are like Sundays in these saw-toothed hills, "San Lunes" (Saint Monday) in the popular argot, and it was nearly 10 o'clock by the time the 60-man death squad was all assembled on the basketball court up by the school, the weapons distributed, and the killing plan agreed upon. 20 men would stay by the road and gun down anyone who fled the attack down below. In what their military trainers had taught them was a "hammer and anvil" maneuver, the rest would move slowly down the steep, overgrown hillside from three directions and surround the refugee camp set below on a flat promontory that overlooks the long valley.

The Abejas had been chosen for sacrifice after the December 17th ambush of Agustín Vázquez Secum. Survivors claimed that they recognized some of his assassins as being Abejas recently driven out of Quextic by the PRIistas. Vázquez and his associates were alleged to be hauling stolen Abejas coffee for sale in Pantelhó when they were hit.

Antonio Vázquez Secum was a big man in Quextic, and Agustín had been the favorite of his 18 sons and daughters. Now the PRIistas met at the old man's home clamoring for vengeance. A delegation from Los Chorros led by Antonio López Santiz, a well-to-do PRI coffee farmer with a lot of guns, showed up to plot the punitive expedition. This time they would teach the Zapatistas and their Abeja pals a lesson they would never forget.

Now the men, dressed in dark uniforms and red Zapatista-style paliacates, stomped through the damp underbrush past the hand-lettered sign planted just below the road that pleaded "Peace Neutral Zone," firing as they descended. For a while the men seemed content just to demonstrate their firepower to the refugees crouched on the promontory below, but when a detachment of state police pulled into the school 200 meters above, the signal was given to advance down the hillside.

By mid-morning, Acteal was mostly a women's camp—the men had gone off to salvage what they could of their coffee. Most of the Abeja women were clustered around a clapboard chapel where they picked through a load of old clothes donated by the diocese. Others prayed fervently for peace with the zone's lead catechist, Alonso Vázquez, who had called upon the devoutly Christian Bees to celebrate three days of prayer and fasting in preparation for the marking of Christ's birthday.

Alonso had been forewarned of the coming violence but had stubbornly refused to leave. One day before, an Abeja from Quextic who had been captured by the PRIistas to cut and haul the stolen coffee, had escaped his kidnappers and come down to Acteal to warn of the death squad's preparations, but the catechist would not run. "We have done nothing wrong."

Now the Abejas had to run, but there was no place to run to. In the prayer circle, Alonso's wife was one of the first to fall. "Women! Women! Do not leave me!" the catechist pleaded as eight AK-15 slugs were pumped into his back. Christian legend has it that Alonso Vázquez gasped, "Forgive them for they know not what they do," before he expired. Manuel, his 10-year-old son, who was hidden in the underbrush, remembers what happened next: "The killers stood there laughing at my mother and then they killed her again and took out a knife and cut open her stomach and took out the baby that was in there and threw it away..."

Manuel's mother was one of four pregnant women slain at Acteal and the catechists in the area have always counted her baby as an additional victim. The Mexican government debunks this horrific story, which invokes the genocidal campaigns of Guatemala's Kaibiles, but the autopsy ordered by the Chiapas state prosecutor's office lists a number of abdominal wounds caused by sharp instruments. Corpse #16, for instance, was "a female cadaver, approximately 32 years old, who died of perforation to her abdominal viscera by a cutting instrument— the abdominal cavity was opened up and the product of approximately 28 weeks extracted."

With the bullets raining down on the wood-board chapel, the Abejas were rat-trapped out on the ledge of the promontory. Many dashed wildly downhill into the leafy gully, at the bottom of which a thin ribbon of an arroyo gurgled. Some sought cover behind boulders or in a cleft of the mountain that forms a sort of cave, their attackers methodically advancing in pursuit, hunting the victims down with automatic weapons and mutilating their bodies with machete cuts. The massacre was slow and systematic, the men in the red masks taking their sweet time. Short bursts of gunfire echoed off the hillside well into the afternoon.

By the time the solstice-shortened sun had begun to drop from the sky, there were 45 dead at Acteal: seven men, 19 women, and 19 children, 46 say the catechists.

Who were the dead? Like their killers, they were impoverished Tzoztil Indian farmers and their families. Unlike their killers, they were not supporters of the Mexican government and the party that had controlled that government for seven decades.

María Ruiz, for instance, had just returned empty-handed from the local government clinic. Although she had been hemorrhaging for two days, there was no blood or anesthesia available, and she had given up and gone back to the Acteal camp. *Ni modo*: there was nothing to do, except to pray, which is what she was doing when she was cruelly cut down.

Micaela, 11, had survived only because her dead mother had fallen on top of her as they bolted for the gully. When the killers were attracted by the squalls of a baby sister strapped to her dead mother's back, Micaela played dead. That's when the paramilitaries killed the baby. "We have to crush out the seed," she heard them laugh.

Some of the victims recognized their killers. Vicente Luna spotted his cousins from Quextic among the butchers. When Armando Vázquez, part of the Quextic killing team, discovered the body of a sister of a woman who had once spurned him, he lifted her skirt and viciously penetrated her with a stick.

In late afternoon, the killers went home and killed a cow, waving good-bye to the police as they climbed back up into the trucks parked by the schoolhouse. Old Antonio Vázquez Secum was overjoyed at the news that so many had died and offered strong drink. Some of the killers went to the Presbyterian chapel to bless their weapons and give thanks to their God.

SIN NOVEDAD

Throughout the massacre, the police had remained posted up by the road where the gunfire was plainly audible. At 11:30, Cornelio Pérez, one of the Zapatista bases who were encamped with the Abejas on the hillside but who had taken cover in the mountain after the warning the day before, ran up to the road to plead with the police detachment to stop the killings. Comandante Roberto Rivas was standing on the lip of the highway, perhaps 50 meters from the death scene, but instead of taking action to stop the bloodshed, detained Pérez. Later, Pérez testified, the police did advance a few feet down the hillside and fired off their weapons into the air briefly before retreating to the schoolhouse. Down below, the killing continued unhindered.

At the same hour, 11:30, José Hernández, another Zapatista partisan, ran to the public phone by the road and frantically dialed the CONAI in San Cristóbal. Gonzalo Ituarte took the information and put in an emergency call to the state secretary of government, Homero Tovilla, in Tuxtla. Tovilla, Laco's successor, seemed unimpressed but promised to check out the "rumor." A call was made to Chiapas public security director General Jorge Gamboa Solís (ret.), who in turn rang up the BOM (Base of Mixed Operations) headquarters at Majomut, close enough to Acteal to have audited the gunshots, and was told by General José Luis Rodríguez Orozco (ret.) that everything was quiet, *sin novedad* in military parlance, "without news."

At 12:30, the Zapatista Hernández picked up the public phone by the side of the road and an unknown caller asked him to go and tell General Julio César Santiago (ret.), who commanded the detachment at the school, to investigate what was going on in Acteal. No investigation was ever made. No one ever called back to find out.

The killing continued until the paramilitaries tramped past the police and went home. Around 18:30 that evening, just before a cabinet meeting with Governor Ruiz Ferro, General Gamboa Solís informed Tovilla that "about four or five shots" had been heard in the area, but otherwise the situation was sin novedad. Tovilla rang up Gonzalo Ituarte to relay the good news. The situation in Acteal was "tranquil." By that hour, most everyone was dead.

In late afternoon, the wounded crept out of hiding and struggled up to the road, where General Santiago ordered trucks to transport them to San Cristóbal. Meanwhile, 150 crack members of the state's Force & Reaction squad were sent from Tuxtla to back up the detachment at the school.

By 20:30, the first wounded stumbled into the regional hospital. Hermann, a medical doctor himself, rushed to speak with the traumatized victims. Doctors told him that the exit wounds were so large that they must have been caused by expanding bullets. Governor Ruiz Ferro's office continued to insist that the situation at Acteal was "sin novedad."

Police scouts had by now descended into Acteal and reported many corpses. Phone calls were made, orders were given. A few hours later, when a Red Cross ambulance from San Cristóbal swung around the bend at Acteal, it was greeted by gunfire. Police would not let the paramedics near the death scene. When the Red Cross workers tried to radio San Cristóbal for instructions, the radio was dead. The reason? A transmitter located at Tzontihuitz mountain, a site protected by army sentinels, had been mysteriously disabled.

All throughout the night the forces of public security labored to rearrange the site. Six trenches were dug down in the gully. The bodies were collected and stacked, perhaps to be burnt. At 4:30 on the morning of the 23rd, Attorney General Jorge Enrique Hernández Aguilar and Zepeda's protégé Uriel Jarquín arrived to control the body count and get the corpses out of Acteal before the press and the human rights groups showed up in the daylight. The ravaged hunks of flesh that had once been the Abejas were slung up in the trucks and carried down to Tuxtla for "autopsies."

THE LIGHT OF DAY

The dimensions of the Acteal massacre dawned slowly on Chiapas and the nation. No reporters ventured out to the site in the dark to measure the blood-letting. The first outsider into the community was an Italian, Massimo Boldini, a solidarity worker who had been visiting in neighboring Polhó when the gunfire broke out and was dispatched by the autonomous council the next morning to investigate. Somehow Boldini (who was later deported) managed to convince the police up on the road to let him through the security lines—they even gave him a password ("condor") to yell at the cops down below.

By the time Boldini reached the center of Acteal, all the bodies had been removed to Tuxtla and the camp was abandoned. Bloody clumps of clothing were strewn everywhere: "There was blood on everything, the path and even the branches of the trees." The houses, which had been shut up by Zapatista bases the night before to prevent looting, were now open and had been ransacked by the police. Christmas lights still winked on and off in the blood-smeared chapel.

Although 45 bodies were now being dissected on the tables of the Tuxtla morgue, the governor's office continued to deny that anything at all had taken place at Acteal until after noon, when a sketchy press bulletin conceded there had been a "confrontation" in the area. In mid-afternoon, President Zedillo offered a brief statement for national television consumption calling the "confrontation" "absurd," promising an immediate investigation, and ordering 5,000 new troops to Chiapas. Most were elements of the GAFE ("Special Air Force Group") who had recently returned from advanced training at the Center for Special Forces in Fort Bragg, North Carolina.

In Chenalhó, municipal president Jacinto Arias thanked Zedillo for showing his willingness "to clear up the violent acts."

"They can't put that on me," Arias responded when asked about the charges that he had armed the PRIistas. "This was not about politics," he spat back, "this was about revenge. It can't be controlled."

THE SADDEST CHRISTMAS

Señores, I want to tell you
what happened on the 22nd
of December in the year 1997
in the town of Chenalhó where
a group of masked men with bullets
interrupted the prayers of those
who are now dead.

Now the survivors gathered at the school in Polhó on a cheerless Christmas Eve to receive what remained of their dead. Don Samuel had intervened to get the bodies back from the state as fast as possible. "Whoever knows the Indians knows they must have their mourning," he demanded of the governor. "Will even this consolation be denied them?" Now the smell of fear and grief was impregnated with death's sweet nauseating gas as the leaky coffins were unloaded one by one from the government trucks. The state, of course, had shipped the victims home in the cheapest containers the budget could buy, "to show what they think the Indians are worth," muttered Padre Gonzalo. There had been no embalming allowance, and instead the morgue men had packed the boxes with ice that was now rapidly melting all over the volunteer pallbearers.

> *45 campesinos, old people,*
> *women and children*
> *were left without life*
> *on that sad morning*
> *My mind is confused*
> *trying to figure out*
> *just what was the crime*
> *for which they massacred*
> *these defenseless people.*

The Abejas vigiled all the night in the frigid schoolhouse, their prayers and sorrow melding into a mournful hum in the early light. At sunrise on Christmas morning the procession formed. Samuel had come to accompany the dead back to Acteal, where they would be buried in the camp because they were Abejas, and the Bees always stayed together.

But about a third of the way to Acteal, at a turn in the road, the mourners were overtaken by a municipal truck that was carrying off sacks of their stolen coffee to sell in Pantelhó. The truck was accompanied by seven state public security officers. The Abejas quickly recognized their killers among the men up in the truck and hiding under the sacks. "*Asesinos!*" they spat, dragging them down and pummeling the paramilitaries to the ground. A mass lynching was threatened right there on the highway. The state police feigned that the men were already in custody, although they were now being escorted out of the county with the Bees' coffee in tow. Samuel asked federal police officers who were assigned to protect the procession to intervene. The state cops and the men in the truck were taken into custody and the mourners continued on to Acteal.

> *What use now is the jailhouse*
> *the grief is left in the houses*
> *among those who live there*
> *you can hear them crying*
> *down in the ravine.*
> *Fly fly my little Torcita*
> *Fly to the Creator and ask Him*
> *where He is hiding*
> *and is He satisfied with this savage killing?*

"Corrido of Chenalhó" collected by Hermann Bellinghausen, Ocosingo, Chiapas, January 12th, 1998

By the time the procession reached the center of Acteal, the hillside, a sort of Tzotzil Dogpatch, was swarming with police and NGO people, mourners, tourists, reporters, and photographers fighting for position to shoot the weeping Indians. The people from the community and the solidarity workers had dug a "communitarian" grave; the Bees would be interred separately but lie together.

The Mass Bishop Ruiz preached that terrible morning was mournful and Christian, reminding the believers that Christ too had been born in such a landscape of oppression and pain. But the Good News of His birth would soon light up the world with resistance and resurrection. The Bishop's eyes filled with tears. "This is the saddest Christmas of our lives," he blurted, his broad face twisted in grief.

Everyone was looking for words to express that grief. There were no words.

The Abejas would not allow their dead to return to the earth naked and savaged. They had first to find their loved ones, to gaze one last time upon their broken faces, but the state, in its stupendous racism, had crassly sent the "coffins" back labeled generically "male adult," "female child," and each box had to be opened to identify who was inside. The stench of putrefaction leaked into the leaden noonday heat, engulfing the gagging mourners in the sweet gas of death.

Now the black flies gathered like a biblical plague. The time was short. There was no way to dress these viciously destroyed bodies, and so the Abejas went and fetched their best clothes, their most brilliant huipiles, their sombreros and their pants and their shoes, and they knelt and kissed them item by item and laid them over the dead in the open coffins, and the coffins were sealed up again and lowered into the freshly dug loam and it was over. It was over.

"This has been the saddest Christmas," old Samuel moaned. "It seems the baby has been born dead."

WHITEWASH

The government whitewash was reflexive and instantaneous: the Acteal massacre was a local affair, almost a family feud, a kind of highland Maya Hatfield & McCoy shoot-'em-up. "These conflicts can be validly characterized as intercommunal or even interfamilial within the context of the constant dispute for power," Attorney General Jorge Madrazo, not an anthropologist, reported on December 26th, not yet 100 hours after the killings. Madrazo's analysis diminished the massacre to a feud between five Chenalhó clans. The president of the Chiapas PRI, Juan Carlos Bonifaz, went Madrazo one better in the quest for ultimate reductionism: Acteal was "just a fight between two families over a sand and gravel pit." Those who had let Acteal happen sought to sweep it under the rug of the local geography, but 45 corpses were hard to hide from prying national and international eyes.

Similarly, the Mexican government would insist over and over again that there were no so-called "paramilitary" groups operating in Chiapas. The paramilitaries simply could not exist, because their existence implicated the military up to its ears in Acteal.

"By no stretch of the imagination" was the Zedillo government culpable of the "absurd" "confrontation" at Acteal by reason of "omission" or "commission," protested Interior Secretary Chuayffet. The accusation that the killers were members of the PRI was a foul calumny against the official party, an offended PRI president Mariano Palacios whined: "The PRI is an institution, and institutions do not commit massacres. These men did not operate under the logo of the PRI."

Of 41 Indians taken into custody in the week after the killings, all identified themselves with either the PRI or the "Cardenista Party," its corrupt subsidiary that had usurped the good name of Lazaro Cárdenas.

The government imposed its dubious spin on Acteal upon the kept press. Full-page newspaper ads and wall-to-wall TV spots were contracted to barrage the masses into buying the whitewash. Jornada columnist Julio Hernández was leaked a copy of TV Azteca reporters' guidelines on how to bamboozle the general public: "(1) Stress that the fight is between Indians. (2) The causes are land [i.e., blame the ejido system] and religion [i.e., blame the diocese]. (3) Stress that the PRD is trying to shift blame [from the Zapatistas] by calling the paramilitaries PRIistas—we cannot approve of calling them PRIistas…" One final caution: "We have to be very careful so as not to inflame the country."

An immediate communiqué from the CCRI challenged the whitewash. The killings had not been the result of a "confrontation" but rather the cold-blooded murder of unarmed civilians by 60 armed paramilitaries "sponsored by the state and federal governments." The EZLN had intercepted police radio communications and had hard evidence that Jorge Enrique and Uriel Jarquín had tried to cover up the killings. The President was "directly responsible for the bloody act— Zedillo will pass into history as a killer of Indians."

Calling upon the Zapatistas to show "responsibility and a constructive spirit," Zedillo tried to smooth over the allegations with evasive platitudes. "Unlike the government, the EZLN has not killed any Indians," Marcos snarled back. "Those who are investigating Acteal are the very ones who planned it…" Curiously, although the interchange was dark and harsh, for the first time since the talks had broken off in August 1996, the two sides had become enmeshed in a dialogue of sorts.

Smarting from national and international criticism, the President made some questionable cosmetic changes. On January 3rd, Chuayffet's chubby head rolled out the door. He was replaced by the agriculture secretary, a sharp-tongued, dagger-thin bureaucrat named Francisco Labastida, terminating Chuayffet's presidential ambitions but greatly enhancing those of his much svelter substitute.

At his first press conference, Labastida pinned Acteal on the EZLN's "unconstitutional and illicit" autonomous municipalities. He pledged a "new strategy" to deal with the San Andrés accords, which he ominously referred to as "proposals." He would meet face-to-face with "Rafael Sebastián Guillén Vicente" as many times as necessary to settle this thing. The army would proactively enforce the firearms and explosives laws in Chiapas and disarm those illegally in possession of weapons. "Everyone must be disarmed," Labastida emphasized, preparing the ground for the invalidation of the dialogue law that had protected the EZLN from such searches since 1995.

The new Interior Secretary's first two appointments were even less auspicious. Emilio Rabasa, the great grandson of Porfirio Díaz's governor of Chiapas, who in 1910 had isolated the state from the Mexican Revolution, became peace "coordinator," replacing the rarely-heard-from Coldwell. Adolfo Orive, founder of Línea Proletaria back in the 1970s and an eternal foe of both Bishop Ruiz and the Zapatista rebels, was appointed Labastida's chief advisor.

On January 8th, the new Interior Secretary ordered Governor Ruiz Ferro to hit the road. The slot was filled by Roberto Albores Guillén, a pear-shaped PRI deputy who represented his party on the revived COCOPA. Albores was Chiapas's sixth governor in seven years and the fourth straight to be imposed on the state from the center of the country (only two had actually been elected). Officially billed as the interim governor for an interim governor, Albores proved a disaster of considerable proportions. Assigned by Labastida to go after the Zapatista autonomous municipalities, the new interim governor, the scion of white Comitán ranchers, would blunder into constant scrapes with the Indians, like a Chiapas version of George Wallace or Orville Faubus.

At this writing, a little over two years after the Acteal holocaust, arrests have been made and convictions obtained. 104 Mexicans are or have been behind bars, 88 of them Tzotzil Indians charged with being the actual perpetrators. Most have received 35-year sentences, although 25 of the cases, including that of ex–municipal president Jacinto Arias, have been returned to the courts for retrial.

Lawyers question the government's failure to prosecute the Acteal 88 as a criminal conspiracy; charging the men individually lowers the profile of the massacre. Rather than a planned, premeditated act, the murders at Acteal are being tried as a casual event, the killers having been convened by serendipity at the top of the road to commit their atrocities.

In addition to the Indians charged with the killings, eight police officers who were up at the schoolhouse December 22nd, including General Julio César Santiago, have received eight-year sentences for failing to take preventive action. Police comandante Felipe Vázquez, who was convicted of protecting arms shipments to the PRIistas, received a seven-year term, but seven other officers were freed by the state of Chiapas. Two former members of the Mexican military who trained the paramilitaries—Mariano Arias Paz, an ex-lieutenant in the 83rd battalion at Rancho Nuevo, and Pablo Hernández, who was responsible for training the group from Los Chorros—received two-year sentences (upped to four years on appeal). It is unknown how many of the charged policemen were Indians.

Most of the non-Indians implicated in the Acteal massacre have escaped prosecution. The director and coordinator of state public security, Jorge Gamboa Solís and José Luis Rodríguez Orozco, are fugitives from justice. 11 state officials, including Laco's successor Homero Tovilla, Uriel Jarquín, and Jorge Enrique Hernández Aguilar, were barred from public office but never saw the inside of a jail cell. Neither did Governor Julio Ruiz Ferro, who could not have possibly been oblivious to the coming massacre. As reward for keeping his trap shut and obediently stepping out of the way, Ruiz Ferro was elevated to agricultural attaché at the Mexican embassy in Washington.

To justify such impunity, the Zedillo government recruited mercenaries to draw up revisionist histories of Acteal. Gustavo Hirales's *Road to Acteal* probably recaps government lies better than any of these volumes.

In a chronicle that rivals the work of the Holocaust scoffers for sheer cynicism, Hirales, a onetime guerrillero and an advisor to Bernal throughout the San Andrés Dialogue, scapegoats "Zapatista expansionism" and the "Pol Pot–like" rebels' "autonomous authoritarianism" for the murders. The EZLN had prior warning that the attack was imminent—why did they not protect the unarmed Abeja camp? he asks rhetorically, suggesting that the Zapatistas set up the Bees. The Diocese and its Fray Bart center were knowing accomplices in this plot to give Mexico a bad name. The fallen catechist Alonso Vázquez was particularly guilty: "The shepherd of the flock facilitated the work of the killers." The government's hands were clean.

PINCHE INDIOS

There is abundant evidence that Acteal was a crime perpetrated by the Mexican state. The involvement of the military with the paramilitary formations is particularly patent and matches the guidelines the Defense Ministry lays out in its "Manual of Irregular War."

On the heels of Acteal, Proceso (January 4, 1998) published a leaked document, the "Chiapas Campaign Plan," drawn up at the 7th Military Region in Tuxtla Gutiérrez in October 1994 by General José Rubén Rivas Pena, a School of the Americas grad, that called for the creation of civil counterinsurgency squads in the 38 Chiapas municipalities in which the EZLN had influence. "We must secretly organize certain sectors of the civil population—our objectives are patriotic—military operations will include the training of these self-defense and paramilitary formations—if no self-defense groups exist, it will be necessary to organize them…"

The Secretary of Defense questions the authenticity of the document. General Godínez, under whose command the plan was drawn up, scoffs that "we would not have waited four years to organize the paramilitaries." Nonetheless, the Chiapas campaign plan was implemented step by step by Godínez's successor, General Mario Renán Castillo, who majored in psychological operations and counterinsurgency warfare while a student at the Center for Special Forces, Fort Bragg, North Carolina.

Military involvement in the Acteal massacre runs from top to bottom. In addition to the high brass, three retired military generals, two of whom have flown the coop, are implicated up to their eyeballs in the killings. A certain Captain Germán Parra (transferred immediately after the massacre to Veracruz) and Major Absalón Gordillo (in charge of the Majomut BOM station) encouraged PRI weapons acquisition and protected deliveries of arms whose possession "pertains exclusively to the armed forces"—freelance journalist Jesús Ramírez Cuevas traced many PRI weapons back to a 1995 state police purchase. Two ex–military trainers were brought in to prepare the paramilitaries for attack.

In addition to this military connivance, civil security agents did nothing to prevent the massacre. Ramírez Cuevas reports that top-secret CISEN agents were gathering intelligence in Chenalhó all throughout November and December; one agent reportedly informed Tovilla of the shootings shortly after noon on December 22nd. Moreover, throughout the build-up, then-municipal president Jacinto Arias's uncle was the director of the state office of Attention to the Indians, the government's antenna in indigenous communities. His successor, Antonio Pérez, was himself a Chenalhó cacique.

But neither the state nor the federal governments had to rely on secret agents to figure out what was coming down. 30 murders (18 PRIistas, 12 PRD-Zapatistas) had been faithfully reported by La Jornada from May 24th on. Ricardo Rocha had bought the matter to the notice of the nation during Sunday prime time.

Acteal, to steal one from García Márquez, was truly a Chronicle of a Massacre Foretold.

So was the Acteal horror a premeditated conspiracy to obliterate the Zapatistas' civil bases and the civil society that sides with them? Probably not—the murders cost Zedillo too much international prestige to have been worth the slaughter. If there was a plan, it was the same old one: get the Indians to kill each other, not a difficult proposition given the tensions in the highlands. Then the military would step in to separate the savages and look like the good guys again. When crunchtime came down, those in charge chose not to notice. Jacinto Arias assured them that everything was under control, and that was all they needed to know. Their exalted positions gave them deniability. They didn't need to appreciate the evil energies at work down on the ground.

In the end, the mal gobierno just let Acteal happen, and when it did, the killing got away from them. Sure, the bloodshed was a little extreme, but that's how it is with these pinche indios.

That's who was at the bottom of the massacre of 46 Tzotzil Mexicans at Acteal, Chiapas December 22, 1997: the Pinche Indios. It had been the same for 500-plus years of poisonous racism and massacre—the Indians were always to blame for their steadfast insistence on being nothing else but Indians. There was no need to look elsewhere.

A FRAGILE SANCTUARY

The horror of Acteal set in motion the massive relocation of Zapatista bases in the highlands. Upmountain settlements hidden in vulnerable pockets of the hills descended to the paved road and set off for sanctuary at Polhó, a silent exodus wrapped in the dense, chill fogs of the mountain.

Volunteer teams risked mayhem to rescue Zapatista families isolated in PRI enclaves like Los Chorros, Pechiquil, and X'Cumunul. Thousands stumbled in from the cold, and Polhó could not hold them. Nearly 12,000 were living under sheets of thin plastic with bad water and little food at the coldest moment of the year, and the babies began to die.

Pedro Arias, 22 days, was the first. Televisa filmed ghoulishly as the distraught father clawed at the mud to carve out his son's grave. Pneumonia and diarrhea raged through the overcrowded camp. The children coughed and whimpered, a chorus of constant misery. Feeder camps, like the one just up the mountain in X'oyep, only spread the misery around. 33 died in the first month.

The relief effort was mired in mistrust even before Acteal. Polhó had refused government aid, turning back Uriel Jarquín's much-advertised blankets. Now the autonomous council was adamant it would only accept relief from NGOs and the diocese, and it wanted the International Red Cross to do the distribution. To Zedillo, the IRC represented dreaded international intervention, and he sent in then–Public Health Minister Juan Ramón de la Fuente to plead with the refugees to allow government doctors and medicines into the camps. "They couldn't kill enough of us with guns, so now they are using poison medicines," young "Luciano," the Polhó council's sparkplug spokesperson told reporters after a Mexican Red Cross truck delivered boxes of medicines that had already exceeded their cancellation dates.

When de la Fuente ventured down the road to Acteal, in the company of the new interim governor Albores Guillén, the Bees would not even let them on the premises. "We don't want your used pants," snorted Antonio Gutiérrez, "we want justice." "Who are you, anyway?" the Abeja representative asked the latest Chiapas interim "governor." "We want to speak to Ruiz Ferro…"

THE WOMEN'S WAR

Zedillo's motives for sending in the troops were patently clear. For two days, the soldiers cajoled and threatened Polhó authorities for permission to enter the camp and "perform social labor," but were repeatedly rebuffed by the women and children, who gathered at the fence and told them, with unmistakable disdain, to just go away.

Finally, the unit folded its tents and headed up the muddy hillside towards X'oyep. There too, the women, carrying their babies tightly wrapped up in shawls on their backs and gripping short, stout sticks, came out to the edge of the settlement to block the troops' advance.

"We have brought you food," the Captain tried to offer, but the women threw the food on the ground.

"Don't be cowards—show your leaders," a corpulent police officer shouted at the enraged ladies. "We are all leaders here," they shouted back in Tzotzil, pummeling and pushing the invaders off the property. Pedro Valtierra captured the moment for history: two young Indian women, their hair flowing down their arched backs, beating up on a grizzled, disgusted soldier, his automatic weapon dangling uselessly at his side. The photograph soon became an international icon.

The first weeks of January were filled with face-to-face resistance in one Zapatista village after another. The military made no pretense of going after the paramilitaries. Instead the soldiers stormed into the Zapatista settlements to "offer" social labor (haircuts, dental care, fixing busted appliances) and to search the houses for "firearms and explosives." Invariably, the women would march out to greet them with insults and stones and big sticks, tempting fresh massacre under the guns of the nervous troops. Most incursions occurred a hundred kilometers from Acteal, down in the Cañadas in the EZLN's autonomous municipalities, where the resistance of the women was resilient.

In San Miguel Yalchiptik, outside of Altamirano, after the military had raided a purported Zapatista safehouse January 1st, ski-masked women in fuchsia Tzeltal dresses and wielding sticks the size of small trees, got into the soldiers' faces. "Get out of here, you black dogs!" they howled. "Stay away from our houses, you snouts of the devil!" In nearby Diez de Mayo, 12 Zapatista women and nine arm babies were injured when troops returned the stones the women had flung to keep the *guachos* (soldiers) away from their houses.

In Chanal, on the Ejido Morelia, in Prado, Garrucha, and 85 other Zapatista settlements in the hundred days that followed Acteal, the women rose up against Zedillo's army like they were starring in a remake of *The Battle of Algiers,* and the

President whined to the New York Times that the Zapatistas were "sending their women and children to hurt our soldiers..."

On January 12th, a day of international mourning and *coraje* (indignation), Zapatista bases from all over the Cañadas converged on Ocosingo to protest the killings at Acteal and demand an end to the escalating invasions of EZLN communities. After the meeting in the town's long plaza, a group of women confronted the hated state police and the cops opened up, wounding two and instantly killing Guadalupe López Méndez, a young Zapatista mother from La Garrucha, whose baby was also hit by a bullet. The incident, unlike Acteal, occurred in full public view (a TV Azteca crew happened onto the scene), and Chiapas's new doubly interim governor was forced to arrest 25 police agents and turn state public security over to the military.

An instant symbol of the resistance of the Zapatista women, Guadalupe López Méndez was buried January 15th at the Aguascalientes in Garrucha, the autonomous municipality of Francisco Gómez. Townspeople first invaded the local army garrison, forcing the soldiers to flee into the jungle. *"¡Adios Zopilotes!"* (so long, vultures) the rebel supporters called after them.

Subcomandante Marcos came to the funeral via "Radio Rebelde" (FM 107) on a 10-watt pirate system smuggled into Mexico for the 1996 Intergaláctica direct from Radio Free Berkeley. "Compañera Guadalupe began to live the day she died," the Sup decreed as the mourners streamed into the wood-plank church.

PARTY POOPERS

The massacre and the military advance in its wake did not put the EZLN in a party mood. When we motored into La Realidad on New Year's Eve for the fourth anniversary celebration of the uprising, the village was dark, and Max, the village's liaison with the outside world, told us all to go back. Just getting in and out of the Cañadas was becoming an increasingly onerous task with military patrols stopping travelers every 10 kilometers to search them and their vehicles and their tangerines from head to foot for "firearms and explosives."

Max had good reason to wave off the outsiders. On January 3rd, military convoys parked at both ends of La Realidad and 200 troops stormed uphill into the mountain, surrounding the EZLN's most famous outpost, above which the general command was encamped. For seven hours, the soldiers moved through the forest, interrogating farmers at gunpoint about Marcos's whereabouts. Helicopters and fixed-wing aircraft flew backup overhead. The painter Beatriz Aurura drove to a pay phone four hours away to inform Gonzalo Ituarte at the CONAI that the EZLN headquarters was under attack, and the priest got the word on the wire right away. By late afternoon, the troops backed off and the Defense Ministry vehemently denied the incident had ever occurred. Aurura's phone call and

Gonzalo's alerting of the press were deemed further proof that the CONAI and its foreign agitators (Aurura is Chilean-born) were in cahoots with the rebels.

The Acteal massacre prompted fresh assault on the diocese and Don Samuel and eventually drove the CONAI out of business. Fray Bart came under renewed fire for inviting the cursed *extranjeros* (foreigners) into the civil peace camps. When CONAI secretary Miguel Alvarez traveled to Milan to raise funds for international observation, Francisco Labastida practically accused him of treason for luring interventionists to Chiapas.

And when, during a sermon in Seville, Spain, Raúl Vera denounced Mexican army training of the paramilitary death squads, the Mexican consul in that Spanish city, Javier López Moreno, an ex–interim governor of Chiapas, demanded to see the bishop's evidence. Upon his return, Raúl was "invited" to testify before a federal prosecutor (most of what he knew about the paramilitaries, Vera confessed, he had read in La Jornada).

On January 9th, General José Gómez Salazar, Renán Castillo's replacement as chief of the 7th Region, called a press conference to display the booty the military had taken at the purported rebel safehouse in San Miguel Yalchiptik: a dozen automatic weapons, radio communication equipment, rubber boots, and several books in Tojolabal published by the diocese—texts on the sacrament of the Baptism and the Rosary, *For the Good of Jesus Christ, the Selected Writings of Samuel Ruiz*—also a copy of the San Andrés Accords on Indian Rights & Culture. Comandante Sammy was once again the supreme chief of the Zapatista Army of National Liberation.

"You can see for yourself, it's obvious," General Gómez Salazar boasted to the press.

THE GLOBALIZATION OF INDIGNATION

Maybe it was the mothers praying as they were gunned down, the stories of the ripped wombs, the images of the shattered children, Christmas Eve, the Noble Savages or White Guilt, but Acteal touched an international nerve. The Pope, trembling with righteous indignation (and Parkinson's disease), protested the "cruel episode in a church in San Cristóbal, Chiapas" in his Christmas message to the world. Washington was even stunned into candor for once. The State Department, rightly assessing that Chiapas was no longer on the foreign policy agenda, demanded an immediate investigation, but when the Zedillo government shot back that it was none of the U.S.'s business how Mexico investigated Acteal, Clinton stepped in to smooth ruffled feathers and praised Zedillo's timely response to the massacre. On Christmas night, a hundred protesters circled in front of the White House.

Other power capitals were not so generous. To U.N. Secretary-General Kofi Annan the killings were a "repugnant crime," French Prime Minister Lionel

Jospin expressed "profound consternation," and the European Parliament debated suspending Mexico's December 8th ascension to interim membership in the EU. Before the free trade treaty had even been finalized, Mexico had violated the democracy clause to which Zedillo had finally agreed. In a stinging slap at the Mexican president, the European Union, which already bankrolled the CONAI, voted funds to sustain the Zapatista-Abeja refugee camp in Polhó.

But the real fury was in the street outside Mexican embassies and consulates, from Tokyo to Togo (where the Organization of African Unity was meeting) to Oslo (blood-red paint on the embassy wall) to Vermont (Ben & Jerry would buy Abeja coffee for their gourmet ice cream). 60,000 marched in Rome, hundreds more in Prague and Portugal. In Hamburg, Zap-symps danced cumbias on the desk-tops at the Mexican consulate. Paris protests were so effective that Le Monde suspended Bertrand de la Grange after he penned a particularly poisonous piece blaming the EZLN for Acteal. La Grange's masterwork on Marcos, *The Genial Impostor,* was distributed by the Mexican government as a tool in its post-Acteal counterattack against the Zapatistas.

When Zedillo flew into Davos for the annual World Economic Summit, he was met with spray paint and loud demonstrations. Latin protesters gathered from the Plaza de Mayo in Argentina to Nicaragua's Plaza Sandino. Everywhere, the protesters carried Pedro Valtierra's photo of the women's heroic resistance at X'oyep, flowers, 45 coffins and crosses, a jar of blood…

Faced with this worldwide "¡Basta Ya!" the Mexican government went into a defensive crouch. The nation's new foreign minister, the Cassandra-like PRIista Doña Rosario Green, bared her teeth at "these unacceptable acts of interference in Mexico's internal affairs, a country that has always stood for the principle of nonintervention…"

But if the Zedillo government sought to dismiss international indignation as proof of criminal foreign intervention, it had a harder time dodging domestic protest. Within hours of hearing the terrible tidings, the Frente Zapatista had gathered under the Angel of Independence with the blessing of the newly-sworn-in Cárdenas mayoral government—Cuauhtémoc visited the camp more than once to offer support and supplies. The 24-hour-a-day vigil under the gilded Angel served as both a collection depot for vital supplies the caravans were hauling south, and a point from which to organize meetings, marches and Masses—on the Sunday after Acteal, Oaxaca bishop Arturo Lona, Samuel's co-liberationist, defied constitutional restrictions by performing Mass on the Angel's steps.

The FZLN was essentially a collection of like-minded cells with no structure or leadership constraints, and protests sometimes got out of hand. When ski-masked students took over popular Pulsar FM radio to lament Acteal and broadcast a message of solidarity with the EZLN, heavily armed federal judicial police surrounded the station and the FZers barely escaped massacre themselves.

On January 5th, mourners deposited their cardboard coffins in front of the Mexican Stock Exchange, halting floor trading for the first hour, although the runners for the brokerage houses just whipped out their laptops and dealt from the median strip. The market itself was not at all upset about Acteal, soaring over 5,000 on the Monday of the massacre.

As the holiday fumes faded, the protests gathered steam north of the border. Knots of young people in ski masks and huipiles, ashen-faced nuns and priests, academics and indocumentados set up in front of consulates in 20 U.S. cities with their crosses and their blood, performing macabre skits that mercilessly taunted Zedillo's governance.

The high point of this globalization of protest came January 12th, the fourth anniversary of the great march that had capped the cease-fire back in '94, the first emergence of the civil society as a force to be reckoned with in the reconstruction of the nation.

Who really knows how many pounded the Mexico City pavement on January 12, 1998? Led by a handful of imported Abejas, the line of march was so lengthy that the last units entered the Zócalo five hours after the first, but because it took so much time to reach the downtown plaza, many abandoned the trek along the way, and those who had arrived in the Zócalo did not hang around. The Zapatistas have never been able to turn out anywhere near such a magnum number since.

According to EZLN totals, between December 23rd and January 13th, pro-Zapatista actions were convened in 130 place names in 25 countries on six continents and on every side of the planet's seven oceans. The "¡Ya Bastas!" boomed like cannonballs pointed at Los Pinos, and the government, like a wounded, dangerous dinosaur, flailed back.

ORCHESTRATING XENOPHOBIA

Knee-jerk fear and loathing of foreigners is practically a Mexican natural resource. Mexico's phobias about annexation, invasion, intervention, incursion, imposition, and other gross violations of national sovereignty would be pathological if they were not so woefully justified. But as patriotism is the sanctuary of scoundrels, those who invoke the phantom of foreign intervention are often those who have sold the Patria to the dogs of foreign capital, the IMF, the World Bank, the WTO, Wall Street.

New Interior Secretary and now top contender for the PRI's presidential nomination Francisco Labastida fingered the non-Mexican NGOs (and those Mexican NGOs that received international funding) for blackening the nation's good name and pledged to "apply the law to international organizations that interfere in what pertains only to the Mexicans." As Interior Secretary, Labastida directed the Mexican Migra.

Curiously, no one had alleged that the NGOs had broken any Mexican laws, but by the third week in January, every stumble-bum PRI deputy in Congress felt it a patriotic duty to take a cheap shot at the internationals and those who aided and abetted their intervention. When a triad of PRD lawmakers took off for Brussels to update the European Parliament on Acteal, the PRI section of the chamber known as the Bronx went carnivorous. "Traitors! *Vendepatrias!*" (sellers of the fatherland) they catcalled, threatening to expel the PRDers from Congress. The PRI swore to send its own "truth squad" to debrief the Europeans.

Bankers and businessmen were prominent in the lynch mob, calling for the application of Article 33—the draconian constitutional provision that gives the President carte blanche to expel any "inconvenient" foreigner without the slightest shred of due process—to all foreign meddlers in Chiapas. Conspiracies of foreign malevolence were conjured up: the World Bank, the Communists, the Protocols of Zion, the Queen of England (said the Larouchites) were behind the subversive NGOs.

The foreigners had set up in Chiapas because it was close to the Oaxaca isthmus, which they coveted to install a new Panama Canal, affirmed then-PRI congressperson Ricardo Montiel. Emilio O. Rabasa, the new peace coordinator's father, recalled how Juárez had executed the French-sent "emperor" Maximilian on Campana Hill above Querétaro and suggested a similar fate awaited Danielle Mitterand.

Chiapas's rookie interim governor, a man so shaped like a croquette that Marcos was soon calling him "Croquetas," was the most loud-mouthed xenophobe in the mob. "Chiapas for the Chiapanecos!" he bellowed at rallies of trucked-in PRIistas, *"Manos Afuera de Chiapas!"* (Hands Off Chiapas!). "Outsiders have been coming to Chiapas to stir up our people for too long," Albores Guillén told 28 PRI mayors from the conflict zone who were demanding the expulsion of Don Samuel and all "foreign catechists" from Chiapas. The Albores government began running radio spots calling upon local patriots to report any suspicious foreigners to immigration authorities. One of Tuxtla's many dailies headlined a story THE SATANIC INTERVENTION OF THE EXTRANJEROS!

It was hard to deny foreign intervention in the Chiapas imbroglio. Important generals had earned their degrees at the gringos' School of the Americas and the Center for Special Forces, and the GAFE, a U.S.-trained special air force group, now patrolled Chenalhó. The U.S. embassy conceded that its military attachés paid "three or four" visits a year to Chiapas, and most of the military hardware in the state had come from Pentagon credits. Given the caliber and the manufacturer of the weapons turned on the Abejas at Acteal, it would not be far off target to affirm that the massacre was "Made in the U.S.A."

Ernesto Zedillo put the presidential seal on the ethnic cleansing in a January 23rd discourse at Kanocín, Yucatán, a Mayan Indian suburb of Mérida. Although the speech begins hopefully—"The government is in agreement with the San Andrés accords" which the President promised to "give form to" (in truth, a devious scheme to impose his own version of San Andrés on the Congress)—Zedillo soon descends into rank extranjero bashing: "The extranjeros who allege human rights violations are directly involved in the conflict in Chiapas—those who are spreading the lies are taking advantage of the government's tolerance—many of those who interfere in our affairs do so not to resolve the problems but to take up a (partisan) flag—these people are breaking our laws even if they hide behind humanitarian causes…"

According to a spurious Interior Secretariat registry, 96 NGOs from 12 countries were working in Chiapas in 1998, although many, like the "Eisenhower Church of Christ" were unknown in the region. The U.S. NGOs, notably Global Exchange and Pastors for Peace, were important conduits for keeping the civil peace camps staffed with eager volunteers. Zedillo's immigration police considered these camps to be chockablock with subversives, and the diocese's role in organizing them was publicly scorned. After Kanocín, Fray Bart ceded the management of the camps to Enlace Civil, a new San Cristóbal magnet that filled the vacuum after the government-induced demise of the CONPAZ coalition.

The first to be snatched up in the new Migra pogrom was Maria Darlington, a 65-year-old North Carolina grandmother who had come to Chiapas with a Pastors' caravan and stayed on for stints in the civil peace camps. Stopped February 7th on her way down to La Realidad at the notorious Zaragoza checkpoint, Darlington was returned to San Cristóbal, interrogated, accused of carrying a sign at a march in Tila a year earlier, put on a plane, and deposited in McAllen, Texas, before anyone even knew she was gone.

The next to go was Edwin Schweitzer, a Pennsylvania art expert who made the great mistake of attending the San Andrés talks as a COCOPA-licensed "observer," although he held only a tourist visa. "Observation," in accord with revised Migra standards, now apparently required a special FM-3 form. The fact that both Darlington and Schweitzer had been thrown out for old crimes was a telltale sign that the INM had loaded up its computers in an orchestrated effort to eliminate foreign witnesses to the carnage in Chiapas.

LOLITA

A singular incident February 13th hit a high bong on the xenophobia meter. That morning, a white helicopter abruptly put down on the school grounds in La Realidad, where the civil peace camp that monitors daily military patrols is housed. No helicopters had ever landed in this key Zapatista outpost before without prior clearance from the community, and the landing was seen as tantamount to an act of war.

Instead of disgorging war-painted soldiers, the whirlybird, which had been rented at great expense to the taxpayers of Chiapas by Governor Croquetas, contained a blowzy late-night talk-show hostess, Lolita de la Vega. Thanks to her husband, the czar of the PRI-run radio and television workers union, Lolita has a lifetime niche at TV Azteca called *Hablemos Claro* or "Let's Speak Straight." Now "Señora Dolores," as the Tojolabales of La Realidad called her with mock respect, had come to answer the burning question: "What Are Foreigners Doing in Chiapas?"

"And what we found out was that foreigners are manipulating our Indians! We were so surprised that strangers with white skin" (Lolita herself is a cadaverous alabaster) "are behind the ski masks of the EZLN!"

The surprise helicopter landing infuriated the townspeople, who gathered around the big ceiba tree while the peace campers, about half of whom were Mexican, tried to tell Lolita that she didn't have the community's permission to be there. A handheld camera inside the craft recorded a man with a Castilian accent asking whom Lolita represented. "We heard English, French, and even German being spoken!"—highly unlikely since Spanish is the lingua franca of the camps. Hermann, who was an eyewitness to this tawdry caper, suggests that de la Vega confounded Tojolabal and Tzeltal with "foreign" languages.

Lolita's producer, burly PRI hack Manuel de la Torre, bailed out of the copter and tried to make friends with the Indians—he later falsely accused the peace people of being armed. After a half hour of such hectoring, Max, the headman, had enough and ordered Lolita and her crew out of town. The international observers removed the branches with which they had hobbled the aircraft. The machine rose violently at an oblique angle, stirring up choking dust and sending the roof of the schoolhouse flying—two kids were cut and a fleeing woman fell and hurt her leg.

The following Sunday, Immigration subsecretary Fernando Solís Camara showed on Lolita's chat fest to thank her profusely for the public service she had rendered by exposing foreign control of the EZLN at last. His hand "would not tremble in applying the law" to these perfidious strangers. Gilberto López y Rivas, now a PRD member of the new COCOPA, who had hesitantly agreed to appear on the program, was so nauseated at this festival of xenophobia that he stalked out of the studio on camera.

"Xenophobia is a useful weapon," mused TV Azteca news director Sergio Sarmiento.

The Lolita spectacular encouraged Immigration agents to set up shop in the San Cristóbal town plaza, demanding IDs from suspicious tourists and following them to their hotels and restaurants and private homes. Solís Camara indicated he had warrants pending for 15 dangerous foreigners in Chiapas. In San Cristóbal, a pair of Spanish bakers of organic bread were taken into custody.

MORE PERFIDIOUS STRANGERS

The next to be snagged by the Migra dragnet was Tom Hansen, past director of Pastors for Peace but then in Chiapas for the Chicago-based Youth Media Project, which distributes camcorders in Cañada villages so that the communities can record their history, and is funded by the Rockefeller Foundation, Harp Helú's bank, and a U.S.-Mexican government cultural fund.

Hansen, a tall, Anglo type, was approached by agents in Altamirano while buying food for a gathering on the Ejido Morelia. They just wanted to check his papers. Would he accompany them to the Immigration post out by the highway *¿por favor?* Tom's abductors first threatened to stow him in the trunk in classic kidnap style, then took him on a dizzying tour of San Cristóbal, Tuxtla, and the Mexico City airport, where he was thrown into a shit-splattered cell overnight. A U.S. embassy official, called in to witness this travesty in accordance with the Vienna Convention, seemed more embarrassed than helpful.

Hansen was charged with feloniously attending the 1996 San Andrés talks while in the country on a tourist visa. Threatened with expulsion under Article 33 by INM mouthpiece Alejandro Carrillo Castro, the former Mexican consul in Chicago who knew Tom well, he was finally put on a plane for Miami and told not to come back for 10 years. To prevent any contact with reporters scouring the airport for him, Hansen was hustled into a van and driven around by agents for an hour before his plane took off. The snatch of Tom Hansen was later explained by Mexico's ambassador in Washington, as "an act of sovereignty similar to the deportation of undocumented Mexicans from the U.S."

On February 26th, the ax fell on Michel Chanteau, the old French priest of Chenalhó, so many of whose parishioners had been butchered at Acteal. Father Michel had been threatened and shadowed since 1995, when Samuel's three foreign priests had been expelled.

On the morning of his detention, Michel had stuffed his errand bag with carrots and cabbages from the garden and jumped into the public van for San Cristóbal to visit with his great friend, the historian Andrés Aubry. The Migra was waiting for him at the checkpoint, asked to see a work visa the government had denied him for years, drove him straight to Tuxtla, put him on a plane, and voilà, Michel Chanteau was in Mexico City being grilled by insistent agents. His sin, he was told, had been to opine to TV Azteca that the Mexican government had organized the paramilitaries at Acteal. This, authorities insisted, was "a crime of opinion," flagrant interference in Mexico's domestic affairs. Article 33 was invoked to punish the padre. The French consul stood by doing nothing, as embarrassed as his U.S. counterpart. Even as Michel was being escorted to the Air France flight, Immigration agents set up a stooge to pretend he was Father Chanteau in an airport press conference, where the phony priest confessed his transgressions.

Others were taken during the February–March offensive: Massimo Boldini, the first foreigner to enter Acteal after the massacre, was rounded up in Tulija, near Chilón, observing a pro-Zapatista demonstration against the military occupation of a local school. Three extranjera women, one a Columbia University student on her Spring break, were also captured. A French sailor, Ahmad Boukara, who had brought sackloads of solidarity messages across the seas in his 30-foot skiff, was dispatched by the ever-vigilant Migra from Puerto Madero. Although it is of little consolation, the Zapaphiles were not the only pernicious strangers being expelled by the Mexican Migra. 63,000 mostly Central Americas were deported to Guatemala in 1997-98, 23,000 of them in the three months following Acteal.

Ironically, at the peak of the INM attack, a large delegation of European civil observers arrived in Chiapas. Although the "Civil Observation Commission" had obtained FM-3 visas, the Europeans still had to weather Migra malfeasance at the checkpoints. In San José del Rio, Zapatista supporters formed a line of resistance to keep agents from grabbing the observers.

The Europeans learned the cruelest lesson first-hand February 23rd in Tila, when an informant, José Tila López, was assassinated by Peace & Justice gunmen an hour after he testified to the delegation. Unable to meet with the CCRI because of military pressures (Marcos would later send a video), the delegates inspected the ghost town of Guadalupe Tepeyac, accompanied by its displaced former residents. The civil observation team's conclusions, dedicated to José Tila López, were eyebrow-raising: "There exist elements to accuse the Mexican government of genocide." "They are lying," snapped Foreign Minister Rosario Green at a special March session of the Euro Parliament called to review charges of human rights abuses in Chiapas.

Into this fulminating sea of xenophobia plunged José Saramago, the Portuguese novelist and humanitarian communist, who had been repeatedly denied the Nobel Prize for literature, a rejection that won him great sympathy in the Spanish and Portuguese literary worlds. Later in 1998, Saramago would finally land his Nobel, an award that heightened the moral authority of his mid-March visit to Chiapas.

Even before he arrived in Mexico, Saramago had advertised that he was going to Chiapas, and head Migra Carrillo warned the author that he too risked expulsion under Article 33 should he be deemed to have intervened in Mexican political affairs.

José Saramago does not cotton much to such authoritarianism. He is a veteran of the Revolution of the Carnations that toppled the Salazar dictatorship, and he so bridled at the Portuguese government's censorship of his controversial work on the real Jesus that he resides in exile in the Canary Islands. An old man of 76 who did not publish his first novel until he was 60, he displays the humility of one to whom success has come late in life.

Although he was "tired and old," Saramago was obligated "to go to where the pain is, or else I am not alive." On March 14th, the author motored into the hills above San Cris, dismounting at the military checkpoints to be searched for "firearms and explosives" and have his documents closely inspected by a pugnacious Migra.

Saramago spent hours in the dust and grinding poverty of Polhó, so crowded that it resembled a breathing Brueghel painting, and sat down with the elders, among whom he was perhaps the oldest. He said little and listened a lot. In Acteal, Saramago said even less, and the Bees told him the story of the massacre and showed him the mutilated children. He took home with him a rock, a piece of the sacred land of the Abejas. "Look, they have let me take a rock," he told his wife Pilar. "He held it in his hand," Hermann wrote, "as if it weighed a century or a lifetime."

Autonomous Zones and Aguascalientes

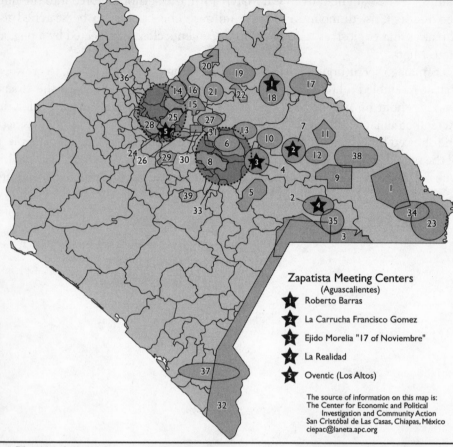

Zapatista Meeting Centers
(Aguascalientes)

⭐1 Roberto Barras

⭐2 La Carrucha Francisco Gomez

⭐3 Ejido Morelia "17 of Noviembre"

⭐4 La Realidad

⭐5 Oventic (Los Altos)

The source of information on this map is:
The Center for Economic and Political
Investigation and Community Action
San Cristóbal de Las Casas, Chiapas, México
ciepac@laneta.apc.org

1.- "Libertad de los Pueblos Mayas";
Municipal seat: Santa Rosa El Copín
In Ocosingo

2.- "San Pedro Michoacán";
Municipal seat: La Realidad
In Las Margaritas

3.- "Tierra y Libertad";
Municipal seat: Amparo Agua Tinta
in Las Margaritas, Independencia,
and Trinitaria

4.- "17 de Noviembre";
Municipal seat: Ejido Morelia
in Altamirano and Chanal

5.- "Miguel Hidalgo y Costilla";
Municipal seat: Ejido Justo Sierra
in Las Margaritas and Comitán

6.- "Ernesto Che Guevara"; Municipal
seat: Moisés Gandhi in Ocosingo

7.- "1 de Enero"; Municipal seat:
Sibaca in Ocosingo

8.- "Lucio Cabañas"; Municipal seat:
Tushakalijá in Oxchuc, Huixtán

9.- "Maya"; Municipal seat:
Amador Hernández in Ocosingo

10.- "Francisco Gómez"; Municipal seat:
La Garrucha in Ocosingo

11.- "Ricardo Flores Magón";
Municipal seat: Taniperlas in Ocosingo

12.- "San Manuel"; Municipal seat:
Ranchería San Antonio in Ocosingo

13.- "San Salvador"; Municipal seat:
Ejido Zapata in Ocosingo

14.- "Huitiupán"; in the territory
of the same name.

15.- "Simojovel"; in the territory
of the same name.

16.- "Sabanilla"; in the territory
of same name

17.- "Vicente Guerrero"; in
the territory called Palenque

18.- "Trabajo"; in the territory
of Palenque and Chilón

19.- "Francisco Villa"; in the territory called
Salto de Agua

20.- "Independencia"; in the territories called
Tila and Salto de Agua

21.- "Benito Juárez"; in the territories called
Tila, Yajalón, and Tumbalá

22.- "La Paz"; in the territories
called Tumbalá and Chilón

23.- "José María Morelos y Pavón"; Municipal
seat: Quetzalcóatl in the territory called
Marqués de Comillas, Ocosingo.

24.- "San Andrés Sacamch'en de los Pobres";
Municipal seat in the territory
called San Andrés Larraínzar.

25.- "San Juan de La Libertad"; Municipal seat
in the territory called El Bosque

26.- "San Pedro Chenalhó"; Municipal seat
in Polhó; in the territory
of the same name

27.- "Santa Catarina"; in the territory
called Pantelhó y Sitalá

28.- "Bochil"; Municipal seat
in the territory of same name

29.- "Zinacantán"; Municipal seat
in the territory of same name

30.- "Magdalena de la Paz"; Municipal seat:
Magdalena, in the territory called Chenalhó

31.- "San Juan K'ankujk"; in the territory
called San Juan Cancuc

32.- "Tierra y Libertad Autonomous Region";
in the territories of Las Margaritas,
Trinitaria, Grandeza, Frontera Comalapa,
Chicomuselo, Porvenir, Siltepec, Mazapa
de Madero, Bellavista, Villa Comaltitlán,
Unión Juárez,
Tapachula, Tuxtla, Chico, and Motozintla

33.- "Tzoj Chuj Autonomous Region"; in the
territories of Atlamirano, Chanal, Oxchuc,
Tenejapa, Cancuc, Huixtán, San Cristóbal,
Amaltenango del Valle, Ocosingo, Abasolo,
and Ernesto Che Guevara

AUTONOMOUS MULTII-ETHNIC REGIONS
(Regiones Autonomas Pluriétnicas– RAP)

34.- "Marqués de Comillas"; RAP in the
the territory of Marqués de Comillas

35.- "Border Region"; RAP
in the territories of Margaritas,
Santo Domingo Las Palmas

36.- "Northern Region" RAP in the territories
of Bochil, Ixtapa, Soyaló, El Bosque,
Jitotol, Huitiupán y Simojovel

37.- "Soconusco Region" RAP in the
territories of Huixtla, Tuzantán,
Tapachula, Cacahoatán y Unión Juárez

38.- "Jungle Region" RAP
in the territory of Las Tazas

39.- Nicolás Ruiz Autonomous Council.

SPRING 1998

ZEDILLO'S BONSAI

In February, on the second anniversary of the signing of the Indian Rights accords, this reporter paid a ritual visit to the meeting house up at San Andrés, where, after arduous months and years of racist government insult and bluster, the EZLN had at last achieved the flawed but historic agreement. A window was broken and had been boarded up. The front door lock had been forced and the furniture looted. Out back, the patio was littered with busted beer bottles and had been turned into a public toilet. The condition of the building summed up the condition of the agreement.

No one seriously believed that the Dialogue could ever be revived, but the government players kept pretending that the renewal of the talks was right around the corner. The Zedillo brain trust, which had already decided it would never sit down with the Zapatistas again, kept proffering "peace" overtures. First Labastida petitioned Marcos for a face-to-face "secret" meeting, which the Sup studiously ignored. Then the Interior Secretary advertised that Zedillo's 29 objections to the COCOPA text left hanging January 11th, 1997 had magically been reduced to just four—actually the four only repackaged the original objections into a 17-page document that was essentially a draft of the President's own soon-to-be-announced Indian Rights initiative.

The re-packaged objections were forwarded to the jungle via the CONAI. Because of heavy military patrols, it took three attempted deliveries to get the document to the comandantes. The EZLN's response was voiced February 16th in San Cristóbal when 5,000 Zapatista supporters marched to demand that "not one comma" be changed in the text. "We want everything or nothing," Comandante Zacarías shouted at the mal gobierno in the cathedral plaza.

At the end of February, the Sup issued several bizarre documents that depicted a banquet attended by a Hieronymus Bosch bestiary of PRI and PAN dinner guests. The final segment, "Amnesia Above (the table) & Memory Below," postulated that the government had never intended to act upon San Andrés, that it had all been (and continued to be) a marketing stunt, and the dialogue was history. The remarks were the last the Sup would make on any matter whatsoever for many months, as the EZLN slunk back into a maddening silence that had only been punctured momentarily by the terrible killings at Acteal.

When, on March 15th, Ernesto Zedillo sent his own shrunk-down version of the San Andrés accords onto the PRI senate majority in Congress for ratification, few legislators dropped their socks. A Zedillo "Indian Rights & Culture Law" had been in the pipeline since Acteal and was a cornerstone of his "new" strategy to unilaterally resolve the conflict without ever having to speak to the EZLN again. Now the military and its paras would keep the Zapatistas busy while the PRI-dominated Congress passed what the President purported was a faithful rendition of the San Andrés accords, effectively discharging Zedillo's obligation to comply with the agreement. A costly TV blitz was activated: "This government will comply with the San Andrés accords."

The President's text picked up where negotiations had broken off a year earlier. Zedillo's law denied autonomy and took pains to delete the word from the initiative. It also negated territoriality, the association of majority Indian municipalities into autonomous regions, the collective use of the land and the environment, and a meaningful justice system conforming to Indian norms that did more than try chicken thieves.

Zedillo's Indian Rights legislation was a bonsai compared to the tree of San Andrés, wrote Luis Hernández, the EZLN's most prominent advisor at the negotiating table. Later, Luis would compare the difference between the PRI legislation and San Andrés to the distinction between "an abortion and a live birth."

The gutted version was circulated first to the new COCOPA, which was invited to integrate its own proposal in the final draft, but PRD reps Gilberto López y Rivas, along with Luis an architect of the original agreement, and La Jornada founder and now senator Carlos Payán walked out, and the effort did not prosper. The legislative commission had been effectively neutralized by the Spring of 1998, and its seal of approval was not essential to the success of Zedillo's Indian Rights bill in the Senate.

Despite the PRI's overwhelming majority in the upper house, the ruling party still fell short of the two-thirds majority it needed to effect constitutional modifications that Zedillo's law required—passage would be even thornier over in the Chamber, where the PRI had blown its absolute majority to the combined totals of the opposition. The PAN would have to be brought on board if the measure was to carry. But the PAN, which has no Indian constituency outside of Yucatán, had its own agenda, a species of municipal autonomy that would defend white, middle-class burghers from the onerous bite of the federal government. Now PAN matched the Zedillo proposal with its own oddly skewed piece of legislation, calling for the creation of *cartas municipales*, a medieval Spanish administrative mechanism by which monarchs granted special dispensations to vassal city-states. The PRI and the PAN disappeared behind locked doors to hash out the fine print.

The PRD, of course, supported the COCOPA version and considered that no law should be enacted until the stonily silent EZLN was heard from. Congressional observers envisioned a ski-masked Marcos addressing a joint session of the Mexican Congress to plead the rebels' case. But the General Command held its tongue at this latest affront to the sacred language of San Andrés, and Labastida was in no mood to wait around for the comandantes to come forward. "So far as I know they are not legislators—laws are not made in the jungle," the bloodless secretary sneered.

Zedillo's thrust on Indian Rights was accompanied by a nest of local laws on the theme that PRI majorities were pushing in state congresses from Chihuahua to Yucatán. The common proposition of these local efforts was to reduce Indian struggles to the smallest possible geographical area. The fragmentation of the issue and the possible passage of the Zedillo bonsai impelled the National Indigenous Congress (CNI) to summon Indians from all over Mexico to the Zócalo for what it heralded as a "National Indian Insurrection."

THE DEEP FREEZE

As an annex to its Indian initiative, the Zedillo government filled the sky over La Realidad and other Aguascalientes with hostile aircraft—Hermann counted nine different craft in the air show over the Zapatista stronghold on the day the legislation was introduced. Villagers at Oventic complained the Air Force was bombarding the ejido with sacks full of poisonous serpents. Zapatista crews were soon planting sharpened stakes on the esplanades of the Aguascalientes to prevent the military from making Lolita-like landings, a self-defense tactic that invoked the Vietnamese resistance.

By the advent of April, the opposition was in the streets. 10,000 marched in Tuxtla against Zedillo's bonsai, and in Mexico City, the CNI swarmed over the plaza fronting the senate, demanding to be let in. How could the solons legislate on Indian Rights without the Indians? Only three out of the 124 senators inside even called themselves Indians, and two of them were PRIistas. But in the inner sanctum, the ruling party was having a hard time convincing the PAN which side their bread was buttered on. Holy Week arrived with no resolution, and the lawmakers headed for the beach.

On April 10th, a day on which the twin crucifixions of Emiliano Zapata and Jesus Christ coalesced, thousands of Indians in town for the National Indian Insurrection from the Zongolica and the Zapotec nation, the Yaquis through the Yucatán inclusive, carried a grotesquely contorted figure of Emiliano Zapata nailed to an enormous cross into that national umbilicus called the Zócalo and pledged not to abandon the great square until Zedillo withdrew his "Indian Rights" initiative.

By now the clock against an April 30th adjournment was ticking. The PAN remained unaccountably aloof, sticking with its cartas municipales as if they were aces in the hole. What did they want? Whatever Labastida offered, it was never enough, and Zedillo's bonsai was dispatched to the deep freeze on April 30th—subsequent sessions of Congress would be overwhelmed with a banking scandal known as FOBAPROA, a veritable Mexican Watergate, that kept Indian Rights on ice for years.

An obscure issue in the first place with a limited constituency (many Indians had a hard time deciphering it), and one that was not número uno on most Mexicans' survival list, Zedillo's bonsai winds up as a footnote to this history.

Given the legislative odds in the first place, the President's true intentions in submitting the Indian Rights measure remain unstated. Marcos had no doubt called it right—this "giving form to San Andrés" had all been a marketing gimmick to wash his hands of the accords. The President was really embarking on a much more dangerous course.

RICARDO FLORES MAGON

The Spring had come hot and tinder-dry to the highlands and the Cañadas, stirring up biblical forest fires that could not be contained. In late March, Environmental Secretary Julia Carabias accused Zapatista cadre in the Chanal region of keeping government firefighters out of the Tzotz Choj autonomous region, an allegation that provoked a rare response from the CCRI (March 28th). The communiqué, sent under Comandante Zebedeo's signature, accuses the mal gobierno of being against nature and setting the fires.

As always, the Spring planting occasioned land invasions and campesino assassinations; the AEDPCH lost several key organizers, among them Rubicel Ruiz, gunned down on a contract hit let by the sinister Sierra cacique Carmen Orantes, an Albores intimate.

As Good Friday and Zapata day approached hand in hand, the CISEN circulated rumors that the EZLN would stage a mass defection to Guatemala April 10th to force international attention upon the stand-off. The Zapatistas had other plans.

Ricardo Flores Magón was a Oaxaca-born anarchist who wrote and published Regeneración, the most influential journal during the early days of the Mexican Revolution. Imprisoned during U.S. sedition raids, he was murdered in Leavenworth federal prison in 1924.

"Ricardo Flores Magón" is also the name of an EZLN autonomous municipality headquartered at the Taniperlas ejido in the east of Ocosingo—the autonomía takes in 50 outlying communities stretching across the northeast corner of the

Montes Azules reserve from the Tulija valley all the way to Naja. The ejido itself was carved from the forest in 1946 by Tzotzil speakers from the mountain cold lands and finally chartered in the 1960s. But by 1998, almost half of Taniperlas was in the hands of newcomers who had affiliated with the PRI when General Absalón was boss of the state. The EZLN came to Taniperlas early, in 1988, offering the original settlers protection from Absalón, and they had been in the rebel fold ever since.

The autonomía of Ricardo Flores Magón was declared in the December 1994 Zapatista advance, but it was a long while before authorities were elected. Now, on April 10th, 1998, the rebel municipality would begin to function at last. What more auspicious day than that of the combined martyrdoms of Christ and Zapata to make autonomous rule a reality?

To mark the occasion, the villagers had painted a bucolic mural on the schoolhouse wall. The colorful project, "The Dream and Reason of the Perlas Canyon," featured fertile fields, kids bathing in the ejido pond, a gaggle of strutting ducks, wandering horsemen, a women's circle, and a kindly, ethereal Zapata hovering above it all: it was coordinated by Professor Sergio Valdez Ruvicalva as part of the Mexico City–based Autonomous Metropolitan University's Tzeltal Education Project. For his troubles, "El Checo" (the professor's cartooning name) would become the first Mexican muralist since David Alfaro Siqueiros to be locked up in prison.

> Ricardo Flores Magón is the name
> of the municipality that was born today
> I'm going to send them a telegram
> to inform the entire nation
> I'm a campesino, I'm a Zapatista
> I'm proud and I have reason to be
> in this land my people have grown
> this is the land that we work
> I helped to build it.

"Corrido of Ricardo Flores Magón" collected by Daniel Pensamento, April 10th, 1998

Not only was the Mexican government prepared to delete the autonomías from the legislation pending in Congress, it was committed to erasing them from the face of the earth. Now the first shots were about to be fired in the Zedillo-to-Labastida-to-Albores war on the Zapatistas' 32 or 34 or 38 municipalities, and those who gathered for the April 10th festivities in Flores Magón were right in the line of fire.

By Spring '98, autonomy had caught on among the EZLN's support networks—Global Exchange was even running reality tours to the Zapatista autonomías (Ejido Morelia, Polhó, Che Guevara, 10 days, $875). Others had come to help on their own. Jeff Conant had given up a San Francisco apartment and set up in San Cristóbal, working on appropriate technology projects in the

Cañadas much in the spirit of Ben Linder, martyred back in Sandinista Nicaragua. He arrived at Flores Magón late on the night of the 10th and hung his hammock in the civil peace camp cabin. Before dawn, he was shaken awake. "The soldiers are here," his compañeros whispered urgently.

Jeff stumbled outside into the pitch-black night A string of Hummers and transport carriers, maybe a hundred in all, were lined up on the road with their lights on—the lead vehicle had run off the jungle track. Now the troops descended from the trucks and jogged towards the village. Jeff took off for the trees and ran right into a bank of heavily armed soldiers, their faces streaked with black war paint.

500 police, 400 soldiers, plus immigration, CISEN, and judicial police agents, participated in the Flores Magón raid. Accompanied by PRI guides from Taniperlas, they entered the autonomía, arresting suspected village officials, and leveling the municipal structures with sledgehammers and setting fire to them. Professor Valdez's idyllic mural was painted over, and he was charged with "usurpation of authorities" and being a member of the autonomous town council. Luis Meléndez Medina, Ofelia's nephew and an observer from the Fray Pedro Lorenzo de la Nada Human Rights Center in Ocosingo, was collared as the autonomía's president. "I was just observing what was going on," he later observed. Along with the authentic Flores Magón authorities, El Checo and Meléndez would spend the next year of their lives in Cerro Hueco before "justice" prevailed.

The fate of the foreigners was just as brusque. Hauled up to San Cristóbal and grilled for 18 hours by hard-boiled Migra interrogators, they were charged with flagrantly violating the Mexican Constitution by setting up a parallel authority. The 12 (four Spanish volunteers, three U.S. citizens, two Belgian observers, two Canadians, and a German) were dragged out of the immigration offices (some went limp) and thrown in a bus to Tuxtla. Photographers from AP and Agence France-Presse (both non-Mexicans) were beaten bloody on the tarmac when they tried to photograph the expulsees as they boarded the plane.

Up in Mexico City, treatment was more cordial (double ham pizzas, Jeff recalls) but the sentences were stiff ones. The 12 extranjeros were now considered "notoriously inconvenient" under Article 33. The foreign minister accused them of crimes against the flag and the national anthem. They were put on separate planes and told they could never ever come back to Mexico, 33ed for life. An unkempt Jeff Conant arrived at LAX customs and was strip-searched because he fit the drug-runner profile.

Albores's explanation of the raid on Flores Magón was all bilious xenophobia and law-and-order mumbo jumbo. "Never again will we allow Chiapas to be taken advantage of by those who do not know the state and have no right to determine our institutional life. We are on an irreversible road! There is no such thing as an autonomous municipality in Chiapas," he thundered. All of these unconstitutionally constituted entities would be dismantled to restore "the rule of law." Polhó would be next. Julio Moguel, onetime EZLN advisor, calculated that, judging by the size of the Flores Magón strike force, it would take 22,000 police and 15,000 soldiers to get the job done.

The remunicipalization of Chiapas had been accorded at San Andrés, the only part of the agreement the government seemed willing to fulfill—as long as it controlled the new municipalities. In May, when Zedillo called for the process to become a reality at last, Albores fetched the bone like a good bulldog and 12 working days later promulgated plans to create 33 new municipalities in the state, 13 of them in Ocosingo, all of which overlapped existing EZLN autonomías, a surefire recipe for chaos.

The Zapatista municipalities did not take the dismantlement of Flores Magón lightly. Round-the-clock civilian patrols were established and an early warning system coordinated in the Cañadas. On the Ejido Morelia ("17th of November") the compañeros encamped around the Aguascalientes to protect it from the PRIs and the soldiers. Where would Croquetas strike next?

TIERRA Y LIBERTAD

Before dawn on May 1st, Albores's huns fell on Tierra y Libertad. Far from the official county seat at Las Margaritas, the autonomía took as its own county seat the hamlet of Amparo Agua Tinta, scant kilometers from the border where Tzeltales, Tojolabales, Mames, Zoques, Mestizos, and Guatemalans have always mixed freely. Tierra y Libertad, with over a hundred communities within its radius, was the largest and best developed autonomía in the Zapatista constellation. Education and health commissions ran clinics and schools, and an efficient civil registry kept track of births, deaths, and other vital statistics. Municipal documents bore the seal of the United States of Mexico, and autonomous officials had taken to issuing marriage certificates, which the police seized as proof of sedition.

Tierra y Libertad has also built a fledgling justice system, and when a Guatemalan refugee was locked up in the autonomía's jail for occupying village lands, the United Nations High Commission on Refugees (ACNUR) communicated the matter to its Mexican counterpart (COMAR), which in turn notified the Governor, who then sent in the troops to rescue the refugee. The compañeros of Tierra y Libertad were astounded that the United Nations had called down the government wrath: "Why does this organization, which is supposed to stop wars, send soldiers to our community?"

56 Zapatista supporters, including all the autonomous council officials, were locked up in Cerro Hueco. Like Attila's hordes, police and soldiers smashed and burnt the municipal offices and looted private homes (PRI houses, which bore the party's logo, were left untouched). Although little of the valuable documen-

tation that Tierra y Libertad had generated in its years of administration was rescued from the uniformed vandals, a singed report of the local education commission fortuitously escaped the torchings. "We the parents pledge to educate our sons and daughters in an integral manner," the subversive document begins, "giving to them the rights of children through which, without using bad treatment, they learn to respect others and not to hurt or disrespect or humiliate their compañeros—we want our children to learn to respect nature and not to use slingshots to hurt animals—we want our children to learn to take care of the health of the environment and not throw garbage in our river—we want our children to learn good words, sweet and respectful, and not ones that hurt others—we want our children to respect the right of others to be different..."

Roberto Albores and his mentors in Mexico City had obviously never attended school in Tierra y Libertad.

TODOS SOMOS ITALIANOS

The Mexican Migra knew it had a problem when, on May 1st, 141 Italian "human rights observers" deplaned at Mexico City International Airport, all wearing neon-green plastic vests that read *Todos Somos Indios del Mundo* (We Are All Indians of the World). Most were members of an Italian support group, Basta Ya! After Acteal, the European support movement had pledged to build an intercontinental bridge of observation to Chiapas, the first installment of which had been the visit of the Civil Observation Commission that had interviewed the late José Tila back in February.

The Italian delegation included five members of the European Parliament, mayors, priests and other professionals, and Immigration had reluctantly granted them 10-day FM-3 observation visas that limited travel in Chiapas to three localities: San Andrés, San Cristóbal, and La Realidad. But the Italians wanted to visit Flores Magón where, reportedly, the men had fled under threat of death from the paramilitaries, leaving nearly 200 women and children at the mercy of the paramilitary MIRAs. "We have to go and see for ourselves," insisted the Italians' spokes Federico Mariani.

The showdown came at the Immigration checkpoint outside Ocosingo, "the gateway to the Lacandón jungle." "¡Alto!" (Halt!), the grim-faced agents barked. The Italians' FM-3s were no good here. "Observation cannot be limited," Mariani argued. The stand-off extended into early afternoon. When higher-ups radioed that only the five Italian Euro-deputies would be allowed to proceed, the Italians chanted, "We are all observers!" The agents protested they could not protect such a large group from possible PRI retaliation. "If the government says it cannot protect us, something must really be wrong," Mariani shot back.

Now the women in the delegation, carrying bunches of purple hyacinths intended for their beleaguered sisters in Flores Magón, linked arms and marched boldly past the startled agents—"a flagrant violation of Mexican law," reported Julia Preston, acting more like a local sheriff then a representative of the international press.

Sweating buckets under their plastic "We Are All Indians of the World" vests, the hikers began to drop like flies, and two Mexican congresswomen (one a PRIista) convinced the Migra to allow the buses the congregation had chartered to pass through the checkpoint and pick up the wilting Italians.

The Basta Yas! arrived in Taniperlas as night was falling fast. Leery of entering the ejido, which reportedly was patrolled by the paramilitaries, the Europeans camped out in the open fields. Few slept, the situation not being conducive to repose—the previous week, a Pastors for Peace mission had been surrounded here by irate PRIs who offered to roast the preachers (many of them of "an advanced age," La Jornada wrote) alive inside their bus.

Early the next morning, the Italians met cautiously with the Zapatista women. The compañeras testified they had been threatened with mass rape by the MIRAs. Suddenly, a club-wielding mob mounted the hill and began swinging. PRD dep Patria Jiménez was clobbered, the mayor of Venice's representative Beppe Gaccia was bopped. The Zapatista women fought back. Once again the Italians linked arms as stones and insults flew. "¡Fuera!" the PRIs whooped, "Get out!"

Hopelessly outnumbered by the Indians, the foreigners surrendered to the surly throng and were escorted through a gauntlet of jeers to the ejido house. Jaime Avilés recorded the tense scene: "The PRIistas kept staring at the green vests and thinking, 'They're not Indians. These are rich people. The Indians of Italy are too poor to travel here.'"

Although lynching was proposed, the Italians were let off with a tongue-lashing administered by Pedro Chulín, a MIRA man. Chulín charged the extranjeros and their Zapatista cuates (pals) with heinous crimes ("disobeying the government") and ordered them to get out of town and never come back. The foreigners were punched and spat upon as they dashed for the buses. Outside of Taniperlas, the caravan was attacked again by rock-hurling PRIistas captained by local deputy Juan Villafuerte.

The brickbats never stopped flying. Back in San Cristóbal, authentic coletos pelted the travelers with eggs and overripe tomatoes. "Italian garbage!" the auténticos hooted.

"Delinquents! Professional provocateurs! Revolutionary tourists!" caterwauled Solís Camara, the Immigration subsecretary. The Italians had failed to obey a lawful order and had gone on to stir up the Indians; now they were liable for awesome sanctions. Those who were not out of the country by Sunday night when their 10-day visas expired would be jailed for 10 years. Mariano protested, but the Italians' options were fast closing down. Some of the visitors slipped over the Guatemalan border in panic, others hopped early flights home. By Sunday midnight, 40 remaining Italians were still stuck at the Mexico City airport when a hundred Migra agents swooped down and herded them off to a holding area, where they were arrested and 33ed from Mexico for the rest of eternity.

Even then, the Basta Yas! were still making demands. They wanted a plane that would fly them to Strasbourg, where the European Parliament would the next day ratify an interim free trade agreement with Mexico, pending detailed item-by-item negotiations. The Mexican government was determined to avoid a Strasbourg stop at all costs and instead rented a Taesa airliner at the exaggerated cost of $260,000 USD to deposit the troublemakers in Rome. Under the watchful eyes of 24 Mexican cops who were installed aboard to head off a possible hijacking to the aforementioned French city, the villains were dead-marched onto the plane and booted out of the country permanently.

"The dignity of the Patria has no price," insisted the INM honcho Carrillo to justify the exorbitant cost of the flight. The removal of the Italians, Carrillo gloated, had been "the most drastic action ever taken in the history of having foreigners in our country."

After their hasty departure, the Italian-bashing got so thick that it became a kind of crime to be caught eating spaghetti in public. But the great wave of xenophobia churned up by Zedillo and those in his cahoots did not have much scratch in the Cerrillo barrio of San Cristóbal if a *pinta* on a wall there was any measure: *Todos Somos Italianos!* it read.

A delegation of Canadian legislators traveled the same route as the Italians in the first days of May. The Canucks were "good" extranjero(a)s who toed the line and spoke respectfully to public officials. Still, they were horrified by what they saw and heard at Polhó and Acteal, and they elicited a promise when they met with Labastida that the government would not dismantle any more autonomous municipalities. The day after the northerners returned home, Interior issued a disclaimer: the decision not to attack the Zapatista autonomías was not Labastida's to make, but rather fell within the province of Roberto Albores, ostensibly the governor of Chiapas.

The Italians did make it to Strasbourg on time after all, bursting into the European Parliament still wearing their green plastic "We Are All Indians" vests—the demonstration was the first ever inside those hallowed chambers, but it did not help the No vote much. The Left was critically divided between those who wanted to let Mexico in so Zedillo could be held accountable under the democracy clause, and those who flat-out rejected the Zapatista-killing Mexican government's presence in the European Union. When the Greens abstained, the Center-Right carried the day and Mexico took its temporary place at the European table.

Although "responsible" human rights NGOs rebuked the Italian hooligans because the group's antics made their work that much harder, the new rules governing human rights observation, promulgated days after the Basta Yas! rowdy departure, had been on line ever since Lolita's landing at the La Realidad peace camp.

The revised regs, which were worthy of a well-oiled dictatorship, stipulated that all applications must be made no less than 60 days in advance of the visit, a waiting period that precluded timely observation of such emergencies as the Acteal massacre. Each group must submit an itinerary and the names of those to be interviewed, a requirement human rights groups could not comply with because it put the lives of informants in jeopardy (witness poor José Tila López). Only 10 observers would be admitted per group, and they would have 10 days maximum in country to complete their investigation. All observers were required to document five years of experience in this rather nebulous discipline. All observer groups must be registered with the United Nations, which, of course, hardly any of the pertinent NGOs are. The new regulations shut the gate on human rights observers as tightly as if Mexico were Tibet.

AN UNSUDDEN DEATH

The death of the patient was not unexpected. Its body had been pierced by quivers of poison darts unleashed by the government archers and its wounds were fatal. The attack on the CONAI and Don Samuel's moral authority had been withering and systematic since Acteal. Labastida's point man in this new campaign of vilification was the just-appointed "peace coordinator." Emilio Rabasa was quite capable of dining with the Bishop (Samuel had been friends with his grandfather) and stabbing Tatic between the shoulder blades the moment he was outside the rectory's doors.

The CONAI was not an impartial mediator, a falsely offended Rabasa and his boss parroted to the press. How could the government do business with this CONAI? "(Samuel) has convoked an international movement to intervene in our domestic affairs," the Interior Secretary admonished. Attorney General Madrazo was instructed to investigate the Fray Bartolomé Human Rights Center for issuing credentials to international peace campers.

The suitcase caper was the capper. Agents unknown had rifled CONAI secretary Miguel Alvarez's suitcase in Rome earlier that year, purloining a privately circulated mediation commission quarterly report that called for "international pressure to bring the Mexican government to reason." A desk-pounding Labastida summoned Don Samuel to Mexico City to explain this latest affront to national sensibilities. When Samuel snubbed the meeting, instead taking out a newspaper ad decrying the witch-hunt and reiterating his call for international pressure, the CONAI's goose was steamed.

The government guns were trained on Samuel all Spring. In March, he had to wear a hard hat to say Mass in Chanal. The brutal murder of Bishop Juan Girardi in Guatemala City, after the prelate accused the military of responsibility in at least 100,000 Indian deaths, had Samuel's supporters calling for him to take cover.

By April, Zedillo was showing up in Chiapas every 10 days, sniping at the diocese from strategic PRI enclaves in the conflict zone. "I seriously doubt that (the diocese) really wants to resolve the situation—they should declare what is the political agenda they have up their sleeve—they are not really concerned about the Indians—the way I see it, they are provoking violence in Chiapas"—words pronounced by the Honorable Ernesto Zedillo Ponce de León, President of Mexico, in Tumbalá, in the Peace & Justice-ridden north of Chiapas, April 15th, 1998.

The President returned to the north state May 29th, to Sabanilla, the most archly anti-Samuel inferno in this infernal region, to assail those who preach "the theology of violence." In this part of Chiapas, where Samuel and Raúl and Heriberto Cruz had suffered an assassination attempt the previous Fall, Zedillo's message could be taken as a license to kill.

The victim died during Sunday Mass on June 7th, R.I.P. It expired in the same cathedral where it had been baptized during Samuel's December 1994 hunger strike. Bishop Ruiz's obituary for the CONAI sounded weary but defiant. "The government continues to dismantle the conditions necessary for dialogue." "The continual aggression against the CONAI" had taken its toll at last. So had the silence of the EZLN, which at first had seemed "comprehensible" but had now become "a great weight" on the restoration of dialogue. "The conditions for mediation have been canceled." First Samuel dissolved the mediation body, and then he resigned as its president. CISEN agents hovered in the back of the crowded cathedral, calling in Tatic's words to Labastida. "We have taken a step closer to peace," crowed Governor Croquetas down in Tuxtla.

Samuel Ruiz was not the whole bowl of cheese. Gonzalo Ituarte and Miguel Alvarez had run the CONAI's day-by-day logistics. Juan Bañuelos and Oscar Oliva had put their lives on hold for four years to give the commission a public face. "The government has entered into the logic of war, and there is no room for the CONAI in this equation," opined Miguel Alvarez to Proceso, recalling that the commission's problems with the Zedillo government had intensified after the EPR's bloody attacks in August 1996. Zedillo had wanted the Zapatistas to play the role of a "domesticated" guerrilla, but the EZLN walked away from the table instead and never came back. "The government blamed us because we could not convince them to return."

The CONAI had been the bridge to the EZLN. Now the government had burnt it down, and there was no way to cross that river again. But in forcing Samuel to shut down the CONAI, the government lost its way. The Zapatistas, or at least those who mattered in intelligence circles, were not talking, and there were no rants from Marcos to be deconstructed by the CISEN. Outside of the overflights and the daily patrols at La Realidad, there was no way to figure out what the rebels were really up to. When, a few days after Don Samuel disappeared the CONAI, the Mexican Army and the Zapatista Army of National Liberation engaged in a full-scale shooting war, the lines to the insurgents were disconnected. The COCOPA, really just a letterhead now, ran to the jungle but could not make contact. Max, the headman in La Realidad, had not seen the comandantes for a long time. "You can leave a note if you want to," he told the lawmakers, but he did not give them a receipt.

Samuel, too, had hung the "out-of-business" sign on the CONAI door and headed off to the jungle himself. Leading pilgrimages down muddy roads (the rains had begun at last) and pronouncing Mass in wood-plank chapels, Samuel moved through the Cañadas saying good-bye to the Indian faithful. On November 3rd, 1999, the Bishop's 75th birthday, he would be obligated under ecclesiastical law to submit his resignation to the Pope—that is, if they were both still alive 18 months down the road.

As the Bishop slogged through the jungle in the June rains, the Indians came to him with concern in their eyes. "Stay with us here, Tatic," they cried. "They will kill you if you go back to San Cristóbal."

GOVERNMENT JIHAD

Despite the government's jihad against the autonomías, Zapatista-like municipalities had begun to sprout all over the Mexican landscape. During the 20-day "National Indian Insurrection," the CNI had declared a score of new autonomous municipalities in five states. Rancho Nuevo Democrático, an Amuzgo Indian formation in the lower Montaña of Guerrero, had been in operation for several years. Nahuas in the Hidalgo Huasteca had declared Atlapexco an autonomía. A trio of Chontal municipalities had been proclaimed in oil-rich Tabasco. Out in Mexico state, San Nicolás Coatepec declared itself autonomous from a constitutional municipality run by Carlos Hank González, and a banner thrown off a pedestrian bridge in the downtrodden Mexico City suburb of Nezahualcóyotl read "Welcome to the Autonomous Municipality of Aragón." The Indian autonomy group ANIPA was working on a national plan that divided all of Mexico up into "pluri-ethnic autonomous regions."

Autonomy fever was in full swing in the Spring of 1998. One of the more curious autonomías was Nicolás Ruiz in the northern valleys of Chiapas, an opposition enclave that synthesized PRD and EZLN credos. Deeply committed to the Zapatista cause, the campesinos also diligently cast their ballots in every election for the PRD—the PRI did not receive a single vote here in 1994, '95, and '97. When Albores ran for Congress from this district, he was shut out in Nicolás Ruiz, a bone he still picked with the local campesinos.

Although it was a constitutionally mandated municipality, the farmers of Nicolás Ruiz declared themselves autonomous in mid-May in solidarity with

Flores Magón and Tierra y Libertad. A handful of PRI families that opposed autonomy were accused of dividing the community and had their ejido rights suspended, giving the governor his justification for retaliation. Under the banner of defending the PRIistas' human rights, Albores Guillén prepared the assault. "We have been prudent until now," warned his new tent-sized Secretary of Government, Arely Madrid, blaming Don Samuel's catechists for the trouble.

A thousand troops and police hit Nicolás Ruiz at dawn on June 4th. Helicopters laid down a dense cap of tear gas, and the security forces stepped briskly through the acrid fog, clubbing down women and children to defend the human rights of the PRIs. The 161 new prisoners rounded up in Nicolás Ruiz broke the bank in Cerro Hueco. Designed for 300 inmates, the penitentiary now held close to 1,100. Every social current that had washed over Chiapas in recent years found a place in the prison complex, occupying entire galleries and creating their own political space. The Zapatista Voice of Cerro Hueco was planted adjacent to the Chinchulines—"Voz" prisoners now included El Checo and all those taken at Flores Magón and Tierra y Libertad. Down the block, the killers of Acteal were neighbors with the 26 cops who had unloaded on Guadalupe López Méndez and her baby at Ocosingo. Zapatistas, PRDistas, PRIistas, traditional Catholics, Liberationists, Evangelicals, a Muslim (the ex-evangelical Domingo López Angel), even six members of the URNG, the Guatemalan guerrilla group that had signed a "peace" treaty in 1996, were on ice in Cerro Hueco.

Behind the prison's big black iron gates, the inmates ran their own restaurants and cantinas and whorehouses and popsicle stands. They held their own fiestas and made up their own rules. They ran the institution as if it were, well, an autonomous municipality.

PUDDLE OF BLOOD

El Charco ("The Puddle") is aptly named, a muddy splat just off Guerrero's violence-riddled Costa Chica in the PRD municipality of Ayutla. Don't look. You won't find it on any map. Like most of the villages that climb from the coast into the Montaña, the habitués of Charco are mainly Mixtec Indians.

It was to this backwater community that, on June 6th, a masked guerrilla band descended from the forest for a prearranged meeting in the bilingual schoolhouse to explain who they were and what they wanted. Some 30 Indian farmers had gathered to hear what the "EPRs" had to say.

But the youthful rebels were not from the EPR, but from a split-off, the ERPI or Revolutionary Army of the Insurgent People, who had annexed the entire People's Revolutionary Army's Guerrero structure, a section more closely identified with Lucio Cabañas's old fighters than with the PROCUP. The latter's penchant for revolutionary terrorism (not to be confused with "revolutionary tourism") had been the point of separation. Tired of just hitting a community and mowing down soldiers and police, a process that brought savage repression down upon the locals, the ERPI wanted to make friends first, to rub elbows with the people for whom it was struggling.

That was the ERPI's first mistake. They had stayed so late making friends with the Mixtecos that they decided to bed down in the school until dawn, along with 15 farmers from outlying settlements. Unfortunately, a *soplón* (informer) had blown the news of their arrival to the military, and the troops were already groaning up the dirt track to El Charco, loaded for bear.

By 4 a.m., the schoolhouse was surrounded. The soldiers called for those inside to throw down their weapons and come out with their hands high. Confusion reigned inside. Some protested they were unarmed. The soldiers opened up anyway, lacing the walls with elaborate mosaics of bulletholes. Two Indians fell, mortally wounded, and the rebels decided to surrender before the whole community was massacred. They stepped cautiously out of the schoolhouse with their hands reaching for the night sky. Each was escorted to the basketball court, thrown down on the rough concrete, and told never to look up. All morning, the guachos executed suspected guerrilleros. 11 rebels died and 16 were taken captive.

Much as with Acteal, the Secretary of Defense described what happened at El Charco as a "confrontation," yet no member of the Mexican Army suffered so much as a scratch. Among the dead was ERPI Comandante "Daniel." When "Daniel"'s mask was lifted, he was identified as Ricardo Zavala, a Mexico City university student active in the fight to stop the privatization of higher education at the UNAM.

The students' time was coming again.

THE BATTLE OF EL BOSQUE

El Bosque—San Juan de La Libertad on the Zapatista map—was like a slow-motion Chenalhó, which it bordered to the east. Homicide had been intermittent in the county ever since Jorge Enrique's helicopter assault at Nichtalacum the previous Spring.

The ambushes begin in April after 34 Zapatista families were burnt out of a PRI enclave called Los Plátanos and their coffee crop was stolen. During the Spring planting between April 18th and June 9th, three PRIistas were gunned down and a dozen Indians wounded in Chenalhó-like road attacks. The El Bosque BOM squad headquarters was also sprayed with gunfire.

"With the law in his hands," once again Governor Albores rose to the defense of human rights. A joint military-police operation even more lethal than the ones that vamped Flores Magón, Tierra y Libertad, and Nicolás Ruiz moved into position for the attack before dawn on June 10th, just three days after Don

Samuel had killed the CONAI. This time the military brought long guns and tanks.

Backed up by the CISEN and the Migra and a platoon of female police to handle the fierce Zapatista women, the strike force rolled into El Bosque ("The Forest") at four neurological points: the county seat, where the autónomos held city hall; Alvaro Obregón, where an environmental institute tied to the diocese was headquartered; and two outlying villages, Unión Progreso down in the draw and Chavajeval above it, where the fiercest fighting would take place.

According to the notarized military report, an army-police convoy took incoming fire around 6:30 a.m. as it ascended towards Chavajeval—a police officer was killed instantly.

The villagers, on the other hand, testify that the security forces pushed their way into Chavajeval, tear-gassing and battering the women as they had the week before in Nicolás Ruiz. In both Chavajeval, where three Tzotziles died, and Unión Progreso (five dead), the Indians agree that some families defended themselves the best way they knew how and got their guns.

Although the press was not allowed into either village until hours later, it is abundantly clear that between 7 a.m. and 9 a.m. on the morning of June 10th, 1998, the low-intensity conflict that the Mexican Army had been waging against the Zapatista insurgency for four and a half years turned into a full-scale shooting war. EZLN fighters opened up with automatic-weapon fire from the nearby hillsides to cover their people's escape from the two settlements below, and the military responded by turning its big guns, tanks, and bazookas on the Zapatista units up in the forest. Helicopters swooped in to give the battle a Top Gun touch: one police copter was hit by ground fire over Unión Progreso, killing an agent, and mortars raked the trees. It had taken a long time, but the real war had begun again.

For a minute.

The battle of El Bosque was distinct from the previous attacks on the autonomías. EZLN fighting units were in El Bosque, prepared to defend their communities from becoming another Flores Magón or worse, Acteal. Reforma published a photo of one of the units, reportedly led by Comandante "Rojo." By fighting back on June 10th, the EZLN was letting the government know that it would be pushed no further, that unlike the Abejas, they were not going to die on their knees praying.

By midday, the ack-ack had trailed off and the villagers emerged to reclaim their dead—besides the eight Indians cut down in Chavajeval and Unión Progreso, the bodies of two police officers (and reportedly one dead soldier) were carried off to Tuxtla along with 53 fresh inmates for Cerro Hueco.

Between El Charco and El Bosque ("The Puddle" and "The Forest"), in a scant 72 hours, government forces had butchered 19 more Indians in a combined bloodbath that topped Aguas Blancas on the massacre meter.

The dead came back to El Bosque on June 13th, and the homecoming was a little like Acteal but without Don Samuel's presence to give dignity to the deaths. "Seven hours of uninterrupted ululation" was how Bellinghausen described the women's grief.

Once again, the remains had been forwarded in cheap, stinking, unmarked cardboard coffins to underscore Governor Albores's great love for his people. But this time, the bodies came back with an interlocutor, CNDH special delegate Adolfo Hernández, who had volunteered to accompany the cadavers to El Bosque.

Now Hernández was cornered up on the truck, the object of dangerous derision. Because there was no other target to personify the "government," Hernández was it. "You murdered our brothers and sisters!" the Indians screamed. The CNDH man denied the charges and tried to explain what he did and who he was.

"Speak Tzotzil!" a man demanded. "I can't," choked Hernández. "Hang around, pendejo, and we'll teach you good." Terrified of being depantsed as the mob was threatening, the pudgy, sweating Hernández conceded that the Army and the police had killed the Indians, but, he whimpered, "I read that in the newspaper."

The villagers refused to accept their dead from the "government." "Take them to your Zedillo so he can have his 'direct dialogue' with them," a woman shrieked. Finally, volunteers from Fray Bart were permitted to unload the bodies. Poor Hernández was kicked and pushed and told to leave, which he did, burning rubber all the way to Tuxtla.

The body count confused the villagers. Seven had been taken from Unión Progreso, six of them still alive, some witnesses say, suggesting that the men were executed on the road to Tuxtla. But only five had been returned (three others belonged to Chavajeval). Moreover, no one could recognize one of the returned corpses. The mal gobierno owed them three of their dead! The stranger was buried along with the others anyway, "because he must have been a Zapatista." Maybe not. At least one of the dead and many of the arrested were PRIistas who shared Chavajeval and Unión Progreso with the EZLN and had joined in the villages' defense.

The government stumbled to explain the new massacre. Emilio Rabasa argued the men had been killed to "prevent another Acteal," echoing the NATO-over-Yugoslavia theorem that the only way to stop genocide is to kill everyone on the ground first. Governor Croquetas laughed off the cartoons that depicted him with bloody hands and dripping knives ("It's a good thing I have a sense of humor"). "Only one person could have authorized this butchery," an inflamed Carlos Fuentes scowled: "The Supreme Commander-in-Chief."

The bones of El Bosque rose up in the usual 20 U.S. cities, and in Congress, Vermont Senator Patrick Leahy had the chutzpah to question Madeleine

Albright about the ongoing massacres south of the border. "We're pressing them for an investigation," the Secretary of State responded, but in Mexico City the press translated the word as "pressuring," and Rosario Green got her back up. "No one pressures us!" she snarled, and Congress, even the PRD, agreed with her that Leahy's inquiry and Albright's response were yet another interventionist attack on Mexico's sovereignty.

After El Bosque, the government reached temporary catharsis. Albores, apparently having sucked up enough red corpuscles (for the time being), promised no more dismantlements (for the time being). Three days after the bloodbath in El Bosque, Zedillo showed up in Las Margaritas to bullshit the Indians about "peace" and "dialogue." "Violence doesn't solve anything," he smiled like a crocodile.

"To Ernesto Zedillo Ponce de León: You are a murderer. *Es todo*," the EZLN curtly snapped back. Rather than being signed by the CCRI, the comunicado bore the rubric of 32 autonomous municipalities.

The battle at El Bosque was the last of the dismantlements. Some observers suggest that Zedillo-Labastida-Albores called off their two-fisted persecution of the autonomous municipalities because the copious bloodshed at El Bosque finally brought them to their senses. I doubt it. If anything derailed the government's enthusiasm to extinguish the rebels, it was the fact that, for once, the EZLN had fired back.

BOOK FOUR

THE TIME OF RE-ENCOUNTER AND RESISTANCE

"We are still here…"
—*Fifth Declaration of the Lacandón Jungle*

SUMMER–AUTUMN 1998

A MADDENING SILENCE

"¿Nos vamos, Tacho?" "¡Nos vamos!" were the comandantes' last words on the video dated March 1st and passed onto the European civil observation commission—and then the Sup was gone again. The curtain rang down and the Zapatista Theater of the Mute resumed.

The silence of the CCRI had been intermittent since Marcos walked away from Zedillo's "observations" in January 1997, but no interval had been less loquacious than the current quiescence. For more than 130 days, nearly 20 weeks, five months, there had been no word from an EZLN comandante other than the March 28th recriminations about the forest fires, and the maddening blackout was getting under everyone's skin. Marcos and the comandancia had simply vanished down the nearest rabbit hole, and not even the CISEN had a handle on where they had gone.

The New York Times reported that Marcos was down with malaria, others that he was wasting away with incurable cancers in a Mexico City hospital. Some whispered the Subcomandante had been captured and was caged up at Military Camp #1, others that the Guatemalan Kaibiles had executed Marcos à la Che, still others that he had been dispatched to the happy hunting ground by the "radical" wing of the comandancia. Javier Elorriaga joked that he'd spotted the Sup at the World Cup matches in Paris—but the truth was that even Elorriaga was stumped.

The silences of the CCRI spanned tumultuous events—the dismantlements and deaths at Flores Magón, Tierra y Libertad, and El Bosque, the dissolution of the CONAI—but no government outrage could bait the rebels into conversation. Fenced off by the Zapatista silence, Labastida and Rabasa and Zedillo adopted the words "direct dialogue" as their mantra and kept repeating the phrase so often—the President pronounced the d-words 44 times in one Marqués de Comillas speech—that it seemed like they were governing by hypnotism. But the more they repeated their call for dialogue, the more of a monologue the muddle became.

Chief monologist Ernesto Zedillo made 12 trips to Chiapas that Summer and Fall, shouting over and over again into the rain for dialogue, but all that ever came back was the echo of his own mean words. Perhaps the President's most spiteful discourse was delivered in a nationally broadcast July 1st address from Simojovel, in which, between obligatory invitations to dialogue directly, he revisited the December 1994 peso debacle and blamed the EZLN all over again for Mexico's economic collapse, heaped fresh abuse upon the hated extranjeros, accused human rights groups of being virtual soccer hooligans, and sprayed imprecations upon Don Samuel's ministry: "Those who call themselves mediators, who promote the intervention of foreigners, speak with forked tongues—the Mexican people reject these messianic leaders, these apostles of hypocrisy…"

The silence itself had by now become the subject of many words. "A Funereal Silence," Proceso front-covered in somber black letters. "An insulting silence," rightist bishop Genaro Alamilla called it. "An eloquent silence, an active silence," responded his ecclesiastical rival Mario López, Mexican provincial of the Jesuits. "Who remains in silence is ungovernable," Luis Hernández quoted the liberation educator Ivan Illich.

But the much-talked-about Zapatista "silence" was really not much of a silence if you listened attentively. Down below the CCRI, the flow of communication from civil Zapatismo generated a dull roar. In one 30-day period from March to April, 15 communiqués—one every two days, received public notice, and May to June was a similarly fecund month. The comunicados and denuncias came from San Pedro de Michoacán, Francisco Gómez, San Juan de la Libertad, and Unión Progreso, from the Ejido Cruz del Rosario, Taniperlas, the ejidos Yuquín and El Censo, the displaced Zapatistas of Los Plátanos, the Zona Norte, the Voices of Cerro Hueco, all of the autonomous municipalities at once in the communiqué calling Zedillo "a killer" ("Es todo") for the massacre at Bosque.

But those who needed to listen turned a deaf and suspiciously racist ear to this groundswell. If Marcos was not on the other end of the line, the EZLN had not spoken.

YEPA YEPA YEPA

By mid-July, the rain, achingly slow in coming, was pelting San Cristóbal ceaselessly, making the old stone city feel more closed down and insular than ever. The comandantes were not writing and no one knew anything. I sucked up my last Bohemia at the Casa Vieja, settled the bar bill, and hopped the night bus for a tryst in Mérida. An hour after I hit the road, the first words from the Sup since Winter hit the striped tablecloths at the Casa Vieja hotel, where the press gathers and where the comunicados usually arrive first.

Both of the long-awaited communiqués bore the familiar curlicue signature of Subcomandante Insurgente Marcos, and both were uncommonly short and oblique. "¡Yepa Yepa Yepa! ¡Andale Andale! ¡Arriba Arriba Arriba! ¡Yepa Yepa!" read the first in large print-out type. Yepa??? The agents of "the Interpol of Paris" and "the CISEN in Polanco," to whom this communiqué was directed, struggled to break the code. The clue was how Marcos signed the note: "Speddy (aka 'Speedy') González," the legendary cartoon mouse who affected a stereotypical serape and droopy sombrero and regularly eeked this battle cry whenever accosted by bandidos—"Speddy" achieved popular antihero status in Mexico in the 1970s.

The second epistle was just as mystifying—11 words in Nahuatl: "!Nemi Zapata! !Nemi Zapata! "!Nican ca namotata, ayemo miqui! !Nemi Zapata!" (Zapata lives! Zapata lives! Your father continues here, he has not died! Zapata lives!" The two short messages were only the door openers.

On July 17th, La Jornada published Marcos's 24-page avalance of pent-up furies and tenderness, "Above & Below: Masks & Silences," a document that showed how closely the comandancia had been watching the events of the past months.

"Masks & Silences" begins with a keen analysis of the just-concluded World Cup soccer matches, then quotes from such eclectic eminences as Hamlet and the Catalán detective writer Manuel Vázquez Montalban and concludes that, despite Acteal, El Bosque, and El Charco, Zedillo's bloodiest crime remained the economic model that was cannibalizing the country.

There were many masks above: the Mask of Modernity ("biodegradable, lite, cool"), the Mask of the Rationalization of Globalization, the Mask of the International War on Drugs, the Mask of the End of the Populist State, and, most insidiously, the Mask of Macroeconomics—the Sup even includes graphs. "Some say that being against globalization is like being against the law of gravity. Ni modo, then—down with gravity!"

It sounded like the same old Sup...

There were masks down below too: apathy, cynicism, silence... But mostly there were victims. Marcos listed seven victims of the government's war on the EZLN: peace and dialogue, the Indians, civil society, the transition to democracy, national sovereignty, the COCOPA and the CONAI. "The government treats the COCOPA as an object of derision. We will not do the same," Marcos wrote, an apparent invitation to reconciliation. The document also mourns the passing of the CONAI—"all the ecclesiastical, political, military, and economic" guns had been lined up against this fragile instance of mediation. Not content with destroying the CONAI, Zedillo now wanted to destroy Don Samuel.

Back again, too, was he of the First Gods, the ones who gave breath to the earth. One Mayan Aesop's Fable tells of how Old Antonio killed the lion by inserting shards of a broken mirror in the heart of a sacrificial calf. When the lion chewed on the heart, he could not distinguish between the blood of the calf and the blood from his own diced tongue, and so he chewed himself to death. In the second, a sort of Maoist morality tale, the lion spots a fat trout he lusts to gobble and asks the gods how to catch it. "Drink up the river," they tell him, and he does. And he drowns inside.

Tongue-tied by this torrent of words words words, the Mexican government responded with a 14-line press release in which the direct dialogue mantra is repeated six times.

LA QUINTA

The Subcomandante's volcanic pen had not run out of magma just yet. On July 21st, the Clandestine Indigenous Revolutionary Committee–General Command of the Zapatista Army of National Liberation, under the hand of Insurgent Subcommander Marcos, offered up the Fifth Declaration of the Lacandón Jungle, a document that begins with a not very rousing preamble: "Today we say we are still here."

"During our great silence, the Zapatistas were watching, and we saw many things...we saw that not all of the government is united in its vocation for death...because we were quiet we could better hear the voices down below, and the winds..." And this Zennish gem: "And we saw too that by not fighting, we were fighting..."

The Fifth Declaration looks at its watch and declares this to be "the hour of the Indian peoples," the hour of the civil society" (Marcos lists 26 components ranging from the disabled to gays and lesbians)—even the hour of Congress and particularly the COCOPA, which can now fulfill "its obligation to the Indian peoples." In a climax that borders on the anticlimactic, the Quinta calls for a National Consultation on Indian Rights and Culture and an End to the War of Extermination, during which the EZLN would bring the gospel of the San Andrés Accords to every municipality in Mexico.

The Zedillo administration's reaction to the Fifth Declaration mimicked the EZLN's silence of many months. Instead of talking, the military brought in five battalions from Tabasco and filled the sky over La Realidad with enemy aircraft. In spite of the rebels' conciliatory tone, Chiapas's cesspool press "reported" that the EZLN was going to attack PRI communities—David and Tacho would lead the assault on Rizo de Oro (Las Margaritas). The ground patrols accelerated.

This new consulta was "unnecessary," Francisco Labastida offered—the government had already consulted with its Indians back in 1995. "Sebastian Guillén" could stay in the jungle "for two or five years," who cares? "We're not his hostages."

The war—at least of words—had been joined again.

A HARD RAIN

After a blistering Spring, during which hundreds of forest fires had blanketed the highlands and the jungle with a choking pall, the sky finally opened up during the third week in June. The somber, pregnant storm clouds hovering over the valley of Jovel, Los Altos, the Cañadas, the selva, and the coast let loose with the vengeance of Chac, the elephant-nosed Mayan rain god, and no one escaped the deluge.

The hard rain fell everywhere, soaking the six refugee camps up at Polhó, where 7,000 Tzotziles still huddled under tentative roofs. The chaos of the camps had stabilized after six months of tremulous sanctuary, but daily life remained uncertain. For example, U.N. refugee guidelines allocate 35 meters of space per displaced person, but up at X'oyep the measure was more like 1.5. Dozens crammed into the narrow galleries at night to sleep, but insomnia prevailed. "No one sleeps here, because they are so nervous about a new attack. They don't want to be caught dead, so they stay up all night," one camp denizen observed to Bellinghausen.

The rains had only aggravated the discomfort. Even with the water pouring down around them, there was not enough to meet their needs. The U.N. suggests 30 liters a day per refugee—in X'oyep, each resident received one. Moreover, the rainy season had brought with it fresh outbreaks of dysentery and respiratory infection for the six overburdened doctors who attended to the hundreds of sick in the camps. Shit floated in the gullies that passed for streets, and inside the hovels the babies breathed fitfully and expired.

The rain fell hardest upon the Abejas, and in June they voted to return to their lands at Los Chorros and Yibiloj. They were farmers and now the rain was falling, and the men and the women of corn had no seed in the ground. They were rootless in the camps, displaced from their only birthright—the land where their dead were buried.

On June 25th, 850 Bees set off from X'oyep singing hymns into the spitting rain, with Don Samuel and Don Raúl in the forefront. But out on the paved road, the Abejas heard whispers: the PRIs were waiting for them in Chorros, the paramilitaries would kill them all again, or kidnap the bishops and exchange them for the killers of Acteal jailed in Cerro Hueco. At Majomut, the Bees called a halt, took counsel, and turned back towards X'oyep. The rain was falling harder now.

Down in the jungle, the hard rain was drowning the milpas in La Realidad. The campesinos had planted three times that Spring. In April, ants had devoured the seedlings, and in May the relentless sun had withered what little had sprouted. Now the deluge had turned the cornfields into mush where little would survive. It was the hungriest time—not even the calabashes had come in yet, and the growling of stomachs drowned out the drone of the military planes breaking from the cloud cover.

The hard rain drummed down on Cerro Hueco too. Packed into the galleries with the downpour flooding the open patio, the Zapatista prisoners began a rolling hunger strike that reached into the other jails around the state. The women came from far-off villages—the structure of the Voz of Cerro Hueco made the prisoners the collective obligation of the community—and laid 85 machetes in front of Albores's government palace: the Strike of the Silent Machetes, they called it. For days, the women encamped under the walls of the prison in the bottomless rain.

The rain fell thick and hard on both sides in this battle. The military patrols slogged through the deep-green landscape in their olive-drab raincapes, the big drops beating a tattoo on their helmets as they eyed the wet underbrush for subversives. No one really knew anymore how many guachos there were in the conflict zone. Before Acteal, researcher Arturo Lomeli had counted 36,000, but after the massacre, the census of military encampments leaped from 129 to over 200 and people began talking about 60,000—a number that had escalated to 70,000 by mid-1998. In congressional testimony, Defense chief Cervantes insisted that troop strength was only around 18,000.

The rain didn't moisten only the Mexican military. On July 27th, in the midst of a blinding rainstorm, two U.S. military attachés, "Elizabeth Krug" and "Thomas Gillam" (probably not their real names), drove into Los Plátanos, the PRI paramilitary enclave in El Bosque, claiming to be lost. The suspicious PRIs surrounded the Yanquis' vehicle. The G.I.s were hauling a number of boxes, and the locals demanded that they open them up. When the North Americans refused, the Tzotziles got testy. Albores had to be summoned before the gringos could drive off. They never did say what was in those boxes.

Whether the hard Chiapas rain fell on U.N. Secretary-General Kofi Annan remains clouded. The Ghanaian flew into Mexico City July 21st, his first trip to the Aztec capital, and quickly quashed speculation that he favored United Nations intervention in Chiapas. Then, although Annan was scheduled to fly back to New York on the 23rd, he abruptly boarded a Mexican Air Force jet to the Oaxaca resort of Huatulco, where Zedillo unexpectedly joined him that evening. On Saturday morning the Mexican president flew to Chiapas, putting down in the Lacandón in the middle of the Montes Azules sanctuary, scant kilometers from where the Zapatista General Command is encamped. Did Annan, who dropped from sight, accompany Zedillo? The image of Zedillo and the Secretary-General hunkered down in some damp jungle camp with the Subcomandante is an intriguing one.

The hard rain tumbled down around the ears of many other dangerous extranjeros that Summer. Hundreds had availed themselves of vacation time to visit the dripping zone, and Global Exchange and Pastors for Peace buses skidded along the slick roads of the highlands and the canyons. From exile, Tom Hansen organized a Tri-Continental (Canada, the U.S., Mexico) contingent that refused to fill out any FM-3s.

The hard rain fell on such notable solidarity workers as Eddie Olmos, rockero Zack de la Rocha, Yvon Le Bot, and a delegation of Chicago congressional reps led by ex–Black Panther Bobby Rush. And the rain fell hard and cold, too, upon Pedro Café's dream.

PEDRO CAFÉ'S DREAM

Pedro Café, aka Peter Brown, is an affable, middle-aged, bilingual schoolteacher from San Diego given to wildly inappropriate ties and crunched fedoras. In 1996, the Zapatista dream of building a "rebel autonomous" secondary (middle) school up at Oventic became his dream too, and he began raising funds and organizing construction brigades to make this dream literally concrete. By July 1998, four classrooms, a computer room with no computers, and a library full of books had been built. California kids shoveled gravel in the rain alongside Zapatista *comuneros*, learned a few words in Tzotzil, and played a lot of basketball. It was like a Summer work camp, the kind the Quakers and other denominations sponsor every Summer all over Mexico.

In mid-July, Pedro Café stood in two rubber boots in the big, drafty, barn-like Oventic auditorium and received from Comandantes Ezekiel and Roberto, in the name of the regional education commission, the planned curriculum for the new school. "We'd like to learn English and, if possible, Japanese," the comandantes explained. Their needs had grown, the Zapatistas said; instead of 200 students, they wanted the new school to board twice that. The large number of kids in the refugee camps obligated them to expand the project. Now they talked about a Zapatista high school, even someday a university. Pedro Café already had $30,000 USD sunk into the school and now he would need another $50,000 to meet the new specs.

Peter ventured down to the cybercafé in San Cristóbal to dial up donors. He was wary of the Migra and returned in the evenings judiciously late, long after Immigration had folded up its nearby checkpoint. But on the rainy evening of July 17th, the Migras were laying for him, gruffly asked for Peter's papers, and snapped on the cuffs. The route was not unknown by now—Tuxtla, Mexico City, back to the Other Side—don't even think about coming back here, pendejo.

Pedro Café had just joined an elite corps of deportees—the 33s, the "inconvenient-to-Zedillo club." Building a school, you see, was a violation of Constitutional Article #3, which relegates absolute control over education to the Mexican state. It was a felony, punishable by deportation if you were an extranjero, to build a school in Chiapas, a state in which 53% of the indigenous inhabitants can neither read nor write.

Like others 33ed before him, Pedro Café contacted his congressperson and even went to Washington to complain. The New York Times noticed his pain and penned an editorial that blasted Zedillo's Chiapas policies. Patrick Leahy introduced a Chiapas demilitarization resolution in the U.S. Senate, and the House Hemispheric Affairs Subcommittee threatened hearings.

Zedillo chose not to notice. During his September 1st state of the union Informe, despite Acteal and El Bosque, a dozen trips to the state, his own perverted rendition of San Andrés pending in the Mexican Congress, and Washington's increasing concern, the President failed once again even to enunciate the name of the place.

And Pedro Café's dream? It is built and stocked. The desks are lined up and the library itching to be used. The "Primero de Enero" rebel insurgent middle school could begin to operate in the morning and might very well do so—despite Albores's threat to pound it into dust if the dream ever opened its doors.

THE HARDER RAIN

In a sordid effort to brainwash the diplomatic corps into believing that the conflict in Chiapas was over and done with, Foreign Minister Rosario Green and Roberto Albores invited 250 people—ambassadors, their wives, and military attachés—to weekend in the state and "get to know its scenic wonders and friendly faces." The all-expense-paid junket would include extravagant hotel suites, a 24-hour free bar, a boat ride down the Sumadero canyon, and even an excursion to an exotic (PRI) Indian village (Chenalhó), where the distinguished guests would never get close to a Zapatista. Zedillo and Rabasa would fly into San Cristóbal to wine and dine with the diplomats September 10th.

But in the first days of September, the hardest rains fell on Chiapas. The state's "scenic wonders" were ripped asunder by the brute ugly force of nature, and the best-laid plans of the Mexican government were washed away.

For 10 days between September 5th and 15th, a "weather system" dubbed "Javier" anchored itself above Chiapas's Pacific Coast and unleashed the densest rains recorded in the 20th century, 588 millimeters in the first three days alone. The coastal rivers filled instantly, flash flooding over their banks and wiping out entire squatter colonies. Up in the sierra, where criminal deforestation had converted calamity into catastrophe, whole settlements were buried under the mud. Motozintla had been rent in two—there were still street signs, but no more streets. Hundreds (officially, 407 corpses were recovered) and maybe thousands of Mexicans and their animals were swept away in the raging waters—days later, you could no longer tell what was man and what was mud, what was animal and what was vegetable. The stench made reporters retch.

"I lived here, because to live here is to have a house, but now I don't have a house or even a mother anymore, and this place smells like death," one 12-year-old told La Jornada's Flaco Garduño.

The September tragedy took place in the Other Chiapas, the one not visited by the caravans and the NGOs, the foreign observers and the Reality Tours. Although this other Chiapas did not much appear on the Zapatista web pages, it is the motor of the state's agrarian export economy, producing a cornucopia of cacao, mangoes, bananas, corn, fish, cattle, and most of all coffee, for the global market.

Coffee is king in the narrow coastal strip running north from Tapachula called the Soconusco, a region settled by Germans and the British and even the Japanese, and one that sometimes regarded itself as a secessionist state. Now the rain effectively separated the Soconusco from the rest of Chiapas. 18 bridges and 400 kilometers of the Pan-American Highway simply evaporated under the "weather system," and half a million Chiapanecos were isolated in what remained of the treetops.

Calling the flooding Mexico's worst natural disaster since the 1985 Mexico City earthquake, Zedillo made repeated trips to the region, ordering even more troops into Chiapas. Rather than moving units from the conflict zone, which were more prepared for war than for relief operations, Defense Secretary Cervantes poured 8,000 fresh soldiers into Chiapas.

"Patience," Zedillo preached as he skated through the coffee-colored rain, the mud-caked flood victims pleading for aid. The aid eventually got to the coast in dribs and drabs, always with the PRI logo attached. Sometimes it was distributed by the PRI candidates—municipal elections were set for October 4th—such as in Huixtla, to which State Government Secretary Arely Madrid reportedly dispatched 10 tons of relief goods in a government truck to her cousin, the PRI nominee for mayor there.

Up to his own chin in water across the state in the Lacandón jungle, Subcomandante Marcos rudely lampooned Governor Croquetas for converting the aid into "a family business" and lavishing relief funds to buy liquor. He reminded the Governor of the fate of Anastasio Somoza Jr. after he similarly purloined aid following the 1975 Managua earthquake, the beginning of the end for his family's dictatorship. The Sup counseled those who wished to donate to use church channels. The EZLN was dipping into the rebel war fund to help out. "This government forgets about Chiapas until it is on the international news," Subcomandante Marcos wrote. "It only knows how to kill Indians—not how to keep them from dying..."

VOTE FOR NOBODY

The October 4th elections for municipal presidents and the state congress was the first test of Albores's questionable mandate. An obese, obstreperous political animal with a fragile ego, the substitute governor for a substitute governor was one of the few citizens of Chiapas who gave a damn about the October elections.

Although a third of the state was still under mud and water (32% of the electorate) and hundreds of precincts were buried in the mud along with thousands of voting credentials and, lamentably, the voters themselves, Albores was determined to go ahead with the balloting. Alianza Cívica and the opposition parties argued to no avail that conditions did not exactly exist for the election. In addition to those too soaked to vote, 36% more of the electorate lived under the threat of armed attack, either from the paramilitaries, the military, or the EZLN.

The pattern of elections in Chiapas was well established by now. The Zapatista bases would abstain and the PRI would win the paper ballot. "We're not going to vote," Domingo Pérez Paciencia explained up at Polhó. "It is not our government that is being elected."

In 1995, the EZLN had boycotted the balloting. In 1997, the rebels had physically assaulted the precincts. Now, the week before the elections, 200 army vehicles rolled through the Cañadas "to discourage disturbances." On October 1st, the CCRI announced that "in attention to civil society's incipient efforts to reestablish a climate of dialogue," the EZLN "will not interfere or otherwise hinder the Chiapas elections."

I covered the vote from Ocosingo. The sun had come out, and I spent much of the morning drip drying in the plaza. In this, the second largest county in all Mexico, one which Albores intended to subdivide into 13 new municipalities to be located smack on top of Zapatista ones, only 24% of the registered voters cast ballots—less than 18,000 out of the 77,000 on the list. Out in Taniperla, one of the proposed new municipalities, voting was reported as low as 14%.

In mid-afternoon, bored with the dribble of voters in Ocosingo proper, most of whom had been paid up to 200 pesos for voting the PRI ticket, I hopped a cab out to La Garrucha, the seat of the EZLN municipality of Francisco Gómez. Instead of voting, the Zapatistas bases were dancing cumbias. October 4th, I had forgotten, is the day of San Francisco and hence the saint's day of the Francisco for whom the autonomía is named, Francisco Gómez, better known as Comandante Ik.

When the ballots were finally tallied all over Chiapas, absenteeism stood at 61%, a near historic low or high, depending from which side of the glass you look at it. Despite the meager turnout, local races were tight, with only a hundred votes or so separating the PRD and the PRI in many municipalities. In San Cristóbal, the authentic coletos narrowly retained City Hall, but in Tuxtla, Manuel de la Torre, Lolita's co-pilot, was crushed by the PAN. Although some

Zapatista bases voted—notably in Altamirano where the PRD was desperately trying to hold on to City Hall —every municipality and district in the conflict zone was won by the Institutional Revolutionary Party, a *carro completo*.

An ebullient Albores labeled the victory "historic" and considered that he now had a mandate to remunicipalize the conflict zone, a dangerous assumption. Marcos was closer to jail than ever, the Governor chortled. In return, the Subcomandante, who considered the October 4th balloting to have been "a grotesque operetta," sent Governor Croquetas a drawing of a bone. "Here, chew on this for a while—I'll be right with you," the Sup needled.

THE CONSULTA CALENDAR

The Fifth Declaration jerked the gears of civil society into motion. The usual suspects gathered at the San Angel Cultural Center in southern Mexico City on September 2nd, the date on which the EZLN had suspended participation in the Dialogue of San Andrés two years back. In addition to the expected mob of Zapsymps, ideologues, and artists (Monsiváis, Poniatowska, Juan Bañuelos, Ofelia Medina, the popular cartoonist Rius, and 68 PRD deputies), the guest list included Juan Sánchez Navarro, a maverick multimillionaire whose brewery confects Corona beer, a liquid export as profitable as petroleum. The civil societarians urged that a meeting be arranged with the comandantes at their earliest convenience to plot out the consulta. Various historical dates were postulated: October 2nd (the 30th anniversary of the Tlatelolco massacre), October 12th ("The Day of Indian Resistance"), and November 20th (the day the Mexican Revolution officially began). "Thank you for giving memory the place in tomorrow that it needs," wrote Marcos, accepting the latter date by return mail.

In assembling the consulta calendar, the EZLN was paying particular attention to another "consulta," the PRD's plebiscite on the mushrooming FOBAPROA banking scandal set for August 30th—these unofficial pulse-takings had become increasingly popular since the Zapatistas' 1995 consultation, and the FOBAPROA vote proved instructive. On the last Sunday in August, 3.1 million Mexicans dissed Zedillo's scheme to dump $80 billion USD in bad bank loans (some of the money wound up in Zedillo's 1994 presidential campaign) on the backs of the taxpayers, a stirring manifestation of popular rejection that, in a better world, would have obligated legislators to mandar obedeciendo. Instead, the PRI and the PAN connived a bank bailout that Mexicans will be paying for the next two generations.

DEAD COCOPOS CAN'T DANCE

The COCOPA had fallen on hard times. The impasse between Zedillo and the EZLN had nullified its effectiveness and drained its credibility. The

Labastida-Orive-Rabasa axis had most of its members on the payroll and the commission was virtually their pawn.

Despite the untrustworthiness of the "new" COCOPA (most of whose members had never seen a Zapatista up close), the Fifth Declaration and the future consulta signaled rapprochement with the legislators—even if few of the Cocopos still supported the commission's rendering of the San Andrés accords—and on October 19th the Zapatistas "reinitiated public contact with the COCOPA" (had there been any other kind?). The communiqué, which lionizes the late Heberto Castillo (many of the new Cocopos had not known Heberto, either) is not exactly a promise of paz: "The COCOPA cannot be a bridge between the EZLN and the government, because the government wants no bridges..."

Nonetheless, armed with this equivocal opening and financed by the Interior Secretariat, which reportedly agreed to pick up the transportation and hotel tabs, the PRI-PAN majority on the commission announced that it would set out for San Cristóbal and La Realidad determined to force a physical meeting with the CCRI. Carlos Payán and Gilberto López y Rivas refused to get on the plane.

The moment was an awkward one. Since the Subcomandante had started talking again, army patrols had intensified exponentially. On October 29th, two long military convoys appeared simultaneously at both ends of La Realidad. When they crossed, the troops heading west to Guadalupe Tepeyac veered off the road into the driveway of the Aguascalientes. Soldiers jumped down shooting— with their video cameras. The simulated massacre had seriously frightened the children, but an urgent note from the CCRI to the COCOPA yielded no relief— all the lawmakers wanted to know was when and where the meeting they proposed would take place.

Marcos headed off the Cocopos just as they were leaving San Cristóbal for the jungle November 6th: because of the intense patrols, it was impossible for the comandantes to come down from the mountain just now, but they would be happy to talk to the COCOPA November 20th-22nd in San Cris, when the CCRI had already scheduled a tryst with Señora Civil Society. The commission was penciled in for 6 p.m., November 20th, at El Carmen convent. Could the COCOPA make the security arrangements to get the comandantes up to the royal city in one piece? If the congresspeople still wanted to visit La Realidad, they were welcome to do so even if the CCRI was indisposed—their presence would no doubt diminish the military patrols.

The EZLN's cleverness was transparent—they would use the commission as cover to insure their encounter with civil society. The Cocopos wondered if they had been sandbagged by the Sup.

RE-ENCOUNTER IN SAN CRISTOBAL

The November sessions stimulated unrealistic hopes. "A window has been opened for peace," Payán rhapsodized, and Nuncio Justo Mullor prayed that no new obstacles would arise to thwart the talks. Luis González Souza, deacon of civil society, exalted the coming re-encounter as "the light of San Cristóbal." In anticipation, CISEN agents bugged the convent where the sessions would be held and the Zapatistas lodged.

As the 15th anniversary of the EZLN's founding approached, Marcos gave his most extensive interview since the silence to La Jornada, a moody look back on a decade and a half of Zapatista survival. Too often, the Sup rued, the rebels had jumped to judgment too quickly and driven off potential allies—his lashings out at the PRD, the EPR, the Church, and some sectors of the PRI and the PAN had unduly isolated the Zapatistas.

Yes, the comandantes' long silences had alienated audiences. "We lost contact when we went inside our submarine." But the EZLN "had said all we needed to say. We decided to let Zedillo do the talking and make a fool of himself, figuring that people would soon get tired of it."

The Sup was enthused about the re-encounter with civil society, but the COCOPA seemed a dead end. There could be no new Dialogue until the government honored San Andrés, and this could not happen until after the consulta, when and if Congress would be obligated by the overwhelming turnout to legislate on the Indians' behalf. The consulta, the Subcomandante underscored, was not merely a referendum but a "mobilization," one that began with this first dual encounter in San Cristóbal.

The departure for San Cristóbal was an extension of the EZLN's 15-year birthday party November 17th at the Aguascalientes. Up in Oventic, there had been a six-hour pageant which included a life-sized papier-mâché tank and Carlos Salinas signing NAFTA in Tzoztil. On the 19th, 28 comandantes—a whole new tier of Zapatista spokespersons under Mayor Moisés' and Comandante Tacho's command—arrived at El Carmen. 3,000 members of civil society and 12 Cocopos were on hand to receive them.

But all was not melba toast and strawberry jam in the rebel camp. Troops had halted two of the International Red Cross vans bringing in the highland representatives at the San Andrés checkpoint; this unexplained stop and the absence of police protection at El Carmen were worrisome signs of a possible Chinameca. Elorriaga organized a noisy demonstration outside COCOPA offices to advertise the Zapatistas' displeasure.

To compound their irritation, the comandantes' digs at El Carmen sorely lacked for creature comforts. There were no mattresses on the humble cots and no blankets, there was no telephone, no fax, the food money was short, the toilets didn't flush, and worst of all, the boiler was busted and there was no hot water. For a weary traveler, San Cris's most redeeming feature is a hot shower.

The 6 p.m. November 20th meeting with the COCOPA did not last long. Four comandantes stomped into the meeting room, glared down at the lawmakers, and expectorated a short list of their complaints. "We're not asking for a luxury hotel or a free bar the public pays for—but we don't appreciate your miserable cots!" Tacho pounded on the table in furious indignation. The legislators were "racists!" he spat. "We will never allow ourselves to be humiliated in this way again!"

A collective gasp went up when the comandantes stomped out. After two desultory years, the long-awaited first meeting with the EZLN had turned into total fiasco. The legislators had been burned by the EZLN, used to reach San Cris safely where the rebels were now holed up with 3,000 fire-breathing supporters, probably plotting new revolutions. ¡Pinche Zapatistas! If they hadn't come to talk to the COCOPA, the cars were ready to take the comandantes back to their jungle!

Carlos Payán, who considers himself a paragon of egalitarianism, was particularly nettled at being labeled a "racist." The EZLN was "undemocratic," he blurted, their performance was "criminal and stupid," their politics were "sectarian" and "Pol Pot–like," and they were "ingrates" too, because the paper he had founded, La Jornada, had dedicated massive amounts of space to their struggle for many years (in January 1994, Carlos Salinas claims Payán counseled him to crush the Zapatistas).

Although La Jornada grossly underreported its founder's intemperance, other more PRI-oriented media did not miss a bleep, among them the NYT's Preston, who wrote the Zapatistas "had picked a mean and gratuitous fight" with the COCOPA and so offended their great pal Payán that he had abandoned their cause and cursed them as *Polpotistas*. The source of the EZLN's whining, Preston reported, had been something about cots that had no mattresses. "The Zapatistas have lost touch with media showmanship," Julia finished the transmission and (unlike the mattressless rebels), crawled into her soft Queen-size at the plush Casa Vieja.

Contact with the civil society was more convivial. Hundreds and hundreds of position papers were read by a cast ranging from farmworkers to folk singers to philosopher kings, and Marcos sent a tape replete with a music track (Pedro Infante, Rage Against the Machine). The Sup's rap splattered FOBAPROA ("just an appetizer/wait for the/multilateral/investment accord.") Civil society was a light bulb, and the juice down below that was making it glow was dimming the lights above.

The details for the consulta were hammered out in three days and nights of strategizing. The balloting was set for March 21st, 1999, the first day of Spring. Rosario Ibarra would head up the coordinating committee. For further information, you could call a certain San Cristóbal number and hear a recorded message from Subcomandante Marcos himself. *"No Están Solos!"* chanted the delirious Zapaphiles, *"No Están Solos!"*

Before the comandantes broke camp, a reconciliation meeting (of sorts) with the COCOPA was brokered by Luis Hernández. Tacho apologized unapologetically for the table-pounding and asked the offended legislators to participate in the consulta on its own version of the San Andrés accords, a decision the commission deferred—most of its members no long supported the original text but did not want to say so to the Zapatistas' facemasks. Instead, the PRIista Javier Gil produced two unmarked white envelopes purported to contain a new peace proposal from Zedillo, but the comandantes refused to accept them, maintaining that it was not the Cocopos' place to deliver letters from the president. Indeed, if the mal gobierno had not quashed Samuel's CONAI, much of the unpleasantness of the past few days could have been avoided.

The two sides lapsed into silence. In the end, after all these years, there was not very much to talk about. The comandantes and the Cocopos promised they would get together soon, but they never did.

The next morning (the 23rd) as the rebels were packing up, Interior flunky Alan Arias showed up at the gates of El Carmen dangling the two white envelopes while Televisa and Azteca whirred away obligingly. No comandante would respond to Arias's theatrical gate-rattling. The EZLN refusal to accept the envelopes was taken as proof that the rebels did not really want peace. Film at 10.

What was actually inside the celebrated envelopes? Proceso's Alvaro Delgado got a look. The gist was that if the COCOPA-EZLN encounter produced direct dialogue with the government, Zedillo would reciprocate with a moratorium on destroying autonomous municipalities and consider repositioning his troops.

A 37-car caravan of supporters escorted the Zapatistas down to La Realidad, and the moment they left, the military roadblocks went up again. The daily patrols and the overflights returned, and the harried residents gulped their Tums and Rolaids. The stress of living in La Realidad is such that most every adult suffers from excess stomach acid, Dr. Bellinghausen observes.

The coda to the season was like an old sad song. During the first week of December, five Zapatista sympathizers were gunned down in three separate incidents. Then on the 13th, an 11-year-old was killed in a road ambush coming out of Los Plátanos, and Albores fingered the EZLN. When, on the 14th, he sent a heavily armed police contingent into Unión Progreso again, 43 Zapatista families fled into the mountain. The year was winding down much as it had begun—with the Zapatista bases displaced in the forest, fearing impending massacre, as the PRIs harvested their stolen coffee below.

WINTER–SPRING 1999

LA SEÑA

They came again on the first morning of winter, the men in dark uniforms and red masks, moving down the leafy hillside, firing off round after round. "¡Viva el PRI!" the masked assassins whooped. Down below, the Abeja women were again clustered around the wood-plank chapel, praying for peace. "Forgive them for they know not what they do," gasped the catechist Alonso before he collapsed, eight bullets in his back.

Bodies writhed in grotesque agonies all over the esplanade, but this year a band of angels and not Uriel Jarquín came to collect them. On every side of the clearing, those who had survived the real massacre prayed like a Greek chorus. Although the automatic weapons of the "PRIs" were made of wood and the detonations of the bullets were simulated by firecrackers, the grief was true to the bone as the Bees marked the first anniversary of the killings.

La seña, a sort of Tzotzil psychodrama, helped to disgorge the pain that was eating the Abejas alive. Depression and lassitude clung to their community like a paralyzing mountain fog. Nursing mothers had stopped lactating and old folks could not eat. One family had already fled north towards the U.S. "They don't want to be Abejas anymore," explained Antonio Gutiérrez, the headman. The seña helped the faithful to distance the devastation and convert it into Christian myth.

Now thousands had descended into this green gully to remember the dead and lay flowers on the little altar in the brick mausoleum that had been raised over the graves. Dripping candles, wildflowers, and a handful of cigarettes (presumably for the dead to puff in their idle hours) were laid out in the niche. Samuel and Raúl together preached the memorial Mass while Indian fiddles and harps scraped mournfully in the high noon heat.

The disgrace that was Acteal still had resonance. At Pine Ridge on the Lakota reservation in South Dakota, Indians mourned the 46 Abeja martyrs in a traditional ceremony. Mourners held hands outside St. Patrick's cathedral on Manhattan's Fifth Avenue at the height of the Christmas frenzy. All over Europe, protesters got out their coffins and their crosses and their jars of blood and read the names of the dead in public.

As if to institutionalize its ill repute, the Zedillo administration issued "The White Book of Acteal," a volume that added little to Attorney General Madrazo's December 1997 whitewash. The killings were still chalked up to "intercommunal" and "interfamilial" tensions. The establishment of a Zapatista autonomous municipality at Polhó was at the bottom of the mass assassination. "The White Book of Acteal" all but blames the Abejas for their own torment because they had not broken with the Zapatistas soon enough.

In all of this monumental construction of premeditated denial and racism, no civilian officials of the Ruiz Ferro administration are held to account, and the word "paramilitary" is not written once.

Mexican immigration authorities contributed to the spirit of the first anniversary of the massacre by deporting nine out of the 70 non-Mexicans who had come to the hillside Mass December 22nd. Meanwhile the annual coffee harvest had begun, and despite the presence of 5,000 soldiers in Chenalhó—one for every six residents—the PRIs were again stealing the Abejas' crop.

FIVE YEARS FIVE

1998 had not been a grand year for the EZLN. Acteal had been the keynote and it never got any better. Four autonomous municipalities had been attacked by military and police, dozens of other villages invaded, and 10,000 Zapatista bases displaced from their land. The CONAI had died and the rebels had quarreled bitterly with the COCOPA. The San Andrés accords were more out of reach than ever, paramilitaries roamed the canyons and the highlands, and the Army had the EZLN's armed wing pinned down in the mountain. Politically, the Zapatistas were boxed in between elections, with the opposition already so mesmerized by its prospects in 2000 that the Zapatista struggle had disappeared from its screens.

The EZLN's growing isolation was alarming. Their protracted silences had short-circuited contact with the outside world, and Marcos, in his gloomiest moments, spoke of coming extermination. Veteran political analyst Adolfo Aguilar Zinser wrote that the rebels were "languidly drifting into irrelevance," a fate even more stultifying than martyrdom. With 65 billion pesos sunk into the conflict zone, Zedillo and Albores were slowly buying up the Zapatistas' base.

The marking of the fifth year of the rebellion was permeated by the sadness of Acteal. "One name sums up the government's position—Acteal," concluded Marcos on a scratchy New Year's Eve tape.

The young men of La Realidad who five years ago that night had fallen upon Las Margaritas and captured General Absalón, were no longer so young anymore,

Hermann mused. Five years had taken a toll on their illusions. Now many were fathers and farmers, and peace seemed an excruciatingly long way off.

The marimba of San José tinkled "Las Mañanitas" and the Zapatista hymn to mark one more turn around the sun in this endless war against oblivion. Up at Oventic, where the party was livelier, 11 Global Exchange "revolutionary tourists" were nabbed by the Migra and "invited" to leave Mexico.

Despite the bleak auguries, the EZLN had its sights set on '99. If 1998 had been "the year of war against the Indian communities" ("the government is drunk on Indian blood"), this next year would be one of mobilization and movement, the Sup scratched. The Consulta would be not just a one-day paper balloting but a continuing mobilization that would keep San Andrés alive into the next millennium. There would be two ways of doing politics in 1999: the boring old party-style and the new exciting peoples' politics of the Zapatista Consulta. ¡Vamonos, compañeras y compañeros! There was much work to do before the Spring equinox.

INVENTING THE CONSULTA

In standard EZLN operating style, the rebels tossed their pebbles into the pool and watched the ripples spread outward into civil society. The comandantes set simple parameters. The ground rules invited all Mexican 12 years and older to participate in the plebiscite. The international ballot—unlike in the 1995 consulta—would be restricted to Mexicans living outside the country.

As in most "popular consultations," the four questions asked were loaded ones: (1) Should Indians be included in Mexico's national project and take an active role in building a new nation? (2) Should peace be achieved through dialogue and the Mexican military returned to barracks? (3) Should the government obey the will of the people and abide by the results (of the Consulta?) (4) Should Indian rights be recognized in the Mexican Constitution with the integration of the San Andrés accords offered by the COCOPA?

It would not be politically correct to say no to any of the four questions.

A fifth question was added for Mexicans in the Diaspora: do you agree that Mexicans living outside of the country should take an active part in the construction of the new Mexico and have the right to vote in elections? With a year to go until the 2000 presidential elections, the vote of Mexicans living in the U.S. had become a galvanizing issue in the exile communities north of the border. If granted suffrage, about 3,000,000 Mexicans might turn out to vote July 2, 2000, enough to decide a close election. Having already voted with their feet against economic and political travesty in their homeland, most of the voters would go to the opposition.

Marcos exhorted "the raza, the batos, the Chicanos, the Mexican Americans, the carnales and the bandas" (but not the cholos) to build the Consulta in Gringolandia. His voice had scratch. By the end of the '90s, the Zapatistas had become icons of Chicano America, revered by such style setters as Carlos Santana and Guillermo Gómez-Peña. Although Cecilia Rodríguez's National Commission for Democracy in Mexico was in tatters, brigades of concheros and shamans ("Danza Azteca," "Harmony Keepers of the Nation of Aztlán"), as well as mainstream white groups like Global Exchange, would accompany the Consulta to fruition.

Marcos promoted the Consulta flagrantly. "Here it comes! The Zapatista Consulta! Not starring Sharon Stone, Leonardo DiCaprio, or Gwyneth Paltrow! Brought to you by Yepa Yepa huaraches —the only globalized huarache!"

By late February, the phone was ringing off the hook at the San Cristóbal contact office. Volunteers registered 50 new brigades a day—1,100 such groups, totaling 27,000 promoters, would eventually sign up. Most brigades were composed of friends from school or the neighborhood, and much like the affinity groups of the U.S. anti-nuke movement of the 1980s, the brigadistas gave themselves fanciful names—from the Soaked Parrots, the Yepas, Chawak (Tzoztil for thunder), and the Cristo Reyes through the Che Guevaras and the Serpent Woman to the Foolish Men.

All over the globe, from Norway to Patagonia ("pole to pole" noted the Sup) by way of Israel, South Africa, South Korea, and Singapore, exiled Mexicans prepared to vote. A ballot box was even set up in Dublin so that Carlos Salinas, should he still be a Mexican, could suffrage.

When Juan Xun, a Chamulan, visited the contact office, he was stunned by all the colored pushpins stuck in the wall maps of Chiapas and Mexico and the world. "The Consulta is like a tree," he told Bellinghausen, "its roots are Chiapas, its trunk is Mexico, and the branches reach all over the world."

5,000 Zapatistas, 2,500 men and an equal number of women, would pair off and visit as many of Mexico's 2,500 municipalities as would have them. Coordinating bodies were established in every state to raise funds to get the rebels to their destinations, to house and feed them, and most crucially, to provide for their security. Although the federal government had pledged safe passage, 5,000 masked Zapatistas were fanning out to states and cities, counties and colonies, where any beat cop, judicial police, madrina (stool pigeon), PRIista, or freelance assassin might want to make his or her day by bagging a "Chiapaneco" on the hoof.

The COCOPA, as it had telegraphed, copped out of the Consulta, and the piqued comandantes retaliated by forbidding contact with the lawmakers during the Zapatistas' sojourn. The CCRI also elicited technical backup from the Rosenblueth Foundation, an NGO intimate with the PRD. The foundation would count the votes and issue the official results.

Many of the votes would not be deposited in ballot boxes at all but rather recorded in traditional communal assemblies. In Chiapas, the questions were translated into seven Indian languages, including the Guatemalan Kakchiquel.

In Oaxaca, the Consulta would be conducted by uses and customs in 412 major-ity indigenous municipalities.

By carrying this debate on Indian rights to every corner of Mexico, the EZLN was committing itself to wage political battle. In many regions, few non-Indians would care much about Indian rights, and others would be hostile and racist. The Zapatistas would have to argue and convince. Such a mission, in effect, trans-formed the Zapatista Army of National Liberation into the sort of political organ-ization participants in the rebels' 1995 consulta had contemplated. But the Zedillo government stubbornly refused to recognize this sea change. "Laws are not made in the jungle," Labastida reiterated. The EZLN was just trying to "insert itself in the 2000 election," peace coordinator Rabasa chimed in. Anyway, the Zedillo government was not bound by the results.

ENERVANTES

Opposition was more active on the ground. Although Albores conceded the EZLN did enjoy the right to transit freely within his state and beyond, pro-Zapatista Indians were arrested and tortured by authorities when trapped at the checkpoints. José Angel and Daniel Gómez were beaten and denied food in Ocosingo jail for four days after a picture of a ski-masked José Angel, taken at the UNAM during the visit of the 1,111, was found in his wallet. One man was jailed for wearing olive-drab pants, another because "you look like you know about the Consulta." When Consulta promoters approached PRI communities to invite their participation, the military would warn the PRIistas that the EZLN was com-ing to kill them, and troops would occupy the settlement. The paramilitary MIRA reportedly organized an anti-Consulta brigade to keep communities in the Cañadas from voting.

Up in Los Altos, the military mounted War on Drugs raiding parties to further malign the "narco-Zapatistas" and their useless Consulta. In mid-January, a 37-car convoy led by two generals, eight operations chiefs, 42 officers, and 451 troops (including military police and the Fort Bragg–trained GAFEs), hit Aldama, an Albores-designated new municipality bordering San Andrés and Chenalhó, where the Zapatista-PRI balance is delicate but generally peaceful. Civil Zapatistas, convinced that the Army had come to bivouac permanently on their lands, tried to block the incursion, and a pre-dawn scuffle, the most violent face-off between the EZLN and security forces since El Bosque, ensued. Tear gas flew and the MPs turned on their spooky electric shields. "Sons of Satan!" the women screamed, "Go away!"

"We have come to destroy the *enervantes*," General Jorge Isaac Jiménez tried to explain as an old woman beat upon his chest. "Enervantes" (stimulants) was not a familiar word to the Tzotziles. "We do not want these plants. They are not ours. We do not eat them. We'll cut them down ourselves," rebutted the local

Zapatista leader, "Jacinto." After hours of mutual insults, the Army was allowed to take 58 scrawny marijuana plants grown on plots protected by PRI families. In lockstep, TV Azteca and Televisa ran stories about Zapatista dope growers that night.

"Do what the mal gobiernos may do, 5,000 Zapatistas are leaving here and going to visit every municipality in the country," Marcos made it clear. "The people are going to get to know the Zapatistas, not just through the television or the newspapers, but in the flesh."

THE HOMECOMING

Congregating at the five Aguascalientes on March 10th, the 5,000 Zapatistas awaited transportation to their assigned regions for a week's worth of proselytizing, to culminate in the March 21st balloting. Most would travel by land—3,000 representatives were bound for the center and north of the country, and the remaining 2,000 would cover Oaxaca, Chiapas, and the Yucatán peninsula. 24 delegates heading for Tijuana and Ciudad Juárez on the U.S. border would fly to their destinations.

Assignment of the number of Zapatistas allotted to each region was determined by demographics—more than 800 would canvass Mexico City's 16 boroughs, but only two were sent to the tiny Pacific Coast state of Colima. Destinations were largely the luck of the draw: some would spend the week on the beach in Acapulco, others in the lost cities in the misery belts girdling Mexico City. Still others were invited to breakfast at the Industrial Club, where beer tycoon Juan Sánchez Navarro hosted a get-together of powerful businesspeople, bankers, and curious diplomats in swankiest Polanco.

Rosario Ibarra escorted four ski-masked Zapatistas to the breakfast at the Marriott Hotel. Usually, the only way an Indian can get into these salons is with a mop, backgrounded Hermann. Things went badly from the outset. First, Sánchez Navarro's wife approached the rebels wagging a fat finger and snarling that no one was allowed to wear a mask in her house—the elderly tycoon had to restrain the matron. Then Israel Chertorovsky, president of Bacardi Mexico, jammed the rebels about prohibiting alcohol sales in their communities. "You grow marijuana, don't you?" the Bacardi man fumed.

From the moment the Indians disembarked from the buses they were filmed and harassed by all kinds of police. The masks provoked most of the mayhem. In Vicente Guerrero, Durango, Judiciales threw two Zapatista delegates to the ground and stripped off their ski-masks (and the rest of their clothes, too). Twice in Mexico City rebels were stopped by cops on suspicion of being kidnappers. Agents prevented a delegation from canvassing Guadalajara's upscale Plaza del Sol shopping mall, and persons unknown shot out the windows of the Carmelite convent where the Zapatistas were lodged in that city. In Celaya, Guanajuato, state police with drawn guns surrounded a bus carrying 30 Zapatistas. When the delegation from La Garrucha went to the Tuxtla airport to fly north to the U.S. border, authorities asked them what they thought they were doing there. "This isn't the bus station," they were told.

Despite the racism and the police pressures, Zapatista delegations went to work nonstop in Mexico City—80 meetings a day were listed out on the delegates' agendas. The rebels visited unions (the Mexican Electrical Workers, which is battling privatization of that industry) and schools (the UNAM, where drastic tuition hikes were about to trigger a mammoth student strike). There was an obligatory sit-down at the counter of Sanborn's House of Blue Tiles, where the first Zapatistas had once supped in a famous photograph in the glory days of the Revolution. Now ski-masked neo-Zapatistas sipped coffee they may well have picked themselves at six pesos a kilo, and which Sanborn's owner Carlos Slim, the richest man in all Latin America, sold at 15 pesos a cup.

Wherever the delegates went in the land, it was a homecoming to a place they had never been before, a Mexico they had never known. They exchanged high fives with skinheads and mohawked punks at the Saturday morning rock n' roll bazaar near the Mexico City train station. Leather-clad bikers escorted them through the streets of Guadalajara, where the EZs even put in an appearance at a Hard Rock Cafe.

A goodly number of delegates evaded big-city chaos and headed for the hills. Up in Chihuahua's Tarahumara, Leonardo (17) and his sister Lisette (13) danced all night with the Raramuri in Rejogochi. "If we support you, it is because we support ourselves," said the head of the assembly, commending a yes vote.

In more mestizo Sisoguichi, where folks knew the EZLN only through what bad things the television said about them, townspeople worried their presence would bring down repression. In San José del Pinar, the assembly only approved three of the four questions because the locals did not want the Army, which they thought protected them from the narcotraffickers who infest the sierra, to be returned to barracks.

At the other end of Mexico, on the Yucatán, ski-masked Zapatistas visited the sun-scorched towns on the peninsula to drum up votes. One couple stayed with my friend Timoteo Pook in Tetiz, a Mayan village an hour out of Mérida. "They never took off their ski masks the whole time they stayed, and it's so hot here...after a few days, my kids got used to having them around," Timoteo recalled a few months later. "At first we could not understand how they talked, but then the words became clearer...the words in their Mayan and ours are really not so different..."

5,000 Zapatistas fanned out to every state in the Mexican union, most of the provincial capitals, more than half of the municipalities, both coasts, and every border. 18 rebels got so close to the United States at Tijuana that they could touch it. Supporters had come down from Los Angeles and San Diego to greet the insurgents, among them three of the 33'd—Peter Brown and a pair from the Flores Magón 12, Michael Zap and Travis Loller. There were tears in everyone's eyes when they touched hands with the rebels through the oxidizing border fence. Then solidarity workers from Alta California read from Marcos's hot-selling *Story of Colors* in English, and the book was handed through the hole in the wall to the Mexicans, who read it in Spanish on the other side.

THE STORY OF THE STORY OF COLORS

The story of *The Story of Colors* is not a pretty one. Marcos penned *La Historia de Los Colores* in October 1994 so that this Mayan fable might elevate the dull gray consciousness of Ernesto Zedillo about the multi-cultural composition of the country he was about to become boss of. One of the first of the Old Antonio stories, *Colors* tells how the macaw gained its brilliant hues, not from the first gods but from second-string deities who were always quarreling. Bored because the world was only black and white, they capture the primary colors, paint the planet with them, and, as an afterthought, splash them all over the macaw's feathers to remind future generations of the many different peoples and ways of thinking in the world.

If Zedillo didn't seem to get it, others did. The Colectivo Callejero ("street collective), a contingent of artists in Guadalajara, published a paperback edition of *The Story of Colors*, wildly illustrated by the Mazateca artist Domitila Martínez. Later, Bobby Byrd, whose El Paso–based Cinco Puntos Press is a beacon of regional hand-to-mouth publishing, bought the U.S. rights (for the art; Marcos is assiduously anti-copyright). Byrd then applied to the National Endowment for the Arts (NEA) for half a grant—$7,500—to produce a bilingual version.

The NEA check was literally in the mail when Julia Preston, who had received a review copy, called NEA chair William Ivey to question the agency's sponsorship of a children's book (it is not really a children's book) written by a dangerously ski-masked subcomandante. Ivey, who was appointed to serve as a kind of condom to protect the beleaguered Endowment from the sort of homoerotic penetration that would provoke Jesse Helms' thunder, had scant knowledge of *The Story of Colors*, but now that his attention had been drawn to the tale by the Times, he canceled Bobby's grant before noon the next day, because it was "not an appropriate use of U.S. taxpayers' money"—i.e., NEA bucks might be going to the Zapatistas.

Byrd protested that his only contract was with Colectivo Callejero, and neither he nor the NEA had any responsibility beyond that—actually, the Callejeros contributed about $1,000 USD in groceries and medicines to the EZLN, returns from THEIR edition of the story. But Ivey, whose most prominent cultural sinecure prior to the NEA gig had been as chairman of the Country Music Hall of Fame, refused to relent. His act of censorship was warmly applauded by the

Mexican embassy, which considered that Marcos's "violent tendencies" made *The Story of Colors* "unsuitable" for North American youngsters (*The Story of Colors* is not a children's story).

Preston, whose inquiries had sunk Cinco Puntos' grant, scored a Times front-pager (below the fold) on the 10th and, as always, notoriety brought swift reward. Cinco Puntos sold 6,000 *Stories* in 48 hours, and a liberal foundation in Santa Fe doubled the lost grant. Still, it was a cheap shot, thought Byrd, a slow-drawling poet in real life. "The NEA chickened out. This book is about tolerance and multi-culturalism, and it is the NEA's mandate to promote those exact values."

Nonetheless, for a quick minute, the NEA had made Subcomandante Marcos into the hottest children's story author in the U.S.

The Story of Colors is not a children's story.

FOREGONE CONCLUSIONS

On the first morning of Spring, consultees streamed into 12,000 polling places across Mexico and 26 foreign countries. 3,000 votes were cast by exasperated motorists in the cramped traffic lanes leading up to the Tijuana–San Ysidro border gate. Mayan villagers voted in impressive numbers all along the southern border. In Santiago Zalizintla, the Nahua hamlet closest to the spewing crater of the Popocatépetl volcano, Indians went door to door with an ambulatory ballot box to avoid military patrols.

The Consulta was unabashedly a numbers game. The answers to the four or five questions were a 90%-plus *Sí* foregone conclusion; the only suspense was in the size of the turnout. The EZLN had to weigh in considerably stronger than the 1.3 million votes it garnered in 1995 and also equal or better the 3.1 million votes accumulated by the PRD in its August FOBAPROA plebiscite.

The totals came close to the mark: 2,830,000 votes were tallied in country and 65,000 in the Diaspora, about 2.9 million in all, which more than doubled '95 and came in just a shade under the PRD's referendum—unlike Zapatista sympathizers on March 21st, voters in the FOBAPROA consultation were not filmed by military and police when they cast their ballots.

With 461,000 votes tabulated, Chiapas was the king of the Consulta—the numbers topped the PRI's 406,000 cast in Albores's "historic" October 1998 elections. The Consulta was probably most pertinent in Chiapas because it opened doors to previously inaccessible PRI villages. The EZLN even encouraged soldiers to vote. "Most of them are Indians," a promoter on the Ejido Morelia argued.

"The specialty of the Zapatistas is to open spaces and convoke actors," Marcos had told Bellinghausen before the election, mumbling something about bringing the results to Congress. But hopeful as the numbers were, they were not big enough to force Congress "to obey the will of the people."

I watched the Consulta from Farmington, New Mexico, a coal-mining town abutting the Navajo reservation in the Four Corners region. Exactly four Mexicans cast ballots—but despite the tiny turnout, they were excited about taking part in social struggle in their own country and enthusiastically endorsed a vote for expatriate Mexicans in the 2000 presidential elections.

Despite the near-100% Consulta victory for suffrage and passage of a bill to that effect in the opposition-controlled lower house of Congress, on July 1st, 1999, the PRI-dominated senate, thumbing its nose at the will of the people, killed any chance of an overseas vote for 3,000,000 Mexicans in the 2000 presidential elections. So much for all this mumbo jumbo about "mandar obedeciendo."

The PRI's veto of the overseas vote was a measure of how much attention it would pay to the Consulta. The ruling party had other priorities—its presidential primary was primordial. Not even the COCOPA would raise a finger to present the results—an overwhelming endorsement of the San Andrés accords—to Congress. It was a foregone conclusion that there could be no motion on Indian Rights until after the presidential election. After March 21st, the Consulta had little scratch with Mexico's political class.

JUNGLE VAUDEVILLE

Roberto Albores Guillén (whose name was now reduced to RAG by the local press) was designated to lead the counter-consulta. RAG's Spring '98 dismantlements of the autonomous municipalities had graduated to his remunicipalization crusade of Spring '99—the creation of eight new constitutional municipalities—including Amparo Agua Tinta, Patihuitz, Taniperlas, Roberto Barrios, and Aldama—was ratified by the governor's stooges in the state congress. Albores also pushed ahead with an "Indian Rights" law that made Zedillo's bonsai look like a sequoia.

To celebrate the first anniversary of Acteal, Governor RAG had offered an amnesty law: in exchange for turning in their guns and pledging allegiance to the institutional way, "armed groups" (the government euphemism for paramilitaries) would be rewarded with farm tools and cattle. The amnesty bill was directed at absolving friendly paramilitaries, but Albores used the gimmick to try and disarm his EZLN enemies as well.

One week after the Consulta, on March 29th, carefully culled media representatives were stuffed into a state helicopter and gyrated to a resort on the bank of the Jatate river just outside of Ocosingo. While lounging on the verandah partaking of the open bar with Governor Croquetas, not a teetotaler, the fourth estate was treated to a stirring bit of jungle vaudeville. Across the river, 16 masked men in Zapatista-like costumes broke from the brush, waded across the knee-deep Jatate, and presented the portly governor with 11 battered rifles. Their leader read a declaration asserting the unit's defection from the Zapatista Army of National Liberation. Then the men plunged back into the river before any questions could be asked. Both Televisa and TV Azteca led their nightly news with footage of the reputed EZLN "desertions." Most other reporters questioned the masquerade as one more instance of Albores's maladroit management of the Chiapas circus.

Who were these masked men? The autonomous authorities of San Manuel knew them by name: they were PRIistas guided by one José Alfredo Jiménez, an Ocosingo City Hall employee and Albores operator. He had driven a city truck laden with forbidden guns and ersatz Zapatista uniforms through two military checkpoints dedicated to ransacking all vehicles for "firearms and explosives," picked up the fake deserters in La Trinidad in the canyon of Las Tazas, and driven them back through the same two checkpoints for the rendezvous with RAG on the banks of the Jatate river resort.

The local leader of the group, Vicente Pérez, had a reputation in his ejido as a car thief and a highwayman and was purportedly hooked up with the paramilitary MIRA, to which, Marcos affirmed, the turned-in guns were later returned. Proceso reported that five of the 16 "deserters" had once been Zapatistas (one for just a month) but had abandoned the struggle in the wake of Zedillo's February '95 offensive. The rest had just come along for the ride.

For the counterfeit rebels, their performance at the Jatate river proved a profitable pantomime. In return for the theatrics, Albores Guillén gifted them with 10 Swiss cows, four calves, a tractor, and an ambulance that Vicente Pérez soon converted into a catch-a-Zapatista paddy wagon.

VOTAN-ZAPATA RIDES AGAIN

For his next act, Governor RAG would move against—of all places—San Andrés Sakamchién de los Pobres. Early on the morning of April 7th, Albores sent 300 state police to take back the government "palace" from autonomous authorities who had occupied the premises since December 1995. Agents found the two concrete-block rooms empty and quickly installed PRIista Marcos Díaz as municipal president. Díaz's first act was to hang up portraits of Albores and his two immediate (interim) predecessors—Julio Ruiz Ferro and Javier López Moreno.

Albores's timing was impeccably poor. He had sent his goons into Sakamchién virtually on the eve of Votan-Zapata's resurrection and just three days before the first anniversary of the destruction of Flores Magón. Sakamchién wasn't just any Zapatista pit stop—it was the site of the torpedoed peace talks and the center of Tzoztil creation, the place where the People of the Bat had been born.

RAG did not get to gloat long. By noon the next day, 3,000 Zapatista supporters were massing on the plaza of San Andrés, and 150 cops left behind to protect the presidencia for the PRI fingered their tear gas launchers and then thought better of it. A sea of women in red huipiles pelted the guardians of Albores's law and order with garbage and rocks as they scrambled up on the trucks to escape. Marcos Díaz has "governed" from Tuxtla Gutiérrez ever since.

The Zapatista authorities took down the portraits of Croquetas and Ruiz Ferro and López Moreno, tore them into strips, and set fire to their torn faces. Emiliano Zapata's visage was rehung in its proper place, and a white banner fluttered from the roof that simply said, "We're back!"

The crowds on the plaza just kept getting huger. By April 10th, 10,000 Zapatista Indian farmers were on hand to remember Votan-Zapata, chanting their *"vivas"* and their *"mueras,"* praying and partying in the Spring sun. Yamahas and marimbas trilled. Albores was the target of endless jokes: "The governor is so stupid that he thinks 10,000 Zapatistas have come to Sakamchién to defect!" mocked Marcos in a much-read communiqué.

MEETING MARCOS

On April 20th, the student General Strike Council (CGH) hung up the red-and-black flags, occupied 40 UNAM schools, and began a strike that would not end anytime soon. The spark had been the rector's disastrous decision to raise tuitions from two US cents a semester to $60 USD at the massive (270,000 students) institution, the oldest and largest in all Latin America and the nation's "Maximum House of Study." The CGH charged that Zedillo, with World Bank complicity, intended to privatize the national university. The EZLN expressed immediate solidarity: "No Están Solos!" Marcos wrote, returning the cry of support that had so often been directed at the EZLN.

On May 10th, dozens of striking students arrived in La Realidad to attend the latest EZLN "encounter with civil society," a sequel to the November meet in San Cris that had planned the Consulta. Now a second encounter had been called to exchange experiences, evaluate the effort, and figure out the next step. 1,700 civil societarians journeyed to the heart of the jungle for the first public get-together at the Aguascalientes since the August '96 Intergaláctica; among them, besides the striking students, were "democratic electricistas," brigadistas from the Tarahumara, Chicanos determined to keep question five alive, a brigade of Bancomer tellers ("please don't mention our names"), Hector, a *niño de la calle* who had hooked up with the Consulta in Cuernavaca, and the "Chuchu el Rotos," an inmate group named for a Mexican Robin Hood, which had tabulated 756 votes at the Eastside Penitentiary and added a distinct fifth question that had gotten some of the Chuchos thrown in the hole: "Are we going to keep paying bribes to the guards?"

But many of the attendees came from the ejidos just down the canyon and up in Los Altos. The men from Nicolás Ruiz told how the PRIistas had at first rejected the Consulta and then voted in it. The musicologist René Villanueva, a Zapatista to the bone, wandered over to ask if there were any flute players on their ejido.

Many who participated in the second encounter were new adepts brought aboard during the Consulta. Most had never been to Chiapas before. Not a few knew the Subcomandante only as a national icon. 18-year-old student strikers had barely turned pubescent when the rebellion first came to town. It was not out of character that when Marcos rode into La Realidad on the 11th, strong women and grown men swooned.

The Sup had not attended a magna function since the Intergaláctica, and the last time reporters had spoken with him in a group was January 1997, when he rode off into an 18-month silence. Marcos had not gone to Mexico City with the 1,111, had not gone out to Mexico for the Consulta, had not shown up at the encounter with the civil society. Nonetheless, while he had been out of circulation, thousands of Zapatistas had traveled all over Mexico and across the water to Europe.

Absence had not dimmed the Subcomandante's charisma. He delivered up Old Antonio's "Story of Calendars" in his familiar nasal tenor, re-created a tale from the Popol Vuh, and identified Rosario Ibarra de Piedra as the Mayan Mama Ixmucané. For Mexican Madres' Day, he presented his surrogate mom with a bouquet of wild jungle orchids.

For the Migra the encounter with civil society was business as usual. The agents posted themselves at the mouth of the cañada and gobbled up a dozen extranjeros when they emerged from the encounter. The 13th victim of the purge, Jens Goltsciot, a Danish sculptor, had come to Chiapas to donate an eight-meter-tall, two-ton, black copper phallus-shaped structure, "The Column of Infamy," to the Abejas.

When Goltsciot got up to the Chenalhó checkpoint with the giant copper column loaded up onto a rented winch truck, soldiers inspected the piece, which is formed by writhing naked figures, from tip to toe.

"Which one is Marcos?" one asked.

Although Galtsciot was allowed to erect the Column of Infamy by the side of the road in Acteal, the sculptor was busted when he came down the mountain and given six days to get out of Dodge. But Jens was on his way to Brazil anyway, to do a column for the Sem Terras. He did one every year, he told me, and put them up at massacre sites around the world. It was like a global happening. Even the Mexican authorities' xenophobic foaming-at-the-mouth had been part of the piece.

The CCRI had called the Consulta workers to La Realidad for a reason. Marcos advanced a seven-step program to consolidate the contacts made during the voting. Through the Consulta, the Zapatistas and their supporters had made contact with hundreds of local struggles that ranged from trying to close a mine in San Luis Potosí to battling exorbitant water rates in Chilpancingo, Guerrero, to the striking students at the UNAM and the electricistas' resolve to keep electricity generation public. The ties needed to be deepened and joined at the base into a national network. The offices of contact would continue to function: "If something happens in Baja California, we want Yucatán to know about it right away."

The EZLN's extension of the contact offices beyond the Consulta seemed to spell *el fin* for the FZLN as the Zapatistas' political organization, although Elorriaga vigorously denied it. But long after the Consulta was boxed up and laid to rest, the contact committees were still in business and the FZ was reduced to a sort of auxiliary to the UNAM strike.

The EZLN's emphasis was now on building alliances, but not necessarily via its own mass structures. The tryout for this tack would be a national coalition against privatizations whose first tasks would be to support the right to a free public education and oppose the transnationalization of the electricity industry. In the next months, Marcos would meet in La Realidad with dissident schoolteachers and anthropologists fighting privatization of the nation's monuments and great ruins, in order to consolidate new alliances.

Little mention of the San Andrés accords, the underlying reason for the Consulta, would be made in the recordable future. There was no political time before the elections to revive the negotiations, and less will to do so. Indeed, on May 18th, Labastida resigned as Interior Secretary and announced his availability for the presidency. Although Pancho L. was obviously Zedillo's designated choice as successor, for the sake of appearances, the President chose to absent himself from the country on the day Labastida flung his sombrero into the ring. Instead, the President flew off to California, where homegrown Zapatistas chased him from Sacramento to San Francisco to L.A. with giant puppets.

JUST DESERTS

Despite the setback at San Andrés, Albores, a species of jungle Rudy Giuliani, was forever on the attack. New "desertions" were announced almost every other day. 139 PRI families were trucked into old Guadalupe Tepeyac to give up. Farmers in Maravilla Tenejapa were so poor they had only nine tattered ski masks to turn in. 439 Tojolabal farmers and their families abandoned the EZLN on the 20th of November ejido in Las Margaritas. Most, of course, had never been Zapatistas. The group from Margaritas had long shopped the Left for the best offer. Now that the PRI was handing out cattle and tractors to "deserters," they were only too happy to turn themselves in.

Albores boasted that 15,000–20,000 Zapatistas had defected or were in the process of doing so. "The EZLN no longer exists!" boomed Governor Croquetas. For years the government had claimed that only 500-600 hard-core Zapatistas had ever existed. Mmm, let's see now, calculated Marcos: 5,000 from five or six hundred? Maybe Croquetas was right—the Zaps were already extinct. Marcos, Tacho, and Moisés were the only true Zapatistas left! But wait! Had not 461,000 Chiapanecos just voted up the Zapatista Consulta? At Albores's stated rate of desertion (3,000 in a year), it would take 150 more years to make all the Zapatistas in Chiapas disappear.

Still, the increasing number of desertions was nothing to sneer at. The Mexican government had committed many billions of pesos to the conflict zone to buy the allegiances of very poor people who had, to some degree or another, once sympathized with the EZLN. Most of these monies were dedicated to winning over the wafflers—waffling was a growth industry in the Cañadas. Stalwart PRI communities whose loyalties were assured got nothing and stayed just as poor.

The bribes came in various sizes: farm machinery, tortillerías, cows, stoves, roofing materials, hot meals, haircuts, liquor, basketball courts, cash money, even a sterile fruit-fly factory in Amparo Agua Tinta. Most every Zapatista settlement in the canyons now contained a few PRI families, or at least families that had accepted Procampo farm subsidy checks. In most places, the Zapatistas and the neo-PRIs got along, but in others, accepting the checks meant becoming the military's eyes and ears inside the villages. Even in La Realidad, three to five families (out of a total 200) had taken the government money. Mainly they stayed to themselves in one corner of the settlement—Julia Preston spent hours trying to get them to speak ill of the EZLN during the second encounter, which she ostensibly was in La Realidad to cover.

But the deserters sometimes got their just deserts too. In La Trinidad, unknowns stole all the Swiss cows from the Jatate 16 and punched out the tires on the tractor. Local Zapatistas said the "deserters" had fallen out amongst themselves and were stealing each other's cattle, but the PRIistas accused the rebels of the misdeeds. Rustling is a high crime in Chiapas, and Albores sent 750 soldiers and police storming down the canyons, invading a dozen EZLN communities in the first two weeks of June to find the cows.

In addition to the cattle search, the security forces were sent in to break up an alleged Zapatista roadblock at Nazareth. The rebels insisted it was all a pretext; there were no roadblocks. And truly the roads didn't need much to block them. By late June, they were rapidly becoming swampland as the Summer rains collapsed on Chiapas again.

SUMMER–AUTUMN 1999

ON THE ROAD

The *bolo* (drunk) snoozed beatifically, face down, on the muddy if newly streamlined boulevard between San Miguel and La Garrucha. Five years ago, the bolo would probably not have been drunk in this then-alcohol-free zone, but then five years ago, the road was just a pot-holed slough that didn't allow the beer trucks to pass through either.

The building of roads that would enable Indian farmers to move their corn and their coffee to market had been prominent among the 34 demands the EZLN presented to the Salinas government during the 1994 conversations in the cathedral. The prospect of dicing up virgin Lacandón tracts with access roads so aggravated eco-guru Homero Aridjis that he blasted the rebels in a celebrated New York Times op ed, tagging them with a bad enviro-jacket at the very beginning of their public relations game.

The Zapatistas' road karma came back to haunt them. Federal refurbishment of the perilous tracks curling down the canyons smoothed the way for the February 1995 army invasion and brought "Progress" and "Civilization" to deep jungle communities.

The EZLN soon had a bellyful of what this P & C was all about: troop convoys, truckloads of prostitutes leased from the great whorehouses of Margaritas and Ocosingo and San Cris, beer wagons, and bolos lying dead drunk or just dead in the middle of the newly built road.

By 1998, the arrival of "Progress" and "Civilization" was accelerated by the completion of the final 45 kilometers of paved freeway riding the border all the way from Tapachula to Chajul, where the Guatemalan frontier elbows north. The stretch had been driven through dense jungle mountain by *ingenieros-fusileros* (riflemen engineers) in the name of national security, a bogus bulwark against the mountains of Colombian cocaine and tidal wave of desperate Central Americans that cascade in from Guatemala. The final miles of highway had one further bonus: they skirted the Sierra of the Colmena (the Beehive) on the south, a presumed sanctuary for the Zapatista CCRI.

Meanwhile, civil road builders were hooking up the Cañadas. The key was the bridge across the Jatate at San Quintín, a bush town that had mushroomed with the arrival of the military into a mud-caked strip mall of bars and bordellos. The new bridge allowed army convoys to penetrate the cañada of Garrucha from Ocosingo and swing west through La Realidad, Guadalupe Tepeyac, and on back to civilization at Las Margaritas. The Zapatista high command suddenly found itself sandwiched between the frontier freeway and the brand-new inter-cañada road.

The next step was to connect up the dots inside the sandwich. By the Summer of 1999, Albores and the Feds were cutting 56 rural roads in the region. Some would tie Governor RAG's new PRI municipalities to the Ocosingo-Margaritas trunk road. Others connected far-flung garrisons for patrol and re-supply. The rains and Zapatista objections did not much slow the construction frenzy. Albores's m.o. was to send "promoters" into the jungle to sign up pockets of PRIistas who welcomed the arrival of "Progress" and "Civilization." Armed with the petitions, the road builders went to work.

On May 3rd, the authorities of San Pedro Michoacán warned RAG against the continuing incursions. On June 10th, the mestizo villagers of San José del Rio expropriated topographical instruments from road surveyors. On July 18th, ski-masked Indians burnt road-grading machinery near Rizo de Oro. On the 21st, a construction company pick-up was torched near La Realidad. Albores sent in state police to protect the construction crews. Zapatista "retrogrades" were not going to keep him from delivering "Progress" and "Civilization" to the Chiapas outback.

One track that the military and the civil authorities seemed obsessed with was a 19-kilometer length running northeast of San Quintín along the edge of the Montes Azules biosphere into the Amador Valley to the village of Amador Hernández and, it was rumored, if the Army got its way, on through the Montes Azules itself, further opening up this delicate region to the exploitation of precious hardwoods, the depreciation of rare species, and the theft of its biodiversity. The suggestion that Amador and the adjoining sanctuary sat on a lake of oil added to the area's allure. When, in July, for the first time in this unabating war, Zedillo sent 7,000 young cadets into the Montes Azules on a "tree-planting" expedition (the President joined them for an afternoon), Zapatista paranoia jumped another notch.

The Tzeltal settlers of Amador Hernández, a jungle cluster a short crow's-flight from the first Zapatista camp at Lake Miramar, came to the Lacandón in the land rush of the 1960s when the PRI was the only party in town—the village is named for a PRI campesino "leader" whose claim to fame is arranging the massacre of 23 coconut farmers in Acapulco in 1963. Despite their ruling-party roots, the villagers of Amador are civil bases of the EZLN, which has long defended them when the government has talked eviction from the fringes of the receding biosphere.

When, on August 11th, the Zapatista campesinos of Amador bumped into a surveying team taking measurements for the new road, the cow's-horn cacho was blown and the village summoned to ponder resistance. The next day, a delegation was dispatched to advise the interlopers to leave, and by the 13th, military police paratroopers began drifting down from the sky to back up the road builders.

30 kilometers west at La Realidad, Subcomandante Marcos was immersed in a "National Encounter in Defense of the Nation's Patrimony," a gathering of 400 anthropologists, students, and indígenas called together to stop a PAN-inspired constitutional amendment concessioning wondrous Mexican citadels like Palenque and Teotihuacán to the highest bidder.

"The Army is at our backs!" the Sup stunned the anthropologists when the news of the paratrooper landing at Amador had been confirmed. Marcos urged volunteers to set off for the village at once.

Ofelia Medina and a group of 30 activists, mostly from the General Strike Council at the UNAM, waded through snake-laced, nose-deep jungle mud and reached Amador on the 14th. The situation had deteriorated into open confrontation in a swampy forest bog now divided by spirals of concertina wire. Wildly dressed indígenas with big sticks pushed at the nervous troops in a reenactment of the famous resistance at X'oyep. The appearance of the outsiders triggered tear gas attack—spent grenades, manufactured in Pennsylvania, bore the admonition "for the exclusive use of the U.S. Army." Suddenly the battle lines had been drawn, with rebel Indians and striking students on one side of the divide and a U.S.-backed military determined to cram "Progress" and "Civilization" down the throats of the locals, on the other.

RAG'S RAGE

Governor RAG, always spoiling for a fight, plummeted into San Quintín on the 18th to defend the honor of Chiapas against Ofelia Medina, her student vandal ultras, and their insidious foreign backers. Met on the ground in a lukewarm downpour by a brace of comely PRI Tzeltaleras, the paunchy, sopping RAG raged at the outlanders who had been sent by "the center" (of the nation presumably) to thwart "the development and tranquillity of our state," and ordered arrest warrants drawn up for Medina and her mob on charges of "inciting to riot," "attacks on the armed forces," "sedition," and "blocking the channels of communication" (although the road had not been built yet).

Military roadblocks were reinforced to grab the agitators when they were flushed from the jungle. PRI mobs were organized to beat up on the outsiders. A Mexican doctor and two Spanish volunteers who had been working in the villages were stopped by enraged PRIistas near Nuevo Momón, slugged, robbed, groped, and nearly raped before they escaped. Military checkpoints set up on both ends of Momón never saw a thing.

When Ofelia Medina finally made it out of the jungle and back up to San Cristóbal, the coleto town council declared her persona non grata and gave her 72 hours to get out of the city.

Bathed once again in the national spotlight, Albores went into orbit, "inviting" all out-of-state young people to leave Chiapas under suspicion of being striking students. Police and immigration agents visited San Cristóbal hotels in pursuit of resident ultras. Bus stations were rousted and Croquetas threatened to stop all incoming agitators at the state line. "Chiapas for the Chiapanecos!" he foamed, pleading with Zedillo to let the "Chiapanecos" settle their own hash. To back up this demand for a free hand, Albores staged a self-congratulatory parade of acarreados "Por la Paz" in Tuxtla on the 21st (the paz-ifists received a torta, bottled water, 50 pesos).

The next day, 6,000 Tzotziles stomped into San Cristóbal in solidarity with their Tzeltal comrades on the Amador Hernández line and demanded Croquetas' immediate abdication. The Indians were led by a starving mongrel with a hand-lettered sign around its scrawny neck: "Albores, don't be like me."

Among the few non-Indian marchers was that famous ultra Ofelia Medina, who at the hour that her 72-hour get-out-of-town-or-else order expired, fearlessly mounted the kiosk in the central plaza of San Cristóbal, just yards from the coleto mayor's office, and slowly sipped a cup of coffee.

As voices calling for RAG's removal increased in volume, Zedillo, although embarrassed by the governor's excesses, was boxed in by past disgraces. How could he replace Albores with a replacement for a replacement for a replacement without looking very foolish?

Meanwhile, tensions were on a hair trigger in Amador Hernández. On one side of the concertina wire, students and Indians challenged the clench-jawed soldiers without fear. "Think, reflect, little soldiers, you are Indians too," a barefoot man from inside the Montes Azules lectured the troops. "Come over here and fight on the side of the people so you will not look so sad there on the other side of that wire." "¡Culeeeeeros!" crooned the students.

Sometimes the Zapatistas came with big sticks and sometimes they came with flowers and affixed balloons to the concertina wire, sang corridos, and danced cumbias in the mud. Meanwhile helicopter after helicopter ferried fresh troops, politicos, and the bought press into the jungle camp on this road to nowhere.

With the comandancia pinned down in nearby mountains, Marcos went off-line and, for the first time since the February 1995 offensive, the communiqués were signed by David and Felipe, the highland leadership. "This is not the first time the blows have been directed to keep us silent and separated from the principal movements of resistance in the country," the Sup wrote the first chance he got. Luis Hernández figured that the government's efforts to keep Marcos in the mountain were a measure of Zapatista success in building alliances.

LA ESPERANZA

Things got out of hand August 25th after pro-Zapatista villagers prevented an army patrol from entering San José de la Esperanza, 20 kilometers southeast of La Realidad in San Pedro Michoacán. Frustrated troops seized three farmers they encountered on the road to Rizo de Oro, but furious comrades soon arrived with stones and machetes and slingshots to set the men free. For the first time since El Bosque, the military opened fire on the Zapatistas. Although the Defense Secretariat maintained the shots were fired in the air to "dissuade aggression," two elderly men were shot in the legs.

The three arrested indígenas were trussed up and transported to the nearest garrison, beaten for 24 hours, and then turned over to civil authorities in Tuxtla. The military claimed that seven soldiers had been wounded by machete blows— including patrol leader General Pedro Cervantes Aguirre, brother of Zedillo's defense chief. Why was so prominent a military man out shooting Indians in some backwater Chiapas town?

For once, the Indians, whose swollen faces testified to torture, were freed quickly, and General Cervantes immediately vanished from the Chiapas Theater of the Absurd.

The shootings hot-wired the recumbent COCOPA into action. As monthly president, Carlos "Pol Pot" Payán pestered Labastida's replacement as Interior Secretary, Diodoro Carrasco, whose debut Zapatista crisis this was, into temporarily suspending the roadwork. But when Payán flew into Amador two days later and spoke through the concertina wire with Albores's political operator inside the new compound, Ivan Camacho told him nope, he hadn't heard anything about the suspension of the project. Yes, the troops were there to protect the road builders.

So the stand-off was joined and remains in place even as we go to press a year later. The military has dug in with hard structures and surrounded their camp with *cazabobos*—booby traps armed with sharpened sticks and steel traps. Although Rabasa denies their material existence, Global Exchange flew one of these cazabobos to Washington. Now the military is considering labeling the traps in English to prevent the accidental maiming of foreign observers.

The *plantón* (sit-down) had hardened too, with neighboring communities coming in to spell the exhausted Amadoreans for a week at a time. An occasional student still stands arm-in-arm with the Zapatistas, still chanting "¡Culeeeeeros!"

At first, the Zapatistas played tapes of Subcomandante Marcos explaining that the rebels "were not opposed to roads that bring us hospitals and schools, but the roads you bring have no benefit to us…with your roads come the vehicles of war, your prostitutes, your alcohol, your venereal diseases…with your roads, the *coyotes* (middlemen) come to buy our crops at an even cheaper price and steal our precious forests…" When at dusk, before they went home, the Zapatistas would sing the national anthem and their own hymn, they noticed that the soldiers' lips were moving too.

The military soon put an end to this subliminal fraternization, installing even louder speakers than the rebels' and filling the jungle with the stentorian rancheros of Chente Fernández, the noxiously grandiose piano of Richard Clyderman, and even, as the season tilted into Autumn, operas like *Carmen*, adding yet another Fitzcarraldian touch to this strange interlude in Mexican history.

GOLD IN THEM THAR HILLS?

It was obvious. The ulterior motive for the military occupation of the Amador Valley and the Montes Azules biosphere was "the richest oil deposits in the world," which, Subcomandante Marcos confided in a lengthy early-September communiqué, lay just under the Lacandón floor. The Sup's revelation fueled conspiracy theories that explained the Amador escapade as the first phase of a coming resource war.

30 years ago, PEMEX had mapped the Cañadas for geological formations that could yield black gold. It was a reasonable endeavor. Just across the border in Guatemala, Texaco and a handful of other transnationals pump modest quantities from the "Zone of the Generals" in the Petén.

But no one was bringing in any gushers on the Lacandón side. The drilling station at Nazareth in the Corralchén, where Zapatistas first went up against the Mexican military in the Spring of '93, produced only 400 barrels a day before it was capped. On the other hand, closed PEMEX stats obtained by Houston oil expert George Baker indicate Nazareth was capable of churning out 4,000,000 cubic feet of natural gas daily. Even though PEMEX is committed to expanded natural gas production, infrastructure would be an onerous security task to build and protect during a rebellion. "Political disturbance is more of a hindrance to extraction than the geologic formations," Barreda quotes a World Oil magazine analysis of the region's potential.

If it is true that the villagers of Amador Hernández are swimming in Persian Gulf–sized oil wealth, then future shock must be now. The possibility of black gold extraction provides a plausible explanation for the road-building frenzy other than encirclement of the Zapatista high command, and gives the government justification for the presence of tens of thousands of troops in the canyons of the Lacandón jungle.

AN OPEN AND SHUT LETTER

When Ofelia Medina, fresh from thumbing her nose at the coletos, best-selling author Laura Esquivel, and actress Jesusa Rodríguez dolled up like indígenas and squatted down on the median strip opposite restaurant row in the posh Polanco district of the capital to pat out tortillas, no one paid them much mind. Even when they hit the lunchtime crowds to beg coins for Ofelia's newest do-good enterprise, SOS Chiapas, few heads turned. "But what do they want, mommy?" one curly-headed *escuincle* (brat) asked. "They're just from Chiapas, dear," she was told, "eat your quiche."

Ernesto Zedillo seemed to be paying just as much attention. For the third year in a row, the President omitted mention of Chiapas in his state of the union Informe (his fifth and penultimate) September 1st, a document that deliberately avoided social realities—the now five-month-old UNAM strike did not rate a mention either.

Then, a week later, the Zedillo administration played its final Chiapas gambit when substitute Interior Secretary Diodoro Carrasco published an open letter to the EZLN in every newspaper in the nation. Although there was no prospect of a pre-election settlement, the rebels were entreated to return to the bargaining table anyway. "I am prepared to go wherever I must go to reinitiate this dialogue," deadpanned Carrasco. Each Interior Secretary has sought to put his own mark on the Zapatista imbroglio, and the ex-governor of Oaxaca was no exception.

The Interior Secretary addressed items the EZLN had raised for years. Three years to be exact. Carrasco's missive arrived just a few days on the far side of the third anniversary of the EZLN's suspension of the San Andrés Dialogue and appeared to be a sort of response to the five conditions the rebels required to get them back to the negotiating table. It had taken the Zedillo government over 1,000 days to respond. A lot had changed in the interim.

Here was the deal: Carrasco offered to investigate all EZLN claims of human rights abuses committed by armed groups against rebel bases—a tacit admission that the government had never taken such complaints seriously before. He offered to free 100 Zapatista prisoners not accused of blood crimes—this was a whole new crew of prisoners than those for whom the EZLN had asked release in 1996. Many had been illegally detained during the dismantlements of the autonomous municipalities and were about to be released for lack of evidence anyway. The Interior Secretary also "invited" the EZLN to "calendarize" the initiation of government-financed "productive projects," i.e., the issuance of Procampo checks which had so divided Cañada communities.

The Zedillo government pledged to create a new blue-ribbon mediation panel composed of "impeccable" Mexicans (no foreign interventionists need apply) and to reconstruct the COSEVER, the oversight commission, although the commission still had no Indian Rights law to oversee.

The two most salient conditions put forth in 1996 remained unanswered: implementation of the San Andrés accords and a military pullback. As to the first, the EZLN was invited to submit the COCOPA version to Congress, where it would be presented jointly with Zedillo's bonsai (or maybe amalgamated with it—Carrasco's language is unclear). The Interior Secretary's proposal was a stinging slap at the Consulta, in which 3,000,000 Mexicans had voted to make the COCOPA version the law of the land. On the question of a military pullback to positions held before February 9th, 1995, there was no offer.

The government's final offer was all for show, a backhanded admission that Ernesto Zedillo would never lift the nation out of the Chiapas quagmire before his six years in office elapsed. Yet another mass propaganda campaign—*Un Paso Más Por la Paz* (One More Step for Peace)—was loosed to once again try and convince an unconvinced public that yes, *sí*, Zedillo had complied with San Andrés after all.

Not to be outdone, the Foreign Relations secretariat printed up four-color, four-language Un Paso Más fold-outs for European distribution as a vote on the EU free trade treaty came down to crunchtime. Un Paso Más was followed by an even more insidious spot campaign depicting a naked Indian child in a jungle clearing, the voice-over imploring "Let us speak Mexicano to Mexicano"—the soundtrack was recorded with an echoplex, and there is a dramatic tremolo on the second "Mexicano" that lingers long after the image has faded from the screen.

On September 13th, the EZLN Consulta committees in Chiapas blocked highways across the state to reiterate demands for the fulfillment of San Andrés—but up to this point in time, the EZLN has never formally replied to Carrasco's open letter.

¡GOYA! ¡GOYA!

By Independence eve, when a quintet of Zapatistas from Amador and San José de la Esperanza journeyed up to Mexico City to celebrate with the striking students, the national university had become a desolate and foreboding enclave. The *Grito* (the traditional *"¡Viva México!"*) and the *goyas* (the university's sporting yell) seemed freighted with fear and loathing. As in Amador, the barbed-wire motif was de riguer at the UNAM—only it had been the strikers themselves who had strung it up. The sharpened coils surrounded the towering rectory building, ran up Insurgentes and turned the corner all the way to the Copilco metro station, effectively sealing off the barricaded campus. General Strike Council (CGH) vigilantes equipped with large clubs protected the chokepoints.

The barbed-wire fixation extended to interior decoration, the strands stretching wall to wall in the Che Guevara auditorium to keep opposing factions from assaulting the microphone during dusk-to-dawn assemblies. By September, the hard Left had taken control of the Strike Council. The so-called "ultras" were a loose coordination of Maoist and Sendero-ist bands—its most prominent leaders were Alejandro Echeverría, "El Mosh," a dreadlocked punk rocker, and 53-year-old economics professor Mario Benítez, "El Gato."

From the outset of the strike, the ultras and mega-ultras had been tougher and better organized than the "moderates," whom they despised and "exiled" from the strike council. The most visible moderates were aligned with the leaders of a 1987 tuition strike at the university, who had now attached themselves to the PRD and even occupied key positions in Mayor Cuauhtémoc Cárdenas's administration. The ultras' rancor at the mods turned pathological when Cárdenas unloosed his police on strikers during violent off-campus confrontations—in respect for campus autonomy, which barred outside interference in university affairs, the mayor steadfastly refused to send his cops onto campus.

The feud with the PRD sharpened October 14th when, without a strike council vote, ultras, who were prone to parade around half naked with red-and-black strike symbols daubed on their butts to moon motorists, blocked the city's most strategic traffic artery during the rush-hour peak. Although Rosario Robles, who had taken over for Cárdenas when he declared for president in late September, sent the riot squad into battle without guns, truncheons, or tear gas, the riot cops still managed to maim students with their Plexiglas shields.

Somewhere in the Lacandón jungle, Subcomandante Marcos stared with disbelief at the Jornada photo of Alejandra and Angel P., teenage strikers beaten bloody to the pavement by the PRD police. He asked painful questions: "How old were Alejandra and Angel when they were beaten? How old are they now? Did the federal district government beat them for being ultras? For being *universitarios*? For being young? Because politics dictated it? To win the approval of Televisa and TV Azteca? To prove the PRD can govern?

"Every time I see this picture, I want to take a rock and throw it far and break the silence above," Marcos exhaled, reliving his days as a campus radical.

TIO MARCOS

In the name of the EZLN and the CCRI–General Command, Marcos had been up to his pronounced nose in the *huelga* (strike) since it was declared in April. Over the months, the Sup issued 10 communiqués of support, Old Antonio and Durito stories. He passed along incriminating World Bank documents that proved the tuition hikes had been ordered by that unloved institution. He urged support from those whom the EZLN also supported—"democratic" schoolteachers and electrical workers. When students at the Metropolitan University offered the EZLN 21,000 pesos in donations, Marcos asked them to turn it over to the *chavos* (guys) at the UNAM —"they look like they could use some pozol."

The Subcomandante and the students had bonded in May at the encounter with civil society, and in June several busloads of strikers showed up in La Realidad to meet with Tío Marcos, who if he is who they say he is, is himself a graduate of the Philosophy and Letters faculty, traditionally the most radical of the UNAM's 40 faculties. "None of the students came to ask us what to do (*qué bueno*, because we don't know) but rather to tell us their word, so we would know it and give them our support." The EZLN had "decided not to intrude in the student movement," but the Sup had one *consejo* (piece of advice) for the strikers: stick by your demands.

The student demands had now grown to six. In addition to wiping the tuition hikes off the books, the strikers' petition included the university's disassociation from a government-imposed testing program, automatic passage of students enrolled in the UNAM's high school system into the university, amnesty for activists, a rescheduled academic year, and the convening of a university-wide congress. But the strike council's insistence that all six demands be met before negotiations could begin on disoccupying campus buildings, stymied dialogue between the strikers and Zedillo's rector, a nervous, scratchy-bearded chemist named Francisco Barnes who did not seem cut out for protracted conflict.

When Barnes made the tuition raises voluntary in June, the strike council did not budge. Nor did it flinch when Barnes conceded a university congress to reform the UNAM. Even after the rector resigned, rattled and babbling, in November, the strikers offered no movement. Indeed, each concession by the administration only increased the strife within the CGH. By its sixth month, the UNAM strike had slid into low-intensity conflict, with bloodied noses and black eyes now the main agenda of the marathon meetings—from which the press, even La Jornada, which had carried the blow-by-blow for months, was physically barred.

By October, the ultras' intransigence had so soured the world beyond the barbed-wire barricades that a handful of respected academics who sympathized with the student demands but feared Tlatelolco-like massacre if some resolution was not in sight, offered a modest proposal to shift resolution of several of the demands to the promised university congress. The proposal was met with derision from the ultras and chiding from the jungle. All six demands must be met before the congress is called into session, the Sup insisted; the Zapatista experience with the mal gobierno at San Andrés proved that it would never "complete its word." Marcos figuratively jammed his fingers into the eyes of the eight emeritus professors who had suggested the compromise: all of their degrees together were worthless when it came to social struggle.

The fact that several of these honored academics—notably Luis Villoro and Pablo González Casanova—were EZLN advisors at San Andrés and had supported the rebels throughout their public trajectory (Casanova, the only communist rector of the UNAM ever, had been a member of the CONAI) did not seem to diminish Marcos's zeal for unmasking their collaborationist proclivities.

The aspersions cast between the Sup and urban intellectuals who had once so fervently supported the EZLN, were all over the pages of La Jornada. Marcos refused to respond to Adolfo Gilly's tempered criticism because Gilly was a paid Cárdenas advisor and Cuauhtémoc's police beat strikers. But the Sup did go head-to-head with Carlos Monsiváis, stubbornly insisting the students were going to win just because "they are right." "They've already won," Monsi shot back, only the ultras won't admit it, because they're afraid they will lose their power in "the concentration camp of ideas" that the "Republic of the Strike" had become.

The government disparaged the EZLN's "contamination" (Rabasa) of the student strike. But the EZLN was not the only radical group to be accused of exploiting the CGH for its own ends—Francisco Labastida, now the odds-on candidate for the PRI presidential nomination, charged that the EPR and the ERPI were stockpiling guns on campus. The sighting of the ultra-left Independent Proletarian Movement and the Francisco Villa Popular Front on campus spawned fresh accusations of outside agitation. On the other side of the Left, the PRD was equally immersed in the troubled UNAM waters, as was, it goes without saying, the Institutional Revolutionary Party, which had always run the university as a kind of advanced day-care center for its trainee lawyers and political "scientists." With only a couple of hundred days left until the presidential election, the contamination of the UNAM strike by the political parties was inevitable.

THE FIX IS IN

Not a few political illuminati considered that the July 2000 Mexican presidential election had been handed to Labastida near midnight September 29, 1999, when the right and left opposition front-runners walked away from building a coalition candidacy and drifted down parallel paths to apparent defeat. Both the PRD and the PAN had learned the hard lesson that the only way to beat the PRI was for the opposition to put its votes together. Indeed, in virtually every election since the 1997 midterms the combined totals of the Right and Left buried the PRI every time. Yet few formal coalitions had ever been attempted.

Coalition between the Right and the Left is not alien to the Mexican continuum. Historian Lorenzo Meyer reminds us that in 1821, the Black liberation warrior Vicente Guerrero joined forces with the conservative Catholic Iturbide to throw off the Spanish colonial yoke, and in 1910 Francisco Madero, a wealthy hacendero, crossed class lines to align with the wild peasant leaders Emiliano Zapata and Francisco Villa and jump-start the Mexican Revolution. But apparently neither Cárdenas nor Fox experienced a similar sense of urgency to find common ground in 2000.

To be frank, neither was built for coalition. Vicente Fox's campaign persona was that of a boastful macho huckster who affected hand-tooled cowboy boots and a big silver belt-buckle and marketed himself as if he were still selling Coca-Cola (he once headed Coke's Latin American operations). Fox was not about to cede his quest to be CEO of Mexico to Cuauhtémoc Cárdenas, the staid two-time loser whose tunnel vision and messianic mission to follow in his beloved father's footsteps, stunted his room to reach compromise. Cárdenas's disappointing stint as Mexico City's first elected mayor seemed to seal his political fate, but still he could not bring himself to abdicate. Besides, asking PRDers to cast a ballot for the crypto-fascist Fox was just asking for a suicidal split in the party he had founded.

Ernesto Zedillo was a weak president with shallow roots in his own party, and his power to impose a successor through the traditional *dedazo,* or "big finger-point," was severely shortened. Instead, he devised the PRI's first-ever primary to guarantee the nomination of Francisco Labastida, former governor of narco-riddled Sinaloa and title-holder at Interior, where he had failed abysmally to defuse the time bomb that was Chiapas.

About the same time as its presidential primary kicked off in June, the longest-ruling political party in the known universe began calling itself the "new" PRI. It was the sort of repackaging that usually signals a failing product. Although the primary was supposed to infuse the "new" PRI with "new" improved democratic vim and vigor, the party was really too old to start all over again.

All Summer and Fall, the PRI primary rated so much prime time that it appeared to be the real Mexican presidential election, which was exactly the impression the ruling party wanted to convey. Labastida and his only real rival, the corrupt governor of Tabasco, Roberto Madrazo, hurled invectives at the speed of sound-bites, the ugliest being the mutual accusation that each was the son of Salinas—the negative campaigns were created by such Washington scumbags as James Carville and Dick Morris, whose dark talents NAFTA now licensed to operate in Mexico. At last, on November 7th, Labastida creamed Madrazo in a not very cleverly rigged balloting. Party officials boasted that 10,000,000 votes had been cast in the primary, an impossible figure given the stark absence of voters at the polls.

Pancho Labastida was Roberto Albores's *gallo* (fighting cock) and Governor RAG would make sure that he swept Chiapas, rolling out the red carpet each time the candidate barnstormed the state. Despite the admonition of his party's hierarchy not to take sides in the primary race, public funds were dispensed freely to promote Pancho's campaign. When the PRI slapped RAG on his thick wrist, he only brought in more acarreados. And when La Jornada reported RAG's peccadilloes, his communication director Manuel de la Torres (Lolita's co-pilot) sent agents out into the streets to buy up every issue of La Jornada in Chiapas when the Mexico City gazette was flown into Tuxtla at noon each day.

On November 7th, the "new" PRI rubber-stamped Zedillo's candidate just about everywhere but in Chiapas, where the oily Madrazo took three out of four electoral districts. Oops.

RAG's embarrassing loss of the state for Labastida made his tenancy in the governor's seat more tenuous than ever. When a mysterious crony of Moctezuma's, Vicente Granados, began prowling the aisles of the state congress, buttonholing impeachment votes, Albores sent a hundred state cops into the impressive edifice to sanitize the precinct.

RAG called out the acarreados, his supporters in the state trucking confederation blocked every highway in Chiapas, and Zedillo backed off, if only because firing Albores would reflect poorly on Labastida. The joyous governor's mood swing was terrifying: "The Zapatistas have always counted with my greatest respect," Croquetas confessed. "After all, without them, I wouldn't still be governor…"

"And which of the candidates do you like in next year's presidential elections, Subcomandante?" the CNN-Europe correspondent asked, somewhere in the Lacandón jungle. "Listen," the Sup winced, "we didn't make this revolution to vote for a political party…"

HELLO, MRS. ROBINSON

Although José Hidalgo vanished from the streets of San Cristóbal de las Casas June 10th, 1999, his face could still be seen on every lamppost. The Hidalgo family, unwavering supporters of Don Samuel and of the EZLN, mobilized quickly, put out posters, and tried to light a fire under the uninterested police. José, who dealt in used cars, had gone off to show a customer an item and never returned—family members remembered that the "customer," a bulky, mustached man, looked like a cop (Juan López Vázquez, ex-military intelligence and judicial police madrina, remains at large).

In the days that followed José's disappearance, his brother Manuel, leader of the San Cristóbal barrio group BACASAN, received many phone calls from surrounding towns, informing him of the discovery of bodies and bones all over Los Altos. None of the leads panned out. Then on June 24th, the police came to the door with a box containing José's clothes and a gleaming white skull that appeared to have been dipped in acid to clean it of gristle and meat. That was José, the police said.

In July, Manuel told this story to Asma Jahangir, United Nations special rapporteur for extrajudicial executions. He feared that death squads were loose in San Cristóbal. But the really frightening thing was not the coleto death squads so much as the great number of unclaimed bones he had found all over the mountains in his search for José.

When U.N. High Commissioner for Human Rights Mary Robinson arrived in San Cristóbal in late November, Manuel was still searching for the rest of his brother.

The Mexican government resents international snoopers, and the United Nations is no exception. Zedillo had told Kofi Annan to butt out, and Mexican government delegations to Geneva meetings of U.N. commissions on torture and indigenous rights endlessly stonewall investigations and recommendations. Often, the Zedillo government would show outright contempt, such as in mid-July when it dispatched PRI deputy Norberto Santiz, the reported MIRA founder, to Switzerland to sit in on a U.N. session looking at paramilitary activity in Chiapas.

The Zedillo administration was nervous about the imminent arrival of the High Commissioner, whose invitation (U.N. officials must be invited to country) had been twice deferred. Not only would Mary Robinson visit Chiapas, but she would meet with indigenous women who now charged 14 unanswered cases of rape against the military.

High-level U.N. investigators had never been kind to Mexico. A 1997 probe by special torture rapporteur Nigel Rodley had generated a scathing report that the Mexican government refused to acknowledge. Jahangir, a sharp-tongued Pakistani who was charged with preparing the ground for the Robinson junket, so disaffected the Zedillo people that the Foreign Relations Secretariat threatened a diplomatic note of protest.

Reporters caught up with Asma Jahangir on the way to Acteal (she was on the massacre site tour—Aguas Blancas, El Charco, El Bosque, and Acteal). "Of course all these cases are extrajudicial executions, even if Mexico wants to deny it," she insisted. "If the Mexican government does not want to know this, why did they invite me? They could have just hired a mathematician to count the number of corpses." During the rapporteur's eight-day stay, so many "extrajudicial executions" took place in Chiapas (Chamula, Tapachula, Ixtapa, El Portal) that state Attorney General Eduardo Montoya claimed a plot was afoot to give the state a bad name while the United Nations was in the region.

Even if the Zedillo inner circle had been hesitant to bring Mary Robinson to Mexico, commercial opportunism outweighed national sovereignty cautions. The free trade pact with the European Union (the TLCUE) was now completed point by point and would be ready for ratification by early 2000. A favorable report by Mrs. Robinson could grease the skids—although the U.N. official's evaluation would not give Mexico a clean bill of health, at least she could attest that the government was trying.

But the High Commissioner's hosts were taking no chances. Mrs. Robinson was flown to country aboard a Mexican Air Force jet—the Mexican Air Force, specifically the GAFE group, is the subject of a torture and extrajudicial execution complaint currently before the Organization of American States' Inter-

American Human Rights Commission (CIDH). The ex-president of Ireland was quickly surrounded on the tarmac by Rosario Green and her team and whisked off for hermetically sealed meetings with Zedillo and other prominent PRI officials.

According to a hush-hush Foreign Relations Secretariat (SRE) strategy plan obtained by La Jornada, Mrs. Robinson would always "be accompanied by a functionary who will be prepared to intervene at any moment." The visit was to be meticulously scripted—when Mrs. Robinson would ask Attorney General Madrazo about Acteal, he would dip into his desk and offer her "The White Book." Press contact would be kept to a minimum, and "friendly pens" were encouraged to write glowing columns about human rights progress while the High Commissioner was in country. Un Paso Más Por La Paz spots would blanket TV transmission.

But the government plan to brainwash Mrs. Robinson was bollixed by a groundswell from the civil society, which reached out to her as an international icon of justice and redress and demanded to be heard—independent human rights groups, the families of political prisoners, union members betrayed by their leaders, the relatives of dead migrant workers, inner-city tenants claiming "social genocide" (10 evictions a day in PRD-run Mexico City). Taxi drivers posted billboards atop their vehicles that welcomed Mrs. Robinson and complained about permit abuses, and small business groups offered testimony of how NAFTA was violating their human rights. UNAM strikers invaded a press conference at U.N. headquarters to read off their grievances. The High Commissioner needed six cardboard boxes and two new suitcases to haul back to Geneva the tapes and video depositions that the civil society showered on her.

There was one conspicuous absence on the roster of social organizations that had reached out to welcome Mary Robinson: the Zapatista Army of National Liberation.

During Jahangir's tempestuous Summer passage through Chiapas, she had received an unusual communiqué from the EZLN spelling out the rebels' refusal to meet with her. Coming on the heels of United Nations approbation of NATO bombing of Yugoslavia, "it would be unethical for us to accept human rights intervention" by the U.N. There were local reasons as well—U.N. refugees commission complicity with Albores at Tierra y Libertad in May 1998. "The U.N. has lost its moral authority." The "real U.N." was the NGOs, Amnesty International, Global Exchange, the independent European Civil Observation Commission that was again tramping through Chiapas.

The blunt Zapatista declaration set an international precedent: in a post-Kosovo world, a group victimized by government persecution had refused to talk with the U.N. on ethical grounds. During the U.N.'s half century of assuaging world conflict, most beleaguered national liberation movements had always cried out for an audience with the United Nations.

Governor RAG tied up Robinson so long in Tuxtla that she had to cancel a drive-by to Acteal, so the Bees came down the mountain to San Cristóbal and slipped a bright red huipil over the High Commissioner's head. "Now when you are working in Geneva, you can wear the dress of the women who were murdered at Acteal," the Abeja leader Antonio Gutiérrez told Mrs. Robinson gravely. Dodging her government handlers, Mary Robinson met twice with the indígenas raped by the military.

The High Commissioner's final press conference left the SRE bureaucrats grinding their teeth. "What the government told me and what I saw in Mexico are two very different realities." Many of her concluding remarks were directed at the military. Mrs. Robinson urged a pull-back in Chiapas, accountability in crimes committed by the military against civilian populations—particularly women—even a military ombudsman to watch out for the rights of enlisted men.

The day Mary Robinson flew out of Chiapas, a 55-vehicle convoy slithered through La Realidad for the first time in a week, and soon after, the military and the new super-duper Federal Preventive Police (PFP) initiated "Operation End-of-the-Millennium" to protect PRI communities from fictitious EZLN attack. Despite Robinson's admonishments the following March, Mexico signed a free trade pact with 14 out of 15 European Union members—the lone holdout was the lower house of the Italian parliament, some of whose members had been barred from Mexico for life.

GLOBALPHOBICS OF THE WORD, UNITE!

"Globalization offers us a choice between two wars, not between war and peace. It's a lie! We don't have to consume in this market of mortality. We don't have to take sides between stupidities…"

Taking a principled stand on the Yugoslav conflagration ("the war that money has sown in the heart of Europe") reaffirmed the EZLN's commitment to building "the Internationale of Hope."

Although their influence within Mexico had been considerably reduced after a half decade of low intensity conflict, the Zapatistas more than ever belonged to the world, emblematic of the growing resistance of indigenous peoples everywhere on the planet against the commercial homogenization the global moguls seek to impose upon the world from the Parnassian heights of the "World" Trade Organization, the "World" Bank, the "White" House, the "International" Monetary Fund, and similar divine institutions.

On the lip of the millennium, the EZLN's legend was being sung from world stages by such universal troubadours as Carlos Santana, whose time had come again, Manu Chau, the iconoclastic European world beat sensation, and Rage Against the Machine, inciters of international youth rage, led by the grandson of a miner from the Cananea copper pits in the north of Sonora where, in 1906, the Mexican labor movement was born in a geyser of blood.

José Saramago, perhaps more than any visitor, sensed the global nature of the Zapatistas' very local struggles. In the faces of those who had survived the massacre at Acteal he saw the survivors of all the massacres in history. In their wounded eyes he saw the "logic of power" of the new globalized world order. His Nobel year winding down, Saramago came again to Chiapas in December and motored out to Oventic for an afternoon, where he listened to Comandante David talk about the Zapatista dead. "Put some dirt in your pocket," Marcos counseled the old writer, "and sprinkle it wherever you go. For some reason science cannot explain, it spreads resistance everywhere…"

Some of that dirt must have gotten sprinkled on the streets of Seattle, Washington, in early December, when the World Trade Organization convened for what it grandiously marqueed as "the Millennium Round" of global free-trade talks, and 40,000 "globalphobes" sat down in protest—steelworkers, students, Buddhist monks, Catholic nuns, bewhiskered rabbis, food purists, farmers, do-gooders, anarcho-punks, indígenas, and environmentalists costumed as turtles and butterflies staged a "carnival against capitalism" that disrupted the WTO's gala celebration of its overblown self-importance and sent representatives from 135 trading nations home with a taste of tear gas on their tongues.

The EZLN, whose Intergaláctica had pioneered the globalization of resistance, was not physically present on the streets of Seattle, but many a ski mask was spotted dodging the pepper spray and the rubber bullets, dancing amidst the swirls of tear gas, flashing a fist from the shell of a gutted Starbucks or trashed Niketown. Many activists in the line of march had visited Chiapas via Global Exchange or on their own private walkabouts, a mandatory way stop on the road to the new resistance.

"The world we thought was stuck in a swamp has begun to move again at last. What happened in Seattle could be the sign of new times. Curiously, this motion has not come from us here in the south," pondered Saramago as he left Chiapas. "Or maybe it has…"

Staring in horror out of the Seattle Westin Hotel lobby windows at the billowing banks of tear gas that blanketed the center of the city, Herminio Blanco, Mexico's Secretary of Commerce, expressed his disgust. The incorporation of labor and human rights considerations in future WTO negotiations, the minimum goal of the insouciant multitudes outside, would only "contaminate free trade." Ernesto Zedillo sadly concurred. "This has been a tragic day for world commerce," he told the American Chamber of Commerce in Mexico City.

Not a week after the Battle of Seattle, Mexico City globalphobics, Zap symps, UNAM ultras, and punks from the Saturday rock n' roll bazaar marched on the U.S. embassy to protest police brutality in Bill Gates's city and were themselves brutalized by the Mexico City police—but not before they busted out 10 embassy windows at the cost of $4,000 USD each.

The Internationale of Hope has taken many trains since Seattle. One of the first stops was Belem in northern Brazil, where, during the second week of December, globalphobics staged the Second Encounter of the Americas in Defense of Humanity and Against Neo-Liberalism. "We'll be there if the piranhas of imperialism let us through," Marcos had promised months before, and now "Lucía" and "Abraham" joined a motley congregation of Amazon Indians, U.S. Black Panthers, gays, Greenpeacers, hordes of anarcho-punks, and union bureaucrats in Belem, a city ruled by the Party of Labor (PT), the Brazilian equivalent of the PRD, which ran the encounter on a tight string—the Sem Terras, who had been promised sponsorship of the event at the Spanish Intergaláctica, huffily chose not to show up. Tensions wafted in the tropical breeze.

The Zapatista presence temporarily patched the warring Brazilian factions together as rapt attendees heard Marcos on tape celebrate "the bridges and tunnels that unite us" and spin yet one more Old Antonio yarn. But once the tape had spooled out, the parts split into opposing camps and stayed there, the PT politicos at one encounter, the punks and Indians at the other. Closely chaperoned by the PT handlers, "Lucía" and "Abraham" were not allowed to mingle.

The battlers spread out from Seattle in diverse directions, visiting Montreal for world bio-security talks setting trade standards for biogenic "Frankenfoods"— killer tomatoes rioted. In Davos, Switzerland, the Alpine ice mountain where the Masters of the Universe gather each January to bask in the warmth of their mutual power, Zedillo toasted Mexico's ready supply of cheap labor and cursed the globalphobics (he popularized the term) while outside, ski-masked activists fought Swiss cops in the snow-clogged streets. Meanwhile, in Bangkok, at the United Nations Commerce and Development annual meeting, another globalphobe mushed retiring IMF director Michel Camdessus with a biotic cream pie.

And in Washington the following April, 10,000 phobes took on both the IMF and the World Bank at its semi-annual joint meeting. After spending a night in DC jail, Mike Saltz, an Oregon university student, blamed it all on the EZLN. The Zapatistas had first gotten him to think about global activism, he confessed to the New York Times. Now here he was, an ex-convict on the Globalphobe Express.

Some of the more vivid detours on the road from Seattle have taken globalphobia back to the wellspring of Indian America. In Ecuador, in January 2000, *dolarización*—the globalization of the national currency—so infuriated that tiny nation's indígenas (half the population) that they took over the national Congress and, in concert with nationalist military officers, actually ran the president out of office for a few hours, the first globalphobic overthrow of a globalphile government in Latin American history. Ojarasca's Ramón Vera, an eyewitness, reported that some of the rebels wore carnival masks when they entered Congress, a reiteration of the resistance-as-celebration spirit of Seattle.

ADIOS TATIC

Piping flutes, pounding skin drums, and strumming harps, the catechists from the Zapatista autonomía of "10th of April" led thousands of Indians through the cobbled streets of the old city. Dressed in their church-going finest, the marchers wove themselves into a living huipil of fabric and flesh, flower and song, the soft murmur of their footfalls sliding over smooth stone as they stepped the final mile of Don Samuel's long good-bye on November 3rd. For 18 months, the old Tatic had been bidding adios everywhere in the jungle and the forests and the mountains at the limits of his immense diocese. San Cristóbal was the last stop.

Canon law requires that all Mother Church's bishops submit their resignations to the Holy Father when they reach 75 years of age, and Samuel would post his tonight, reluctantly, a few ticks before midnight, in a letter that begins "Being of sound mind, that is, I'm not crazy..." Painful as it was to leave the throne of de las Casas after 40 incandescent years, Tatic was heartened that the People of God would soon be in the able hands of his successor, Raúl.

Inside, the cathedral was cool, *juncia* (pine boughs) had been spread out over the floors, marimbas were singing, and copal incense swirled into the heavens. Although the house was packed, many invitees were nowhere in sight. The Bishops of Tapachula and Tuxtla, the two adjoining Chiapas dioceses, for instance—in fact, no member of the Mexican Bishops Conference showed up save for Samuel's old co-conspirator Arturo Lona. Lona himself would retire the next year, virtually closing down the Liberation Church in Mexico.

Also not on hand: representatives of local, state, and federal governments— Samuel had done battle with seven presidents, 13 governors, and too many municipal presidents in his multiple decades at the wheel of this ship. Nor did the Zapatista Army of National Liberation send a bouquet or a communiqué or even a *por qué* to the Tatic who had saved their ass on so many occasions.

Don Samuel, Don Raúl, Arturo Lona, and the Bishop of San Marcos from Guatemala, stood alone on the altar—save for Tatic's four bodyguards, who were posted discreetly at the back. But the People of God were here, packed shoulder to shoulder before the Tatic. Samuel looked down and saw in the lines of the Indian's faces the story of the 40 years he had spent in this magic place and his heart was tranquil. Raúl had indeed been brought here by God to guide the Indians to their liberation.

Moreover, there was a plan. The five-year-long diocesan synod that had been the crowning glory of Samuel's religious work provided a road map for the diocese's transition into the new millennium. The 600 pages of the synod's conclusions were ironclad. There could be no deviation in the diocese's option for the poor or the continuing construction of the indigenous church.

"If they ever try to change the direction of this church, they are going to have to fire hundreds of priests and nuns, 300 deacons, 10,000 catechists, and close down Fray Bart," Miguel Alvarez, Don Samuel's longtime personal secretary, told me the next day at the Tuxtla airport. He never actually said the name of who the theys were.

Perhaps Samuel chose not to read the signs posted along the road to his personal Calvary, or maybe he just did not want to give his enemies the satisfaction of watching him mourn his dream of Raúl's succession as it went down the drain. But there were plenty of signposts. The Pope himself, flying into Mexico in January 1999 for the Synod of the Americas, labeled Samuel's indigenous church a Marxist front. During the Pontiff's last sojourn to the land of the Aztecs, Francisco Labastida had cornered Vatican secretary of state Angelo Sodano, said to be the real power behind the degenerating John Paul II, to lay out the reasons why Raúl should not be named successor to Comandante Sammy. Rabasa had visited the Vatican to reinforce this vision. Foreign Minister Rosario Green spent three hours there in July, huddled with Sodano. Even the coletos had gone to Rome to thwart Raúl's elevation. It was like a full-court press.

By mid-December, Don Samuel had to concede that an "unholy alliance of non-ecclesiastical forces" was threatening Vera's succession. Aligned with the unholys was the so-called "Club of Rome," a power clique that included two out of the three Mexican Cardinals and key "Prigione boys" who had always backed up the ex-nuncio's manic schemes to rid the Church of Samuel.

When, during his long good-bye, Samuel publicly anointed Raúl as his successor, the CEM distributed a snippy press bulletin admonishing the San Cristóbal diocese that the appointment of a new bishop was the exclusive province of the Holy Father. Now, the rumors swarmed like abejas. Raúl would be upgraded to Cardinal. He would be summoned to Holy Rome. He would become the Bishop of Saltillo, in the desert at the other end of the country on the U.S. border. Vera assiduously carried with him the Pope's letter of appointment as Samuel's coadjutor, which stipulated the right of succession. He displayed it at press conferences. He would automatically become bishop once John Paul accepted Samuel's resignation. The only way this might not happen, the coadjutor explained, was if, God forbid, he died before the Pope got around to accepting Tatic's renunciation, or else if he was removed from the diocese before Samuel had been officially retired. Suddenly, there were a lot of big ifs on the table.

On December 22nd up at Acteal, Raúl preached Mass on the second anniversary of Mexico's My Lai. The man who would be Tatic blessed the new coffee harvest and the three wounded children who had just returned from treatment in Washington (the Mexican government had tried to block the trip). Raúl prayed for their recovery, he prayed that the paramilitaries' hearts would be changed, he prayed for the fulfillment of the San Andrés accords, and he prayed that the EZLN (he did not mention them by name) would continue to struggle peacefully for justice. Most of all, he prayed that he really would become the new Tatic. The Abejas even offered to go to Rome and plead his case before el Papa.

One week later, on December 30th, scant hours before the millennium came crashing down upon planet Earth, the Vatican issued a terse press release congratulating Raúl Vera on his designation by Pope John Paul II as the new Bishop of Saltillo, Coahuila, about as far away from San Cristóbal as you could travel and still be in Mexico. The papal nuncio called the move a "promotion." The CEM pledged total obedience. So there it was. Raúl had been driven off into the desert. There would be no new Tatic. Samuel's dreams had crashed in flames. God's work was done here in San Cristóbal.

WINTER–SPRING 2000

THE ANTI-MILLENNIUM

There were no popping champagne corks, dazzling fireworks displays, metric tons of confetti, midnight countdowns, giant screens, worldwide hook-ups, or frenzied mobs paying obeisance to the new global millennium in La Realidad, Mexico, on New Year's Eve 2000. There weren't even any comandantes or messages from them. Instead, Claudia, the representative of the community, read a modest message in halting Spanish repudiating the international ballyhoo that rang in the Third Millennium: "The rich and the powerful celebrate our humiliation while they lie to us and steal from the Mexicans…the mal gobierno just wants to keep us poor for another thousand years."

For the Zapatista Army of National Liberation, January 1st, 2000 marked the dawn of the seventh year of their war against oblivion, nothing more—or nothing less.

Deep in the heart of the Lacandón on an inky night, with only a pulsating Orion's belt to find our cosmic bearings, we had no clue as to how the rest of the world was behaving or whether or not the dread Y2K bug had paralyzed the planet. We may be the only survivors, Hermann and I surmised.

For better or for worse, we were not. The next morning, the first army convoys of the millennium were snaking through La Realidad and Air Force planes circled in the neighboring sky. The Zapatista air force counterattacked in Amador Hernández on January 1st, launching paper airplanes, confected from leaflets urging the soldiers to defect, over the barbed-wire barricade in that now institutionalized face-off on a road to nowhere.

Out on the highways, the Migra snarled at Mexicans and non-Mexicans alike. 43 nons were hauled in for consorting with the enemy, mostly up at Oventic, a new Migra record for a single night's activity; among the detainees were Kerry Appel, the Colorado coffee-bean seller, who had been tossed out of town three years earlier. Now the Mexican government threatened 10 years' imprisonment for returning without their permission, but Fray Bart went to court and stopped the proceedings. Still the mal gobierno's ardor to toss out nosy foreigners during an election year, when the world might be more or less watching, was an ill omen for fraud-free presidential elections on July 2nd.

IN RECEIVERSHIP

Indignation at Bishop Vera's removal pervaded the diocese. Raúl was one more martyr of a church persecuted by both the Mexican government and the Vatican. The Abejas wept that they had been orphaned yet again and proposed to accompany Raúl to Rome to protest. Instead, he went alone, somehow obtaining an audience with the Pope, who (according to Vatican insider journalist Carlos Fazio) claimed he had been cut out of the loop on Vera's banishment to the desert. Not to worry, the Pontiff assured, he would pick a suitable successor.

Samuel's people were hardly convinced. "Our faith has been shaken," vicars Gonzalo Ituarte and Felipe Toussaint inscribed in a joint press statement. To the vicars, the removal of Raúl was "a military victory." They intimated that the Vatican had conspired with the Zedillo government, so infuriating the nuncio Mullor that he refused to attend celebration of Samuel's 40th year on the throne of de las Casas.

January 25th was supposed to have been Samuel's last day on the job, but with Raúl now removed, he had no successor. Moreover, John Paul had not accepted his resignation, a process that could take years. "At least we will have him here for a little while," his great friend Andrés Aubry rejoiced as we bought our Jornadas that brisk winter morning.

13 candles, symbolizing the 13 days of Mayan creation, were ablaze upon the altar, and 13 bundles of pine boughs spread upon the floor. Three planeloads of well-wishers flew in for the Mass, as did Vicente Fox, who showed up "to steal the camera." But most of the hierarchy of the Mexican church stayed away, and the CEM was repped by the two Felipes, Arizmendi of Tapachula and Aguirre of Tuxtla.

The names of Samuel's possible successors floated by like lost balloons. One day, it was the bishop of Oaxaca and the next, the Yucatán bishop. Onésimo Cepeda, the golf-playing, PRI-loving prelate from Mexico state, a charter member of the "Club of Rome" that had engineered Raúl's leave-taking, offered to give up his sumptuous cathedral if John Paul should call upon him to go to Chiapas and clean out that rat's nest of liberationists in San Cristóbal. The probability that Samuel would be replaced by a bishop dedicated to destroying his work was palpable.

Now, with Tatic gone and the threat of a successor who had no feel for the situation, many prophesied the war would come again. "We have gotten rid of Raúl Vera and Samuel Ruiz. Now it is time for the government to get rid of the Zapatistas," was how Juan Sandoval Iñíguez, the cranky Cardinal of Guadalajara, saw it.

In mid-March, Raúl Vera set out for Coahuila, accompanied by Samuel and representatives of the diocese's four language groups. La Jornada reported that business groups in his new bailiwick were troubled by the Bishop's imminent arrival. The Interior Secretary assigned Vera a brace of bodyguards.

Then on March 30th, the Pope launched his dedazo. Don Samuel's resignation was accepted and Tapachula's Felipe Arizmendi would be moved to San Cristóbal. It was not the best scenario, but given what could have come down, Samuel's people blew a sigh of relief. At least Arizmendi knew Chiapas. "I do not go to San Cristóbal to destroy or compete," he soothed in his first press statement—but Arizmendi did not promise to continue the Tatic's work either.

Although he had exhibited little option for the poor in Tapachula, a diocese through which pass 100,000 desperate Central American migrants a year, Felipe Arizmendi had sometimes come to Samuel's defense, refusing to join Prigione's 1993 "Marxist gospel" purge and resisting Salinas's efforts for condemnation of the San Cristóbal bishop in the early days of the uprising. He had also protested Zedillo's calumnies that Don Samuel preached the "theology of violence."

Arizmendi himself had twice met with the Zapatista comandancia—once with Marcos in the cathedral during the 1994 negotiations, and again at San Andrés with Comandantes Tacho and David, but he was by no means a fan—"violent," "radical," and "intolerant" were about the nicest words he had for them.

Unlike Samuel's birthday celebration and the January anniversary of his four decades at the head of the diocese, Arizmendi's coronation was attended by 50 bishops, three Mexican cardinals, and the new papal nuncio—Mullor, having completed Prigione's mission to replace Samuel, was awarded Mexico's most prestigious medal and returned to Rome. Also on hand: the authentic coletos, led by mayor Mariano Díaz and his hatemonger father Ricardo, attending their first Mass in the former Cathedral of Peace in several decades. But not all of Don Samuel's enemies were assuaged by Tatic's leave-taking. "The seed still remains," Peace & Justice's Marco Albino ominously off-the-cuffed to the vicious anti-Samuel daily Cuarto Poder.

Arizmendi's May 1st coronation emptied the stage and silenced the city. Although Samuel lingered on in San Cris until the end of the month, the cathedral remained locked much of the day, and there were no lines of visitors at the rectory doors begging for the old bishop's blessing. "The owner doesn't live here anymore," sighed his friend Aubry sadly over the counter of the newspaper store. The House of Samuel had passed into receivership.

But the diocese's peculiar magic had not dried up entirely. In his first weeks as bishop, Felipe Arizmendi set out to get to know his new flock. His first stop was Cerro Hueco, a hopeful sign. On May 7th, Tatic's successor ventured out to Chenalhó and even spent a few hours at Polhó, where he met with the Zapatista autonomous counsel. That night, he bedded down with the Abejas in Acteal.

Death was fresh in the Spring zephyrs when the Bishop arose on the morning of the 8th. Another road ambush a few miles north in Pantelhó had taken three lives—two PRIistas and an Abeja. A coffee-harvest cash heist was a probable motive. Right on cue, military vehicles began racing up and down on the country highway fronting Polhó. Helicopters conducted night missions. 500 federal preventive police (PFP), the newly organized superpolice force, were ordered into the highlands to patrol the mountain trails. A shaken Felipe Arizmendi returned to San Cristóbal to mull what the Indian woman had told him at Polhó: "Welcome, but you do not know how it works here yet." Now he was beginning to get the idea.

Several days later, in his first face-to-face with substitute Interior Secretary Carrasco, Arizmendi pleaded for a military pull-back in Chiapas, and several days after that, in his first diocesan assembly, the new bishop appointed Samuel's most trusted priest, Joel Padrón, as his personal secretary. Aubry was heartened. "Here the people teach their bishop how to behave," he joked as we stalked our morning Jornadas.

NOT QUITE TLATELOLCO

The new super-dooper Federal Preventive Police sprang from the loins of several suspect agencies: 700 spooks from the CISEN and 3,500 elements of the Federal Highway Patrol, a force with a black history of drug corruption. But the backbone of the PFP was 5,000 military police drawn from a crack riot-control battalion. Some considered that the new police force had been constructed to quell any trouble that developed after the July 2nd election.

The new force was mandated to fight organized crime (kidnapping, car theft, drug and body-parts trafficking) but its debut came in Guerrero in October 1999 with the arrest of several key ERPI commanders. After that, the PFP's deployment in Chiapas seemed inevitable. But first the PFP would be utilized to put the UNAM "strike without an end" out of its misery.

By the new year, the lingering student revolt was infecting electoral discourse. Cárdenas and Fox blasted the PRI gobierno for its failure to take charge of the deteriorating situation. Labastida talked about gun caches on campus. Zedillo had replaced Francisco Barnes with health secretary Juan Ramón de la Fuente (who had been sent in to neutralize the Zapatista refugee camps after Acteal), and now the new rector drew up a plebiscite demanding that the bedraggled strike council fold up its red-and-black flags and return the faculties to the university. About a third of the UNAM community voted and overwhelmingly endorsed the new rector's ultimatum. Armed with their endorsement, de la Fuente sent his goons into the schools to physically wrest them from a CGH that no longer could muster up enough rank-and-filers to prevent the take-backs.

After a particularly cruel battle at a university prep school February 3rd, in which the rector's paunchy thugs were mashed into the pavement by young rebels, Zedillo sent in the PFP; 251 students, many of them underage, were rounded up and charged with terrorism. For the first time since 1968, a university facility was occupied by the military—albeit thinly disguised as the new police. The endgame was closing fast around the strikers.

Before dawn on the 6th, the robocop-like military police swarmed into the UNAM, entrapping what was left of the CGH in one final marathon meeting and hauling off anything that moved, including the two ringleaders, El Mosh and Professor Benítiz, street kids who had taken refuge on campus, Argentinean tourists, and Indian construction workers who were living in the shell of a building they were working on. In a little over three days, Zedillo had taken a thousand "students" prisoner.

Down in La Realidad, Hermann reported the villagers huddled around their radios, stoically absorbing the salient details of "university Sunday." *"Están chingando los estudiantes"* ("they are screwing the students"), one unhappy rebel gravely confirmed.

But the February 6th crackdown was not quite Tlatelolco. Despite the mass arrests, no one had been killed, and the worst weapons discovered on campus were a dozen scraggly marijuana plants. Still Zedillo's strikebreakers stirred memories of the '68 massacre, and in the end, the government's ham-handedness united all the factions that had been bickering for months. Even as cleanup squads moved through the recovered buildings, whitewashing out murals of Che Guevara and Uncle Ho, Chairman Mao and Subcomandante Marcos, the contingents were forming on the Paseo de la Reforma for the most voluminous response of the civil society since the Acteal outrage, and the well-worn refrain from 1968 acquired fresh urgency: *"¡Presos Políticos Libertad!"*

Once again, the UNAM was full of soldiers and the jails were stuffed with students Subcomandante Marcos taunted from the jungle. "The PFP is Zedillo's new excellence in education plan."

"AN INCIDENT IN HISTORY"

Reporters accompanying Ernesto Zedillo on a European jaunt to celebrate Mexico's new trade pact with the European Union at the end of January could hardly believe their ears when the Mexican president repeatedly dismissed the Zapatista rebellion as just "an incident in history" and justified his veto of the San Andrés accords as "a minor matter." After six years and hundreds of deaths, 20,000 refugees, 70,000 troops permanently based in the jungles and highlands, billions of pesos in bribes, social programs, and military hardware, and trillions of words expended to stanch Mexico's hemorrhaging credibility, Chiapas was just an incident in history.

"An incident?" raged José Saramgo. "Zedillo is the incident!" Actually, thought the Nobelist, we are all incidents in history, but "no one is incidental." Marcos soon began writing from "the incidental mountains of the southeast."

Zedillo was the history part, and the EZLN was not yet an incident but would be one soon if they did not rejoin the dialogue, argued Emilio Rabasa. The debate about who was the history and who was the incident was stacked against the Mexican president.

Ernesto Zedillo spent a good deal of his last year in office boasting of the accomplishments of his administration. In Zedillo's world, everything had to come up roses: The economy, the drug war, the environment, Chiapas—where peace now reigned. Sure there had been some nastiness there in the past, but social harmony had returned to the state by the Spring of 2000. The Indians were still poor, but less poor due to the enormous resources the government had showered upon them. "Chiapas used to be a paradigm of criminal contempt for the state of law," the President beamed at Roberto Albores, but RAG had changed all that. Between his efforts and those of his bulldog governor, the accords on Indian Rights and Culture had been implemented!

During the months of buildup to the election, Ernesto Zedillo visited this incident in history six times, armed with a blizzard of statistics that proved beyond a shadow of a doubt that he had fixed everything. The truth diverged from this vision. In the first six months of 2000, sometimes on the very day that the President visited the state, 23 Indian and mestizo farmers and police had been gunned down in Chiapas and another 24 wounded. The murder sites—Chenalhó, Pantelhó, El Bosque, Chavajavel, Chilón—were familiar ones to students of the Zapatistas' endless war against oblivion.

Not everyone agreed with Ernesto Zedillo's assessment of his achievements. On April 3rd, the President, on his 32nd visit to Chiapas, addressed several hundred schoolgirls assembled on the front lawn of a Chiapas university extension in Comitán, Roberto Albores's hometown. The students had been bused in and forewarned not to shout "vivas" for the EZLN. One slender 16-year-old, Tania Ocampo, the possessor of the deepest brown eyes in all of southeastern Mexico, borrowed a sheet of paper from a compañera's notebook and wrote big: "Comply with the San Andrés Accords!" Zedillo spotted her right away and interrupted his speech to argue that he had complied. "It's the others that haven't." An official tried to rip the sign from Tania's outstretched hand. Albores glared at her malevolently—"It was the most horrible look I've ever seen," Tania later fretted.

After he had done, the President approached young Tania to defend his record. "Comply with San Andrés!" she shouted, and Zedillo stomped off, muttering "They are the violent ones!" according to the Reforma reporter at his side.

After the confrontation, Tania Ocampo was overwrought, still shouting that Zedillo must comply. "What would it cost him?" she asked reporters. "There's no peace here like he says. Where is his damned peace?" "They are leaving everything for later, and by then it will be too late," the trembling teenager sagely deduced.

EVICTION FROM EDEN

Peering through the hole in the gathering rain clouds, Nuevo San Gregorio seemed a phosphorescent pinprick in the vast green wilderness of the Montes Azules biosphere reserve, 331,000 hectares of lush, virgin jungle UNESCO had long ago declared a world heritage site. In the spring of 2000, the Mexican government was accusing the Mayans who lived within the reserve, mainly sympathizers of the EZLN, of burning the Blue Mountains down.

Closer to the ground, Nuevo San Gregorio was muddier but no less Edenesque. Howler monkeys ululated under the vibrant canopy, crimson macaws gabbled at the crowns of colossal caoba trees, deadly four-nose nauriaca snakes lurked in the underbrush, and fierce red ants stripped meat down to the bone in a matter of seconds (gringo flesh was a delicacy). There are American crocodiles (*caimanes*) in the crystalline Río Negro. Hermann was impressed: "One feels really inside here in this sanctuary of Indians and butterflies."

Although the forest had been a sanctuary for displaced Mayans for three millennia now, the Mexican government, its environmental ministry (SEMARNAP), police, and military apparatus, were fixated on getting rid of the Indians—the butterflies could stay.

In a meticulously coordinated campaign, cheered by near-daily newspaper appeals, Secretary of the Environment Julia Carrabias accused 32 communities situated inside the biosphere—some with deeds dating back to the 1930s—of illegally invading, cutting, and burning this international treasure. Mendaciously claiming that the Montes Azules would be desert in 14 years if the present rate of destruction continued, Carrabias demanded the voluntary relocation of the settlements. If they did not negotiate their evictions in good faith, the Federal Preventive Police would be summoned.

The secretary had tony allies in this endeavor—the World Wildlife Fund and Conservation International, a private trust fund that had bought up a piece of Mexico's swelling foreign debt in exchange for the preservation of a swatch of the Montes Azules. Also on board Carrabias's eviction team were SEMARNAP forestry subsecretary Jorge del Valle, Bernal's confederate at San Andrés; Agrarian Reform secretary Eduardo Robledo, onetime governor of Chiapas; and poet–eco guru Homero Aridjis, who never failed to accuse the Mayans of ecocide.

Settlers in Montes Azules had been resisting expulsion for decades. In 1972, President Luis Echeverría deeded the entire forest to 66 Lacandón Maya families, who promptly subleased it to ruthless rip-and-run loggers. The Lacandones, while the longest-lived Indians in the forest from which they take their name, were hardly the only Mayans living there.

When, in 1978, President José López Portillo delineated the boundaries of the Montes Azules biosphere and ordered non-Lacandones to move on—threatening, as Carrabias would two decades later, to bring in the Army and the police—resistance hardened, and the Zapatista Army of National Liberation, then doing business as the FLN and encamped inside the sanctuary themselves, joined the settlements in resisting the evictions. Zapatista influence inside the biosphere went back a generation.

The EZLN presence "inside" whetted the interest of the military as much as that of the new police. Sprawling bases at San Quintín and Monte Libano sat right on the borders of the reserve around which the military had wound a skein of access roads such as the one the soldiers had attempted to drive through Amador Hernández. In fact, the Army was inside the sanctuary "planting trees" and protecting corporate interests of the Savia project (a joint venture of Mexico's leading cigarette tycoon, Alfonso Romo, and the U.S. Monsanto Corporation) near Lake Suspiro, where scientists were reportedly genetically mapping Lacandón vegetation for commercial sale.

Andrés Barreda, the UNAM strategic resources expert, thought the push to evict the Indian settlers was grounded in such resource exploitation—in addition to rare genetic materials, petroleum, timber, and exotic species trade was incentive enough to despoil the Mayans of their forest.

But the 30 families of Nuevo San Gregorio were not going anywhere. Tzotzil speakers, a rarity in the jungle, they had once been *acasillados* (serfs) on a highland finca near Huixtán. When the land played out, young men like Manuel R. migrated to the German coffee plantation Liquidámbar in the central sierra, where they worked from dark to dark for chits redeemable at the hacienda store. "We were like slaves," Manuel remembers.

Inspired by Tatic Samuel's liberationist preachings, the young families of old San Gregorio had set out for the jungle to build a better life. A year of biblical exodus later, they founded new San Gregorio here in "the desert of solitude," as the Spanish explorers had described the heart of the Lacandón. Now their fathers were buried in the reserve, and they were not moving on.

In late May, a handful of environmentalists, civil societarians, and intrepid reporters flew into San Gregorio for a forum "In Defense of Life, the Land, and Natural Resources," an effort arranged by the ARIC-Independiente, the indigenous farmers' "rural collective interest association" that shares the EZLN's vision, if not its penchant for arms. 12 worried communities along the Río Negro sent delegates—twice in March the PFP had put down in Candelaria, just up the river from San Gregorio, demanding that the Mayans accept relocation or face forced expulsion.

All spring, Carrabias had been spreading false alarms, alleging that 200 fires were burning out of control in the Montes Azules due to Mayan slash-and-burn agricultural techniques. But the ARIC and the EZLN settlements inside the reserve were pledged not to burn their forests, composting instead to nurture the fragile jungle soils. In fact, there was only one forest fire burning out of control in the Blue Mountains in the Spring of 2000, and that was near Lake Suspiro, where the Savia project was plotting the jungle's genetic makeup—it was probably started by a careless soldier puffing away on one of Romo's cigarettes. The Indians insisted the military, not they, held responsibility for damaging the delicate balance in and around the sanctuary, having fouled the streams and clear-cut a 10-acre hillside during the soldiers' lengthy stay in Amador Hernández.

Gathered at dusk in front of the one-room jungle schoolhouse, the children of Nuevo San Gregorio crayoned posters of parrots and jaguars for their guests. "We have a right to live here with our animals and our plants," one read. "Señores of the environment, do not evict us."

Then young Porfirio Encino, the indefatigable ARIC organizer, read the Declaration of New San Gregorio, which demanded that transnational corporations stop stealing the secrets of their jungle. "We demand respect for our traditional knowledge! We say no to free trade in genetic materials!" The document designates the Mayan settlers as "the guardians of the Montes Azules." The Declaration of Nuevo San Gregorio was sent on to a U.N. biodiversity conclave in Nairobi, Kenya, where a nervous environmental secretary Carrabias was forced to defend her eviction plan.

Now the rain was falling fast, and the village catechist arose to close the meeting with a prayer in Tzotzil—Samuel had not retired in this jungle—and the Indians sang the ARIC hymn of resistance, which shared lines with the Zapatista anthem, and everyone dashed for cover. The big drops would extinguish the government's mythical fires and moot that pretext for the PFP presence. The summer rains had come again, slowing down the mal gobierno's persistent march to obliterate the Zapatistas and their friends.

EPILOGUE

OBLIVION & THE ELECTIONS

The EZLN studiously avoided the presidential elections as long as it could. Marcos's many communiqués coyly skirted the subject. He wrote the Argentinean poet Juan Gelman about ballistics, bade anthropologist Fernando Benítez farewell as he passed on to the spirit world, advised musicologist René Villanueva to take his medicine, and congratulated Pablo González Casanova for resigning from the UNAM to protest the jailing of the students. A book-length schmooze with Catalan writer Manuel Vázquez Montalban was published, as was a volume of the Subcomandante's writings, *From the Mountains of the Southeast.* Neither work addressed the electoral season.

In April, to mark Votan-Zapata's resurrection, Marcus issued a charming children's story, *The Memories of Zapata's Horse,* as told by the Caudillo's steed to one of the EZLN horses, El Marinero, all about the famous battles he had ridden into and how he saved the first Zapata at Chinameca.

The memoirs of Zapata's horse end with a refrain repeatedly spotted at the foot of the Sup's correspondence that spring: "I'm off to *las playas de trigo* (beaches of wheat) where La Mar (the sea) sleeps." La Mar, as it soon became evident, was a sentient being, Marcos's newest compañera, Mariana, a cipher the comandante asks interviewers to leave up to the readers' imagination. Isolated as they were in their mountain camp, Marcos and Mariana were a rough-hewn image of domesticity, even attending the "Mad Hatter's tea party" (really coffee and animal crackers) on La Mar's birthday (letter to González Casanova). In none of these correspondences was the July 2nd presidential election alluded to.

***

But if the EZLN was not addressing the elections, everyone else in Mexico seemed to be. From the first of the year onwards, the campaigns so deluged the media that there was no other news. Zedillo's boy, Labastida, surged out of the gate with a 47% rating and then nose-dived into a 40-40 dead heat with Coca-

Cola king Vicente Fox Quesada, a PANista charlatan with a silver tongue that seemed permanently disconnected from his brain, with less than a month to run until July 2nd.

The third (of six) candidates in the race, Cuauhtémoc Cárdenas, had never caught fire. The only principled contender in the bunch, Cárdenas vowed to implement the San Andrés accords and kick the military and the new PFP federal preventive cops out of Chiapas; he even campaigned at Polhó and Acteal. But despite his great nobility compared to the other lamebrains on the ballot, his cant was old and his day was done.

Panicked by the prospect of a Fox victory, the PRI cranked its vote-buying machine into overdrive. Zedillo toured 20 states in 60 days, dispensing 300,000 pesos each hour in public works funds to purchase allegiances. Among the projects inaugurated was the frontier superhighway that had been in operation for over a year.

In Chiapas, Pablo Salazar charged, the government was handing out 300 million a month in Progresa poverty program checks, along with Vote Labastida leaflets. Alianza Cívica documented home visits by PRI officials to advise recipients that the checks would disappear if Labastida lost the election. 13 million Mexicans were enrolled in the Progresa program.

As in 1994, Procampo agrarian subsidies were paid out just prior to election day. Long lines of Indian farmers formed outside the banks in Ocosingo to cash their checks and swear allegiance to Labastida.

Meanwhile the PRI dominated media coverage—76% of all electronic media election news in Chiapas. When Fox decapitated Labastida in two television debates, Albores ordered the state's newspapers to run eight-column headlines declaring the PRIista the winner.

The dynamic between the three top candidates had an edge of Machiavellian backbiting and ambush. The PRI successfully manipulated Cárdenas into attacking the PAN rather than going after a ruling party that had killed 600 of his followers in the past 10 years, while Fox wooed (ex) PRDistas like the duplicitous Porfirio Muñoz Ledo. Every vote for Cárdenas would be a vote for the PRI, chanted the PANistas. Every vote for Fox was a vote for fascism, the leftists chanted back. Although the interchanges were a lot more scintillating than the Gore-Bush dull-men's contest up north, none of it sounded good to the Zapatistas.

A Labastida victory July 2nd portended demolition for the EZLN. As the post-Acteal Interior Secretary, Pancho Labastida had presided over the massacre whitewash, sandbagged the San Andrés accords, murdered Samuel's CONAI, crippled the COCOPA, allowed Ruiz Ferro to escape to Washington, and ordered his proxy, Albores, to dismantle Zapatista autonomous municipalities at gunpoint.

Fox, who bragged he would settle the conflict in Chiapas "in 15 minutes"— he never said how—was not a promising alternative. Although he spoke of a military pull-back, he had zero clout with the brass. Instead, a Fox presidency meant the military would inevitably flex its muscles to define its influence within the new regime—and in July 2000, Chiapas was the place where the military had muscle to flex.

July 2nd presented a physical threat to the integrity of the EZLN leadership. If Labastida won, Zedillo would be sorely tempted to take out the snotty Indian guerrilla that had taunted him every day for the past six years and eliminate the problem for the next PRI tenant of Los Pinos. On the other hand, if Fox took the cake, the military was likely to move on its own.

***

By June, the EZLN could no longer avoid the snakepit into which it was about to stumble, and warned its supporters that oblivion was on the national agenda again. "The government's war against the Indian peoples advances in these lands. On one hand, the machinery is cranked up to insure the imposition of the new lord of war Francisco Labastida. On the other, they are preparing a definitive military offensive. In the highest spheres of government, they speak of an agreement between Zedillo and Labastida..." to annihilate the Zapatistas.

Several hundred veterans of the civil society met under a tent in the puddle-drenched Zócalo on June 9th to once again try to stop the war. Six years previous and at this same near distance to the presidential election, many of these suspects had traveled to the jungle for the first time to meet Marcos, write a new constitution, and organize the post-electoral struggle at the first National Democratic Convention. Now they were far fewer in number, and it was way beyond their energies to deter an impending attack on the EZLN by stimulating a civil society hypnotized by elections three weeks hence.

A frustrated Mama Piedra, as Marcos now called Rosario Ibarra, chewed out the damp handful of supporters for not having kept their word to the rebels, but her rage lit no fires. Everyone there—Ofelia Medina, Luis Hernández, Elorriaga, González Casanova, Memo Briseño, the CNI, the human rights defenders, Rosario, all the others—had spent the last six years of their lives rescuing the Zapatistas from oblivion, and the assault was still coming...

Just outside the tent, Aztec concheros fumed because the civil society was taking up too much of their assigned space on the Zócalo floor. "We are the real Indians here," they argued, beating upon their war drums and displaying credentials from the government.

***

The EZLN's paranoia about imminent provocation and military obliteration soared June 12th after a murderous mid-morning ambush on the rutted back road between El Bosque and Simojovel, in which seven municipal police officers were cut down with brutal precision. Some of the attackers wore red paliacates, others reportedly caked their faces with clay. Over 200 rounds had been pumped into the police pick-up, and some of the cops had received the coup de grâce.

The attack occurred, ominously enough, on the second anniversary (plus two days) of the June 10th, 1998, massacre at Unión Progreso and Chavajavel in El Bosque—and one day after folksinger Oscar Chávez and the civil society sang for peace at Oventic (where the First of January rebel middle school was at last up and running).

The Army rushed in and put a clamp on the highlands. GAFE units combed the hills from the air and on the ground. Troops ransacked Las Limas, the settlement closest to the massacre site, and the Tzotziles fled into the mountain. Everyone held their breath as the long-predicted final offensive took shape.

Then, abruptly, the investigation, coordinated by state attorney general Eduardo Montoya, veered away from the Zapatistas—rustlers, dope growers, gavillas even the EPR were fingered. Meanwhile Marcos broadcast a personally signed appeal avowing the EZLN's innocence—the extreme violence of the cop killings was just not the Zapatista style. "Our investigations point towards a provocation to increase military presence" and induce the famous "vote of fear," accused the Sup.

"Only a sick mind" could deduce such a conclusion, Montoya shot back, but days later, warrants were sworn for an El Bosque PRI firebrand and 58 associates—the accused had all the earmarks of being one of the paramilitary bands whose existence the Mexican government continued to deny.

***

The fresh massacre in El Bosque was less than a blip on the screen of a nation hopelessly overrun by the electoral contagion. The tightest presidential race in Mexican history steamed towards the wire with the front-runners in a dead heat and reduced to flipping over every rock in the nation in their manic search for votes. On June 14th, both Labastida and Fox at last turned their high beams on Indian Mexico. The PRIista bused 30,000 PRI Indians up to the "Otomí Ceremonial Center" on a Mexico state hilltop—a sci-fi-like setting built by petro pesos back in the fabulous '70s—for the usual PRI palaver. The little man (Labastida had had to stand on a box to debate Cárdenas and the six-foot-four Fox) strutted the specially-built runway, promised the PRI Indians better and bigger Progresa checks, and dissed the San Andrés accords.

Almost at the same hour, Vicente Fox summoned representatives of the nation's 56 indigenous peoples to the Fiesta Americana hotel (formerly the Holiday Inn) near the Christopher Columbus traffic circle in downtown Mexico City—14 showed up. With 17 days to the election, for the first time in three years of campaigning, the rangy right-wing rancher endorsed the San Andrés accords.

***

The EZLN unexpectedly plunged headfirst into the electoral fray on the 24th, but the major Marcos communiqué got a little lost in the reportage of Cuauhtémoc Cárdenas's difficult day at the UNAM. Although that campus had been the scene of some of his most historic rallies, by late June 2000, the "Moral Authority of the Mexican Left" had been declared persona non grata at the UNAM by what remained of the General Strike Council, for having manhandled student rebels the year previous.

"*¡Cárdenas Fascista!*" it screamed in huge freshly painted letters everywhere at the university. Up on the rectory esplanade, a rowdy gang of radical toughs rained down eggs and garbage and balloons filled with yellow paint upon the PRD aficionados gathered to hear out Cárdenas. "*¡Hijo de puta!*" hollered the rads as Cárdenas woodenly recited a speech advocating free public education. "*¡De Puta! ¡De Puta!*"

The Marcos-authored communiqué, dated June 19th but not published until five days later, was one of the few intelligent documents delivered during the dumbed-down blitzkrieg of glitzy gimmick marketing that U.S. carpetbaggers like Carville and Morris, amongst other glorified horseshit salespersons, brought to the Mexican electorate in 2000.

Squinting at a 12-inch black-and-white tube in a mud-splattered mountain camp 20 kilometers from the Guatemalan border, Subcomandante Marcos became as acute a media philosopher as Rafael Guillén had ever been, lamenting the "scandal, the insult, the infamy, and the banal gossip" that passed for political discourse in a campaign in which the media was czar.

"A citizen no longer makes a decision before distinct political options but rather what the media offers," the Sup critiqued. "The exercise of political power has not passed from the elite to the citizenry but rather to the publicists…" The huckersterism was a clue that July 2nd would be a very undemocratic election.

Vote buying had been extravagant, sighed Marcos, but the Zapatista bases were not for sale. Indeed, the Tzeltales of the Ejido Morelia ("17th of November") had just turned 19,000 pesos in Procampo monies back to the Feds, the campesinos complaining that they were not for sale and demanding respect for the San Andrés accords.

Bellinghausen reported that the Zapatistas of La Realidad were being offered 500 pesos to vote up Labastida—although few had valid voting credentials (the Federal Electoral Institute frowns upon masked voters).

Marcos did not discount a Fox victory—but even such a historic shuffle at the top did not guarantee the long-awaited "transition to democracy." In a country that suffers the scourges of terminal "presidentialism," the Sup posited that an election in which all attention is riveted upon the presidency was self-defeating. Congress needed to be strengthened to fend off the presidential evil—and not just any Congress but a non-party citizens' Congress that, it goes without saying, would make San Andrés the law of the land.

The EZLN spokesperson also urged the left not to be bamboozled by the Coca-Cola man's invitation to cast a "useful" vote "for change" instead of throwing it away on the sure loser Cárdenas. Designating himself as chair of the "Committee for a Useless Vote," the Sup urged Cuauhtémoc not to renounce his candidacy at the last minute in favor of Fox, because Mexico required a left political option—"the last option for peaceful change."

Nonetheless, although Cárdenas was the only principled candidate in the race, the EZLN would make no endorsement. The communities could vote or not vote, and there would be no sanctions. The rebels would not interfere with the installation of voting stations in the conflict zone and would not "sabotage" the July 2nd balloting.

The communiqué also warned that Mexico had more armed groups "than any other country in Latin America." The EZLN was not responsible for the post-electoral conduct of the EPR and the ERPI, nor of the two new entries in the field—the Villista Army of Popular Revolution (EVPR), whom no one had ever seen (although they sent abundant e-mail), and the FARP, or Armed Forces of Popular Revolution, which actually waved weapons around at a La Jornada photo op in Xochimilco in April, threatening war if the PRI won again.

"The electoral hour is not the hour of the EZLN," the Subcomandante underscored, "but maybe it will be someday, when there is peace and respect for the indigenous people."

***

On July 2nd, for the first time in their modern political history, Mexicans went to the polls without knowing who their next president would be. Most everywhere, election day was a kind of quantum leap into the unknown, but in Chiapas, the script had been rehearsed many times. In the cluttered plaza up at San Andrés, the ballot boxes were filled up by the PRIs, and the autonómos stayed home (over the mountain at Acteal, the Abejas dared to vote for Cárdenas).

Down in the Cañadas, the voting stations had been set up adjacent to military bases and PRI communities where Cárdenas supporters would not dare set foot. On an ejido near the sprawling military complex at San Quintín, Bellinghausen spotted a PRI cap set atop the ballot box to remind voters of their options.

In the jungle, the choice was PRI or PRD or nothing at all—the PAN had no presence in the zone. Between them, ruling-party pressures and Zapatista prickliness often made voting for Cárdenas an act of bravery. On election morning, Ana Lidia, a Tzeltal mother of six, walked for three hours down a heavily patrolled jungle road to cast a ballot in the schoolhouse at Patihuitz. Back in her home community, Zapatista loyalists suspected that anyone who voted was a PRIista, but Ana Lidia, who was affiliated with the ARIC Independiente, was going to vote for Cárdenas anyway. "How can we change things if we don't vote?" she asked Reforma's Teresa del Riego, looking nervously around her for witnesses. "*Ojalá* (let's hope) that God will bless us and the PRI won't win."

But despite Ana Lidia's touching faith, at the end of the day, the PRI had won 11 out of 12 federal districts in Chiapas, and Labastida had carried the state by a comfortable margin.

***

As usual, Chiapas was marching to a perverse drummer. All over the center and north of Mexico, voters stormed into the polling booths July 2nd, in some places literally chanting for change (and not one that leaned left, either). The presidential election was no dead heat as the pollsters had intimated. 71 years of PRI dictatorship had instilled in the Mexican electorate a great cautiousness that the intrusive gringo techniques of the inquisitors could not penetrate. Most of the so-called "undecided" (10 to 19%) proved to be very decided for El Fox.

All day, the PANista built up a huge lead, winning Guadalajara, Monterrey, and Puebla—the nation's second, third, and fourth largest cities—plus provincial capitals from León, Guanajuato, to Mérida, Yucatán, and shaving 700,000 votes from the PRD majority in Mexico City (where Andrés Manuel Lopez Obrador eked out a narrow victory in the mayor's race). The tide seemed irreversible. No PRI finagling out in the countryside—the celebrated *voto verde* or "green vote"— could concoct big enough numbers to steal the election back from the Fox juggernaut. The hard-won independence of the Federal Electoral Institute—for which the EZLN had once battled—seemed to have insured an honest vote count at last. The PAN was on its way to winning the governorships of two states, majorities in the lower house of Congress and the capital's legislative assembly (both by an eyelash), and the presidency of the Mexican Republic.

***

As anticipated by all but the most rabid fanatics, Cuauhtemoc Cárdenas was demolished by the right-wing bandwagon—the PRD would lose 60% of its congressional delegation. But the PRI was the biggest loser July 2nd.

Inside the Institutional Revolutionary Party compound out on Insurgentes Norte, the railroad men and the lottery ticket hawkers, the ambulantes, and the bused-in colonos gathered early to cheer on Labastida. All afternoon, the PRI masses blew their plastic cornets, clacked their traditional *matracas* (wooden noisemakers), and yelled themselves hoarse at their party's impending victory.

But after voting closed at six, the exit polls and the quick counts began to kick in, and the results looked ominous for the still-ruling party from the get-go. The crowd slumped into a sullen silence. As dusk closed in, rain clouds blotted out the sky and a dank wind gusted through the compound, icing the ambiance with doom. Orders were given and the celebration discreetly canceled. The PRI rabble folded up its Labastida banners and trudged off into the uncertain night.

Since noon, Francisco Labastida had been holed up in the bunker of the PRI tower trying to console his supporters. Now he descended to street level and dead-marched into the Plutarco Elías Calles auditorium where, not so many years before, Luis Donaldo Colosio had been laid out. But that was another funeral.

Suddenly, Ernesto Zedillo was conceding the Fox victory direct from Los Pinos on the big screen, and the only dry eye in the house appeared to be Labastida's. When, with a silly little grin of embarrassment permanently pasted to his ferret-like face, the first defeated PRI candidate ever for the presidency of Mexico admitted, "The results do not favor us," the party leaders could no longer contain themselves, and their sobs and anguished bellows filled the auditorium to capacity. Mourners embraced and bewailed their collective fate—how could they survive without the PRI's lock on the state? Suicides and vendettas were contemplated…

The longest-ruling party in the known universe no longer ruled!

Outside in the compound, the poor, upon whose backs the PRI had built its sinking empire, had gone home to consider other options. The mariachis had packed up and the stage had been torn apart. The sound system that had been contracted to bring "The Fiesta of Triumph" to the nation was dismantled. Only the garbage wafting in the doomed wind remained, the garbage and a strobe light someone had neglected to unplug, raking the compound from one dark corner to the next, hunting for survivors, as if the Titanic had gone down all over again.

***

When those Mexicans who went to sleep Sunday night, July 2nd, opened their eyes the morning after, the dinosaur that had dogged their lives from the cradle to the grave for seven excruciating decades had disappeared, or at least was grievously wounded. The sky was blue. All over Mexico, the first day without the PRI was one of dizzying speculation and bashful self-satisfaction at the collective empowerment that had brought the once perfect dictatorship to its knees. Like the fall of the Wall, the crumbling of the PRI became an instant building block in the memory of the Mexican people.

Under the Angel of Independence and basking in the heat of victory on election night, Vicente Fox had been startled by the chanting supporters beneath him—"Do not fail us!" they warned, "do not fail us!" One could not but be struck by this demand for accountability from a barely elected president, this injunction to mandar obedeciendo. The EZLN had something to say after all.

The days to come will be enlivened by change and counterchange. Chiapas remains stuck in the muck the PRI left behind, and the horizon is troubled by the prospect of renewed violence. The wounded PRI dinosaur and its military and paramilitary assets will not abdicate voluntarily. The new president will not easily find common ground with the Zapatista Army of National Liberation. Like the first Zapata, who in 1910 struck an alliance with another rancher from the north named Francisco Madero to get his village lands back, the EZLN and the first post-PRI president of Mexico may agree to a halt in hostilities, but when the president fails to deliver, as did Madero, the rebels will inevitably dig up their guns again and resume this war against oblivion...

What is certain at this uncertain moment, as old Efren Capiz never tires of insisting at public meetings, is that the struggle will go on and go on and go on and go on and go on and go on and go on and go on and go on and....

TO BE CONTINUED

BIBLIOGRAPHY

Books, Theses, & Reports

Barreda Marin, Andrés: "Atlas Geoeconómico y Geopolítico del estado de Chiapas," doctoral thesis, Universidad Nacional Autónoma de México (UNAM), April 1999

Bernal Gutiérrez, Marco Antonio and Miguel Angel Romero Miranda: *Chiapas, Crónica de una Negociación*, volumes one and two, Rayuela, 1999, Mexico

Centro de Derechos Humanos Fray Bartolomé de las Casas: "Update on the Human Rights Situation in Chiapas" (1999); "Executive Summary: Acteal Between Mourning and Struggle" (March 1999); "A Special Report on Executions in Chiapas" (July 1999); "Chiapas, ¿Un Incidente en la Historia?" (March 2000), San Cristóbal de las Casas, Chiapas

Centro de Derechos Humanos Miguel Agustín Pro: "Chiapas, La Guerra en Curso," Ciudad de México, 1998

Centro de Información y Análisis de Chiapas: "Chiapas, Cronología de un Conflicto 1998," "Chiapas, Cronología 1999," San Cristóbal de Las Casas, Chiapas

Centro de Información y Analisis de Chiapas and Coordinación de Organismos No-Gobernamental CONPAZ: "Para Entender Chiapas: Chiapas en Cifras," San Cristóbal de las Casas, Chiapas, 1997

Chanteau, Miguel: *Las Andanzas de Miguel*, privately published, San Cristóbal de las Casas, Chiapas, 1999

Conant, Jeff: "The Poetics of Resistance: Strategy and Symbol in the Communiqués of the Zapatistas," Master's thesis, New College, San Francisco California, 1998.

De la Grange, Bertrand and Maité Rico: *Marcos: La Genial Impostura*, Alfaguara-Aguilar, Ciudad de México, 1997

Durán de Huerta Patiño, Marta, with Massimo Boldini: *Acteal, Navidad en el Infierno*, Times Editores, Ciudad de México, 1998

Ejército Zapatista de Liberación Nacional (EZLN): *Documentos y Comunicados*, Volumes 1–3, Ediciones Era, Ciudad de México, 1995, 1996, 1997

——*Shadows of Tender Fury: The Communiqués of Subcomandante Marcos and the EZLN*, Monthly Review Press, New York, 1994

——EZLN Communiqués: "Memory From Below," "Masks and Silences," "Navigating the Seas" (English, separate pamphlets), AK Press, San Francisco, 1998

Elorriaga Berdegue, Javier: *Ecos de Cerrohueco*, Planeta, Ciudad de México, 1996

Global Exchange: "Foreigners of Conscience: the Mexican Government's Campaign Against International Human Rights Observers in Chiapas," San Francisco, 1999

Gutiérrez, Maribel: *Violencia en Guerrero*, La Jornada Libros, Ciudad de México, 1998

Harvey, Neil: *The Chiapas Rebellion: The Struggle for Land and Democracy*, Duke University Press, Durham and London, 1998

Hernández Navarro, Luis and Ramón Vera Herrera: *Acuerdos de San Andres*, Ediciones Era, Ciudad de México, 1998

Hirales, Gustavo: *Camino a Acteal*, Rayuela, Ciudad de México, 1998

Katzenberger, Elaine (editor): *First World, Ha! Ha! Ha!: The Zapatista Challenge*, City Lights, San Francisco, 1995

La Jornada, *Memorial de Chiapas*, La Jornada Libros, Ciudad de México, 1997

Le Bot, Yvon: *El Sueño Zapatista*, Plaza y Janes, Barcelona, 1997

López, Mario, with David Parvón: *Zapatismo y Contra-Zapatismo: Cronología de un Enfrentamiento*, Grupo Omega, Turala Ediciones, Buenos Aires, 1997

López y Rivas, Gilberto with Jorge Luis Sierra and Alberto Enriques del Valle: "Las Fuerzas Armadas Mexicanas al Fin del Milenio," Grupo Parlamentario del Partido de la Revolución Democrática (PRD), Ciudad de México, 1999

"Marcos," Subcomandante: *Desde las Montañas del Sureste Mexicano*, Plaza y Janes, Ciudad de México, 1999

——*The Story of Colors*, Cinco Puntos Press, El Paso, 1999

Oppenheimer, Andrés: *Bordering on Chaos: Guerrillas, Stockholders, Politicians, and Mexico's Road to Progress*, Little Brown, Boston, 1996

Ross, John: *The Annexation of Mexico: From the Aztecs to the IMF*, Common Courage Press, Monroe, Maine, 1998

——*Rebellion From the Roots: Indian Uprising in Chiapas*, Common Courage Press, Monroe, Maine, 1995

Rovira, Guiomar: *Mujeres de Maíz*, Ediciones Era, Ciudad de México, 1997

Tello Díaz, Carlos: *La Rebelión de las Cañadas*, Cal y Arena, Ciudad de México, 1995

Vázquez Montalban, Manuel: *Marcos, el Señor de los Espejos*, Aguilar, Ciudad de México, 2000

Womack, John: *Rebellion In Chiapas: A Historical Reader*, New Press, New York City, 1999

Newspapers and Magazines

Expansión (Mexico City), special Chiapas issue, April 1998
El Financiero (Mexico City), January 1994–February 1995
La Jornada (Mexico City), January 1994–July 2000
Los Angeles Times (Los Angeles), occasional, 1994–2000
Milenio magazine (Mexico City), 1998–2000,
New York Times (New York), January 1994–July 2000
Nexos (Mexico City), special Chiapas issue, January 1999
La Palabra (San Cristóbal de las Casas), monthly publication of El Centro de Información y Análisis), 1998–2000
Proceso (Mexico City), January 1994–July 2000
Reforma (Mexico City), February 1995–July 2000
El Tiempo (San Cristóbal de las Casas, Chiapas), January 1994–July 2000
Universal (Mexico City), occasional, 1994–2000

A

Aamilla, Genaro (Bishop), 283
Abejas, 14, 219, 235–237, 239–255, 286, 297–298
Abuela Trini, 126
Aburto Martínez, Mario, 61
Acarreados, 123
ACNUR (United Nations High Commission on Refugees), 169, 286, 326
Acteal Massacre, 14, 202, 239–255, 253–254, 297–298
AEDPCH (Chiapas Assembly of Indians and Campesinos), 82, 86, 112, 127, 165–167, 211–212
Agrarian Reform Secretariat, 5
Agrarian subsidies, 79
Agribusiness, 7
Aguas Blancas massacre, 132, 182
Aguascalientes: CND, 75–78; destruction of, 107; Fall 1996, 206; map of, 262; reclamation, 119, 152–153
Aguilar, Daniel, 84
Aguilar Camín, Hector, 62
Aguirre, Felipe, 334
Ajustes de cuentas, 62
Albino, Marco, 238
Albino Corso, Angel, 141
Albores Guillén, Roberto "RAG": appointed governor, 247; attack on San Juan de la Libertad (El Bosque), 15, 277–280; attack on Tierra y Libertad, 269–270; move against San Andrés, 306–308; road construction, 313; support for PRI communities, 310–311; weekend in Chiapas, 289; xenophobia, 315
Albright, Madeleine, 279–280
Alcántara, Juan Manuel, 176
Alfaro Siqueiros, David, 267
Alianza Civica, 136–138
Althusser, Loius, 108
Alvarez, Luis H., 120, 204, 207
Alvarez, Miguel, 253, 273, 274, 331
Amnesty bill, 306
Amnesty International, 24, 326
Amuzgos, 40
ANCIEZ (Emiliano Zapata National Association of Indian Farmers), 7
Angel, José, 301
Angel de los Santos, Miguel, 175
Angeles Duharc, Tomás (General), 122
ANIPA (National Assembly of Indian

Peoples for Autonomy), 146
Annan, Kofi, 253, 287, 325
Appel, Kerry, 160
Araujo, Octavio, 136, 138
Arellano Félix brothers, 58
Arias, Alan, 296
Arias, Jacinto (Indian Attention office), 92, 145
Arias, Jacinto (municipal president), 220, 235–237, 243, 247, 249
Arias, Pedro, 250
Arias Paz, Mariano, 248
Aridjis, Homero, 312, 339
Arizmendi, Felipe (Bishop), 334–336
Arrieta (General), 106
Article 3, 288
Article 27: discussions at the Jornadas, 54; goals of the EPR, 184; government rejection of changes, 161; modification, 13; revision of, 7; revocation of changes, 150. *see also* Land reform
Article 33, 256
Asesinos, 34
Aspe, Pedro, 62
Assembly of Barios, 177
Aubry, Andrés, 259, 334
Aurura, Beatriz, 252–253
Autónomos, 142, 191
Autonomous municipalities, 275
Autonomous Pluri-ethnic Regions (RAPs), 86, 146, 262
Autonomy: building of municipalities, 217–219; goals of the EPR, 184; Zedillo objections, 264
Avendaño, Amado: campaign for governor, 68, 74–75, 81; Chiapas governorship, 92–93; EZLN letter to, 31; government-in-rebellion, 86, 94–95; injuries from fall, 229; invitation to San Andrés VII, 145; looking to Europe, 131; newspaper editor, 19, 67; recognition as governor, 100
Avilés, Jaime, 274

B

Baker, George, 317
Banamax, 23, 57
Banco Interacciones, 98
Banderas, Antonio, 137
Banque de France, 98
Bañuelos, Juan: on CONAI, 89, 120, 203; on the election commission, 80; Forum on

15th anniversary, 294–296; an incident in history, 337–339; and elections, 342–350; future of, 344; timeline, 13–15. *see also* Specific events, issues and people

Subcomandante Marcos

ABOUT THE AUTHOR

The author at Ovantic   **Photographer: Faith Attaguile**

John Ross is a Latin American correspondent who regularly con-
tributes to the *Los Angeles Weekly* and *San Francisco Bay Guardian*. A
novelist (*Tonatiuh's People—a Novel of the Mexican Cataclysm*) and poet
(*jazzmexico*) as well as a social activist, John Ross "is a new John Reed
covering a new Mexican revolution" (*La Jornada.*) He is also the author
of *The Annexation of Mexico—From the Aztecs to the IMF*, *Rebellion From
the Roots*, *In Focus: Mexico*, and editor of *They Came to Play*, an anthology
of basketball stories. His weekly electronic reportage "Mexico Barbaro" is
greatly praised. Ross resides in Mexico City's old quarter, once the Aztec
Island of Tenochtitlan.